PRAISE FOR
THE PATIENT PRIORITY

The Patient Priority is one of the best books on health care that I have ever read. It takes the concept of value-based health care from rhetoric to actionable frameworks for strategy and operations. Readers' understanding of how health care should evolve will be deepened by analyses of the best paths forward for different stakeholders and broadened by examples drawn from around the world. The insights from this book will be valuable for managers who are helping their organizations adapt to change and for leaders who are focused on moving health care forward.

> **—THOMAS LEE, MD,** Chief Medical Officer of Press Ganey Associates, Inc., Professor at the Department of Health Policy and Management at the Harvard T.H. Chan School of Public Health, and Editor-in-Chief of *NEJM Catalyst*

The Patient Priority is intelligent, insightful, and intriguing. If you care about health systems organized around what matters to patients and that deliver better care at affordable cost, you should put this book on your must-read list. Stefan Larsson, Jennifer Clawson, and Josh Kellar provide a fresh, well-documented, and inspiring investigation into how to make value-based transformation a moonshot target for national health systems.

> **—FRANCESCA COLOMBO,** Head of the Health Division of the Organisation for Economic Co-operation and Development (OECD)

Imagine if health care were founded on ever-increasing volumes of patient data that drive a deeper understanding of health and disease. *The Patient Priority* offers a compelling action plan for realizing that future through the systematic tracking and continuous improvement of the health outcomes that matter to patients.

> **—JAMIE HEYWOOD,** CEO of Alden Scientific and Founder, former Chairman, and CEO of PatientsLikeMe

The Patient Priority is not only a vivid account of the current state of progress in value-based health care around the world; it also lays out a compelling road map for the future in which public-private partnerships work together to accelerate the value-based transformation of the world's health systems. Highly recommended for anyone interested in improving health systems.

> **—SHYAM BISHEN,** Head of Health and Healthcare at the World Economic Forum and former Deputy Director of Global Health at the Bill and Melinda Gates Foundation

America's health care system is one of the best in the world, made clear by the doubling of life expectancy over the past century. But the world and our way of life have changed dramatically over this time, requiring the health care system to evolve to fit today's needs, while also ensuring it's primed to meet the challenges of tomorrow. *The Patient Priority* is an insightful read for anyone interested in learning more about the industry or in leading its transformation.

—**BRUCE D. BROUSSARD,** President and CEO of Humana, Inc.

The Patient Priority is a must-read book for anyone interested in value-based health care and healthcare transformation more generally. It combines a lucid analysis of the central issues that beset health systems with well-chosen case studies emphasizing practical approaches to addressing the challenges we face.

—**CHORH-CHUAN TAN, MBBS, PHD,** Chief Health
  Scientist and Executive Director of the Office of Healthcare
  Transformation at the Singapore Ministry of Health and
  Chairman of the National University Health System

The Patient Priority is the book that we have all been waiting for. Twentieth-century health care has run its course, and today's stand-out providers are doing things differently and providing better care as a result. From their unique vantage point, Larsson, Clawson, and Kellar distill a tangible vision for health systems centred on patients and driven by value. Their book lights the path ahead and brings us to a tipping point. It will be a catalyst for change and a cornerstone for everyone involved in the future of health care.

—**RUSSELL GRUEN, MBBS, PHD,** Dean of the College of Health
  and Medicine at the Australian National University

Health care is a human right, and people's expectations for better health are ever increasing. Yet the world's health systems are facing an existential crisis. *The Patient Priority* is a must-read for anyone looking at ensuring that health systems will deliver better value to patients in the future.

—**CHRISTOPHE WEBER,** President and CEO of Takeda
  Pharmaceuticals

The Patient Priority offers an inspiring, comprehensive, and transformative approach to delivering better outcomes and value in health care by focusing on the patient journey.

—**FRANS VAN HOUTEN,** CEO of Royal Philips

The Patient Priority is an important read for anyone aspiring to improve the US health system. The book's powerful, well-researched narrative outlines the need for the systematic measurement of health outcomes to drive the value-based transformation of health systems. As someone who has led health care organizations in the academy, government, and the payer and provider sectors, I wholeheartedly endorse the thesis of this book that the key to improving health care value is to systematically measure and continuously improve patient health outcomes.

—**PATRICK CONWAY, MD,** CEO of Care Solutions at Optum, UnitedHealth Group, and former Director of the Center for Medicare and Medicaid Innovation (CMMI) at the US Department of Health and Human Services

Larsson, Clawson, and Kellar deliver a much-needed call to action for public and private sector stakeholders to build a better health care delivery system focused on patient outcomes, with a practical plan for treating patient health outcomes data as critical infrastructure.

—**ANEESH CHOPRA,** President of CareJourney and former Chief Technology Officer of the US Federal Government

The Patient Priority is a timely account of how to redefine health care in the coming decade. Internationally recognized pioneers in the field of value-based health care, the authors link that concept to the pivotal domains of modern care delivery, change management, payment incentives, and digital technologies with the sole aim of building heath systems that deliver improved health outcomes that matter to patients. This book will serve as a cornerstone for clinicians, managers, economists, and politicians striving to shift the world's health systems from volume to value.

—**CHRISTOPH A. MEIER, MD,** Director of the Department of Internal Medicine at Universitätsspital (Zürich, Switzerland)

The Patient Priority provides a comprehensive overview of the journey to value-based, patient-driven care. The authors put the continuous improvement in health outcomes that matter to patients at the very center of the global movement for value-based health care. In addition to charting the considerable progress made in the last decade toward that goal, they also tackle the common challenges that still exist worldwide, regardless of the type of health system, in making the vision a reality. An important contribution that should be read by health care CEOs and senior leaders around the world.

—**GARY S. KAPLAN, MD,** Senior Advisor and Senior Vice President of CommonSpirit Health and former CEO of Virginia Mason Franciscan Health

The Patient Priority provides a compelling rationale for why value-based health care represents the most comprehensive solution to the challenges faced by health systems around the world and a clarion call to action for all who care about the sustainability of health care delivery. The authors' proposed model for value-based health systems and coherent road map for action will resonate with patients, clinicians, and payers alike. A must-read for anyone who cares about the future of health care.

—**ELIZABETH KOFF,** Managing Director of Telstra Health and
former Secretary of Health of New South Wales, Australia

The administrative burden experienced by health care workers has grown exponentially. Although the intention has been to secure value for money, the outcome for staff and patients has often been the opposite. There is an urgent need to change management culture in health care. *The Patient Priority* provides inspiration for how to do it.

—**JAN NILSSON, MD,** Professor of Medicine and former Dean of
Lund University Medical School (Lund, Sweden)

Compared to other countries, Japan's universal health-insurance system has been relatively successful at controlling costs. But in the face of new trends such as rapid technological change and population decline, Japan like other countries faces the simultaneous challenge of ensuring high-quality medical care even as it makes the health system more cost efficient. In an age when the conventional rules for managing national health systems no longer apply, *The Patient Priority* will become an indispensable textbook.

—**TOSHIHIKO TAKEDA,** Former Director-General of the
Health Policy Bureau of the Ministry of Health, Labor,
and Welfare of Japan

THE
PATIENT
PRIORITY

THE
PATIENT
PRIORITY

Solve Health Care's Value Crisis
by Measuring and Delivering Outcomes
That Matter to Patients

STEFAN LARSSON, MD, PhD
JENNIFER CLAWSON
JOSH KELLAR, PhD
with ROBERT HOWARD

New York   Chicago   San Francisco   Athens   London   Madrid
Mexico City   Milan   New Delhi   Singapore   Sydney   Toronto

1 2 3 4 5 6 7 8 9   LCR   27 26 25 24 23 22

ISBN   978-1-264-74162-5
MHID   1-264-74162-6

e-ISBN   978-1-264-74135-9
e-MHID   1-264-74135-9

Library of Congress Cataloging-in-Publication Data

Names: Larsson, Stefan (Advisor in healthcare), author.
Title: The patient priority : solve health care's value crisis by measuring and delivering
    outcomes that matter to patients / Stefan Larsson, Jennifer Clawson, and Josh Kellar
    with Robert Howard.
Description: New York : McGraw Hill, [2023] | Includes bibliographical references and
    index.
Identifiers: LCCN 2022029772 (print) | LCCN 2022029773 (ebook) | ISBN
    9781264741625 (hardback) | ISBN 9781264741359 (ebook)
Subjects: LCSH: Medical care—Cost effectiveness. | Medical care—Quality control. |
    Medical care—Cost control. | Patient-centered health care—Evaluation. | Medical
    care—Evaluation.
Classification: LCC RA399.A1 L37 2023 (print) | LCC RA399.A1 (ebook) |
    DDC 362.1068/1—dc23/eng/20220805
LC record available at https://lccn.loc.gov/2022029772
LC ebook record available at https://lccn.loc.gov/2022029773

McGraw Hill books are available at special quantity discounts to use as premiums and sales promotions or for use in corporate training programs. To contact a representative, please visit the Contact Us pages at www.mhprofessional.com.

McGraw Hill is committed to making our products accessible to all learners. To learn more about the available support and accommodations we offer, please contact us at accessibility@mheducation.com. We also participate in the Access Text Network (www.accesstext.org), and ATN members may submit requests through ATN.

To the love of my life and my best friend, Lotta, and our two wonderful children, Andrea and Pontus. To my late parents, Margareta and Sven-Olof, and my brothers, Jerker and Urban—for their values, determination, and love.
—SL

To Pedro and to our children, Pedro, Rob, and Anna, for giving me boundless encouragement and support, and to my parents, for instilling the passion to explore and embrace new challenges.
—JC

To my family, who has instilled in me a love of learning and a responsibility to use knowledge to make the world a better place.
—JK

CONTENTS

FOREWORD
by Michael E. Porter   **ix**

PREFACE
The Patient Priority   **xiii**

CHAPTER 1
The Three Crises of Modern Health Care   **1**

CHAPTER 2
The Power of Outcomes   **31**

CHAPTER 3
Organizing Care Delivery Around the Patient   **69**

CHAPTER 4
Meeting the Change Challenge   **105**

CHAPTER 5
Paying for Value Instead of Volume   **137**

CHAPTER 6
Harnessing Digital Health to Improve Patient Value   **175**

CHAPTER 7
A Moonshot for Value-Based Transformation   **209**

CHAPTER 8
The Value Leadership Agenda   **237**

ACKNOWLEDGMENTS   **259**

NOTES   **265**

INDEX   **297**

FOREWORD
by Michael E. Porter

O ver 20 years ago, I began working in the field of health care, with my Harvard Business School strategy colleague Elizabeth Teisberg, on our 2006 book, *Redefining Health Care: Creating Value-Based Competition on Results*. In that book, we built on earlier research to define a strategic vision for what we termed *value-based health care*, in which care-delivery models and payment systems are rebuilt around the fundamental goals of improving outcomes that matter to patients for their medical conditions, while efficiently managing costs over the full cycle of care for the patient. We put forward a strategic agenda for health care providers that includes (1) the creation of integrated practice units, (2) the measurement of patient outcomes and costs, (3) the adoption of value-based payments, (4) the implementation of systems integration across facilities, (5) the expansion of excellent care across geographies, and (6) the use of new information technology focused on value for patients.

In the 16 years since *Redefining Health Care* was published, we have been thrilled to see the emergence of a growing international movement of clinical leaders and provider institutions who are defining their goals around delivering better patient value, making steady progress in tracking the health outcomes that matter to patients, and moving toward bundled and capitated payments based on value.

With contributions from thought leaders such as Dr. Thomas Lee, Professor Robert S. Kaplan, Dr. Thomas Feeley, and Dr. Mary Witkowski, we have deepened our understanding of the essential steps and management processes involved in a transformation to value-based care in primary care, and also for specialty, condition-based care. At the Harvard Business School, we have written numerous case studies on care-delivery innovation, institutional change, and dynamic leadership at providers such as Cleveland Clinic, Vanderbilt University Medical Center, Children's Hospital of Philadelphia, innovative primary care provider Oak Street Health, European leader Martini Klinik, and dozens of other organizations elsewhere across the globe that have moved such delivery innovations forward.

An early partner in this effort has been Boston Consulting Group (BCG), whose commitment to value in health care was led by Dr. Stefan Larsson. In my first meetings with Stefan in 2010, it became clear that we not only shared a view on the dysfunctional and unsustainable structure of today's approaches to health care delivery, but also that Stefan and I shared a personal passion and set of values, which became the foundation for more than a decade of close collaboration in advancing this work.

One important early milestone was to cofound the International Consortium for Health Outcomes Measurement (ICHOM), together with Martin Ingvar of the Karolinska Institute. ICHOM was established as a not-for-profit organization working with patients and clinicians on moving to value by defining international standards for sets of health-outcome measures that matter most to patients for each medical condition. As of 2022, ICHOM has published more than 40 outcome-measurement sets for a broad range of medical conditions and patient population segments. ICHOM is currently catalyzing the efforts of health care delivery organizations around the world to measure outcomes and drive improvements in care equitably across the globe.

Stefan and I have also worked together over time with the World Economic Forum (WEF) and its distinguished global group of physician leaders, corporate partners, and ministers of health, who are actively embracing the value-based-health-care movement. Jointly with the WEF, we have established the Global Coalition for Value in Healthcare, which has worked actively on the value transformation of health care delivery systems around the world.

Stefan and his coauthors, Jennifer Clawson and Josh Kellar, have worked closely with other organizations around the world on making value-based health care a reality. In *The Patient Priority*, they synthesize over a decade of experience, combining theory and practice to chart the progress of value-based health care to date and to define a detailed road map for its future. They argue that the comprehensive measurement of health outcomes that matter to patients is the key to addressing the health sector's systemic value crisis, of uneven outcomes despite rising costs, and to unlocking continued momentum in health care transformation. In addition to profiling leading value-based innovators across the various sectors of the global health care industry, the authors describe the growing engagement of governments across the world such as in the Netherlands and Singapore in the value-based transformation of national health systems. *The Patient Priority* presents a compelling vision for the creation of digital learning platforms on a global scale to improve value delivered to patients and describes the key leadership challenges that health care leaders face in an increasingly value-based world, with concrete action steps for tackling the remaining organizational and systemwide obstacles to the dissemination of value-based care.

We at Harvard Business School, along with other scholars, have taught thousands of clinicians and health care managers from all over the world, and continue to work to train the current and future generation of health care leaders on the transition to value-based health care. Health care delivery is now being revolutionized around the world, and medical education is in transition with a growing number of programs instituting course work on the principles of value-based health care, including the Harvard Medical School, where health care delivery and leadership is part of the required curriculum for medical students. As we continue to pursue the goal of delivering high value care and equitable outcomes for all, this book will become a valuable reference for leaders, with its comprehensive road map for industry transformation.

PREFACE
The Patient Priority

This book is about the future of a complicated industry, but it has a simple message. The $10 trillion global health care sector, the world's largest and, in many respects, most complex industry, suffers from serious—and growing—problems of cost and quality. In order to address them, health care leaders need to go back to first principles. Specifically, they need to put the continuous improvement in the delivery of health outcomes that matter to patients at the very center of how they manage their organizations, and how countries manage their national health systems. This is what we mean by "the patient priority." How to make it real is the subject of this book.

The idea that health care suffers from an interconnected set of stubbornly persistent performance problems isn't new. Indeed, signs of those problems, and attempts to address them, have been accumulating for decades. Despite years of focus on cost containment, costs continue to grow at an unsustainable rate, outpacing growth in GDP. Despite an increasing preoccupation with improving the quality of care, the health outcomes delivered to patients remain remarkably inconsistent—across countries, across regions within the same country, across different socioeconomic and racial groups, and even across multiple hospitals and clinical sites within the same locale.

To be sure, the accelerating sophistication of clinical medicine, the global pharmaceutical industry, and the medical technology (med-tech) sector has led to a proliferation of important and, in many cases, life-saving and life-changing new treatments. But it has also contributed to dysfunctional complexity in health systems, leading to the fragmentation of the patient experience and to a systematic misalignment of incentives across the industry's many stakeholders to a degree rarely seen in other industries.

The paradoxes of the current situation abound. The health care sector is increasingly reliant on rapidly growing quantities of health-related data, making it a twenty-first-century knowledge industry *par excellence*. And yet, it consistently lags other sectors of the economy, such as retail or financial services, in the exploitation of powerful new digital technologies. Billions are spent on the education and training of a highly specialized professional workforce. And yet, health professionals experience unprecedented levels of stress and burnout far beyond that experienced in other fields. Last but far from least, despite the genuine heroism of the response to Covid-19, the pandemic has made a series of chronic problems painfully acute—in the process, revealing critical structural weaknesses, such as serious underinvestment in public health, prevention, and the treatment of chronic disease.[1]

We don't believe the problems plaguing the global health care industry are somehow the result of bad actors. Of course, health care, like any industry, has its share of greedy or self-interested people.[2] But we work with health care leaders around the world: physicians leading major hospitals and health systems, clinical staff on the front line of care delivery, research directors at leading university medical centers, C-suite executives at pharmaceutical and med-tech companies, and policymakers who guide the evolution of national health systems. In our experience, the vast majority of people in the sector are well-meaning. They have been drawn to health care for positive and, in many cases, even noble reasons. They care about patients, are proud of their contributions to human health, want to tackle the big problems of disease, and hope to improve the health of the world's population. But they are rational actors caught in what too often feels like an irrational system. In order to change their behavior, we have to change the system.

Despite the considerable problems facing health care today, we are actually quite optimistic about its future. Indeed, we believe that the industry is on the cusp of a fundamental transformation. For more than a decade, we have been part of an emerging movement to change how the health care sector is organized and how care is delivered that is known colloquially as *value-based health care*. The basic principle is to shift the health care sector from a system that is managed primarily on inputs (for example, the volume of services and procedures delivered, or adherence to guidelines and budgets) to a system that is managed primarily on the health outcomes delivered to patients for the money spent. We have worked closely with organizations across the industry that are innovating new patient-centered and value-based models of care.

We have also witnessed how the pandemic, despite (or perhaps because of) its painful costs, has been an extraordinary catalyst for innovation.[3] The global response has been far from perfect; many mistakes have been made.[4] Nevertheless, in the face of crisis and despite the system's complexity, clinicians, researchers, private corporations, government regulators, and patients adapted quickly to mobilize around a single goal. Epidemiologists systematically tracked cases and deaths on a global basis. Providers reached out to help and learn from each other and shifted nearly overnight to incorporate new practices such as telemedicine (in the United States, it grew from 1% to 40% of patient visits). Pharmaceutical companies and regulatory agencies developed, tested, and approved vaccines in record time. In the process, the pandemic has made urgently clear the importance of more agile and more coordinated approaches to managing the full cycle of care. Stakeholders across the industry are open and ready to contemplate fundamentally new ways of working together; they also understand that a new wave of investment will be necessary to rebuild the world's health systems in the wake of Covid-19.

But sustaining the innovations of the pandemic period will require broad systemic changes in how health systems operate.[5] In order to materially impact the future evolution of the health care sector, value-based health care needs to become a shared transformative project—not just at the level of individual health care organizations but at the level of entire national health systems and, indeed, of the global health care sector as a whole. Our book defines a road map for that project.

WHAT VALUE MEANS IN HEALTH CARE

The term *value-based health care* was introduced by Michael Porter of Harvard Business School and his colleague Elizabeth Teisberg in their

2006 book, *Redefining Health Care: Creating Value-Based Competition on Results.*[6] Porter and Teisberg's book was an early attempt to rethink the health care industry from the perspective of the customer—that is, the patient. They argued that, seen from the patient's perspective, the ultimate measure of performance in any health system ought to be the delivery of health outcomes that matter to patients for a given cost along the full cycle of care. A key insight of Porter and Teisberg's work was that, too often, what passes for competition in health care markets is really competition over the wrong things. According to them, if markets for the provision of health care were reorganized around the shared objective of delivering better health outcomes for specific patient groups, competition would unleash innovation that delivered benefits both to patients and to the system as a whole.

In the 16 years since Porter and Teisberg's book was published, the idea of value-based health care has become widespread and, in the process, acquired a variety of different (and sometimes contradictory) meanings. For some, improving health care value is merely the latest euphemism for cost-cutting. For others, it is synonymous with eliminating waste by getting rid of low-value care.[7] For still others, especially in the more commercially oriented US health system, value-based health care mainly refers to alternative payment models that, in contrast to the traditional fee-for-service payment system, put provider compensation at risk depending on their ability to deliver cost-effective quality care.[8]

Our book will address cost containment, quality care, alternative payment models, and other issues associated with the term. But our concept of value-based health care hews closely to Porter and Teisberg's original definition. By *value* in health care, we mean simultaneously the value delivered *to the patient* in the form of better health outcomes and the value delivered *by the health system* in terms of the most efficient use of society's limited financial and other resources.

What's more, we believe that systematically tracking health outcomes by disease or patient segment is critical to improving performance not only in commercially oriented health systems such as that of the United States, where competition plays a more central role. It is relevant to *all* national health systems, including those in which health care is seen as less of a business and more of a public service. After all, continuously improving the health outcomes delivered to patients for the money spent is—or ought to be—the ultimate purpose of any health system and the closest thing to a genuine objective function around which all stakeholders should align. In this book, we will show that embracing the shared goal of delivering better outcomes for the same, or in some cases even lower, cost can become a powerful engine for continuous improvement, innovation in clinical research and practice, and step-function improvements in health equity, productivity, and performance.

We also believe that the principles of value-based health care are relevant not just to provider organizations but to all stakeholders in the health system, including payers, suppliers in the pharmaceutical and med-tech industries, health technology companies, patient organizations, and government policymakers. In our book, we strive to take a holistic, systemwide approach to our subject, because we believe that providers will succeed in improving patient value only if other parts of the system—payments models, government regulations, digital infrastructure, and the like—are aligned with their efforts.

Finally, we are convinced that the shared objective of improving health outcomes is the key to making actionable many of the admirable visions for the future of health care. Recent decades have seen a dizzying proliferation of ways to describe the desired future state of health care: evidence-based medicine, precision medicine, personalized medicine, patient-centered care, deep medicine, the triple (and now quadruple) aim, 4P medicine (for Predictive, Preventive, Personalized, and Participatory), just to name a few.[9] But in order to realize these laudable goals, industry stakeholders need a simple shared objective against which they can assess their contribution and their progress. Continuously improving health outcomes for the money spent is, in our view, precisely the right objective.

A ROAD MAP TO HEALTH-SYSTEM TRANSFORMATION

According to our definition, no national health system in the world today is entirely value based. And yet, many leading health care organizations and even some national health systems are putting aspects of the value-based model into practice with extraordinary results. They are measuring and tracking the health outcomes delivered to patients, categorized by disease, condition, or risk category. They are analyzing the data, increasingly with the help of powerful digital tools, to identify and disseminate solid evidence for innovations in treatment that are proven to deliver the best outcomes for a given patient group. They are also using comprehensive outcomes data to develop a more integrated model of care delivery for specific patient groups and population segments—for example, focusing as much on prevention as on treatment, and combining traditional clinical interventions with nonclinical interventions to address the social and behavioral determinants of health. And they are reinventing the clinician-patient dialogue to incorporate a more nuanced consideration of individual preferences in treatment choice.

The challenge, now, is to accelerate these changes and, in particular, to expand them beyond individual organizations to the system as a whole. Doing so will require the systematic collection of comprehensive data on patient health outcomes on a global scale, the development of new approaches to payment and reimbursement in order to encourage the right kind of behavior on the part of all industry players, major investments in digital-health technologies to transform the global health sector into a genuine learning system, and new approaches to regulation, governance, and public-private partnership.

Most of all, it will require bold leadership. Leaders of provider organizations, health insurers, and pharmaceutical and med-tech companies will need to develop strategies for competing in an increasingly value-based world and innovate new value-based business models. At the same time, they will need to look beyond their immediate economic and organizational interests to develop a common sense of purpose and cooperate in the shared task of health-system transformation.

In the pages that follow, we tell the story of the innovators on the front lines of value-based health care and provide a road map for how health care leaders in both the private and public sectors can accelerate the value-based transformation of the world's health systems.

In Chapter 1, we begin by defining the problem. In particular, we dig deeper into the challenges confronting the health care sector today and frame them in terms of three interrelated crises. The core crisis is a crisis of *value*, characterized by a disconnect between money spent and outcomes delivered. This value crisis is exacerbated by a growing crisis of *evidence*, characterized by an expanding gap between research and clinical practice. Finally, both these crises are contributing to a crisis of *purpose*, characterized by a misalignment of incentives and a growing conviction on the part of many participants in the industry that the current imperatives of the system are in contradiction with the fundamental values and motivations that brought them into health care in the first place. We conclude Chapter 1 by making the case for why focusing on the continuous improvement of health outcomes is the best way to cut through this tangled Gordian knot.

In Chapter 2, we show the power of outcomes measurement and transparency to stimulate the continuous improvement and innovation of clinical practice and to improve health outcomes that matter to patients. To illustrate this principle, we do a deep dive on a type of health care institution that plays a vital role in improving health outcomes but remains relatively unknown to the broader public: national quality registries. And we describe a now 10-year initiative by leading clinicians and patient-advocacy groups around the world to create international standards for health-outcomes measurement for major diseases, conditions, and population segments.

In Chapter 3, we turn to the story of leading value-based innovators in the provider sector who are using the principle of systematic outcomes measurement to transform how they deliver care to patients. Through in-depth case studies, we describe how pioneering providers are tracking health outcomes systematically and creating integrated end-to-end care pathways in which multidisciplinary clinical teams match clinical interventions to patient needs.

In Chapter 4, we look at how more traditional provider organizations are working to adopt value-based approaches to clinical practice and, in some cases, to change fundamentally how they organize to deliver care. We also explore some of the distinctive challenges in making value-based change in traditional health care institutions.

In Chapter 5, we shift gears from individual provider organizations to address some of the key enablers of value-based transformation at the level of entire health systems—starting with how providers and suppliers, such as pharmaceutical and medical technology companies, are paid. In this chapter, we look at new models for value-based payment and argue that in order to be successful, such models need to be designed carefully in combination with other changes in a value-based health system.

In Chapter 6, we look at the promise of digital technology to make it easier for practitioners to routinely collect, share, and analyze outcomes data and, ultimately, to create digital learning platforms on a global scale. A key component of these platforms will be powerful techniques associated with artificial intelligence that radically improve clinical decision support and individualized care. Making this vision a reality, however, requires the development of global standards for the cybersecurity, interoperability, and ease of use of health information systems.

In Chapter 7, we emphasize the leading role that governments have to play—as chief payer, regulator, and convenor of industry stakeholders—in accelerating the value-based transformation of national health systems. We argue for a moonshot initiative in which the governments of the world play a more active role, both on their own and in cooperation with each other, to create the value-based health systems of the future.

Finally, in Chapter 8, we describe the leadership challenges facing health care leaders in an increasingly value-based world—both to prepare their organizations to survive and thrive in an industry defined by value delivered to patients and to cooperate across industry boundaries to create new value-based health ecosystems.

A MANIFESTO FOR INTERNATIONAL COLLABORATION

The Patient Priority is a product of more than a decade of research and consulting that we have conducted at Boston Consulting Group (BCG) with health care organizations around the world. Although there are some exceptions, most English-language books about health care take the US health system as their primary (and, in many cases, sole) reference point. It's understandable, given the uniqueness of the US health care industry and the distinctive challenges the US national health system faces, as well as the way that outsized US investments in biomedical research, and new innovations emerging in the US health system, drive developments in the sector internationally. But it can also come at the price of a certain myopia about what the American health sector can learn from other countries around the world.

In our book, by contrast, we take a resolutely global perspective. To be sure, we address many of the much-discussed problems of the US health system, even as we feature many US health care institutions that are leading innovators in the field of value-based health care. But we also draw on examples and developments from other national health systems around the world—both public and private, as well as from both high- and low-income countries.

This global perspective is a direct product of our focus on improving health outcomes delivered to patients suffering from the same disease or condition, irrespective of where those patients happen to live. After all, as the pandemic has painfully reminded us, disease respects no national boundaries. Just as the symptoms and etiology of diabetes or heart disease or cancer are the same everywhere, so too are the principles and best practices that deliver the best health outcomes. Indeed, part of our argument is that standardized outcomes measurement will contribute to the eventual rise of a global learning system and a gradual convergence around effective care and payment models in health systems around the world.

At a time when geopolitical conflicts and socioeconomic challenges, combined with the travails of the coronavirus pandemic, make it tempting for countries to retreat into a narrow nationalism, we believe strongly in the imperative of international collaboration on health-outcomes improvement and value-based health-system transformation. It's time—past time—for national health systems around the world to start learning more systematically from the best that each has to offer.

CHAPTER 1

THE THREE CRISES OF MODERN HEALTH CARE

The development of the modern health care sector is a remarkable human achievement. In the century lasting roughly from the late 1800s to the late 1900s, it was responsible for a doubling of life expectancy—an extraordinary accomplishment first reached in the high-income countries but then increasingly extended to low- and middle-income countries.[1] Social and organizational innovations in the domain of public health effectively controlled—and, in some cases, eliminated—the threat of infectious disease. Scientific breakthroughs in the understanding of the molecular and genetic determinants of health and disease allowed clinicians to prevent, treat, and, in some cases, cure diseases and conditions that were not treatable before. Progress toward universal access to care allowed millions to benefit from these advances. In the process, the world's national health systems became cornerstones of citizen well-being, national competitiveness, and indeed human civilization itself.

Will the next century see equivalent progress? The world invests more resources than ever in biomedical research and development (R&D); we estimate a little more than $400 billion in 2020 alone.[2] That investment has fueled rapid progress in the understanding of health and disease. Figure 1.1 charts the exponential growth in the number of scientific publications as recorded by PubMed, the global repository containing more than 33 million citations in the biomedical literature. This massive increase in scientific knowledge has been the catalyst for new treatments and clinical interventions.

FIGURE 1.1 **Biomedical knowledge is growing at an exponential rate.**

Number of publications (millions)

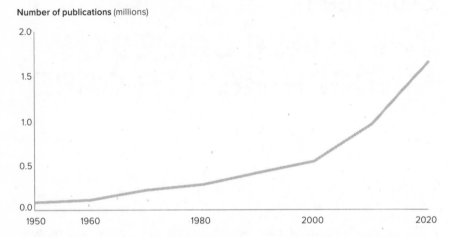

Since 1950, the number of scientific publications added every year to the PubMed database has exploded—from about 85,000 in 1950 to more than 1.5 million in 2020.

Source: *PubMed*.

In recent years, however, the signs of what society is getting for all this investment are troubling. Since at least 2014, life expectancy in the United States has been in decline.[3] So too in the United Kingdom and other high-income countries.[4] And the coronavirus pandemic has, of course, had a major negative impact on life expectancy around the world.[5] Some may argue that these are temporary indicators or reflect society-wide factors beyond the control of national health systems. And yet, we think they are also symptoms of persistent problems and systemic dysfunctionalities in the health care sector itself that risk undermining its ability to sustain its record of progress.

In this chapter, we diagnose those problems and dysfunctionalities and suggest how to address them. Specifically, we argue that the world's health systems are experiencing what we call a triple crisis. The core crisis is a crisis of *value*, characterized by unsustainable costs, substantial waste, and a growing disconnect between money spent and the health outcomes delivered to patients. This value crisis is made worse by a parallel crisis of *evidence*, characterized by a disconnect between research and clinical practice. Finally, the value crisis and the evidence crisis contribute to a corrosive crisis of *purpose*, characterized by the growing dissatisfaction of both health professionals and patients as they struggle with the accumulating dysfunctions and misalignments of an increasingly complex health sector.

These three interdependent crises of modern health care are mutually reinforcing. The only way to cut through the tangled Gordian knot of dysfunction that they create is to reorient the world's health systems around value delivered to patients by improving the delivery of health outcomes that matter to patients for a given level of spending. We conclude this chapter by introducing our model for what a genuinely patient-centered and value-based health system would look like. How innovators in health systems around the world are putting that model into practice is the subject of the subsequent chapters in our book.

UNSUSTAINABLE COSTS, EXTRAORDINARY WASTE

The most visible sign of health care's value crisis will be familiar to many readers for the simple reason that it has been a major focus of discussion and debate in recent decades: the vertiginous rise in health care spending, which, despite decades of cost-containment initiatives, continues to significantly outpace the rate of growth in GDP in most high-income countries. For example, in the 20 years between 2000 and 2019, aggregate health expenditures in 36 Organisation for Economic Co-operation and Development (OECD) countries, measured as a percentage of GDP, grew by a third—from 9% to 12%. (See Figure 1.2.) And according to a 2017 estimate in the leading medical journal *The Lancet*, by 2040 the world will spend approximately $24 trillion every year on health care—which represents a 4% annual increase from the $9 trillion spent in 2014.[6]

In the near term, the costs of the coronavirus pandemic and its aftermath will only increase such numbers. For example, for US providers the first quarter of 2022 was one of the worst in recent memory, with losses driven by extraordinary wage growth, as well as growth in the cost of supplies, a product of both the pandemic and subsequent inflationary spiral.

FIGURE 1.2 **The growth in health care costs is outpacing growth in GDP.**

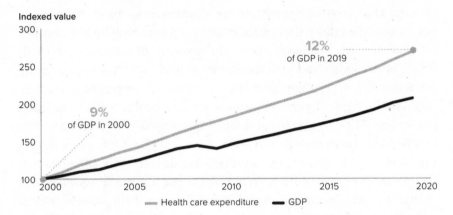

The chart compares the growth in health care costs to growth in GDP across 36 member countries of the Organisation for Economic Development and Co-operation (OECD). Between 2000 and 2019, the share of health costs, as a percentage of GDP, grew from 9% to 12%.

Note: Index based on US dollars adjusted for purchasing-power parity.

Source: *OECD.*

Escalating costs are putting severe pressure on national health budgets and exacerbating inequities in access to care. It also is placing significant burdens on individuals trying to cover health care costs. According to the Kaiser Family Foundation, in 2010 the average annual cost of US health insurance premiums for family coverage was $13,770. By 2020, it had increased by more than half to $21,342.[7] If employers did not cover these premiums, many families could not afford them.

To be sure, much of the recent growth in global health care spending has been in emerging economies, which, historically, have underinvested in health. Spending more on health care in low- and middle-income countries can, of course, be a sign of progress. However, as these countries seek to catch up with more advanced health systems, they run the serious risk of maneuvering themselves into financially untenable situations if they simply try to replicate the current health systems of the advanced economies. Nigeria, for example, has roughly 11% the number of doctors per capita as the average in the OECD countries.[8] To catch up, we estimate that Nigeria would need approximately 12 times as many doctors—at a training cost of somewhere between $13 billion and $37 billion.[9] Needless to say, this is not a feasible option.

Although it may seem surprising to say it, in some respects, the absolute rise in health care costs is the least of the industry's problems. Over the past decade, it has become increasingly clear that a significant portion of health care spending is, quite simply, wasted on low-value and, in some cases, medically inappropriate care.[10] How much? In 2012, an Institute of Medicine report estimated that roughly 30% of what the United States spent annually on health care at the time—approximately $750 billion— was on procedures and services that do not make patients healthier.[11] In 2019, a systematic review of 54 peer-reviewed publications estimated that the annual total cost of waste in the US health system due to failures of care delivery, poor care coordination, overtreatment or low-value care, pricing failures, administrative complexity, and outright fraud and abuse were between $760 billion and $935 billion (roughly 20% to 25% of total spending).[12]

The review also concluded that interventions to address waste were generating savings of between $191 billion and $286 billion every year, so at least some progress has been made in addressing the issue. But it's clear that waste and overtreatment continue to be a serious problem—and not only for the health system in terms of unnecessary cost, but also for patients in terms of medically unnecessary or inappropriate treatment. Doctors seem to agree. Some 2,000 US physicians who responded to a 2017 Johns Hopkins Medical School survey estimated that between 15% and 30% of medical diagnostics and treatments are medically unnecessary, a finding consistent with the academic literature.[13]

Although the United States may be an extreme case, with some unique contributing factors (for example, fear of malpractice litigation), wasteful health care spending is by no means exclusively a US phenomenon. The World Health Organization (WHO) estimates that between 20% and 40% of health spending worldwide is wasted through inefficiency and overuse.[14] The widespread overuse of health services has been documented in health systems as diverse as Australia, Spain, Israel, and Brazil.[15] In South Korea, for example, the introduction of systematic screening for thyroid cancer led to a 15-fold increase in diagnosis of the disease. And yet in subsequent years, mortality from the disease did not decline—and approximately 99% of the detected cancers turned out to be misdiagnosed.[16]

Nor are low- and middle-income countries immune. Take the example of the recent increase in Caesarean sections. Typically, Caesarean deliveries make up roughly 15% to 20% of deliveries. But in Tanzania, between 2000 and 2011, Caesareans grew from 19% to 49% of normal low-risk deliveries.[17] And in rural China, approximately 27% of all hospital admissions are considered by researchers to be inappropriate—compared to 18% to 25% in France and 33% in Germany.

Wasteful spending is not just a result of the overuse of medical services. Underuse contributes to unnecessary spending as well. In addition to being helpful to patients, certain clinical procedures—antihypertensive treatment, say, or vaccinations—provide a good return on investment to the health system. When they are underused, the costs show up in the need for expensive treatments in other parts of the system.[18] Underuse is a serious issue in low- and middle-income countries. But it is also a problem in some high-income countries, such as the United States, where a large segment of the population—the OECD estimates as much as 37%—does not have full access to the health system because of the high costs of care.[19]

Finally, it is becoming increasingly clear that waste in health care not only has significant financial costs to society; it also has a major negative impact on the environment. According to one estimate, "The health care industry is among the most carbon-intensive service sectors in the industrialized world," responsible for roughly 4.5% of worldwide greenhouse gas emissions, and as much as 8% in the United States.[20] The industry's carbon footprint is equivalent to that of the food sector and is only surpassed by the energy, transport, and construction industries.[21]

UNEXPLAINED OUTCOMES VARIATION

The ultimate symptom of health care's value crisis, however, is the broad variation in the health outcomes delivered to patients across countries, regions within countries, between different socioeconomic and racial groups, and even between different hospitals and clinical sites treating the same types of patients—with no clear correlation between money spent and health outcomes delivered.

The World Health Organization assesses the health and well-being of a country in terms of health-adjusted life expectancy (HALE), or the average number of years that a person can expect to live in full health, unhampered by disabling illnesses or injuries. Figure 1.3 compares 163 countries in terms of HALE and the amount of money each country spends per capita on health care. A few things immediately stand out.

FIGURE 1.3   Increased health care spending has diminishing returns on population health.

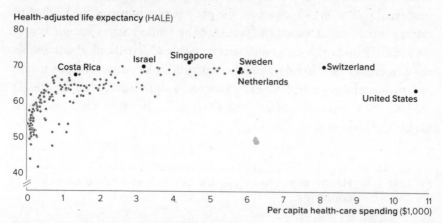

Health-adjusted life expectancy (HALE)

The chart compares health-adjusted life expectancy in 163 countries to each country's per capita spending on health care. US life expectancy lags that of the leading countries, despite spending the most on health care.

Note: All data is from 2019 or later; per capita spending calculated in US dollars adjusted for purchasing-power parity.

Sources: *WHO, World Bank.*

First, the United States is a real outlier in the group, spending more per capita (and in some cases, double or even triple what other developed countries spend), and yet delivering a significantly lower health-adjusted life expectancy: only 66 years, compared to more than 70 years for the countries at the top of the chart. Second, even among those countries that have the highest health-adjusted life expectancy, there are some (for example, Israel) that achieve it while spending considerably less per capita on health care than others (for example, Switzerland). Finally, among the many low- and middle-income countries that still spend relatively little per capita on health care and which often have lower healthy life expectancy as a result, there are some (for example, Costa Rica) that have been able to "break the compromise" between low health care spending and longer life expectancy.[22] They are approaching advanced-economy results without spending at advanced-economy levels.

This variation can also be found in health outcomes for specific diseases. Since 2001 the OECD has published international comparisons of health outcomes by disease in its now 38 member countries. Figure 1.4 shows that for nine common conditions, outcomes vary by at least 1.2 times (five-year survival from breast cancer) to as much as 10.2 times (maternal mortality). Once again, the poor performance of the US health system stands out. Despite the fact that the United States spends nearly 20% of GDP on health care every year (roughly $3.8 trillion), about double the percentage of other developed countries, in key areas such as infant and maternal mortality US health outcomes significantly lag the OECD median. (See also the sidebar "The Disconnect Between Outcomes and Costs: The Case of Diabetes.")

FIGURE 1.4 **Health outcomes can vary as much as tenfold across countries.**

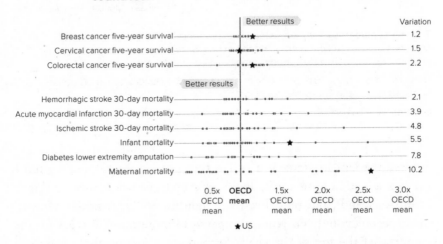

The chart plots the degree of outcomes variation across selected OECD countries for nine common health conditions. In many, US outcomes lag the OECD mean—in the case of maternal mortality, by more than two-and-a-half times.

Note: AMI stands for acute myocardial infarction. Most recent data are from 2016 to 2019 (infant and maternal mortality), 2015 to 2017 (AMI, stroke, and diabetes), and 2010 to 2014 (cancer survival). Not all metrics reported by United States.

Source: *OECD.*

The Disconnect Between Outcomes and Costs: The Case of Diabetes

For a striking example of the disconnect between health outcomes and costs across nations, consider diabetes. Diabetes is a serious chronic disease that is reaching near-epidemic proportions. According to the International Diabetes Foundation (IDF), roughly 463 million adults between the ages of 20 and 79 (more than 9% of the global population in that age group) suffered from diabetes in 2019, and nearly half of those cases went undiagnosed.[23] An additional 374 million adults had impaired glucose tolerance, putting them at high risk for developing diabetes in the future.

In 2019, diabetes caused 4.2 million deaths worldwide, more than HIV/AIDS, tuberculosis, and malaria combined. As a point of comparison, that is roughly equivalent to the total number of deaths from Covid-19 from the start of the pandemic in December 2019 up until August 2021. By 2040, the number of adults with diabetes is expected to grow to 700 million, nearly 11% of the world's adult population. Long-term complications from diabetes include cardiovascular disease, blindness, kidney failure, and poor circulation and neuropathy (which contributes to foot ulcers and eventually, if the condition worsens, to amputation of the lower limbs).

In addition to this widespread human suffering, diabetes represents a growing economic burden. Treatment for diabetes and related complications currently accounts for about 12% of global health care spending. IDF estimates that diabetes-related health expenditures will increase from $760 billion in 2019 to $845 billion in 2045. What's more, the lion's share of the costs associated with the disease is incurred treating patients with serious complications, which makes prevention and progression control critical to both delivering good health outcomes and minimizing the costs of care.

The prevalence of diabetes and the costs of diabetes care vary widely across national health systems. (See Figure 1.5.) The key metric for comparing rates of diabetes is what the IDF calls *age-adjusted prevalence*, which adjusts for differences in the distribution of age groups among nations and includes estimates of the percentage of the population with undiagnosed diabetes. In 2019, the age-adjusted prevalence of diabetes in the US adult population was 10.8%. In

Sweden, by contrast, that number was less than half as large—4.8%. What's more, not only is the prevalence of the disease substantially higher, but diabetes patients in the United States are significantly more likely to suffer from serious complications. For example, in 2010 (the most recent year for which comparable data is available), Sweden had 3.2 diabetic amputations for every 100,000 people; the equivalent US number was 17.1—more than five times as high.[24]

FIGURE 1.5 **The prevalence and cost of diabetes vary widely across countries.**

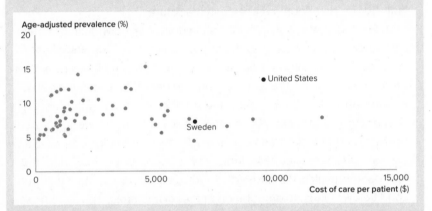

The chart compares the age-adjusted prevalence of diabetes in the United States and 57 other countries to the cost of care per patient. Sweden has much lower diabetes prevalence than the United States, despite spending considerably less per patient.

Note: Per capita spending calculated in US dollars adjusted for purchasing-power parity.

Source: *IDF Diabetes Atlas.*

Because complications drive the majority of costs, the higher US complication rate helps explain why the annual cost per patient of diabetes treatment is roughly a third higher in the United States than it is in Sweden—$9,506 versus $6,643. Based on IDF calculations, we estimate that if the United States could bring its prevalence rate down to Sweden's, it would save nearly a third of what the US health system spends annually on diabetes care, or about $103 billion. Alternatively, if the United States could bring its cost per patient for treating diabetes down to the Swedish level, it could save even more—about $190 billion, or almost half of current annual diabetes-related expenditures. Doing both would lead to cumulative annual savings of about $235 billion. These numbers reflect only direct savings in health care costs; they do not include the considerable indirect savings in terms of limiting lost productivity due to illness or the indirect economic benefits of diabetes patients living longer lives—let alone the improved quality of life due to reduced human suffering.

Widespread variation in health outcomes isn't just a phenomenon among countries. Such variations also exist between regions within countries, between different socioeconomic and racial groups in the population, and even between hospitals in the same region or the same city.

Socioeconomic factors and patient behavior explain some of the observed outcome variation. For example, in recent years, increasing attention has been paid to below-average health outcomes for certain socioeconomic and racial groups due to inequities in access to care or to receiving low-value care. In 2021, the *Journal of the American Medical Association* (*JAMA*) published a special issue on the stubborn persistence of racial and economic differences in both access to care and in health outcomes in the United States. For example, a national survey of nearly 600,000 people found that in the two decades between 1999 and 2018, low-income Black individuals had the highest estimated prevalence of poor or only fair health (nearly 30%), while high- and middle-income white Americans had the lowest (only about 6%).[25] What's more, there was no significant decrease in the gap over time—despite the 2010 passage of the Affordable Care Act. As is the case with rising health care costs, Covid-19 is also exacerbating health inequities across the world.[26]

But even when one controls for racial and other demographic differences, outcomes variation among different hospitals or clinical sites remains widespread. In 2016, we were part of a research team led by Dr. Barry Rosenberg in BCG's Chicago office that participated in a major study of outcomes variation in the United States, together with Dr. Atul Gawande of the Brigham and Women's Hospital in Boston and researchers from the Harvard T. H. Chan School of Public Health, the Johns Hopkins School of Medicine, University of Michigan Medical School, and the University of Rochester Department of Public Health.[27] Probably the most comprehensive analysis of health outcomes variation in the United States to date, the study covered 22 million hospital admissions across states that account for over half of the US population, and included information from both the federal government's Medicare and Medicaid programs and from private insurance companies.

We found that health outcomes vary dramatically across hospitals. Patients in low-performing hospitals (the bottom 10% in our sample) were 3 times more likely to die and 13 times more likely to experience complications than those in high-performing ones (the top 10%). Even a hospital that has excellent outcomes for treating heart attacks, for example, might have far worse outcomes in treating a condition like diabetes.

We looked at specific health outcomes, including for many common illnesses such as cardiovascular disease and pneumonia. And even after extensive risk assessment, which allowed us to adjust the results for factors such as patient comorbidities and age, income, and other demographic and social determinants of health, we found that large variations in performance persisted across geographies.

Let's take just two examples. Even after risk adjustment, the probability of dying in the hospital after an acute event, such as acute myocardial infarction (AMI), commonly referred to as heart attack, was more than twice as high at low-performing hospitals as at those in the top 10%. (See Figure 1.6.) And patients were nearly 20 times more likely to experience central-line blood infections at low-performing hospitals than at high-performing ones.

Moreover, the variation persists even within states or among hospitals in the same metropolitan area. For example, if you have an AMI in Los Angeles, which has 17 hospitals, an ambulance might take you to a hospital with a 6% death rate or one with a 22% death rate. And it's not just down to socioeconomic factors. We found regions with low-performing hospitals that serve high-income, largely white populations and many regions with high-performing hospitals that serve low-income, minority populations. In other words, the variation we found was not primarily driven by the patients being served but rather by differences in organization and clinical practice across the hospitals.

This is the variation in health outcomes that we know about. But there is likely a great deal of hidden outcomes variation that we *don't* know about, simply because health systems do not systematically track the outcomes. We'll address the need for more comprehensive tracking of health outcomes in Chapter 2.

FIGURE 1.6   **Health outcomes vary widely across regions in a single country.**

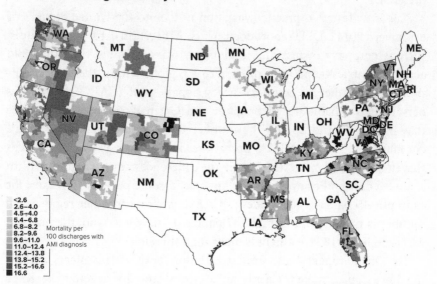

The chart maps mortality levels for every 100 discharges with a diagnosis of acute myocardial infarction (AMI) in 1,295 hospital service areas (HSAs) in 18 US states for which data was available. The darker the shading, the higher the mortality.

Source: *Barry L. Rosenberg et al., "Quantifying Geographic Variation in Health Care Outcomes in the United States Before and After Risk-Adjustment," PLOS ONE 11, no. 12 (December 14, 2016): e0166762,* https://doi.org/10.1371/journal.pone.0166762.

UNWARRANTED PRACTICE VARIATION

The finding of our study that outcomes variation is, in large part, driven by differences in clinical practice sheds light on the considerable research in the medical literature showing that there is widespread *practice* variation in how clinicians treat their patients. Ever since the pioneering work of Dr. John Wennberg and the Dartmouth Atlas of Health Care Project, it has become increasingly clear that a significant portion of this variation is unwarranted or medically inappropriate. The project, which used publicly available information from the US Medicare program to track variations in treatment received by Americans over the age of 65, highlighted that much of the widespread variation in per capita spending, resource allocation, and service use across Medicare hospital-referral regions is unwarranted because it cannot be explained by illness or patient preference.[28]

Nor is widespread practice variation unique to the United States. For example, a 2014 OECD report documents that certain cardiac procedures, such as coronary bypass and angioplasty, vary by more than threefold across countries—and even more across regions within the same country.[29] The number of coronary-artery-bypass-graft (CABG) procedures per 100,000 inhabitants in Belgium and Germany is more than twice that in France and Spain. The number of percutaneous-transluminal-coronary-angioplasty (PTCA) procedures in Germany is twice as high as that in Italy. Even more striking are the differences among regions within a single country. For every 100,000 people in some parts of Germany, for example, 45 patients will undergo CABG; whereas in other regions, the number is nearly twice as high (87 patients). In Switzerland, the regional variation in CABG treatment is more than threefold.

The OECD report shows similar variation for other treatments, including knee replacements, Caesarean sections, and hysterectomies. Knee replacement rates not only vary widely across countries, they also can vary as much as threefold across regions within a single country (for the example of Germany, see Figure 1.7). This variation is not limited to surgical procedures; the report documents similar variations in diagnostic procedures (such as MRI and CT scans) and hospital admissions.

Of course, some degree of practice variation is entirely appropriate, reflecting legitimate differences in patient mix, needs, or preferences. But according to Wennberg, the Dartmouth Atlas, and the OECD, a significant portion of practice variation is not. In particular, Wennberg has described three common types of unwarranted practice variation.[30]

The first is the underuse of *effective care* in which the benefits of treatment clearly outweigh the risks, mainly due to poor care coordination.[31] The second is variation in *preference-sensitive care*—for example, elective surgery.[32] Finally, unwarranted practice variation can be a function of *the overuse of supply-sensitive care or services* that are directly related to the supply of physicians, health care facilities, and medical equipment.[33]

How big a contributor is unwarranted practice variation to health care's value crisis? Wennberg estimates based on Dartmouth Atlas benchmarks that if the entire US health care system followed the practice patterns found in the high-quality, low-cost regions of the country, it would save 40% of resources spent on chronic illness.[34]

FIGURE 1.7 **There is considerable practice variation across countries and across regions within a single country.**

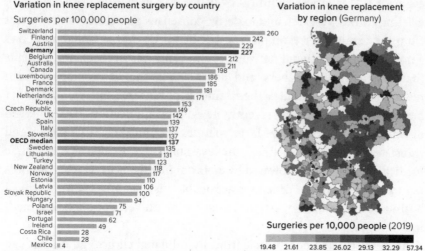

Variation in knee replacement surgery by country

Surgeries per 100,000 people

Variation in knee replacement by region (Germany)

Surgeries per 10,000 people (2019)

19.48 21.61 23.85 26.02 29.13 32.29 57.34

The bar chart on the left shows the variations in the number of knee replacement surgeries per 100,000 people in 30 OECD countries. The map at the right shows the variation in the number of surgeries per capita in different regions of Germany.

Sources: *OECD Health at Glance 2021; Statistisches Bundesamt, DRG-Statistik, 2020.*

A PARALLEL CRISIS OF EVIDENCE

Health care's value crisis is made worse by a parallel crisis in evidence. In a nutshell, the evidence crisis is the paradoxical product of the explosion of biomedical knowledge in recent decades and the resulting increase in the complexity of clinical practice. The more biomedical knowledge available, the more diagnostic and therapeutic options to choose from. But the more options to choose from, the more clinicians risk suffering from information overload, and the less clear it becomes how best to apply our growing knowledge in any particular case, matching the most appropriate treatment to the circumstances of a given patient. This uncertainty is a key factor in the phenomenon of practice variation that Wennberg and others have identified.

In response, the medical profession has increasingly embraced so-called evidence-based medicine, or the idea that medical practice and care should emphasize the practical application of the findings of the best available current research.[35] An entire industry has grown up to gather, evaluate, and synthesize clinical evidence by conducting meta-studies of existing clinical research and to derive consensus guidelines for treatment from the results. For example, the UK-based Cochrane Collaboration is a nonprofit international network of clinicians, researchers, and patients that systematically gathers and summarizes the best evidence from research and disseminates them among physicians, nurses, and other health professionals. More recently, new digital applications have emerged in which computers analyze large volumes of clinical research papers and translate them into guidelines. One example is Dr. Evidence, a real-time medical search engine powered by artificial intelligence (AI) that, according to its developers, "generates actionable insights and answers critical business and research questions based on the universe of published medical information."[36]

To be sure, adherence to scientifically validated clinical guidelines can be an important mechanism for reducing unnecessary practice variation. In their book *Noise: A Flaw in Human Judgment*, Nobel laureate Daniel Kahneman and his coauthors Olivier Sibony and Cass R. Sunstein describe how diagnostic and treatment guidelines can be an important "decision hygiene strategy" for reducing unexplained variations in judgment in medical decision-making.[37] But there are considerable limits to clinical guidelines as they are currently developed.

First, despite the exponential growth in clinical research in recent decades, the scientific evidence just doesn't exist yet for many clinical interventions. In a review of 3,000 interventions used to prevent and treat common clinical conditions, the journal *BMJ Clinical Evidence* found that half of these interventions had insufficient evidence of effectiveness.[38]

What's more, the evidence supporting those guidelines that do exist is often remarkably weak.[39] In 2009, a research team from the Duke University Clinical Research Unit analyzed the 53 practice guidelines, encompassing more than 7,000 recommendations, issued by the American College of Cardiology and the American Heart Association between 1984 and September 2008.[40] Among the guidelines that had been updated at least once by the end of this period, the number of recommendations had increased by about half. And of the 16 current guidelines that reported the underlying evidence, only about 11% of the recommendations were classified by the researchers at the highest of three levels of evidence (defined as a minimum of two supporting randomized controlled trials or meta-analyses), whereas nearly half the recommendations were classified at the lowest level (based only on expert opinion, case studies, or existing standards of care). What's more, the proportion of recommendations for which there was no conclusive evidence grew over time.

What explains the relatively poor scientific support of many clinical guidelines? Partly, it is a matter of the daunting complexity of human biology. The fact that only about 14% of drug candidates in Phase I trials ever reach the market is a telling indicator of how much we still have to learn about the biochemical mechanisms of human health and disease.[41] But the main reason is that despite the approximately $400 billion that the world spends each year on biomedical R&D, relatively little of that money targets the comparative effectiveness of different treatments for the same condition or disease. (See the sidebar "Why Growing R&D Spending Isn't Solving the Evidence Crisis.")

Why Growing R&D Spending Isn't Solving the Evidence Crisis

The R&D and innovation system that has evolved over the years in health care is focused on generating new knowledge used to identify new drugs, new diagnostics, new treatments, and other interventions. Only a relatively small fraction of the money spent on R&D is devoted to understanding the comparative effectiveness of different treatments or therapies and on identifying the most effective interventions for specific groups of patients, thus contributing to new evidence for better clinical guidelines. As a result, the world's health systems lack adequate evidence to judge which interventions contribute to high-value care (and for whom) and which do not.

A 2013 analysis in *The Lancet* estimates that in 2009, worldwide spending on biomedical research was in the neighborhood of $240 billion.[42] Using that analysis as our starting point, we estimate that annual R&D spending has grown by about 6% per year since, reaching just over $400 billion by 2020, with private industry (mainly the pharmaceutical sector) responsible for a dominant and growing share—64%, or nearly two-thirds of all spending.

Very little of this money, however, targets research on the comparative effectiveness of different treatments or interventions. For example, the vast majority of pharmaceutical-industry-funded Phase III clinical trials test the efficacy and safety of a single product (the company's own) against a placebo.[43] Some test the so-called "noninferiority" of the drug candidate in question—that is, they attempt to demonstrate that the new treatment is not unacceptably worse than the current standard therapy. Such studies are useful for helping a new product navigate the drug approval process, but they tell clinicians little about its comparative effectiveness versus other potential therapies or where it delivers demonstrably superior health outcomes to patients.

The pharma industry does sponsor some head-to-head studies that compare the relative effectiveness of two or more drugs or clinical interventions, but the vast majority of these studies have only a single industry sponsor (and, perhaps unsurprisingly, the results typically favor the product of the industry sponsor).[44] According to various estimates in the scientific literature, head-to-head studies sponsored by multiple sponsors represent as few as 1% to 3% of all industry-funded clinical trials.[45]

Earlier studies of head-to-head trials typically focus on studies sponsored by the largest pharmaceutical companies. We have attempted to update these numbers in a much larger sample, using data on all clinical trials from Phase II and later that are registered at the US government website clinicaltrials.gov, the most comprehensive global database of active clinical trials. In 2022, the site covers almost 400,000 studies, of which just over 50% were registered outside the United States.[46] But despite this larger sample and the expanded number of studies analyzed, we came to remarkably similar conclusions as earlier studies: only about 3% of industry-sponsored clinical trials compare more than one product and are sponsored by more than one company.

The roughly 25% of health-related research funded by public entities also suffers from other imbalances that contribute to the perpetuation of the evidence crisis. The vast majority of public research dollars in medicine funds basic and applied research on the biomedical mechanisms of disease. The biomedical model has resulted in remarkable advances in clinical medicine, including the development of antibiotics, mRNA vaccines, organ transplantation, and cures for some cancers. But it has also led to a proliferation of therapeutic options, many of which are expensive, or only marginally better, or in some cases, not useful at all. And as Stanford psychologist Robert Kaplan has pointed out in his book *More Than Medicine*, the dramatic imbalance between the massive research dollars spent on the biomedical determinants of health and disease comes at the cost of a relative neglect of the social and behavioral determinants that according to one estimate account for roughly 60% of the factors contributing to premature death.[47] Kaplan shows that between 1999 and 2002, the budget of the US National Institutes of Health (NIH) more than doubled and by 2018, had increased to more than $37 billion. But the vast majority of the increase was targeted at specific biomedical programs—Alzheimer's disease, cancer, universal flu vaccines, and the like—while "none of the expansion was targeted at social, behavioral, and environmental determinants of health that account for most premature deaths in the United States."[48]

Finally, from a global perspective, the fact that the vast majority of biomedical R&D—estimates suggest as much as 90%—takes place in rich countries, with the United States accounting for fully half of global R&D spending, creates another major imbalance. Most research focuses on diseases that are common in wealthy countries (for example, cancer) rather than on diseases that represent the largest burden of preventable mortality in poorer countries. Research has shown no correlation between the global burden of disease and the corresponding quantity of randomized controlled trials in a given disease domain.[49]

Even when guidelines are supported by strong clinical evidence, the arduous process of validation—in which a critical mass of clinical studies must first be completed, peer reviewed, and published, the initial studies then replicated and validated by other researchers, and finally, the implications for clinical practice synthesized in comprehensive meta-studies—can often take so long that once the guidelines are launched, their relevance to fast-evolving clinical practice has decreased.[50] According to one estimate, it takes approximately 17 years on average for newly developed treatments to be fully introduced to and accepted by clinicians, even when they clearly outperform the old options; in addition, only about half of all evidence-based recommendations get implemented into care.[51]

Even when scientifically validated guidelines are successfully implemented, medical knowledge is moving so rapidly that guidelines tend to
have a relatively short shelf life and by the time they are finally implemented
may be out of date. According to one meta-analysis, systematic reviews of
randomized trials have a median "survival time" of 5.5 years before needing an update, with 23% requiring an update within 2 years.[52] Another
study reported that about half of the guidelines published by the Agency
for Healthcare Research and Quality needed updating within 5.8 years.[53]

Last but far from least, because of the growing cost of care and con-
cern about variations in clinical practice, guidelines are increasingly used
by payers and regulators to enforce adherence or to link guideline compliance to reimbursement. Not only does this contribute to the erosion
of purpose and autonomy among clinicians (a topic that we will address
in the next section of this chapter), forced compliance to general standardized guidelines also risks coming at the expense of local clinical
innovation and meeting the specific needs of individual patients. Needless to say, there is a major difference between adhering to guidelines that
have been conclusively linked to improved patient health outcomes and
adhering to guidelines when it isn't clear whether they deliver improved
outcomes or not.

To cite one concise summary from the biomedical literature: "In short,
clinical practice guidelines are limited in their ability to deliver what our
health care system needs: a way to promote greater care standardization
that accommodates patients' differences, respects providers' clinical acu-
men, and keeps pace with the rapid growth of medical knowledge."[54]

The goal of evidence-based medicine is too important to allow it to
rely on what is increasingly a broken innovation model.[55] Scientific rigor
is critical, but in a world characterized by an exponential increase in the
number of studies published and increasingly rapid iterative cycles of
agile innovation, it's imperative to pose the following question: Are there
better ways to organize the generation of clinical evidence, to speed up
the process of validation and translation into clinical practice, to reduce
the occurrence of inappropriate care, and, most important of all, to better
arm clinicians on the front line of care with decision support to help them
match the right treatments to the right patients? A more robust innovation system would not only address the evidence crisis, it would also be an
important weapon in the fight against health care's value crisis. Finally,
it might even renew a sense of purpose for health care professionals in

an industry where many feel they are losing touch with the reasons that brought them to health care in the first place.

A CORROSIVE CRISIS OF PURPOSE

There is a final crisis confronting health systems around the world that is simultaneously more subtle and yet perhaps even more corrosive than the two we have discussed so far. We call it a crisis of purpose, and it has to do with what it feels like to work in today's health systems and to receive care as a patient in them. Francesca Colombo, the longtime head of the Health division at the OECD, told us: "If I had a mandate to define the priorities for the OECD ministers of health, at the top of my list, especially in the light of the coronavirus pandemic, would be addressing health care's growing people crisis."

As a way in to charting the dynamics of this crisis, consider the much-discussed topic of clinician burnout.[56] For years, a great deal of attention has focused on the extremely high rates of stress and burnout in the health professions. For example, surveys suggest that roughly half of US physicians report that their morale is either somewhat or very negative and that they often or always feel burnt out.[57] Estimates suggest that the cost of physician burnout to the US health system is roughly $5 billion per year due to reduced clinical productivity and increased physician turnover.[58] Again, the problem isn't just a US problem. Eighty percent of doctors in a 2019 British Medical Association survey were at a high or very high risk of burnout, with junior doctors most at risk.[59] Burnout is a problem in health systems in low- and middle-income countries as well. And, as Colombo points out, the profoundly destabilizing impact of the coronavirus pandemic has only made the problem worse.[60]

When physicians are asked about the causes of burnout, they cite a variety of reasons: excess bureaucracy, long working hours, lack of respect from colleagues (and increasingly from the public), the negative impact of the computerization of clinical practice, insufficient compensation, and a lack of clinical autonomy.[61] All these factors are certainly important. But we think they are merely symptoms of a deeper reason having to do with long-term trends in the evolution of the health care sector—trends that produce a disconnect between the values and motivations that have brought many to work in the industry and their day-to-day work experience.

Our perspective on this purpose crisis has been deeply influenced by the work of two of our BCG colleagues, Yves Morieux and Peter Tollman. Yves is an organizational sociologist and the head of BCG's Institute for Organization; Peter is a health care expert who used to lead BCG's People and Organization practice in North America. For more than 20 years, they have been working with organizations to help them cope with rapidly expanding business complexity.[62] We think their views on business complexity shed light on health care's purpose crisis; but before describing precisely how, let's explore their general perspective.

Morieux and Tollman argue that complexity is an unavoidable aspect of the contemporary business environment. It is driven by the proliferation of performance requirements; the increase in the number of customer segments, local markets, and competitors; the growth in the number of relevant stakeholders and business partners; the multiplication of categories of specialized knowledge and expertise; the faster pace of innovation and change; and the higher levels of uncertainty and volatility.

Complexity may sound like a problem, but Morieux and Tollman point out that, in fact, it can be an enormous opportunity—if organizations can learn how to take advantage of it. The more complex the business, the more ways to create value by breaking compromises among heretofore conflicting objectives or goals and by combining diverse skills and capabilities in unprecedented ways.

Problems arise, however, in the typical way that most organizations try to manage complexity. They use traditional organizational mechanisms such as reporting relationships, formal processes, detailed rules and guidelines, and key performance indicators (KPIs) to dictate how employees should behave in the face of complexity. The more goals and objectives multiply, however, the more the rules, processes, and guidelines proliferate in an effort to manage complexity and control what people do. The paradoxical result is to add unnecessary layers of organizational complicatedness on top of necessarily complex tasks. Increasingly complicated organizations restrict autonomy and make it more difficult, not less, for people to work together to manage complexity effectively.

According to Morieux and Tollman, the key to effective performance in complex work environments is to encourage autonomy, not to restrict it. After all, autonomy is the freedom to exercise one's judgment in the completion of a task. In situations where the task is simple and the goals clear, autonomy isn't really necessary; the organization can create a rule or an algorithm that people can follow. But in situations where individuals and teams need to make trade-offs among multiple objectives or multiple ways of achieving them, all the rules in the world cannot dictate the most appropriate solution for the specific situation. The only way to manage a growing number of increasingly complex trade-offs is to establish a few simple global objectives and goals, give people the autonomy to exercise their judgment in realizing those goals, provide them access to relevant information and data so they can effectively exercise their autonomy, and then measure and reward them for the results.

But autonomy alone is not enough. The more complex the work environment, the less likely that any one individual or group will have all the answers. Rather, people, teams, and entire organizational units need to work together to get to the best result. It's therefore also essential for an individual's autonomy to be deployed in the service of cooperation with others to realize shared goals.

Cooperation may sound like a feel-good term, a self-evident value in any organization. In reality, cooperation is a complex social process, hard to create and easy to destroy. The fact is, many people avoid cooperating if they can get away with it, and they will often use whatever autonomy they have to do so. To truly cooperate with others requires people to adjust their individual goals for the greater good of the organization or, put another way, to align their individual goals to the shared goals of the organization. Cooperation involves tension, the confrontation between different but equally valid perspectives and priorities, and sometimes considerable conflict. (Indeed, *absence* of conflict is often the first sign that cooperation isn't taking place.) The challenge, therefore, is to find ways to make cooperation and the adjustments it imposes on people's goals not only a worthwhile organizational objective but also a rational strategy for individuals.

We think Morieux and Tollman's perspective on business complexity and how to navigate it is relevant to any industry. But it is *especially* relevant to health care.[63] Few work environments today are subject to as much complexity as those in health care. Rapid advances in biomedical science have led to an exponential increase in the understanding of health and disease and in new tools for diagnosis and treatment. But they have also led to increased specialization, more complex clinical decision-making, and a concomitant fragmentation of care, which can make it difficult for clinicians to work together to take a truly integrated approach to patient health. The paradox of specialization is that it makes cooperation more necessary even as it makes it more difficult to achieve.

Complexity in health care is exacerbated by the industry's many stakeholders. Payers, providers, drug makers, and medical device companies are separate but interdependent members of an increasingly intricate complex adaptive system.[64] So are institutions that are not typically thought of as part of the health care industry at all—for example, university research labs, patient advocacy groups, public health and social service organizations, health technology companies, and the like. All these various organizational entities contribute to patient care and, ultimately, to the health outcomes delivered to patients, but diverging goals and misaligned incentives stand in the way of effective cooperation.

Like many businesses, health care has also witnessed a proliferation of new performance requirements in recent decades. Increasingly, clinicians are asked not merely to treat the patient and cure disease but also to control costs, maximize capacity utilization, minimize wait times, and ensure patient satisfaction, among other important goals. Multiple performance requirements further increase the complexity of the task.

As is the case in many other sectors of the economy, the way that traditional health care institutions try to manage this complexity too often only makes the problems worse. Much like managers in other industries, health care leaders have put in place more and more standardized processes, rules, guidelines, and KPIs. They focus on compliance but at the price of significantly eroding the professional autonomy that clinicians used to enjoy while at the same time making it even more difficult for them to work together to make the trade-offs necessary to deliver value to patients.

Consider the typical approach to cost control. Payers try to control costs by imposing constraints on medical decision-making and patient choice in the form of utilization reviews, drug formularies, prior authorization, restricted provider networks, rationing, and the like. In response, many provider organizations focus on process efficiency, imposing top-down performance measures to increase their control over clinical practitioners. It's an understandable impulse. But the result is that highly qualified and experienced clinicians end up feeling micromanaged, caught between the demands of payers to contain costs, of hospital administrators to maximize the use of expensive medical technologies, and of themselves as professionals to provide the most appropriate treatments to their patients.

Clinicians still have the responsibility for making life-and-death decisions. But they are increasingly subject to bureaucratic controls that erode their capacity to exercise their own expertise and judgment in the best interest of their patients. The stress of bearing that distinctive emotional burden, with less and less control over the outcome, often leads to frustration, cynicism, and mistrust.

Given these broad systemic dysfunctionalities, it's little wonder that health professions have some of the highest levels of dissatisfaction and burnout. At its worst, this situation can lead to a growing divide between management and clinical staff and to an organizational and professional culture of cynicism in which poor performance or breakdowns are blamed on others, rather than being occasions for reflection, cooperation, innovation, and continuous improvement.

Of course, patients, too, feel the impact of the purpose crisis. It is reflected in their own experience of the dysfunctional complexity of many current health systems. Too many patients feel like cogs in a machine in which highly specialized caregivers focus on one aspect of their condition, while no one takes responsibility for the whole. People are, with good reason, increasingly being asked to take more responsibility for their health. They are also having to pay out of pocket for a growing share of treatment costs. And yet, they face extreme asymmetries of information about the health outcomes delivered by different providers, making it extremely difficult—and in many cases impossible—to make informed choices among providers or treatment options.

The complexity of modern medicine and the modern health care industry isn't going away. Indeed, given the expansion in biomedical knowledge, that complexity is only likely to increase in the future. The only way to effectively manage that complexity—and to cut through the dysfunctional organizational complicatedness of the industry today—is to give autonomy back to caregivers and at the same time channel that autonomy toward new kinds of cooperation across medical disciplines and across the different sectors of the health care industry, in the service of clearly defined shared goals.

The basic idea behind value-based health care is to align industry stakeholders around the shared objective of improving measurable health outcomes delivered to patients for a given cost and then to give those stakeholders the autonomy, tools, and accountability they need to meet that objective.[65] We believe that outcomes improvement is the shared goal that can align all the players in the industry and renew a sense of purpose for health professionals. When all stakeholders focus on that goal, renewed commitment, robust clinical innovation, and, ultimately, better outcomes for patients will follow.

WHERE TO BEGIN? TACKLING HEALTH CARE'S THREE CRISES

In the last few decades, there has been a proliferation of formulas for describing the kind of goals that the global health care system should aspire to. We have already considered one—evidence-based medicine—but there are many others. For example, the Triple Aim proposes three broad goals that address roughly what we have described as the value crisis: improving the experience of care, improving the health of populations, and reducing the per capita costs of health care.[66] And in a direct response to what we have termed the purpose crisis, the Quadruple Aim adds a fourth: improving the experience of those providing care.[67] Other formulations emphasize the importance of health equity, universal access, quality, the personalization of care through precision medicine, or ensuring that our health systems are patient centered.[68] Finally, some attempt to combine all these worthy goals—for example, the "4P Health Spectrum," in which the four Ps stand for Predictive, Preventive, Personalized, and Participatory.[69]

But the question remains: How to translate these goals into practice? In a complex adaptive system such as health care, no single entity or authority can decree, impose, or force compliance to the necessary changes. Rather, all stakeholders must work together to define a limited but comprehensive set of principles—what system scientists call "simple rules"—to reshape the organizational context so that it encourages new behavioral patterns and new dynamics of healthy competition and purposeful collaboration.

The literature on complex adaptive systems suggests that four types of rules are especially important:[70]

1. The system needs a clearly articulated purpose or mission around which stakeholders can align.
2. Individuals and institutions in the system need access to data and information directly relevant to that purpose in order to inform their actions and interactions with others.

3. Resources and incentives aligned with the purpose need to be made available to make it easy for the right kind of behaviors to emerge.
4. Regulations need to encourage autonomy, innovation, and self-organization—but also to establish guardrails against self-dealing and abuse.

How might we apply these four simple rules to health care? From 2016 through 2018, we worked with public- and private-sector health care leaders associated with the World Economic Forum on what was known as the Value in Healthcare project.[71] We'll say more about this project later in the book. But here at the beginning, we want to introduce one particular output from the project: a "greenfield" model for a future value-based health system. Rather than being constrained by how the health sector is organized today, our goal for the model was to focus on what would encourage the right kind of behaviors to emerge and flourish. (For a schematic illustration of our model, see Figure 1.8.)

FIGURE 1.8   A conceptual model of a value-based health system.

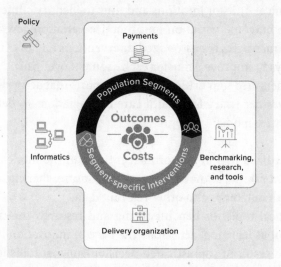

The model describes the building blocks of a health system designed to improve patient value. At the core is the systematic measurement of outcomes and costs for defined population segments, supported by complementary enablers.

Source: *World Economic Forum.*

At the center of the model is a definition of what we believe should be the ultimate purpose and objective of any health care system: to deliver the best possible health outcomes to patients for the money spent. This objective puts the individual patient at the very center of the health system. It also serves to reconnect clinicians and other health professionals to the sense of purpose that attracted many of them to the industry in the first place. Put another way, in a value-based health system, patient value becomes what evolutionary biologists call the "selection principle" against which the contribution and performance of all institutions in the system is assessed and their collective results evaluated.

The systematic measurement of health outcomes that matter to patients, as well as of the costs required to deliver those outcomes across the full cycle of care, is the all-important data that industry players need in order to fulfill the mission of continuously improving patient value. The relevant outcomes tracked for any individual patient at a given moment in time depend on their profile matching to a specific population segment—for example, all patients suffering from a specific disease, such as diabetes, or groups that share a similar risk profile, such as the frail elderly. Tracking outcomes and costs by population segment makes it possible to compare clinical units or locations and thus to identify clinical best practices, reduce outcome variation and practice variation across providers, and develop increasingly customized interventions and ever more precise care pathways to improve value for each segment over time.

We also identified four critical system supports that define the resources and incentives necessary for health care organizations to deliver on this value-based care model:

1. Standardized digital platforms (captured in the model by the term *informatics*) that allow for the routine capture, sharing, and analysis of health outcomes and other relevant data

2. Analytical tools for benchmarking and research that will support continuous learning, accelerate the pace of innovation in the industry, and result in sophisticated decision-support tools for clinicians and patients

3. Value-based payment models that create incentives for continuous improvement in patient value by rewarding clinicians for improving value, not just for increasing volume—for instance, through prevention and better cooperation along the care pathway

4. Organizational models and roles that allow networks of providers and suppliers to deliver better access to appropriate care, engage clinicians in continuous improvement, and adapt to new opportunities and innovations

These four enablers of value-based health care are interdependent. They need to work together and be assessed by their contribution to patient value. In this respect, they represent a holistic framework for health care system reform.

Finally, a value-based health system also requires the development of an important governance and regulatory context: new public policies and legal and regulatory frameworks that, through the design of a limited set of enabling guardrails, encourage value-based innovation across all the components of the health system and accelerates the transition to value-based health care.

Described in so skeletal a fashion, our model may seem abstract. And, of course, no health system today has all these components in place. In subsequent chapters, however, we will describe the logic behind each of the elements of this model, how they connect to each other, and how innovators across the health care sector and around the world are putting them in place—sometimes in a single organization, sometimes across multiple organizations, sometimes at the level of an entire national health system, and sometimes on a global scale.

The place to begin our journey is at the very center of the model: by demonstrating the power of outcomes measurement to unleash innovation and continuous improvement and to deliver better outcomes to patients, often for the same, or even lower, cost.

CHAPTER 2

THE POWER OF OUTCOMES

No industry can improve its performance unless it has some objective measure against which it can analyze and assess its efforts. Systems of performance measurement and management have proliferated across industry in recent decades, and health care is no exception. Clinicians have been subject to a bewildering variety of metrics to measure performance. The problem, however, is that most of these metrics do not really get at what ought to be the fundamental purpose of any health system: to continuously improve the health outcomes delivered to patients for a given level of financial investment.

Therefore, the first critical step to unlock value in health care is to reorient performance measurement around the systematic collection, sharing, and analysis of health-outcomes data. When the outcomes providers deliver become transparent, health systems can know where they stand in comparison to regional, national, and global benchmarks; identify innovations in clinical intervention and treatment; and adopt those practices that are proven to deliver superior outcomes.

In this chapter, we will make the case that the best way to think about results in health care is in terms of the delivery of health outcomes that matter to patients and argue that health systems around the world need to measure health outcomes more systematically and comprehensively.

Next, we'll describe what is probably the best example of how systematic tracking of health outcomes can become a powerful catalyst for performance improvement: national quality registries that collect comprehensive data on the health outcomes in a population of patients with the same condition or who have undergone a common medical procedure.

Finally, we'll conclude the chapter by examining a nonprofit initiative known as the International Consortium for Health Outcomes Measurement, or ICHOM, which brings together clinical experts and patient representatives from around the world to create consensus global standards for health-outcome measures that support international networks for learning and continuous improvement.

HOW TO MEASURE RESULTS IN HEALTH CARE

Health care providers have been tracking an increasing number of metrics in recent years, often in response to requirements from payers or regulatory agencies to improve cost efficiency and the quality of care delivered to patients. In addition to tracking a patient's initial conditions and the key health indicators in a patient's medical history, they track organizational and financial metrics such as staff-to-patient ratios or whether a given unit is on budget. They track treatment protocols such as time of biopsy, time-to-diagnosis, surgical technique used, radiation treatment settings, medication administered, and other process measurements that monitor adherence to clinical guidelines. Increasingly, they measure patient satisfaction, using patient-reported experience measures (so-called PREMs) to assess patient perceptions of everything from the patient-provider interactions and the length of waiting times to the quality of hospital food and the general cleanliness of the facility.

The proliferation of new metrics in health care has provoked something of a backlash on the part of many clinicians.[1] They are, rightly, worried about the growing administrative burden of providing the data to track all these new metrics, which can take valuable time away from clinical practice and interaction with patients. They are also concerned that even when such metrics are well-intentioned, their proliferation can lead to a perfunctory "check-the-boxes" approach to care. Another common objection is that organizations will use the growing body of metrics to assess clinician performance (and even determine their compensation) based on factors over which they do not have complete control. In the worst-case scenario, linking payment to performance on a given set of metrics can lead to the systematic gaming of the metrics as organizations focus more on documenting so-called quality care (for financial purposes) rather than actually delivering it to patients. Finally, some argue that too much of a focus on what can be measured inevitably squeezes out clinical judgment, making it difficult for clinicians to navigate complex trade-offs in treating patients, and too often comes at the neglect of critical but hard-to-quantify aspects of the healing professions. Or as one Swedish general practitioner put it, "You can't measure empathy and compassion."

We're sympathetic with these concerns. And yet, measurement is not only central to the scientific method; it is also foundational to any organization's ability to learn from experience and improve its performance. As such, it is a prerequisite for progress not only in, say, molecular biology or the development of new drugs but also in how health systems are organized, care is delivered, and the overall system is managed. In this respect, effective measurement is critical, not so much for reasons of managerial control but for organizational learning.

It may be true that "you can't measure compassion." Yet, however important compassion and empathy in the doctor-patient relationship are (and, in certain situations, they are vitally important), in the end they are only means to the end of delivering the best possible health outcomes to the patient. What's more, it is definitely possible to measure the *impact* of compassion and empathy—for example, in whether patients feel listened to and have their preferences respected, whether they trust their doctors and have confidence in their advice.

So, the critical issue is not *whether* to measure but *what* to measure and especially, *how* to measure what really matters to the fundamental purpose of health care organizations: improving the health outcomes delivered to patients. The key problem with performance measurement in health care today is not so much that there are too many metrics (although there are) or that their use is often inflexible or mechanistic. Rather, it is that so many of these metrics really are poor substitutes for measuring the actual health outcomes that matter to patients.[2] Process efficiency may make a department more efficient and save costs, but if it comes at a decline in the health outcomes delivered to patients, it is not really contributing to patient value. Ensuring that patients have a good experience when they receive care or visit the hospital is admirable, but what is the value of a great patient experience if the actual health outcomes that result are below average?

The relative lack of measurement of actual health outcomes is also a problem when it comes to the way that most health systems typically measure quality. With relatively few exceptions, the idea of quality in health care has been defined in terms of compliance with evidence-based practice guidelines. For example, a 2016 analysis of the nearly 2,000 quality indicators in the National Quality Measures Clearinghouse of the US federal government's Agency for Healthcare Research and Quality found that only 139 (7%) were actual health outcomes, and only 32 (less than 2%) were patient-reported outcomes.[3] The biggest category of measures, making up more than half of all the measures in the clearinghouse, were process-related measures such as adherence to guidelines. (See Figure 2.1.) As we discussed in Chapter 1, although adherence to scientifically validated clinical guidelines can be an important mechanism for reducing unnecessary practice variation, there are many limitations to using adherence to guidelines as a proxy for the actual health outcomes delivered to patients.

We did a similar analysis of the 70 measures used in the Health Effectiveness Data and Information Set (HEDIS), a set of performance measures developed by the US National Committee for Quality Assurance that is used by the US government to rate the quality of US health insurance plans. The results were slightly better but broadly similar: only about 12% of the HEDIS metrics are outcomes measures. Meanwhile, nearly three-quarters are process metrics.

The purpose of this analysis is not to criticize all process metrics, many of which are quite useful. Rather, it is to demonstrate that, although there are some exceptions which we will discuss later in this chapter and in subsequent chapters, most health systems do not routinely track health outcomes for all patients beyond basic mortality statistics and adverse events (complications, medical errors, and the like).[4] Even fewer are able to link outcomes to the cost or even to the key cost drivers of the full cycle of care delivered to patients. And the outcomes measures that do exist often vary from institution to institution, making it difficult to compare outcomes across institutions, regions, and countries.[5]

This is a major obstacle to the improvement of health care value. The systematic measurement of health outcomes is critical to assessing the

FIGURE 2.1 **The vast majority of US quality metrics do not measure health outcomes.**

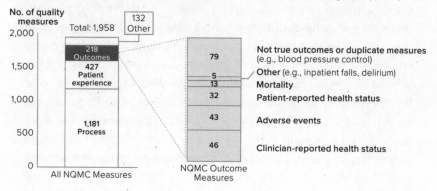

Categories of Quality Measures Listed in the National Quality Measures Clearinghouse (NQMC)

The bar on the left categorizes the nearly 2,000 quality measures in the US National Quality Measures Clearing House. Only about 10% are categorized as health-outcomes measures—and of these, more than a third are either duplicate measures or not really health-outcome metrics.

Source: *From NEJM, Porter, Larsson, and Lee, "Standardizing Patient Outcomes Measurement," Volume 374, Pages 504–506. Copyright © 2016 Massachusetts Medical Society. Reprinted with permission.*

ultimate results of the health system; identifying gaps in clinical protocols, knowledge, and capabilities; learning from experience; and more quickly revising and updating clinical guidelines over time. When outcome metrics are designed by clinicians in cooperation with patients and used as an asset for learning, it can be a powerful tool for increasing clinical autonomy and innovation, and for continuously improving health outcomes delivered to patients. (See the sidebar "Measuring Outcomes Versus Measuring Costs.")

For an example of what we mean, consider the experience of national quality registries.

Measuring Outcomes Versus Measuring Costs

In this chapter, we focus on measuring health outcomes delivered to patients, not on the costs required to deliver those outcomes. We do so not because we think that tracking costs is unimportant. Sooner or later, every provider organization needs to understand what it costs to deliver quality health outcomes to patients.

There has been so much focus on cost containment and cost efficiency in health care in recent years, however, that the lion's share of attention has gone to optimizing the efficiency of discrete pieces of the system (witness the popularity of "lean" approaches to process improvement), too often in isolation from the ultimate results that the system as a whole delivers to patients. We want to shift the focus of attention from narrow cost containment to outcomes improvement because we believe the only way to get a comprehensive handle on costs is to understand them in terms of the total costs required to deliver quality health outcomes to a given patient group. Put another way, even when an organization aspires to cost efficiency as one of a number of important goals, the best and most appropriate way to achieve it is first, by focusing on the precise health outcomes the organization hopes to achieve and only then, on the costs required to deliver those outcomes.

In our experience, improving health outcomes often saves money by eliminating unnecessary or inappropriate care. When organizations focus on outcomes improvement, they also often come up with less expensive and more efficient ways of delivering the same, or even higher, quality of care. And even when improvements require additional investment, the ultimate impact on health outcomes should always be the result against which the effectiveness of such investments are judged.

Once organizations start focusing on improving the health outcomes delivered to specific patient groups or population segments, there is a growing body of quite sophisticated methodologies for tracking total patient-group costs.[6] As health systems increasingly move in the direction of value-based payment (a subject we will address in Chapter 5), it will become increasingly important to know their costs by patient groups and population segments.

As important as measuring outcomes and costs for specific patient groups and population segments is, however, it cannot tell a health system how best to allocate scarce resources across patient groups and disease areas or what share of a nation's health care spending should go to, say, new generations versus the elderly, or sufferers of acute diseases such as stroke versus sufferers of chronic diseases such as diabetes. This is ultimately a public policy decision that is beyond the scope of this book.

QUALITY REGISTRIES: AN OUTCOMES-BASED LEARNING SYSTEM

We first witnessed the power of outcomes measurement as a catalyst for the continuous improvement of patient health in 2009, when a group of senior public and private-sector health care leaders in Sweden asked BCG to study that country's extensive network of quality registries.[7]

Quality registries are clinician-led organizations that collect comprehensive data on the health outcomes in a population of patients with the same condition (for example, those who have suffered from acute myocardial infarction, or heart attack) or who have undergone a common medical procedure (for instance, cataract surgery). Typically, they are established by the relevant professional society of specialists in a given field, although as we will see later, in some cases, registries have been organized by patient advocacy organizations. Registries are not the only way to track health outcomes, but they are a powerful example of the positive impact that transparent outcomes measurement can have on clinical practice.

Quality registries can be found all over the world. But Sweden has been an international pacesetter in the establishment of registries, with some dating back to the 1970s. Today, the country boasts more than 100 quality registries. About a third collect patient data on more than 90% of all Swedish patients diagnosed with a given condition or undergoing a common procedure, and many have been in place long enough to provide longitudinal data of a richness that is rarely found in other countries.

Most descriptions of registries make them sound like large databases— and they certainly are that. But the key insight from our early research was that registries are far more than simply repositories of data. In fact, the best registries are dynamic national networks of leading clinicians that function as engines of continuous improvement and innovation in clinical practice, while ensuring methodological and scientific rigor.

The process works like this: The initial launch of a registry becomes an occasion for clinical leaders in a given domain to come to some kind of consensus about what ought to be measured. Once a standard set of metrics is agreed to, the accumulation of registry data over time from all relevant providers across the nation makes it possible to identify how health outcomes vary across clinical sites. This enables researchers to analyze the root causes of those variations, establish the degree to which they are caused by variations in clinical practice, and codify the best practices and the latest clinical innovations that produce better patient outcomes.

What's more, making the data and analysis transparent (in the first instance to clinicians but eventually also to the public) then becomes the catalyst to refine clinical guidelines and encourage the adoption of best practices across the system, reduce practice variation, and improve median health outcomes. In addition, systematic quality improvement of this type often has the positive side effect of lowering total health care costs for some medical conditions because unnecessary procedures are eliminated, expensive complications occur less frequently, and repeat treatments are avoided by "getting it right the first time." (For a graphical depiction of this virtuous circle, see Figure 2.2.)

FIGURE 2.2   The value-based health care improvement cycle.

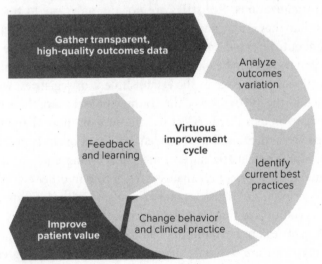

The graphic visualizes the process by which the collection and analysis of transparent, high-quality outcomes data can improve clinical practice and lead to better patient value.

Source: *BCG analysis.*

Swedeheart: A Quality Registry in Action

For an example of how registries achieve such improvements, consider the case of Sweden's heart attack registry, which was first established in 1991 and since 2009 has been part of Swedeheart, a consortium that groups together Sweden's six cardiovascular-disease-related registries. (One of the early leaders in the development of the registry was Dr. Lars Wallentin, a leading expert on unstable coronary artery disease and one of the most highly cited cardiologists in the world.)

Since 1995, Swedish hospitals have succeeded in lowering the average in-hospital, 30-day, and one-year mortality rates for patients under the age of 80 who suffered an acute heart attack by 60%, 68%, and 65%, respectively. (See Figure 2.3.) Such improvements have made Sweden a global leader in cardiac-related health outcomes. For example, a 2014 study published in *The Lancet* compared 30-day mortality after acute myocardial infarction in the United Kingdom and Sweden and found that the Swedish rate was 37% lower than the UK rate.[8]

FIGURE 2.3   **Swedish hospitals have steadily reduced mortality for heart attack patients.**

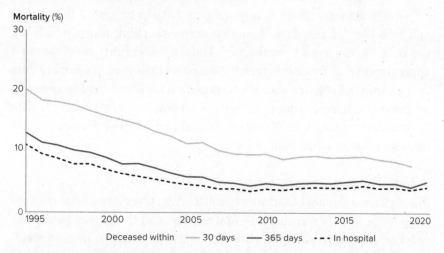

The chart tracks the continuous reduction in mortality for Swedish patients who suffer from an acute heart attack. In recent years, however, the rate of improvement has hit a plateau.

Source: *Swedeheart 2020 annual report.*

What role did the Swedish heart attack registry play in this improvement? In our research, we identified three factors that in combination prove especially important.[9]

Comprehensive, High-Quality Data

The registry collects comprehensive data from all 74 of the nation's major hospitals and covers nearly all patients (96% of those under the age of 80) in Sweden who suffer a heart attack. In addition to tracking well-accepted clinical-outcome measures such as 30-day and one-year mortality rates, the registry collects data on the severity of disease, patient risk profiles, medical and medical-device treatment, and any complications from the time of intervention for all procedures, and surgical interventions performed. It also tracks adherence to clinical guidelines but, importantly, informed by the actual impact of those guidelines on health outcomes.

In addition to the data it collects on heart attack patients, Swedeheart also covers all Swedish patients undergoing angiography, angioplasty, transcatheter aortic-valve interventions (TAVI), and cardiac surgery. For patients diagnosed with acute coronary syndrome (ACS) admitted to coronary-care units, the registry collects baseline data on 106 variables, with another 75 variables relating to secondary prevention collected after 12 to 14 months. The data are registered online directly by the caregiver.

Swedeheart researchers also go to great lengths to ensure the quality and reliability of the data. Automatic error-checking routines validate the data for range and consistency. Trained Swedeheart monitors visit approximately 20 randomly selected hospitals each year to compare data entered into the registry with the information in the medical records of a selection of randomly chosen patients. Such practices ensure that the data is extremely robust. A 2007 study of Swedeheart's data-validation process demonstrated an agreement of 96%.[10]

A Bias Toward Transparency

The registry does more than simply collect data. Over time, it has increasingly made its data transparent—first to peers and then to the public—in order to encourage accountability and focus clinicians on improvement. For example, in 2005, in response to a media debate about variation in survival rates for cardiac patients at Swedish hospitals, the registry created a quality index that tracked how well the nation's hospitals were complying with clinical guidelines that were associated with better outcomes. At first the registry published only aggregate data at the regional level. In late 2006, however, it decided to make public the index scores for each of the country's 74 hospitals.

Public disclosure, and the accountability that came with it, was instrumental in spurring a significant improvement in hospitals' scores on the quality index. From 2005 through 2007, the period before and immediately after the data became public, the average hospital quality index score improved by 13% per year. However, the hospitals whose scores were below the average improved by only 7% per year, on average. In other words, the quality gap between above-average and below-average hospitals was widening. (See Figure 2.4.) From 2007 through 2009, however, during the period after all the data were made public, the average annual rate of improvement jumped to 22%. But below-average performers improved their scores by nearly twice as much—40% per year—decisively narrowing the gap between the worst-performing hospitals and the best.

FIGURE 2.4   Transparency drives continuous improvement.

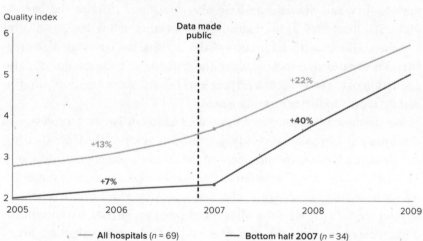

The decision to publish hospital rankings on a national quality index not only increased the rate of improvement but also narrowed the gap between the worst-performing hospitals and the best.

Sources: *"Use of 13 Disease Registries in 5 Countries Demonstrates the Potential to Use Outcome Data to Improve Health Care's Value,"* Health Affairs *31, no. 1 (January 1, 2012): 220–27,* https://doi.org/10.1377/hlthaff.2011.0762; *Register of Information and Knowledge About Swedish Heart Intensive Care Admissions (RIKS-HIA) annual reports, 2005–2009.*

Karlstad Hospital, located in southwestern Sweden, illustrates how data transparency can inspire clinical engagement, tighten focus on a clear goal, and in the process transform care. In 2005, Karlstad had high AMI mortality and one of the lowest scores on the quality index. In response, the hospital reorganized the total care cycle and improved its adherence to clinical guidelines, raising its rank to forty-third out of Sweden's 74 hospitals by 2007. Once the performance data became public, however, Karlstad boosted its ranking to twenty-second, cut its 30-day mortality rate from 9% to 4%, and improved its one-year mortality rate from 13.5% to 5.2%—well below the national average.

Today, the transparency of Swedeheart's data allows hospital administrators, public authorities, and the general public to make informed comparisons between hospitals and between regions. Individual clinicians can also compare their results against an average for other providers in their hospital or for all providers in the country. Transparent data also makes it possible to assess the effectiveness of new medical devices or different treatment strategies.

What's more, as Swedish cardiologists have improved their performance, they and Swedeheart have also continued to raise the bar. As Figure 2.3 illustrates, around 2010, AMI mortality in Sweden began to hit a plateau. This is partly a function of the fact that the coverage of the registry has expanded to include older and higher-risk patients. But it is also a function of the fact that at a certain level of care, there are simply diminishing returns to further improvement.

We discussed this phenomenon with Dr. Stefan James, a professor of cardiology at Uppsala University, scientific director of the Uppsala Clinical Research Center, and president of the Swedish Society of Cardiology. "The interesting thing," said James, "is that as we have improved mortality, we have come to recognize that there are important health outcomes beyond mortality itself. So in all of Swedeheart's registries, we have introduced new types of quality measures having to do with patient quality of life as well as the burden of the specific condition."

For example, in 2011 the registry introduced a new index that incorporates critical preventive measures into patient tracking and hospital quality assessment—for example, the degree to which patients participate in smoking cessation or exercise programs and receive routine blood pressure monitoring. And more recently, the Swedish cardiology community is focusing on generating more refined outcomes data to assess new therapies for at-risk patient segments such as those who suffer cardiogenic shock. This trend at Swedeheart illustrates an important general principle. The relevant outcomes to track for a given patient group aren't static; rather, they should evolve over time to incorporate new clinical knowledge and the latest progress in the standard of care.

Active Engagement with the Clinical Community

Transparent registry data functions as something of a stick, exposing poor-performing hospitals to a degree of professional and public censure. More important, it is also a kind of carrot, a resource that harnesses healthy competition and clinicians' natural desire to do the best for their patients to the purpose of organizational learning and improvement. Swedeheart has become a key partner in the efforts of Swedish cardiologists to improve health outcomes. Registry staff and university researchers who study registry data work closely with hospitals to engage physicians and other clinical staff in the shared task of improving the quality of care, and the registry itself serves as a clearinghouse for the dissemination and sharing of best practices.

This kind of close collaboration has been demonstrated to significantly improve clinical outcomes. In 2002, the Uppsala Clinical Research Center ran a controlled experiment of quality improvement in Swedish coronary care.[11] The study selected 19 hospitals as sites for a quality improvement intervention, pairing them with 19 other hospitals with similar populations and treatment profiles. Although the latter were recipients of registry data, they received no intervention (indeed, they were not even aware of the study).

Quality-improvement teams, consisting of registry experts, the research team, and hospital clinicians, worked to help the intervention hospitals optimize their use of registry data. The registry, meanwhile, offered these hospitals rapid feedback and continuous measurement of their efforts, including real-time national comparisons, analyses of local time series, and performance-level measurements. By the end of the study, the intervention hospitals showed significant improvement in all five of the quality parameters the researchers tracked, whereas the reference hospitals did not. Since then, this type of collaboration between the registry and local cardiac-care clinicians has become standard practice.

It is this combination of high-quality data, transparent results, and close collaboration around continuous improvement that helps explain

Swedeheart's success. As one of the cardiac-care physicians at Karlstad put it in describing the hospital's performance improvement, "The media coverage played an important role in our improvement work, but the foundation was our collaboration with the registry."[12]

In fact, Swedish cardiologists, in general, seem to acknowledge the registry's role in improving the health outcomes for cardiac care. In a 2016 survey of 115 physicians and nurses who are the formal contacts for the Swedeheart registry at Swedish hospitals, 93% of respondents agreed to a "high" or "very high" degree that registry data was useful for identifying potential areas for clinical improvement, 89% that the data captured the most relevant and important metrics for quality of care, and 67% that registry data contributed to actual improvements in clinical practice.[13] However, only 39% agreed to a high or very high degree that their clinical leaders regularly requested access to the results, suggesting that there is still considerable room for improvement in integrating registry data in the management of clinical practice in Sweden.

APPLYING SCIENTIFIC METHOD TO EVERYDAY CLINICAL PRACTICE

As registries accumulate large amounts of data on patient outcomes and the gathering of this data becomes part of the daily routines of all clinics, the data is also becoming a valuable resource for research on the comparative effectiveness of both existing and new clinical interventions and therapies. As such, they represent one potential solution to the evidence crisis that we described in Chapter 1.

A dramatic example of the potential of registries to generate critical evidence for clinical guidelines occurred not long after the 1998 approval by the US Food and Drug Administration (FDA) of a revolutionary new class of drugs known as tumor necrosis factor (TNF) antagonists. The drugs, which block a specific molecule in the immune system, delivered radical health improvements for sufferers of autoimmune disorders such as rheumatoid arthritis (RA) and Crohn's disease—so much so that some RA sufferers who went from being bedridden to fully mobile, dubbed the new therapies the "Jesus drug."

The human immune system, however, also plays a critical role in the defense against cancer. In the early years after the introduction of the TNF antagonists, there were some worrisome reports that patients taking the new drugs had an increased risk of developing lymphoma, a deadly hematological cancer.[14] These concerns led the FDA to consider withdrawing approval of the drugs until better evidence for its safety and risks was available.

Because the Swedish rheumatoid arthritis registry had been collecting data on Swedish RA patients since the mid-1990s, researchers were able, with only a few weeks of analysis, to publish a comparative study of more than 53,000 RA patients, of whom 4,160 were being treated with TNF antagonists. The study demonstrated that while RA itself did double the risk of both lymphoma and leukemia in RA patients, that risk was not made worse by treatment with TNF antagonists.[15] Given the size and quality of the data in this registry study, the FDA decided not to withdraw approval of the drugs.

In addition to this type of retrospective study, the accumulation of registry data also makes possible an alternative approach to prospective, pragmatic, randomized clinical trials: so-called registry-based randomized clinical trials, or R-RCTs.[16] In an approach pioneered by Stefan James and his team, R-RCTs use an existing clinical registry as the infrastructure and database for conducting and reporting the trial. Because registry-based studies are done as part of normal clinical practice, they can more easily recruit a larger number of patients. And because their patient panels are taken from the normal pool of patients, R-RCTs better reflect the underlying makeup of a targeted patient population. What's more, R-RCTs are typically less expensive because patient recruitment and randomization can be integrated into day-to-day routine health care visits. Finally, the existence of an established registry research team and infrastructure means that the results of R-RCTs can be developed much faster and the conclusions more quickly integrated into everyday clinical practice, allowing for more rapid updating of clinical guidelines and more effective monitoring of compliance to them.

In 2013, the first R-RCT (known as the TASTE trial) used Swedeheart registry data to test the effectiveness of coronary-artery thrombosis aspiration, a technique that was being used (along with percutaneous coronary intervention, or PCI) with increasing frequency for patients suffering from a type of heart attack known as ST-segment-elevation myocardial infarction (STEMI).[17] The trial prospectively enrolled 7,244 STEMI patients who were to receive routine care at Swedish hospitals and whose outcomes would be monitored by Swedeheart's coronary angiography and angioplasty registry. The patients were randomly assigned to receive either manual thrombus aspiration followed by PCI or PCI alone. The study found that routine thrombus aspiration before PCI did not significantly reduce mortality and therefore did not contribute to improved health outcomes.

The finding had an enormous impact on cardiac-care clinical practice in Sweden. In the years before the registry trial, thrombosis aspiration had become an increasingly common intervention at Swedish hospitals, reaching its height during the period when researchers were conducting the registry trial. Within months of the study's publication, however, the use of the technique dropped precipitously, with no negative impact on 30-day mortality.[18] (See Figure 2.5.)

FIGURE 2.5 **Registry-based randomized clinical trials can have a major impact on clinical practice.**

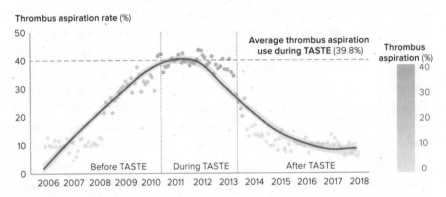

The graph shows that after the publication of the results of the TASTE registry-based randomized clinical trial, the use of thrombosis aspiration by Swedish doctors declined rapidly.

Source: *Sergio Buccheri et al., "Assessing the Nationwide Impact of a Registry-Based Randomized Clinical Trial on Cardiovascular Practice: The TASTE Trial in Perspective,"* Circulation: Cardiovascular Interventions *12, no. 3 (March 7, 2019): e007381;* https://www.ahajournals.org/doi/10.1161/CIRCINTERVENTIONS.118.007381

The *New England Journal of Medicine* described the thrombosis-aspiration randomized registry trial design as a potential "disruptive technology in clinical research" that "transforms existing standards, procedures, and cost structures."[19]

Since that initial thrombosis study, Swedeheart's registries have been conducting many more R-RCTs, involving some 50 of the country's 72 hospitals that provide specialized cardiac care. These studies are assessing the effectiveness of recent innovations as well as evaluating new-treatment indications for certain drugs and medical devices, sometimes as part of a formal regulatory-approval process. What's more, the R-RCT model is being used in other countries and for other conditions—for example, in the domain of cancer care, where there is a wide variety of treatment options, often with no clearly superior approach and where traditional clinical trials are especially complex, expensive, and difficult to organize. In Australia, which benefits from the existence of a number of cancer registries, R-RCTs are currently being conducted to assess various treatment options in metastatic colon cancer, glioblastoma, and prostate cancer.[20]

DO IMPROVED HEALTH OUTCOMES LOWER HEALTH CARE COSTS?

One way to think about the registry experience is as the health care industry's version of the total quality movement that swept through manufacturing in the 1970s and 1980s. A core tenet of that movement is that boosting quality often has the beneficial side effect of lowering costs—a principle captured in the aphorism "Quality is free."[21] In our research, we found many instances to suggest that this phenomenon may also apply to outcomes measurement, quality registries, and quality-improvement initiatives.[22]

Take the example of total hip arthroplasty, the replacement of a hip joint with a prosthesis. As people live longer, it is becoming an increasingly common operation. Although generally effective, the procedure fails for some patients, either because of postoperative infection or normal wear on the prosthetic hip. In such cases, a second procedure, known as a revision, is required to repair or replace the implant. Undergoing a revision is disruptive for patients. It's also expensive. The only comparative figures that we could find in the literature are by now quite old, but in 2003 the average cost of a revision in Sweden was about $18,500 per operation; in the United States, the average at the time was roughly 15% higher: $21,224.[23]

Since the founding of the Swedish hip arthroplasty registry in 1979, Sweden has reduced its revision burden, calculated as the ratio of implant revisions to the total number of arthroplasties in a given year, to 10.2% in 2014, one of the lowest rates in the world at the time.[24] Nearly 40 years of data helped Swedish hip surgeons identify not only the best clinical practices but also the highest-performing implants.

In our study of the Swedish quality registries, we used registry data to estimate that in the decade between 2000 and 2009, Sweden avoided some 7,500 revisions that would otherwise have taken place if Sweden's revision burden had been as high as that of the United States at the time.[25] That represents approximately $140 million, or $14 million per year, in avoided costs. The amount was equivalent to about 8% of the total cost of total-hip arthroplasty in Sweden during this period.

The most comprehensive analysis of the costs of total hip arthroplasty to the US health care system was published in 2007.[26] At the time, demand for primary total hip arthroplasties was expected to grow by 174% by 2030, and hip-revision procedures projected to double by 2026—a key factor in driving cost increases from the roughly $6 billion spent on the procedure in 2005 to an estimated $24 billion by 2015. Based on these assumptions, we estimated that if the US health care system could lower its revision burden to Sweden's 2014 level of 10.2%, it would avoid $2 billion of the expected $24 billion in total costs.[27]

Interestingly, the American Joint Replacement Registry (AJRR) was established by the American Academy of Orthopaedic Surgeons in 2009 and has been reporting revision burden data since 2012. The registry's data suggests that the revision burden at participating institutions has declined from a high of 12.7% in 2013 to a low of 4.1% in 2019—less than half the 2019 Swedish rate of 8.8%.[28] Although such improvement may reflect the impact of the registry itself, these numbers should be taken with a grain of salt. Participation in the AJRR is voluntary and in 2016, only captured 28% of arthroplasty procedures performed in the United States, compared with nearly 100% in most national registries, including Sweden's.[29] So, the low AJRR revision-burden number may reflect an unrepresentative sample of American hip-replacement surgeries.[30]

Given the potential of quality registries both to improve health outcomes and in some cases also to limit the growth in health care costs, in September 2011 the Swedish government announced a five-year program to strengthen Sweden's registry network. The program more than tripled the annual public budget in support of registries from 96 million Swedish kronor (approximately $13.5 million at then-current exchange rates) in 2011 to 320 million kronor (approximately $49 million) by 2013. This targeted investment was dedicated to expanding the registry network and to developing new tools that use data on outcomes to inform clinical decision-making, improve relevant information available to patients, and serve as the foundation for value-based payment.

REGISTRIES AROUND THE WORLD

Few countries have as extensive a network of quality registries as Sweden does. But excellent registries can be found all over the world—including in the United States, with its more complex and fragmented national health system. The National Institutes of Health (NIH) lists some 80 US-based registries, established by organizations such as the American College of Cardiology, the Society of Thoracic Surgeons, and the National Cancer Institute's Surveillance, Epidemiology, and End Results (SEER) program. Indeed, one of the oldest—and most successful—registries we have studied was established in the mid-1960s, even before Sweden's registries, by the US Cystic Fibrosis Foundation, a patient-advocacy group.

Cystic fibrosis is a rare genetic disease; only about a thousand American children each year are diagnosed with it, less than 1 of every 3,000 newborns. That rarity poses a challenge in researching the disease and developing improved treatment guidelines. But in 1964, the US Cystic Fibrosis Foundation gave a University of Missouri pediatrician by the name of Warren Warwick $10,000 to collect reports on every patient treated at the then 31 cystic fibrosis centers in the United States.[31] That initial investment has grown into a quality registry that today collects systematic outcomes data on all US patients suffering from the disease. More than 31,000 living patients are enrolled in the registry, which collects data from the approximately 120 certified cystic fibrosis centers in the United States.

The registry's work has been instrumental in improving the average life expectancy of a newborn diagnosed with cystic fibrosis. That life expectancy was three years in 1964. By 1966, it had risen to 10 years and by 1972, to 18. Today, average life expectancy for a newborn diagnosed with cystic fibrosis in the United States is 46. Until quite recently, most of that improvement has come from sharing best practices across cystic fibrosis clinics rather than from the introduction of new drugs to treat the disease.

Like other registries around the world, the cystic fibrosis registry collects comprehensive, high-quality data—for example, on patient growth, genotype, lung function results, pancreatic enzyme use, transplantation, complications such as lung infections, diabetes, liver disease, and, of course, on mortality. And like Swedeheart, as the registry has helped improve basic health outcomes (such as mortality), it has expanded its focus to include patient quality-of-life outcomes. For example, in one sign of the life-changing progress in health outcomes for the disease, the registry's patient-reported-outcome-measures (PROMs) survey now tracks young adults' degree of confidence about having children and raising a family. Although until relatively recently center-level data was kept confidential, in the past decade the cystic fibrosis registry has, like other registries, gradually moved toward full data transparency to jump-start improvements in clinical practice and over time, in patient outcomes.

For example, a common complication of cystic fibrosis is infection by *Pseudomonas*, an opportunistic pathogen that is one of the most serious and difficult-to-treat hospital-acquired infections. *Pseudomonas* colonizes the lungs of patients with cystic fibrosis, contributing to the progression of chronic pulmonary disease and the high death rate associated with the condition. Since 1995, the *Pseudomonas* rate in US cystic fibrosis patients has declined by nearly one-third, and there are indications that efforts by the registry were an important catalyst in this improvement.

Between 1995 and 1999, the decline in *Pseudomonas*-positive sputum cultures was relatively modest—from 60.3% to 59.3%. However, in 1999, the registry began providing each center with data on its own performance compared with a national benchmark; in 2006, the data were made available to the public. With greater visibility and, therefore, increased focus on this key indicator, the decline in the *Pseudomonas* infection rate accelerated significantly. In 2009, a decade after the registry first began providing centers with comparative data, it had dropped to 51.7%. Ten years later, in 2019, the percentage of patients with *Pseudomonas*-positive sputum cultures had declined even further to 44.2%.

Like other registries, the US cystic fibrosis registry also works closely with centers around the country to improve their performance. It has a formal benchmarking team made up of clinicians with strong reputations in the cystic-fibrosis medical community and strong ties to the various centers. The team identifies top performers, documents best practices, and encourages site visits to high-performing centers to observe patient management and identify novel diagnostic and therapeutic approaches. The registry, like many of the others we studied, also spreads best practices nationwide through a regular program of national conferences, local meetings, newsletters, and word of mouth.

In addition to helping cystic fibrosis centers improve their outcomes, the registry also collaborates with patients to encourage their adherence to treatment plans and to assess the overall value of care. Physicians have found that sharing registry data with individual patients can enable frank dialogue about the implications of patient behavior for future survival. It also helps patients understand how they can influence the life cycle of their disease.

Finally, the registry has also invested in research partnerships with biotech companies to discover new therapies for curing the disease. Because the registry has compiled extensive genetic profiles of cystic fibrosis patients, its data can be used to track a relevant study population relatively easily and cheaply in R-RCTs. As a result, clinical trials can happen faster, accelerating drug approvals by as much as three to four years. Registry data has been used in clinical trials for new antibiotics and in drug-effectiveness research to determine which medications and treatments yield the best outcomes. Registry participation in such projects has even become an important revenue stream for the nonprofit Cystic Fibrosis Foundation, allowing it to earn income from licensing its data for postmarketing and Phase IV clinical trial information, and from royalties and rights collected on new drugs approved on the basis of registry-based research.

REGISTRIES GO GLOBAL

Until recently, quality registries were mainly a regional or national phenomenon. But in recent years, there has been a growing trend toward international collaboration among registries that focus on the same condition or disease. It makes sense. Although living conditions and health care systems differ across the planet, a specific medical condition is the same irrespective of where we live. The more collaboration and data-sharing there is among international registries for a given disease, the bigger the sample population of patients that researchers and clinicians can analyze to identify the sources of outcomes variation and spot emerging best practices. And the bigger the sample size, the more confidence that researchers and clinicians can have in the statistical robustness of their conclusions.

For example, the European Registry of Quality Outcomes for Cataract and Refractive Surgery, known as EUREQUO, connects surgeons from 13 EU countries and 2 non-EU countries in a web-based platform that allows them to audit surgical results, identify best practices, adjust their techniques, and improve their outcomes.[32] Since it was established in 2008, more than 3 million cataract surgeries have been recorded in the system. And the International Society of Arthroplasty Registries, or ISAR, brings together hip-replacement registries from more than 20 countries to develop common standards and data sets. In 2018, an ISAR working group called for a standardized benchmarking system to allow hip surgeons to compare the performance of different artificial hip implants. "A global benchmarking system can enhance international public safety and cost effectiveness through the identification and subsequent use of higher performing arthroplasty prostheses," the working group wrote.[33]

Such a system would transform the terms of competition in the device market, promoting innovations that result in better outcomes for patients. For an idea of what this trend might look like, consider the 2010 recall of Johnson & Johnson's DePuy ASR XL Acetabular metal-on-metal hip implant by the FDA. Studies have shown that wear on metal-on-metal hip implants can leave behind dangerous fragments of metal that may not be discovered for years and can eventually lead to death. The recall followed a British study showing that the DePuy device had a five-year failure rate of approximately 13%, or one in eight patients.

In Australia, however, despite the fact that the country's population is only one-tenth that of the United States, the data collected in its national hip-replacement registry allowed Australian researchers to identify problems with DePuy's ASR implant, warn surgeons not to use the device, and eventually prompt a voluntary recall from the Australian market by the manufacturer in December 2009—a full seven months before the device was recalled by the FDA.

Of course, international collaboration of the sort illustrated by EUREQUO and ISAR depends on the development of common measurement standards. In order to share and compare their data, clinicians in different countries need to be measuring the same thing. And when they do, the total universe of data expands so that it is easier to identify important safety risks, as well as the clinical best practices that result in superior health outcomes. Imagine how much faster researchers might have identified the problems with the DePuy device had they had access to standardized outcomes measures on a global scale. For all these reasons, creating common global standards is the current frontier of the movement to measure health outcomes.

"THE GSM OF HEALTH-OUTCOMES MEASUREMENT"

The model of national quality registries working together across international borders is one effective way to organize systematic health-outcomes measurement on a global scale. But it is not the only way. In countries where such registries do not yet exist or are underdeveloped, individual health care organizations can commit to measuring outcomes across disease domains and to sharing their data directly with other health care institutions around the world. When they do, researchers can aggregate massive quantities of data and institutions can learn from each other—not just within a single region or country but on a global scale. For such a model to work, however, the measurements used need to be standardized across multiple institutions in multiple countries so health systems are comparing apples to apples and not apples to oranges. Think of it as one big global registry, covering most countries and institutions.

To make such a vision a reality, in 2010, Stefan reached out to Michael Porter, professor at Harvard Business School and head of its Institute for Strategy and Competitiveness. Porter, of course, is the doyen of competitive strategy, but he is also something of the grandfather of value-based health care. His 2006 book, *Redefining Health Care: Creating Value-Based Competition on Results*, written with Elizabeth Teisberg, launched the concept of value-based health care and emphasized the importance of tracking health outcomes by disease and condition. Porter had heard about BCG's research on quality registries in Sweden from a former BCG consultant attending Harvard Business School and was interested in the new evidence the work could provide for the concept he and Teisberg had laid out in their book.

That initial conversation became the starting point of a joint project: What if we could bring together clinicians from around the world to create truly global standards for outcomes measurement that would allow global benchmarking similar to what Sweden was doing on the national level? Our mantra became: "Let's create the GSM for health-outcomes measurement."

The analogy is to mobile telecommunications. The Global System for Mobile Communications—GSM, for short—is a technical standard developed in Europe in the early 1990s to describe the digital protocols for second-generation digital cellular networks. The first all-digital standard, GSM became the common standard for European mobile phone networks and ultimately was adopted by many other countries around the world. By the mid-2010s, the GSM standard had achieved over 90% market share and was operating in more than 193 countries and territories. The great advantage of the widespread adoption of the GSM standard was that it allowed subscribers to use other GSM networks that have roaming agreements with each other. The standard created a "common language" that reduced research and development costs (since hardware and software could be sold with only minor adaptations for local markets) and enabled data-sharing and innovation on a global scale. Could the world's health systems create equivalent standards for outcomes measurement so registries, hospitals, and other health care institutions could share their data, align on targets for patient care, and learn from each other?

In 2012, Stefan and Porter, joined by a third colleague—Martin Ingvar, a neuroscience professor and, at the time, vice dean at Sweden's prestigious Karolinska Institute, the institution that awards the annual Nobel Prize in Physiology and Medicine—founded a nonprofit to do just that: the International Consortium for Health Outcomes Measurement (ICHOM). They brought in a German physician, Dr. Jens Deerberg-Wittram, who had pioneered the use of outcomes measurement at a hospital chain he led in Germany, as president (and ICHOM's first employee) to get the organization up and running.

Based in Cambridge, Massachusetts, and London, ICHOM has a simple but ambitious mission: "to unlock the potential of value-based healthcare by defining global sets of patient-centered outcome measures that matter most to patients and by driving adoption and reporting of these measures worldwide to create better value for all stakeholders."[34] It does so by convening global working groups of registry leaders, clinicians, patient representatives, and other leading experts to define consensus standards for outcome metrics for specific conditions, diseases, and population segments. Such standards, if broadly implemented, would allow clinicians to compare their results, assess the value they are delivering to patients, and learn from each other. (In the interest of full disclosure, BCG has provided financial and in-kind support to ICHOM over the past decade, and Stefan is a member of the ICHOM board.)[35]

In the 10 years since its founding, ICHOM has published standardized outcome metrics and risk-adjustment variables for more than 40 major conditions—ranging from addiction, atrial fibrillation, and breast cancer to lung cancer, psychotic disorders, and recently, Covid-19—representing nearly 60% of the global disease burden. (See Figure 2.6.) In the process, it has developed a distinctive approach to the development of outcome-measures sets that is characterized by four basic principles.

FIGURE 2.6 **ICHOM's outcome measures cover nearly 60% of the global disease burden.**

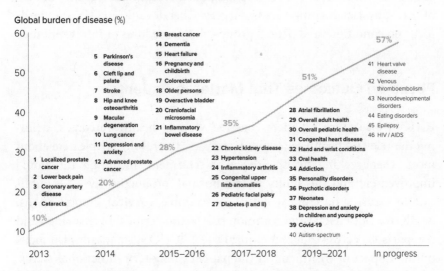

Since 2012, ICHOM working groups have defined more than 40 outcome-measurement sets. The first 39 have been published in international peer-reviewed journals.

Note: Completed measurement sets as of first quarter 2022. Bold text indicates existence of a peer-reviewed publication. Global burden of disease is defined in terms of disability-adjusted life years (DALYs).

Source: *ICHOM.*

Focus on Patient Groups, Not Procedures

In the past, outcomes measures have traditionally been developed by specialty societies and, therefore, tend to focus on specific interventions or procedures. Sometimes, focusing on a specific procedure makes sense. Cataract surgery is probably the best example, because it is the only treatment for patients suffering from cataracts. But in most situations, the ideal health outcomes to track for a given condition should reflect the overall care for a patient's medical condition, in which multiple specialties are usually involved and multiple treatment options are available, so clinicians can assess the relative effectiveness of different types of treatment. Procedure-based registries have played an important role in improving hip and knee arthroplasty, but they can't really address the broader question about the optimal treatment for the underlying disease of osteoarthritis. Or consider a patient suffering from back pain: for that condition, the relevant outcomes measures should be broad enough to assess the comparative impact of, say, physical therapy versus surgery. Therefore, ICHOM's standards focus on conditions and patient groups, not procedures or interventions.

Focus on Outcomes That Matter to Patients

ICHOM also takes a patient-centered view of health outcomes, defining the relevant health outcomes simply as "the results people care about most when seeking health advice or treatment, including functional improvement and the ability to live normal, productive lives." In addition to focusing on clinical status (for example, survival, complications, or adverse side effects) and common risk factors (critical to ensuring valid comparisons across different clinical sites), ICHOM standards also focus on the impact of treatment on the patient's long-term functional status, which can have a major impact on his or her quality of life.

To that end, all ICHOM's outcome-measurement sets emphasize the inclusion of patient-reported outcome measures (PROMs) that are directly reported by the patients themselves, which have taken on a growing importance in health-outcomes measurement in recent years. Since PROMs capture a patient's personal assessment of his or her condition, unmediated by the clinician's influence or interpretation, they provide an important complement to clinical measurements and assessments. (PROMs are distinct from patient-satisfaction and patient-experience surveys or PREMs that ask patients whether they are satisfied with their care experience with a given provider or in the hospital.)

Bring Together Global Leaders in Registry Research with Patient Representatives

A third principle that defines ICHOM's approach is to recruit clinical leaders of global stature, typically leaders of the world's most respected quality registries, to lead and participate in its working groups, and to team them with patient representatives with actual experience of the condition in question. (See Figure 2.7.) Indeed, the organization has made a conscious choice to recruit clinical and scientific leaders to its working groups, as opposed to official representatives from specialist societies around the world, so as to minimize the impact of differences in the organization of national health systems on ICHOM's recommendations. It has also insisted that the patient perspective be an integral part of the measurement-set development process. (See the sidebar "A Patient's Perspective on Measuring Health Outcomes.")

FIGURE 2.7   **ICHOM's working groups have included participants from 62 countries.**

Approximately 1,000 clinical experts and patient representatives have contributed to the development of the ICHOM outcome-measurement sets. Although the majority are from North America and Europe, a full quarter are from Africa, Asia, South America, and Australia and New Zealand.

Source: *ICHOM.*

A Patient's Perspective on Measuring Health Outcomes

Günter Feick is a prostate cancer survivor who serves as a patient representative with the Prostate Cancer Self-Help Association of Germany and the German Cancer Society. He was also one of three patient representatives on the working group that developed the ICHOM outcome-measurement set for localized prostate cancer. In a conversation, Feick offered a patient's perspective on the importance of health-outcomes measurement.

"For many prostate cancer patients," said Feick, "the main issue is that physicians typically don't have the management systems in place to measure, report, and compare the quality of clinical and patient-reported outcomes over the entire period of the disease. As a result, doctors are often ignorant about the results of their work one, two, five years after treatment. That makes patients nervous, because it means they don't have the information they need to compare the effectiveness of different treatments or the performance of different clinics. I've had fellow patients tell me, 'if I want to buy a refrigerator or a car, I have a whole lot of information about the quality of the product, but when it comes to the outcomes of medical treatment, we know almost nothing.'"

Feick also spoke to the importance of collecting health outcomes directly from patients through PROM surveys. From his perspective, PROMs are not only an important source of data for clinicians about the impact of treatment on a patient's quality of life. The very act of responding to PROM surveys also serves to engage patients in their treatment and in the collective task of improving care delivery. "When patients fill out a PROMs questionnaire," Feick said, "they feel observed, respected, and cared for. They also feel like they are doing something that will be useful for future patients. By contributing to outcomes tracking, they are contributing to better long-term results through a better understanding of the patient. That input is critical to the medical profession and to the health system as a whole."

According to Feick, both physicians and patients benefit from collecting the kind of standardized outcome measures in the ICHOM measurement sets. "Physicians get to see the long-term results of all their hard work. And patients have a newfound sense of security because they have the data they need to make more informed treatment decisions." Perhaps most important, said Feick, "what gets measured gets improved."

Aim for a Pragmatic Consensus

Finally, ICHOM working groups go through a structured process: reviewing the scientific evidence from the literature, assessing the experience with existing measures around the world, and ultimately voting on what to include in the measurement set. The goal is not to create new metrics but to select the best among existing and already validated metrics to arrive at a minimally sufficient set of measures that all clinicians should track.

PROFILE OF AN ICHOM MEASUREMENT SET: LOCALIZED PROSTATE CANCER

To see how these principles play out in practice, consider the example of prostate cancer. In developed nations, it is, after skin cancer, the most common cancer in men. More than 1.3 million new cases were reported worldwide in 2018.[36] However, although prostate cancer is the fifth leading cause of death worldwide, fully half of men who die from other causes have been living with prostate cancer, meaning many more die *with* it than *from* it.[37] A full 95% of prostate cancer patients survive for more than five years after diagnosis.

Physicians treating prostate cancer face a complex set of options. The most intensive treatment—prostatectomy—leads to better survival in many cases, especially for high-risk patients. But it also carries risks of loss of functionality for the patient in the form of nerve damage causing incontinence, erectile dysfunction, or both. Other treatment options (such as radiation therapy, chemotherapy, and hormone therapy) present a different set of risks and likely outcomes. Watchful waiting has much lower complication risks but a higher mortality rate for those with an aggressive tumor.

Because individual preferences differ, it is critical that patients have the opportunity to consider how treatments will affect their quality of life.

One patient may opt for surgery based on a strong desire to see his grand-children grow up, while another may choose watchful waiting owing to a strong desire to avoid incontinence or erectile dysfunction. These pref-erences and the data to help the patient make an informed choice should be part of the treatment discussion. Ideally, a set of outcomes measures for prostate cancer should be broad enough both to capture the quality-of-life issues that matter most to patients and to assess the differentiated impact of various treatment options on health outcomes. That is pre-cisely the approach that the ICHOM localized prostate cancer working group took.[38]

Like many of ICHOM's working groups, its work was funded by a patient advocacy organization, Movember, a global charity dedicated to improv-ing men's health. The working group's 28 members from nine different countries included leading urologists, radiologists, radiation therapists, oncologists, and registry experts—as well as three prostate cancer survi-vors, among them Günter Feick. The leader of the working group was Dr. Hartwig Huland, founder and chairman of the renowned Martini Klinik in Hamburg, Germany, a global center of excellence for treating prostate cancer. (We'll learn more about Martini in the next chapter).

Between June and December 2013, the group went through a struc-tured process, consisting of a systematic literature review, iterative cycles of meetings to share their clinical experience, and follow-up surveys and votes on the measures to include in the set of measures. A two-thirds majority was required for a given measure to be adopted.

Sometimes, the debates got contentious. Given the central importance of quality-of-life outcomes to prostate cancer patients, it was critical for the set of measures to include a PROM survey. The goal of the group was to recommend a single PROM instrument in order to make it easier for prostate cancer centers around the world to compare their outcomes. But providers and cancer registries around the world have developed a number of different PROM surveys in recent years, with no compelling evidence for the advantage of one particular survey instrument over another. So, in order to give clear advice to centers and to new prostate cancer registries and in the hopes of moving existing efforts toward alignment on measure definitions over time, working-group members had to use their judgment. A two-thirds majority eventually agreed on a specific PROM instrument (known as the Expanded Prostate Cancer Index Composite 26-question short form, or EPIC-26). Meanwhile, the group recommended that centers not yet ready to adopt the EPIC survey or with compelling reasons to use other instruments, collect the same basic survey domains at the same time points during treatment and then develop "crosswalk" algorithms to allow meaningful comparisons with centers that were using the ICHOM set of outcome measures.

The final result of the working group's collaborative process was a set of 30 data elements across seven alternative treatment options. The data categories cover patient baseline information, including key risk factors, and track health outcomes in three areas: survival and disease control, patient-reported functional health status, and acute complications.[39] The localized prostate cancer set of outcome measures also includes sample timelines for when clinicians should collect the data for each patient, depending on the type of treatment pursued. The timeline extends from a post-diagnosis, pre-treatment baseline to six months, one year, two years, and three years after selected treatment. Some metrics are meant to be tracked annually for up to a decade—or even for the rest of the patient's life.

The result: an internationally agreed-upon method for measuring outcomes that matter to patients, so providers and payers can compare performance globally and the impact of treatment choices on patient outcomes can be better understood.

THE NEXT FRONTIER: IMPLEMENTATION

With some 40 sets of outcome measures and counting, the next frontier in ICHOM's efforts is to accelerate implementation. "As we scaled up to more and more disease areas, it quickly became apparent that our early adopters need advice on implementation," Dr. Christina Rångemark Åkerman, former director general of the Swedish Medical Products Agency and Deerberg-Wittram's successor as ICHOM president, told us. Currently, ICHOM standards are used in some form in approximately 500 hospitals, other clinical sites, and quality registries in more than 40 countries, and ICHOM's working groups have stayed active, testing and validating the measures and providing advice to institutions on their use.

For example, the Erasmus University Medical Center, a leading academic medical center in the Dutch city of Rotterdam, is currently using more than 20 ICHOM outcome-measurement sets in areas ranging from stroke, breast cancer, and localized prostate cancer to cleft lip and palate, congenital upper limb anomalies, and inflammatory bowel disease.[40] (We'll learn more about Erasmus in Chapter 4.) The Aneurin University Health Board, one of seven integrated payer-provider health boards in Wales, has formed a strategic partnership with ICHOM in disease areas such as Parkinson's disease, heart failure, dementia, lung cancer, prostate cancer, and other conditions.[41] The French Ministry of Health and France's national payer have recently launched a pilot at three leading centers for cataract surgery that uses the ICHOM cataract outcome-measurement set in a proof-of-concept demonstration project both for a future national cataract registry and for a standard model and methodology for health-outcomes measurement in France.[42] And the coronary angiography registry in the Australian state of South Australia has adopted the ICHOM set of outcome measures for coronary artery disease, with the goal of eventually incorporating the data into the patient electronic medical record and benchmarking the data with comparable data from ICHOM's global coronary-artery-disease community with participating institutions in North and South America, Europe, and Asia.[43]

Patient organizations are also taking the lead in meeting the implementation challenge. For example, Movember, which helped fund the development of ICHOM's localized and advanced prostate cancer outcome-measurement sets, continues to play an active role in funding the development of prostate-cancer registries that use the ICHOM measures, championing the collection of patient-reported outcomes, publishing benchmark data, and collaborating with clinical and research institutions to identify clinical interventions linked to better outcomes. Among the initiatives that Movember supports are:

- PCOR-ANZ, a large-scale prostate cancer registry in Australia and New Zealand, in which some 250 participating sites are tracking health outcomes for nearly 85,000 patients[44]
- The TrueNTH Global Registry, which aggregates and analyzes localized prostate cancer outcomes data from 13 countries (including baseline patient-reported outcomes from some 50,000 patients)[45]
- The International Registry for Men with Advanced Prostate Cancer (known as IRONMAN), which currently collects prospective data and bio samples for some 2,500 patients (with plans to double that number in the near future) in 16 countries on five continents, including Africa and South America[46]

At some institutions, however, implementing the ICHOM measurement sets has encountered some common obstacles. A significant one is the additional cost and administrative burden of collecting comprehensive health-outcomes data, especially in organizations that lack financial resources to invest in a robust IT platform. We spoke with Dr. John Rumsfeld, professor of medicine at the University of Colorado School of Medicine and former chief innovation, science, and quality officer at the American College of Cardiology (recently, he became director of health technology research at Meta). Rumsfeld is an expert in cardiovascular outcomes measurement and was an active member of the ICHOM working group for coronary artery disease (at the time, he was national director of cardiology at the US Department of Veterans Affairs, which operates the dedicated health system for veterans of the US military).

"The collaboration on the working group was fabulous," Rumsfeld told us. "But, at the VA at least, the challenges came with implementation. In general, the VA health system is ahead of most US health care organizations in terms of standardized data capture. But we didn't have the financial resources to expand beyond what we were already collecting in the course of the clinical workflow. We were able to do some good pilots, but they just didn't take off. There were also important patient privacy issues with regard to data sharing. So, we were never able to implement the ICHOM sets of outcome measures."

According to Rumsfeld, the absence of robust IT platforms and true interoperability across health IT systems is a major obstacle to routine and systematic outcomes measurement. "The concept of systematic outcomes measurement is a great one, but one that is difficult given the heterogeneity and complexity of the US health care system," he said. In the absence of an efficient way to routinely collect outcomes data in the course of care, there is a heavy reliance on manual data collection, which means investing in a dedicated staff to collect and validate the data.

We'll address what it will take to create a digital health platform to automate the collection, sharing, and analysis of standardized outcomes data in Chapter 6. Here, we want to mention that in 2020 ICHOM took a major step in that direction by making its standards "machine readable" so as to facilitate their implementation in existing health information systems.[47] The effort included harmonizing all metrics across multiple diseases in a common "term bank" and mapping those metrics against the leading international medical terminology standards. In 2021, ICHOM announced a new partnership with the Dutch health care analytics firm LOGEX to pilot the world's first global benchmarking platform for health outcomes using the machine-readable versions of ICHOM's sets of outcome measures. ICHOM's digitized sets will simplify implementation, reduce the registration burden in clinical practice, and facilitate the comparison of outcome measures that matter to patients across providers, regions, and nations.

However, there is another, more subtle obstacle to the widespread adoption of outcomes measurement standards—one having to do with the current organizational culture of medicine and the standard approach to care delivery at many health care organizations. So much of health care today is organized around the principle of the efficient processing of volume. Especially in health systems such as the United States where fee-for-service is the dominant payment model, physicians and other clinicians are under enormous pressure to maximize the number of patients they see, tests they order, and procedures they perform. In such an environment, said Rumsfeld, "people don't feel like they have any control." And when people feel out of control, they tend to put their heads down and focus on what is right in front of them. As a result, the typical response to outcomes measures on the part of time-stressed clinicians, added Rumsfeld, is "Sounds great, but now I have to do my job. I just don't have the time." Rumsfeld is hopeful, however, that the ongoing shift in payment models from fee-for-service to value-based payment (a trend that we discuss in Chapter 5) will help shift the focus of provider organizations from volume to value. "At-risk payment models put pressure on the need for longitudinal data on outcomes," he said.

The obstacles that Rumsfeld describes are real, especially in the US health system. And yet, we are confident that there is a growing awareness of the need to reinvent how US payers and providers assess quality, in general, and of the central role of health-outcomes measurement, in particular, in doing so. For example, in January 2022, the health policy journal *Health Affairs* published a call for "the wholesale replacement of our system for measuring health care quality," criticizing the current approach as "ineffective, expensive, burdensome," and "no longer credible"—in large part because it "does not measure health or the outcomes of health care."[48] The author proposed a "national effort to implement a 21st-century measurement system" based on "a common set of outcome-oriented measures and data requirements," a goal that we share and will elaborate on in later chapters of this book. A few months later, the prestigious *New England Journal of Medicine* published a three-part series on the flaws of current approaches to quality improvement in the US health system that among other things, highlighted "the need to improve the quality of measuring quality."[49] Such views may point to an emerging consensus. For example, Dana Gelb Safran, the recently appointed CEO of the National Quality Forum, told us that the Forum is increasingly focusing on the development of what she called "a next generation of measures" that "reflect outcomes that matter to patients, families and caregivers." In particular, Safran emphasized the importance of PROMs that "directly measure how patients are feeling and functioning."

But even in the absence of the kind of comprehensive national system for outcomes measurement that the *Health Affairs* article calls for or of the kind of financial incentives that Rumsfeld describes, there is a lot that individual provider organizations can do now to focus on health outcomes as a way to improve performance. The fact is, many provider organizations around the world are not only committing to systematic outcomes measurement; they are also innovating an alternative model of care delivery that is demonstrably delivering superior health outcomes to patients, as well as higher staff satisfaction, strengthened clinical research, and lower costs of care. This alternative model of care delivery is the subject of our next chapter.

Outcomes Measurement: Action Steps

PROVIDERS

1. **Let clinicians take the lead.** Effective outcomes measurement is clinician driven. Clinicians should lead the measurement initiative and ensure that it produces clinically useful information.

2. **Define key population segments.** Outcomes should be measured for all patients within a well-defined population segment, regardless of how their condition is treated. Define the segments that are most important to your organization.

3. **Measure outcomes across the full cycle of care.** Track every stage of a patient's journey, including prevention, diagnosis, treatment, recovery, follow-up, and long-term well-being.

4. **Measure outcomes that matter to patients.** Make sure to include PROMs to determine whether treatment has delivered what patients care about.

5. **Don't reinvent the wheel.** The more comparable the outcomes data is across providers, the more useful they are, so prioritize standardized metrics that are already widely used.

6. **Avoid measurement overload.** Measure what really matters, not everything. When adding new outcomes metrics, eliminate existing metrics that are poor proxies for health outcomes.

7. **Use outcomes measurement for learning, not punishment.** The goal is continuous improvement, not pointing fingers or punishing outliers.

8. **Don't let perfect be the enemy of good.** When it comes to measuring health outcomes, start small, pilot to learn, and build enthusiasm and excitement among clinical teams.

PAYERS

1. **Measure quality in terms of outcomes, not process.** Incorporate actual health outcomes in all quality metrics.

2. **Pay for outcomes measurement.** Tracking outcomes is real work and important work. Introduce financial incentives that pay providers for measuring outcomes.

3. **Support metric standardization.** Align with other payers and with providers on outcome-measurement standards so that as many providers as possible track the same set of outcomes for defined patient segments.

4. **Minimize administrative complexity.** New data requirements inevitably add administrative complexity. Minimize the administrative costs by supporting common measurement systems across all providers.

SUPPLIERS *(Pharma, Med-tech, Etc.)*

1. **Link outcomes measurement to product development.** Track the health outcomes delivered by new products and services—as early as Phase II clinical trials.

2. **Make superior health outcomes part of the business case.** Be prepared to document how your products and services actually improve health outcomes, compared to existing or competing offerings.

3. **Focus on innovative outcomes-based solutions.** Partner with innovative providers to develop holistic new offerings that provide superior health outcomes.

POLICYMAKERS

1. **Make outcomes measurement and transparency a cost of doing business.** Define policies that make outcomes measurement and the transparency of those outcomes a prerequisite for participation in the national health system on the part of providers, suppliers, and payers.

2. **Support national quality registries.** Through policies and financial incentives, encourage the creation of a national network of quality registries.

3. **Regularly revisit measurement requirements.** Revise current measurement and reporting standards to eliminate ineffective measures and ensure that standards reflect the latest scientific and clinical knowledge.

PATIENTS

1. **Make outcomes part of the doctor-patient dialogue.** Ask your providers whether they track health outcomes, how they do so, and if not, why not.

2. **Know your preferences.** Discuss with your providers the full range of possible health outcomes associated with your condition and decide which outcomes are a priority for you.

3. **Become an active participant in outcomes measurement.** Fill out patient-reported health-outcomes surveys when asked to do so.

CHAPTER 3

ORGANIZING CARE DELIVERY AROUND THE PATIENT

The goal of systematically measuring and continuously improving the health outcomes delivered to patients has profound implications for how health care providers organize care delivery. Put simply, it encourages a more comprehensive and holistic perspective on health and disease thatideally should be replicated in how care is delivered.

Taking a more holistic approach to care delivery, however, can be difficult in the fragmented environment that characterizes contemporary health care. Most health systems around the world are organized around specialized functions. Primary care focuses on basic population health and disease prevention, as well as caring for the chronically ill. Then, depending on the uniqueness or severity of a patient's condition or the need for specialized care, patients are referred to secondary, tertiary, or even more specialized quaternary care centers. In theory, this structure allows patients to find the most appropriate treatment setting based on their condition. Too often in practice, however, each unit of the care-delivery value chain is managed separately, and incentives for clinicians at the various levels can conflict. Organizational fragmentation results in an equally fragmented patient experience.

So, too, inside the typical hospital. Departments are usually organized by medical specialty—for example, cardiology, orthopedics, rheumatology, or radiology. Shared resources, such as the emergency room, intensive care units, or surgery are likewise often organized into their own specialty units. Despite the high degree of formal interaction among departments through referrals for diagnostics or treatment, each unit is measured on its own budget and its own key performance indicators. What's more, the various specialist departments deployed along the patient care pathway typically do not share incentives.

This functional organizational structure made sense in the past, when specialization and the unique expertise of a hospital's clinicians was the primary means of improving care delivery, and choices among diagnostic and therapeutic alternatives were simpler. But over time, the traditional model of care delivery has become increasingly complex and dysfunctional. Specialization is an inevitable and necessary feature of modern health care. But the existence of separate, specialized units in organizational siloes makes it increasingly difficult to manage the trade-offs between different treatment options, to optimize the entire care pathway for a given disease or condition, and to manage costs in an integrated way.

These challenges have accelerated with growing financial pressures. Although individual unit performance and costs can be tracked, no one unit can typically be held accountable or even feels responsible for the health outcomes of a given group of patients across the entire care chain or for the total costs required to achieve them. In fact, negative financial incentives for the clinicians in one unit may dissuade them from collaborating with those in another.

Once health systems start to systematically track health outcomes for specific patient groups, however, an alternative model for organizing care delivery starts to emerge—organized not exclusively around specialist-based functions but mainly around the needs of particular groups of patients. In this new model, care is customized to the distinctive needs of specific population segments; the various relevant clinical interventions for each population segment are grouped together in integrated, "end-to-end" care pathways; and different types of clinicians and associated experts cooperate and work together in multidisciplinary teams to deliver the best health outcomes possible for the patient group.

In this chapter, we focus on how innovative provider organizations around the world are using this patient-focused and value-based approach to organize how they deliver care to different patient populations. We start with a general description of the alternative model of care delivery that is emerging at value-based innovators and revisit the theme of diabetes care to contrast this new model with traditional approaches to care. Then we do a deep dive on three organizations that are exemplars of value-based care delivery:

- Martini Klinik, a "hospital within a hospital" affiliated with the University Medical Center Hamburg-Eppendorf (known, in German, by the acronym UKE), an academic medical center in Hamburg, Germany, that focuses on delivering superior health outcomes for men who suffer from prostate cancer
- Oak Street Health, a US provider organization that is reinventing primary care for a specific population segment: the low-income elderly
- Kaiser Permanente, an integrated US payer-provider that probably more than any other provider organization in the world, has put together all the pieces of the value-based care-delivery model to serve its 12.4 million members in seven states and the District of Columbia

THE VALUE-BASED MODEL OF CARE DELIVERY

The traditional model of care delivery is organized around medical specialties. By contrast, value-based care delivery is organized around population segments. And while it may sound paradoxical, it is precisely this focus on specific populations of patients that makes possible a far-reaching personalization of care.

As we saw in Chapter 2, the simplest way to define the population segments of a value-based health system is to group all individuals suffering from the same condition or disease. To be effective, however, segmentation also needs to consider the risk factors influencing outcomes. The patient population suffering from a condition or disease will typically have subgroups with different risk profiles. For example, within the broader population of all patients suffering from diabetes, some patients suffer from other medical conditions, such as congestive heart failure or asthma, and others do not. These groups will have different risk profiles, as patients with multiple diagnoses will have a greater risk of worse health outcomes than those suffering from diabetes alone.

Over time, as the appropriate health outcome metrics for these patient subgroups become better understood, these subgroups may become clearly defined population segments in their own right (for example, all type 2 diabetes patients with heart failure), with their own clearly defined clinical interventions and specific health outcomes.

Another key dimension of risk concerns individuals who may currently be asymptomatic, but who are at risk of developing a disease in the future. They also represent distinct population segments that any population-based approach must take into account. In some cases, social or demographic factors will be the most relevant segment category—for instance, the population segment of all newborns or of the frail elderly—as such groups are likely to face similar health issues, pose unique challenges, or place special demands on the health system. In other situations, the key risks will be behavioral, as for the population of heavy smokers. Whether or not members of this segment are symptomatic today, their current behavior represents a key health risk and requires certain types of interventions, such as smoking cessation programs, to minimize the risk of future illness.

Finally, an individual's genetic profile may represent a key risk factor for certain population segments. As biomedical researchers accumulate knowledge of important genetic risk factors, certain risk groups are becoming well known, as with the role of inherited mutations in the BRCA1 and BRCA2 genes in creating an increased risk of female breast and ovarian cancers.

Thinking of care delivery in terms of distinct population segments has the advantage of putting patients at the center of the health system. Individual provider organizations may specialize in a particular patient group (such as Martini Klinik's focus on prostate cancer). Or they may focus on the needs of a specific demographic segment (the approach of Oak Street Health for the low-income elderly). Or they may choose to serve a broad spectrum of patient groups in a general population with customized care pathways, depending on the segment (Kaiser Permanente's approach). But no matter the specific strategy, the focus is on organizing care in a holistic manner for clearly defined population segments.

Does focusing on health outcomes for population segments come at the risk of ignoring the unique circumstances of specific individuals, often referred to as "personalized care"? Improvements in health outcomes, on average, could in theory disguise poor outcomes in individual cases. We think precisely the opposite is the case: only when a health system develops a fine-grained and nuanced statistical understanding of the health outcomes for a well-defined population segment based on patient characteristics will it be able to customize treatment sufficiently for any single member of that segment, based on that individual's distinctive risk profile and preferences. In other words, true personalization happens when health systems combine evidence-based customization, informed patient choice, and compassion and personal engagement of caregivers in their dialogue with patients.

For an example of what we mean, consider an innovative "dialogue support" tool, developed by the Swedish national spine quality registry SweSpine, to inform the clinician-patient dialogue for patients who suffer from diseases of the lower back or neck and who face the prospect of spine surgery.[1] The tool relies on a rich database incorporating standardized outcomes data and structured patient profiles drawn from some 140,000 back surgeries. The tool allows clinicians to predict outcomes for future patients based on their particular risk profile, thus providing a valuable base of evidence to help patients make informed choices about treatment options. Through a simple online survey, patients enter their specific back condition, age, sex, and other relevant information that has been shown to impact the outcome of surgical treatment.[2] The tool provides the statistical outcomes from past surgeries as a prediction and support for the patient's dialogue with his or her surgeon.

Once the purpose of a health system is conceived as delivering the best health outcomes possible for distinct population segments, the next logical step is to begin organizing care delivery around integrated, end-to-end care pathways for each segment, so that outcomes and costs can be managed in a more holistic and integrated manner.

Creating such care pathways requires customization along two critical dimensions. First, whereas traditional care delivery typically focuses on diagnosis, treatment, recovery, and rehabilitation, a genuinely integrated value-based approach to care will reach upstream to include interventions that enable prevention and downstream to include the long-term monitoring and management of patients with chronic disease.

Second, moving beyond the traditional clinical setting will allow for inclusion of the kind of behavioral and social interventions that research has shown are critical to addressing the social determinants of health. Behavioral interventions include helping patients modify unhealthy behaviors (for instance, smoking, poor diet, the lack of exercise), comply with treatment guidelines, or increase their individual motivation and willingness to participate in care. Social interventions address issues that have traditionally been the domain of the separate public health or social welfare system (for example, access to housing, immigration status, or food security). In order to improve patient outcomes and overall population health, such interventions also need to be integrated into the care pathway.[3]

An approach to care delivery that integrates both clinical interventions along the entire treatment pathway and nonclinical interventions that encourage prevention and address the social and behavioral determinants of health is not only a more effective way to monitor and treat patients, it also allows for better coordination across multiple stakeholders and gives health systems full visibility of the system costs to make informed trade-offs—for example, investing in preventive care to avoid high treatment costs at later points in the care-delivery value chain. Through standardized measurement of outcomes and thoughtful segmentation and rigorous risk adjustment, new innovations—whether a new surgical technique, predictive analytics like the SweSpine dialogue-support tool, or a system for organizing the delivery of social services, such as housing or nutritious food—will continue to improve health outcomes for each population segment.

In calling for the development of more integrated care pathways, we are not arguing for ending the traditional functional organization of primary, secondary, and tertiary care. There is value in specialization and the economies of scale that this kind of organization makes possible. Nevertheless, value-based care delivery does require clinical specialists to cooperate more closely and work together in new ways. In particular, it relies on a more team-based approach to care in which all the specialists necessary for treating a given condition—general practitioners, surgeons, nurses, physical therapists, social workers, data scientists who analyze outcomes data, social-welfare specialists, and the like—collaborate far more closely on caring for and treating a given population of patients.

This team-based approach to care requires clinicians to give up traditional forms of individual autonomy for a more collective form of team-based autonomy. Or in other words, it asks clinicians to put their own expertise at the service of cooperation in the multidisciplinary team, with shared goals for the outcome of care.

REVISITING DIABETES CARE: A TALE OF TWO COUNTRIES

To see what this new care model looks like in practice, let's revisit a situation that we described in Chapter 1: the large differences in national health outcomes between the United States and Sweden in the domain of diabetes. Recall that in 2019, the age-adjusted prevalence of diabetes in the US adult population was 10.8%, whereas in Sweden it was only 4.8%.

In 2016, we looked at differences between diabetes care in the two countries to see how they might contribute to this wide disparity in health outcomes. How health systems treat diabetes, of course, isn't the only factor determining health outcomes for the disease. Diabetes is largely a lifestyle disease, so patient behavior in terms of diet and exercise plays a central role in its prevalence and progression.[4] For example, obesity is a key risk factor in diabetes, and obesity levels (measured by the age-adjusted percentage of the population with a body mass index of 30 or above) are 70% higher in the United States than in Sweden, mainly owing to differences in diet. Sugar consumption in the United States is 1.5 times higher than in Sweden; according to one recent study, more than half the calories consumed by Americans come from so-called ultra-processed foods that are high in sugar.[5] Such differences between the two countries reflect many things—for example, Sweden's much higher investment in public health and social welfare, compared to the United States, and subtle (and not so subtle) differences in social and cultural values.[6]

Nevertheless, the way the health systems in the two countries organize the treatment of diabetes is another important factor, and that was the focus of our research. To analyze the different approaches to clinical practice in the two countries, we reviewed the scientific literature and interviewed clinical experts and representatives of patient groups. Our goal was to develop a high-level behavioral map of how the two systems typically diagnose and treat diabetes. While there are, of course, exceptions in both health systems and our analysis is not comprehensive, we identified two important clusters of behavioral difference.

Individual-Based Versus Team-Based Approaches to Care

In the United States, individual physicians typically take responsibility for diabetes care. The vast majority of diabetes patients (roughly 80%) are treated by their primary care physician (PCP). It's rare for PCPs to refer diabetes patients to an endocrinologist unless the case is especially serious—and when they do, the specialist tends to take over primary responsibility for the patient's care.

In Sweden, by contrast, clinicians take a more interdisciplinary, team-based approach. A patient's general practitioner (GP) usually makes the initial diagnosis, but that diagnosis immediately triggers the involvement of a variety of other experts, who play different but complementary roles. For example, most primary care facilities in Sweden have access to specially trained, full-time diabetes nurses who play a central role in diabetes care. In the United States, by contrast, diabetes nurses work mainly in secondary care treatment facilities, not primary care. Therefore, they tend to see only the most seriously ill patients.

Swedish GPs also refer diabetes patients to specialists (known as *diabetologists*, a term used in Sweden to describe endocrinologists who specialize in diabetes care) far more frequently than US primary care physicians do. But that does not mean those patients stop seeing their GP. Rather, Swedish diabetes patients move relatively easily between health care providers in the system, from GP to diabetes nurse to specialist and back again in a way that does not happen routinely in the United States.

Finally, Swedish primary care centers often appoint one GP to serve as the designated diabetes "node." In addition to treating his or her own patients, the node oversees the care and disease progression of other diabetes patients in the center, plays a consultative role with his or her colleagues, and in general helps coordinate the movement and care of patients among the multiple caregivers on the interdisciplinary team.

Integrating Prevention and Treatment

This team-based approach results in far more holistic clinical interventions in Sweden than in the United States. Whereas US clinicians focus primarily on medical measures—diagnosing symptoms and then prescribing drugs or performing procedures to address them—Swedish clinicians balance this approach with the kind of educational and behavioral interventions that are critical for managing a lifestyle disease such as diabetes.

These differences are partly a function of how much time primary care physicians spend with their patients. Once diagnosed, diabetes patients in the two countries visit their doctor with about the same frequency— roughly three or four times a year. But the time they spend per visit differs substantially: between 5 and 10 minutes in the typical US office visit, compared with 15 to 20 minutes in Sweden. The additional time that Swedish doctors spend with patients creates more opportunities to educate them on the behaviors needed (such as proper nutrition and exercise) to manage their disease effectively. In contrast, because US doctors are more time constrained, they are forced to focus on the most immediate and acute effects of the illness, reinforcing the overreliance on medical measures compared to educational and behavioral interventions.

But the main driver of the more holistic interventions of the Swedish system is the team-based approach we described previously. Here, the role of the diabetes nurse is key. As soon as a general practitioner makes the initial diagnosis, he or she refers the patient to a diabetes nurse, who conducts an initial one-hour visit to develop a tailored plan and daily routine for managing the disease (including when to take medication and how to measure blood sugar). Diabetes nurses meet regularly with patients in follow-up appointments, where they examine their feet for signs of neuropathy or foot ulcers (key symptoms of disease progression), make any necessary appointments with specialists, such as podiatrists or ophthalmologists, and in general help with the ongoing management of the disease.

The presence of diabetes nurses in most primary care settings also makes it easier for the system to focus its educational efforts not only on patients who have been diagnosed with diabetes but also on those at risk of developing the disease in the future. In other words, the Swedish approach contributes to prevention, not just to treatment and cure. And in general, it seems to integrate the traditionally separate domains of health care and public health better than the US system does.

Even specialists take a broader approach to diabetes care in Sweden. Diabetologists typically focus on the more serious cases, just as endocrinologists in the United States do. But in some Swedish counties (roughly the equivalent of US states and the primary funders of health care), they also offer an intensive four-day program of examination and education for early-stage type 2 diabetes patients, in which they develop a comprehensive treatment plan and then refer the patient back to his or her general practitioner for follow-up. This practice helps slow down the progression of the disease.

It may be tempting to explain these differences in clinical practice in terms of differences in the national or medical culture of the two societies. But that simply begs the question, "*Why* have these different cultures led to different behaviors?" Looking more closely, we can identify at least three aspects of the organizational context of the two health systems that have shaped the differences in approaches to diabetes care: access to comprehensive outcomes data, capitated payment models, and an emphasis on what we call integrator roles.

Comprehensive Outcomes Data

Given our discussion of Swedish quality registries in the previous chapter, it should be no surprise that one fundamental difference between the two health systems is that Swedish clinicians have access to comprehensive data on the health outcomes of diabetes patients nationwide. Since 1996, Sweden's National Quality Registry for Diabetes (known by its Swedish acronym, NDR) has collected comprehensive outcomes data on more than 5 million Swedish diabetes patients. Since 2002, NDR data has been available online, allowing individual clinics to easily compare their own results with national statistics.

Because Swedish clinicians have data on the actual health outcomes they are delivering, they are empowered to identify the most effective treatment options and change their behavior accordingly. And because this data is publicly available to providers, payers, and patients, clinicians have an interest in cooperating with peers to improve their outcomes over time.

Some regional US health systems have active diabetes registries, which they use to identify best practices in care much as Swedish clinicians do. And in 2014, the American College of Cardiology, in partnership with the American Diabetes Association, the American College of Physicians, and Joslin Diabetes Center, announced the launch of the Diabetes

Collaborative Registry, the first national, cross-specialty clinical regis-try designed to track and improve the quality of diabetes care. The new registry represents important progress, but so far its coverage is far from universal. By 2019, the registry had approximately 1.5 million unique patients in its database, which represents only about 4% of the roughly 37 million people with diabetes in the United States.[7] In the absence of comprehensive outcomes data, it is far more difficult for primary-care physicians on the frontline of diabetes care to assess their performance against that of peers, codify best practices, and ultimately improve their health outcomes.

Fee-for-Service Versus Capitation

Another major difference has less to do with care delivery per se than the financial incentives embedded in the two systems. It concerns how care-givers are paid. Despite many changes in recent years, most US clinicians continue to be paid according to some version of the traditional fee-for-service payment model. In Sweden, by contrast, payment for primary care is usually based on capitation adjusted for a primary care center's popu-lation mix.

The US fee-for-service model helps explain why primary care providers in the United States are less likely than their Swedish colleagues to refer patients to an endocrinologist. If a large share of referred patients end up returning to that specialist for their ongoing care, the primary care pro-vider loses the patient and the associated revenue stream. Fee-for-service compensation also encourages US clinicians to focus on medical inter-ventions, which are most likely to be reimbursed by payers.

A capitation-based incentive system, by contrast, encourages autonomy by making it easier to choose from a wider variety of interventions with-out having to get payer approval. As a result, more time and attention go to activities such as patient education. Capitation also gives Swedish clinicians an interest in preventing diabetes and minimizing its progres-sion, because the fewer the cases, the lower the costs and the more the primary care facility will be able to keep within its county-approved bud-get. Finally, the fact that risk-adjusted health outcomes are tracked in a national quality registry and made available to the public greatly limits the risk that capitation will encourage cherry-picking of patients or the rationing of care. (We'll talk more about capitation and other forms of value-based payment in Chapter 5.)

"Integrator" Roles

A third aspect of the Swedish organizational context for diabetes care is the explicit roles that have been created to support the team-based and holistic clinical approach. The diabetes nurse who is a central player in diabetes care and the general practitioner who is the designated diabetes node in a primary care center are both examples of what we call "integrator" roles—actors with an interest in encouraging cooperation who help each member of the organization benefit from the cooperation of others. It is the existence of these clearly defined roles in overall care delivery that helps make Sweden's approach to diabetes care so effective.[8]

There is no reason why the US health system—or any health system, for that matter—couldn't foster an organizational context that encourages comparable behaviors. In fact, some US providers have begun to do just that. A number of leading diabetes-focused clinics in the United States—for example, the Joslin Diabetes Center in Boston—take a team-based approach to care that is quite similar to the Swedish model, and these specialty clinics provide some of the best diabetes care in the world. So far, however, they remain the exception that proves the rule. For example, in 2018, Medicare introduced an innovative "Diabetes Prevention Program" covering similar educational and early-intervention programs that have been demonstrated in clinical trials to reduce diabetes incidence in high-risk people. But the program currently covers only about 4,000 Medicare beneficiaries, due to lack of awareness about the program's existence and cumbersome payment structures.[9] And a recent review of US diabetes care argues that progress in the prevention and treatment of type 2 diabetes has stalled in the past decade—primarily due to poor coordination and low accountability caused by fragmentation in three areas: health policy and governance, payers and reimbursement design, and service delivery.[10]

Diabetes is just one example. Leading innovators around the world are putting the alternative value-based model of care delivery into practice for specific diseases and patient populations—and often in the face of considerable obstacles embedded in the way that various national health systems are currently organized. Let's explore more of these examples to see what we can learn from them.

PATIENT-CENTERED PROSTATE CANCER CARE: GERMANY'S MARTINI KLINIK

For an example of a health care organization that has thrived by focusing relentlessly on the needs of a particular patient segment, consider Martini Klinik, a "hospital within a hospital" affiliated with the University Hospital Hamburg-Eppendorf (UKE), an academic medical center in Hamburg, Germany.

Martini is an example of what Michael Porter and Elizabeth Teisberg have termed an "integrated practice unit" (IPU).[11] Unlike a typical urology clinic, Martini focuses exclusively on a single patient group: men suffering from prostate cancer. The clinic was founded in 2005 by Dr. Hartwig Huland, one of Europe's leading urologists and at the time, the urology chair at UKE (we met him in Chapter 2 as the head of the ICHOM prostate-cancer working group), and his colleague Dr. Markus Graefen. The mission of the new clinic was to create a genuinely patient-centered environment in which each patient receives personal, end-to-end attention from a single physician and his or her team. "It sounds a little bit romantic," Huland told us, "but my main principle has always been to treat a patient in the same way I wish to be treated myself."

By 2019 the clinic had become the largest prostate cancer treatment program in the world, employing 12 surgeons with tenured faculty positions and some 215 associated clinical and administrative staff, treating some 7,000 outpatient cases every year, and performing about 2,500 radical prostatectomies—nearly two-and-a-half times the volume of the second-largest prostate cancer center in the world at Johns Hopkins University and representing roughly 11% of all prostatectomies performed in Germany.

By focusing on a clearly defined patient segment, meticulously tracking health outcomes for that segment, and then using the data from a growing volume of cases to improve clinical practice, Martini Klinik has been able to deliver health outcomes that are by far the best in Germany—and perhaps the best in the world. Take the example of erectile dysfunction, a serious and extremely common side effect of radical prostatectomy. A 2012 study by the German sick fund Barmer found that in Germany, about three-quarters of all patients who undergo the surgery end up with the condition. At the time, the rate of severe erectile dysfunction among Martini patients, by contrast, was less than half the average rate—34.7% one year after operation, as opposed to 75.5%. A more recent 2019 comparison between Martini and a Norwegian urology clinic found that the German clinic's rate for preserving erectile function was more than one-and-half-times better.[12]

So too for other common side effects such as urinary incontinence. According to the Barmer study, the percentage of Martini patients who suffer severe urinary incontinence after surgery was 11 times lower than the German average—0.4% versus 4.5%. And the number of patients who maintain full continence after surgery was 45% higher. Finally, in terms of preventing and avoiding post-surgical complications, results at Martini Klinik were well superior to the German average for pulmonary embolism and thrombosis, ureteral injury, and sepsis.

How is Martini able to achieve such results? Central to the clinic's approach is the kind of rigorous outcomes measurement we described in Chapter 2. The clinic not only collects comprehensive data on each of its patients while they are at the clinic, including baseline information on demographics, comorbidities, tumor stage and characteristics, laboratory data, and functional status, it also tracks their health outcomes long after they leave the clinic, through the systematic collection of patient-reported health outcomes. According to Huland, this is especially important for a disease like prostate cancer that can intimately affect a patient's quality of life. "Normally, when a patient is discharged, the surgeon never knows the ultimate results," he said. "By contrast, we get information long after the discharge from the hospital."

The process starts four weeks after the removal of a urinary catheter when patients fill out a brief four-question survey meant to assess their urinary function. Six months after surgery, they receive an email link to a 30-question survey about complications they may have experienced after surgery, as well as another survey instrument that assesses their functional status in greater detail. The clinic repeats the functional assessment annually for the first 10 years after surgery (subsequently, patients are surveyed only about the long-term oncologic outcomes of their surgery). The response rate for the 2,000 patient surveys that Martini administers each month is in the neighborhood of 85%. More recently, Martini has formally incorporated the ICHOM outcome-measurement sets for localized and advanced prostate cancer, which, as we saw in the previous chapter, Huland played a lead role in developing.

As a result of this comprehensive tracking, Martini has accumulated a database on health outcomes for approximately 35,000 prostate cancer patients that have passed through the clinic—the world's largest database on prostate cancer, providing unique insights on what works and what doesn't that lead to new ideas for improving treatment. "There are some 400 institutions doing prostate cancer surgery in Germany," said Markus Graefen. "But nobody has the outcomes database that we have." By continuously accumulating more and more outcomes data, Martini is able to identify relevant new subsegments within the broader population of prostate cancer patients, do increasingly sophisticated risk assessment, define multiple care pathways for different patient categories, and develop more precise and more personalized care, depending on each patient's risk profile and preferences.

The massive data that Martini collects on each patient also serves as the foundation for a structured process of continuous improvement on the part of the clinic's surgeons. Every six months, the clinic holds a three-hour quality review meeting in which each surgeon's outcomes for the previous six months are compared with the results of earlier years and with those of peers. "If someone is an outlier in a certain domain," Graefen explains, "we discuss it as a group. Nobody is punished." For example, there is no financial penalty for below-average outcomes (although an individual's outcomes data does play a role in whether younger surgeons are eventually promoted to faculty status). "But they might have to team for a period with the best performer in that area until their results improve."

The result of this process is continuous improvement in the outcomes delivered both by individual surgeons and the clinic as a whole. Figure 3.1 portrays data from a 2014 study showing the performance of Martini faculty members in ensuring that their patients maintain urinary continence after radical prostatectomy.[13] Each line in the figure represents a different surgeon, based on the year he or she joined the clinic, and shows the continence rate for each surgeon's patients as the surgeon accumulates case experience. The steady upward trajectory of the lines shows that the clinic's surgeons, including the most experienced, have been continuously improving the continence rate of their patients over time. But even more important, the graph shows that the later a surgeon joins the clinic, the higher the starting point in terms of performance—which suggests that the more senior surgeons in the clinic are successfully passing on their accumulated experience to each new generation, continuously raising the average of the entire team.

FIGURE 3.1   At Martini Klinik, outcomes measurement fosters apprenticeship and rapid learning.

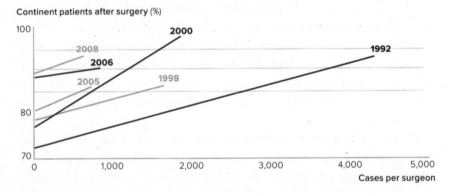

Continent patients after surgery (%)

Each line represents the improving performance of surgeons (categorized by start date at the clinic) in maintaining urinary continence in their patients. Not only does each surgeon improve performance over time; newer surgeons also begin at a higher starting point because their training benefits from the collective expertise of the team.

Source: *Dr. Hartwig Huland, Martini Klinik.*

Another key feature of Martini's value-based approach to care delivery is a team-based approach to care. Academic medicine in Germany tends to be extremely hierarchical. In a typical clinic, the physician-in-chief, known as the *Chefarzt*, sits at the top of a pyramid consisting of senior physicians and below them, assistant physicians. In contrast, at Martini, all the surgeons promoted to faculty rank have equal status and work closely as a team to deliver the best possible care to their patients.

Before surgery, every new patient is discussed by the entire faculty in a weekly tumor board of specialists from surgery, radiation therapy, oncology, and other specialties. Patients have access to a psychologist to discuss any concerns about their surgery and to help them articulate their preferences in terms of desired health outcomes. And in 2018, the clinic started a continuous patient education program.

Because the clinic focuses on a single disease, each faculty member also has the opportunity—and the expectation—to specialize in a particular aspect of the clinic's work and to serve as a specialist resource for the rest. For example, one of Martini's clinicians is an expert in advanced prostate cancer; another is a clinician/computer scientist who is the expert at drawing clinical insights from the outcomes database; a third specializes in robotic surgical techniques (and spends roughly two months each year training his colleagues on the latest developments in that fast-moving field).

In addition to its core group of surgeons, Martini employs approximately a hundred nurses who are specialized in prostate cancer care. And as the volume of patients has grown, Martini has begun to include on its team associate faculty who are trained in nonsurgical specialties that play an increasingly important role in prostate cancer care—for example, medical oncology, radiation therapy, radiology, anesthesiology, psycho-oncology, and pathology.

Martini's data-driven, team-based approach allows the clinic to take advantage of increased specialization even as it provides an integrated patient experience. It also allows the clinic to engage in cutting-edge clinical research. The existence of its outcomes database has contributed to Martini becoming a global leader in research on prostate cancer, with the clinic's surgeons publishing in the neighborhood of 90 publications every year in the biomedical scientific literature.

With advances in molecular diagnostics and genomics, Martini has also linked its outcomes database to genetic and molecular data for every tumor sample. The Martini biobank has more than 72,000 blood, tissue, and urine specimens, allowing the clinic to conduct research that may reveal the links between genetic mutations, molecular indicators, and the growth and spread of prostate tumors. And the clinic leads the project on prostate cancer at the International Cancer Genome Consortium (ICGC), a worldwide initiative to elucidate the genomic changes present in cancers that contribute to the burden of disease throughout the world.

The more data the clinic accumulates, the more it has been able to refine its ability to analyze its practice. "We are increasingly recognizing the value of new data sets," said Graefen. Take the example of robotic surgery. Robotic equipment makes it possible to track the movements of the surgeon throughout the course of an operation. Recently, Martini has been linking this data, as well as image-data from videos taken of individual surgeries, to the outcomes data for the surgeries in order to detect patterns that may explain the differences between good-outcome and poor-outcome surgeries.

Last, but far from least, Martini Klinik's success has fueled a virtuous cycle in which specialization and a focus on delivering superior outcomes has led to a rising volume of patients—and increased volume has led to more data, more clinical experience for its surgeons, and more improvement in the quality of care delivered.

Between its founding in 2005 and 2019, the clinic's case volume grew 9% per year (compared to an historical growth in prostatectomy volume in Germany of about 1%), which represented a near tripling in the number of patients. Martini's global reputation for excellent care has also increasingly attracted patients from across Germany and even from countries all over the world (one sign of the clinic's international scope: its website is in 12 languages). The clinic has negotiated multiple bundled-payment contracts with Germany's leading private insurers. And in 2013, it signed a similar contract with a leading private Swiss health insurer to treat its prostate cancer patients in Hamburg. Martini has since developed a care bundle for international patients that includes surgery, inpatient stays, and travel expenses. As a result, the number of patients coming from abroad quadrupled in the five years prior to 2019 and includes people from some 65 countries.

Growing volume isn't just a result of the clinic's success at delivering superior outcomes. It also reinforces the clinic's ability to improve still further. Radical prostatectomies are among the most complex and riskiest of urological procedures. Research has shown that the volume of surgeries that a surgeon performs is critical to improving health outcomes in prostate cancer surgery. The patients of high-volume surgeons typically have better disease-specific survival and lower rates of surgical complications, incontinence, and impotence.[14] Every faculty member at Martini has personally performed more than 1,500 prostate surgeries and typically performs between 200 and 300 every year. In contrast, about half of all radical prostatectomies in Germany are performed in hospitals where fewer than 50 such procedures are performed in total each year.

In 2023, Martini Klinik will move into a new seven-story building, designed explicitly to support the integrated approach to care delivery that the clinic has pioneered. In addition to expanding the clinic's surgical theaters from five to eight, the new facility will group all the clinic's specialty departments (currently spread across the university) in a single site and include a chemotherapy ward, labs for basic research, a diagnostic department with its own MRI, and even a kitchen to teach patients how to improve their diet. The new building is a sign not only of Martini's clinical success but also its financial health. In fiscal year 2018, Martini generated revenue of €32 million and a profit of €3.4 million, making it the best-performing unit within the UKE system.

For the moment, however, Martini Klinik's approach to prostate cancer care remains unique in Germany. "Our approach is so different from the way that most doctors are trained," said Graefen. "It's not easy to build a group that thinks differently." And yet, that may be changing. The Martini example is already having an impact on prostate cancer care in Germany. The clinic played a lead role in getting the German Cancer Society to adopt the ICHOM prostate cancer outcome-measurement sets as part of the certification process for urology clinics in Germany. Since 2018, clinics need to commit to tracking the ICHOM measures in order to win society certification. And currently, a research study is underway that is using the ICHOM measures to compare the health outcomes delivered by some 122 participating German urology clinics. "It's just a beginning," said Graefen, "but in the future, it will allow centers to regularly compare and learn from their results."

Of course, many factors have contributed to Martini's success. Institutional support from UKE's leadership has been critical to the development and evolution of Martini's innovative care-delivery model. So has considerable financial investment in the IT platform and specialized resources necessary to collect and maintain Martini's growing outcomes database (here, the clinic benefited from an early generous donation from a private German philanthropist). But the most critical success factor has been Huland's visionary leadership.

Markus Graefen tells a story of one of the first meetings of the clinical team to discuss their individual performance on patient outcomes. In one particular aspect of prostate cancer surgery, one of the younger surgeons had achieved significantly better results than Huland, the leader and most experienced member of the team. "There was a lot of tension in the air," Graefen recalled. "How would he deal with this?" Huland's response: "Oh, you're better than me. When you do your next surgery, I want to observe and learn from you." "It made it crystal clear to everybody why we were gathering all this data," said Graefen. And it sent a signal to the team:

"Don't believe you always know what's best." (See also the sidebar "Integrating Around the Patient: Examples from Around the World.")

Integrating Around the Patient: Examples from Around the World

In many respects, Martini Klinik is unique. But other health care organizations in both high- and low-income countries are pursuing versions of Martini's patient-centered, disease-focused, and data-driven business model in other key areas of specialty care.

In the Netherlands, for example, a network of specialty clinics created by the clinical research center Diabeter has used a similar approach to develop comprehensive, personalized approaches to treat children and young adults suffering from type 1 diabetes. As a result, Diabeter's clinics have some of the best health outcomes for type 1 diabetes patients in the Netherlands.[15] In 2015, the company was acquired by Medtronic to become part of the med-tech giant's integrated global offering for diabetes care. The move has fueled Diabeter's expansion. In addition to its five clinics in the Netherlands, Diabeter now has a new clinic in Saudi Arabia and another planned for Spain.

In India, the Aravind Eye Care System has developed an approach to cataract surgery that combines systematic tracking of health outcomes, standardized procedures that make possible the rapid dissemination of the latest innovations in clinical practice, and an integrated approach to care delivery to deliver first-world health outcomes at a cost per surgery that is approximately one-tenth of the cost in the United States.[16] Although Aravind's lower cost is partially due to the relatively low salaries of cataract surgeons in India, it is primarily due to how Aravind organizes care.

Finally, in Africa, an innovative pilot program known as MomCare has created an integrated-care delivery model that focuses on maternal and newborn child health. Developed by the not-for-profit PharmAccess and funded by participating national social health insurance schemes and international donors such as the Child Investment Fund Foundation and MSD for Mothers, MomCare was launched in Kenya in 2017 and has since expanded to Tanzania and Nigeria. The program organizes care around the World Health Organization's guidelines for prenatal and postnatal care and uses a modified version of the ICHOM standard set for pregnancy and childbirth, adapted for local use, to collect both clinical and patient-reported outcomes data. So far, some 50,000 pregnant women have participated in the program, with promising early results.[17]

RETHINKING PRIMARY CARE: OAK STREET HEALTH

It's one thing to organize care around patient groups with clearly defined diseases such as prostate cancer and clearly defined procedures for treating them. But what about in areas of health care such as primary care, where the range of issues that clinicians face is far broader, where diagnosis can be more multidimensional, and where patients often suffer from multiple comorbidities?

The question is especially urgent in the United States. In 2021, the National Academies of Science, Engineering, and Medicine published a report calling for major investments in creating a value-based primary care system. "High-quality primary care is vital but undersupported in the United States," states an article in the *New England Journal of Medicine*, whose authors included a cochair of the National Academies report committee.[18] And the situation is worsening. "The share of the country's health care resources that is invested in primary care is meager and declining." More than half of office visits in the United States are to primary care physicians, but they make up only 30% of the physician workforce and are supported by only 5.4% of national expenditures. They also earn 30% less than other physicians, on average. And yet, the decisions that primary care physicians make have a key impact on the entire costs of the health system.

Precisely for these reasons, primary care is becoming an extraordinarily active site for value-based innovation in the US health system. The last decade has seen the emergence of a variety of new approaches that Patrick Conway, CEO of Care Solutions (the provider network of United HealthCare's Optum subsidiary) calls "intensive primary care."[19]

Take, for example, a relatively new provider organization by the name of Oak Street Health. Founded in 2012 on the north side of Chicago, Oak

Street's mission is to bring comprehensive primary care to residents in medically underserved communities. Since its founding, Oak Street has grown from a single clinic in Chicago's Edgewater neighborhood, where some 16% of households live below the poverty line, to more than 130 clinics serving approximately 150,000 people in so-called health care deserts across 20 states and in cities ranging from Chicago and Detroit to Philadelphia and Providence. (See Figure 3.2.)

FIGURE 3.2   Oak Street is building a national care network focused on the low-income elderly.

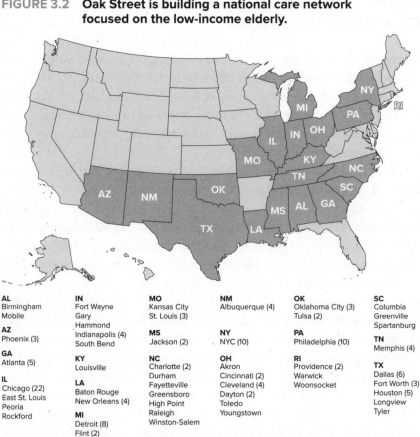

AL	**IN**	**MO**	**NM**	**OK**	**SC**
Birmingham	Fort Wayne	Kansas City	Albuquerque (4)	Oklahoma City (3)	Columbia
Mobile	Gary	St. Louis (3)		Tulsa (2)	Greenville
AZ	Hammond		**NY**		Spartanburg
Phoenix (3)	Indianapolis (4)	**MS**	NYC (10)	**PA**	**TN**
	South Bend	Jackson (2)		Philadelphia (10)	Memphis (4)
GA			**OH**		
Atlanta (5)	**KY**	**NC**	Akron	**RI**	**TX**
	Louisville	Charlotte (2)	Cincinnati (2)	Providence (2)	Dallas (6)
IL		Durham	Cleveland (4)	Warwick	Fort Worth (3)
Chicago (22)	**LA**	Fayetteville	Dayton (2)	Woonsocket	Houston (5)
East St. Louis	Baton Rouge	Greensboro	Toledo		Longview
Peoria	New Orleans (4)	High Point	Youngstown		Tyler
Rockford		Raleigh			
	MI	Winston-Salem			
	Detroit (8)				
	Flint (2)				
	Kalamazoo				

In its first decade, Oak Street Health has grown from a single clinic in Chicago's Edgewater neighborhood to 130 clinics in 20 states.

Note: Locations listed are as of first quarter 2022.

Source: *Oak Street Health*

We've had a ringside seat from which to observe the evolution of Oak Street because its three founders—CEO Mike Pykosz, COO Geoff Price, and Chief Medical Officer Dr. Griffin Myers—are all former consultants in BCG's Chicago office (Pykosz was involved in some of our early work on quality registries).

Oak Street focuses on providing high-value care for a population segment with perhaps the greatest health challenges of all in American society: the low-income elderly. The company's patients are among the most difficult cases found in the US Medicare system, which covers some 52 million Americans who are 65 and older or who suffer from chronic disabilities or end-stage renal disease. Eighty-six percent of Oak Street's patients have multiple chronic conditions such as hypertension, diabetes, congestive heart failure, or chronic obstructive pulmonary disease. Forty percent have a behavioral-health diagnosis.

About half of Oak Street's patients also struggle with one or more social risk factors that are critical determinants of poor health—for example, lack of secure access to housing or to nutritious food. Approximately 40% of its patients are so-called dual-eligible patients—that is, they are eligible not only for Medicare but also for Medicaid, which covers low-income families and individuals. The average income of Oak Street's dual-eligible patients is less than $21,000 per year. Given this complex mix of health and social challenges, it should be no surprise that such patients are especially costly for the US health system. For example, per capita Medicare fee-for-service spending for dual-eligible patients is about twice as high as for other Medicare beneficiaries.

"Oak Street's initial premise," Pykosz told us, "was not to worry about what's billable but instead to focus on what our patients need—and then align resources around those needs." The idea: by engaging in careful risk assessment and focusing on prevention and early intervention, Oak Street could keep people healthy and out of the hospital, thus avoiding, to the degree possible, expensive acute care. As a financial incentive, instead of getting paid for its services according to the traditional fee-for-service payment model, in which providers are paid for the volume of services and procedures they deliver, the company takes on full financial risk for its patients' health needs. Oak Street receives risk-adjusted capitated payments for each patient, either directly from the federal government's Centers for Medicare and Medicaid Services (or CMS, the administrator of Medicare and Medicaid) or from private health insurers who offer capitated plans through CMS's Medicare Advantage program. (We will describe Medicare Advantage in more detail in Chapter 5.) The vast majority of Oak Street's patients come under a capitated agreement.

"Because we have taken financial responsibility for the entirety of care for many of our patients, including primary, specialty, acute, and post-acute care," COO Geoff Price explained to Harvard Business School researchers writing a case about the company, "we can invest in primary care services that have a positive health (and therefore economic) return for our practice."[20] The company's chief clinical officer Dr. David Buchanan, calls this "increasing the dosage of primary care."[21]

Oak Street's approach to care delivery features all the components of value-based care delivery that we described earlier in the chapter. Like Martini, Oak Street has carefully designed its delivery model around the specific needs of its target population segment. The company's clinics are often the first health care providers to open in the neighborhoods that it serves—and often the first new business in years. "Our centers don't look like primary care centers" explained Oak Street chief medical officer Griffin Myers in an interview in *NEJM Catalyst*.[22] "They don't look like health centers. They're not located in medical office spaces. They're specifically built in the neighborhoods we serve in high-traffic areas where people live and work and play, not necessarily where they go to get health care."

In effect, Oak Street clinics function as a kind of community center, a one-stop shop to serve a variety of health and social needs. The standard design includes a self-serve café, a computer lab with internet access, and a community-room event space that hosts a wide array of activities: arts-and-leisure events such as Bingo and movie nights, exercise classes such as senior yoga and Zoomba, and daily educational sessions, including computer classes, book groups, and sessions on Medicare basics and the value of primary care.

Each clinic also has an outreach team drawn from residents in the neighborhood and provides door-to-door transportation services to the clinic and to local hospitals and specialty providers. During extreme weather in the winter and summer, the clinics serve as warming or cooling centers for the neighborhood. And more recently, Oak Street has been increasingly focused on the social and behavioral determinants of health, working with its partners to help patients find resources for food and housing, including hosting produce sales in clinic community rooms.

"Over time, this is our number one focus," said Meyers. "What can we do to bring in the things that we know our patients need that may be outside the exam room rather than on the inside?"[23]

Oak Street also takes a team-based approach to care. Each patient is assigned a primary care physician, responsible for each patient's overall care plan; a nurse practitioner or physician assistant who coordinates the care team; a medical assistant who manages in-clinic workflow and helps patients navigate their visit to the clinic; and a care manager responsible for implementation of the care plan and who coordinates with the patient and his or her family in between clinic visits. In addition, registered nurses assist in care coordination and patient education, and clinical-informatics specialists make sure that all relevant past and present clinical information is available at the point of care. Meanwhile, a team of scribes, phlebotomists, social workers, behavioral health specialists, and some 200 community-outreach workers (such as the drivers of the vans) are shared across teams.

New patients receive an intensive 40-minute initial assessment known as the "welcome visit" to determine their overall health situation. Based on the assessment, each patient is assigned to one of four risk tiers, which are used to determine the frequency of primary care visits and the allocation of care-management resources. For example, the focus for patients in the "good" category is preventive care; for the roughly 30% of Oak Street patients in the "VIP and serious" categories, the emphasis is on early intervention and careful care coordination and management in order to avoid, to the degree possible, the necessity of acute hospital admissions and readmissions.

In addition to its core primary-care delivery model, Oak Street also has developed a number of specific modules for common chronic or acute conditions. Some are performed in-house. For example, the company has a behavioral health program, which gives patients access to social workers and mental-health professionals directly through its network of clinics. And for patients who do need acute care that the organization cannot deliver itself, Oak Street has partnered with external specialists who, in the company's judgment, share their value-based care-delivery model. (While Oak Street assists its patients in the choice of hospitals and specialists, unlike many managed-care plans, it does not restrict patient choice.) Throughout, the emphasis is on providing cost-effective, high-quality care. "Take, for example, end-stage renal disease," said Pykosz.

"Dialysis is expensive, but it's a lot more expensive not to do it and have the patient end up in the hospital. We put a lot of resources against that specific patient group to make sure their condition is controlled in the most cost-effective way."

The arrival of the coronavirus pandemic posed distinctive challenges both to Oak Street's target population and to its clinic-based delivery model. In response, the organization quickly developed a remote-care program that allowed it to conduct the vast majority of its 2,200 daily patient visits by phone or video.[24] Oak Street developed a specific disease-management program for suspected or confirmed Covid cases that used remote monitoring, daily rounding, and evidence-based guidelines for supportive care to simulate an actual hospital stay. Depending on the level of the acuity, typical interventions included a daily nursing phone call, food delivery, access to home-based social work services, and physical house calls for the most acute patients. Meanwhile, the company converted its drivers and vans into a delivery fleet to provide patients with groceries, medical supplies such as digital thermometers and simple pulse oximeters, toilet paper, and other necessities.

Oak Street systematically collects outcomes and cost data, using it to continually refine its integrated team-based approach to care. As the clinical informatics specialist role suggests, the Oak Street care-delivery model is supported by a proprietary IT platform that integrates all clinical information, automatically assigning patients to disease-specific registries, identifying patients at increased risk for admittance to the hospital, and tracking those patients who have missed appointments or who are at increased risk of complications. A patient dashboard incorporates data from payers, hospitals, and partner specialty practices and allows care teams to compare the outcomes of their patients relative to those of all other Oak Street patients. And the company tracks 24 out of the 28 recommended metrics in the ICHOM "Older Persons" measurement set, which defines key health outcomes for the elderly.

Recently, Oak Street has leveraged this digital platform to incorporate machine-learning algorithms into its patient risk-assessment process. Up until 2019, risk stratification at Oak Street was based on historical patient data and the assessment of a patient's clinical team. Although useful, the approach did not really differentiate between types of risks. And other than flagging life-limiting illnesses, it provided little actionable information to clinical teams. As Oak Street has accumulated more and more data on its patients, however, it has begun to use machine learning to develop analytics that more accurately predicts a patient's risk level.

For example, the company has recently developed a machine-learning application called Data IQ that leverages a wide range of data from the patient's electronic medical record (EMR), claims data provided by CMS and health insurance partners, and other sources to predict a patient's risk of in-patient admission, projected 6-month third-party costs, and risk of mortality in the next 12 months.[25] The application has allowed Oak Street to more accurately identify those patients likely to require hospital admission in the future, and access to the predictive data has made care teams more likely to plan early interventions in an effort to avoid preventable hospitalizations.

Through its patient-centered, team-based, data-driven care model, Oak Street has found innovative ways to serve an underserved patient segment. The company's focus on the specific needs of its patient group has won the company a five-star rating on the CMS-sponsored five-star quality rating system that tracks performance against 40 categories for quality and service (based, in part, on the Healthcare Effectiveness Data and Information Set, or HEDIS, which despite the limitations that we described in Chapter 2, remains the accepted standard for comparing US health-plan performance and quality of care). And Oak Street's emphasis on prevention means that patients end up in the hospital less frequently and spend less time there when they do. The company boasts a 40% reduction in hospital admissions, a 52% reduction in emergency department visits, and a 35% reduction in 30-day readmission rates. The company's 90% patient retention rate suggests that patients are satisfied with the care they receive. Last but far from least, Oak Street's risk-adjusted costs of delivery per patient are significantly lower than the amounts allocated by the Medicare Advantage plans under its contracts.

Of course, Oak Street isn't the only health care company trying to create a value-based model for primary care. The trend toward intensive primary care in the United States has attracted a lot of players and potential competitors. For example, Boston-based Iora Health is pursuing nearly the identical business model to that of Oak Street; in 2021 it was acquired by the concierge medical network One Medical. CareMore, another player in this space, was acquired by health insurer Anthem. Other organizations striving to reinvent US primary care include CityBlock, Adelaide, ImagineMD, and Upstream Healthcare.

Mike Pykosz, for one, welcomes the competition. "We are striving to build a scalable, national model." To that end, in the summer of 2020, Oak Street went public in an initial public offering that raised $328 million and together with an $800 million convertible debt offering is funding the company's expansion into new markets, as well as the acquisition of new capabilities to strengthen its offering. "In our first five years, we opened 25 clinics," said Pykosz. "In 2021, we opened 50, and in 2022, we are targeting 70." In 2021, Oak Street also acquired Rubicon MD, a company that does virtual consulting with medical specialists. The acquisition allows Oak Street to have richer and more constructive real-time interactions between its primary care doctors and specialists.

"The more we grow, the more we can invest in our model, in data, and in the patient experience," said Pykosz. "We want to become a kind of Walgreens or CVS of primary care."

PUTTING IT ALL TOGETHER: KAISER PERMANENTE

Organizations such as Martini Klinik or Oak Street Health might be termed "focused players." They are designing value-based care-delivery systems for specific patient segments, defined by disease or by demographic and socioeconomic profile. It's relatively rare, however, to find a full-service provider organization that is organized entirely around the value-based care-delivery model.

The organization that probably comes closest to putting together all the pieces of value-based care delivery is the US integrated payer-provider Kaiser Permanente (KP). Founded in 1945, KP traces its origins to an innovative program to provide health care to workers at dam-construction projects in the western United States during the Great Depression and at the Kaiser shipyards on the West Coast during World War II.[26] Today, it is one of the largest not-for-profit health plans and health care providers in the United States. With more than 12.4 million members (primarily in California but also in Washington, Oregon, Colorado, Hawaii, Maryland, Virginia, and Washington, DC), the KP health system is larger in terms of population than the national health system of Sweden (which has a population of about 10 million people). The organization operates 39 hospitals and 723 medical offices and other outpatient facilities; employs approximately 217,000 people, including nearly 24,000 physicians, 64,000 nurses, and 75,000 allied health professionals; and has an annual operating revenue of nearly $90 billion.

Unusually for the US provider landscape, KP is a fully integrated payer-provider—that is, its members purchase insurance (typically through their employer) from KP's own health plan and KP delivers care through its own network of doctors and hospitals. This organizational structure creates a strong incentive to provide high-value care in the most cost-effective manner possible and has allowed the organization to create an integrated-care delivery model that emphasizes preventive care and the active management of chronic disease, and includes incentives that simultaneously promote excellent clinical outcomes and resource efficiency.

The company describes its "unique business model" as combining "health coverage and care delivery into one coordinated experience." The approach allows KP to provide health benefits that are, on average, 10% to 20% cheaper than traditional managed-care plans, while delivering outstanding quality. In 2019–2020, its health plans took the top three spots in the US National Center for Quality Assurance (NCQA) Medicare plan rankings, and eight of the company's nine commercial plans had a rating of 4.0 or above, indicating higher performance based on Healthcare Effectiveness Data and Information Set (HEDIS), Consumer Assessment of Healthcare Providers and Systems (CAHPS), and NCQA Accreditation standards scores.[27] KP also typically has lower rates of preventable hospitalizations, mean length of stay, and readmission rates for chronic medical conditions such as angina, chronic obstructive pulmonary disease, congestive heart failure, diabetes, and hypertension than are found in some of the world's leading national health systems.[28]

How does KP achieve these results? For one thing, the company has invested heavily in systemwide IT platforms with common standards across all providers and standard methodologies for risk stratification across member population segments. The organization has implemented the largest advanced electronic health record in the United States, known as KP HealthConnect, which integrates each patient's clinical record with appointments, ancillary services, and registration and billing, creating a complete health care business and management system that supports the continuous improvement of the quality of patient care.

KP HealthConnect also integrates data from the organization's extensive network of outcomes registries, which function much like the national quality registries we described in Chapter 2 and some of which have been collecting clinical data from multiple sources since the late 1990s. Since 2001, for example, KP has collected outcomes data on the roughly 35,000 total joint replacements that the system conducts every year in the Kaiser Permanente Total Joint Replacement Registry. KP clinical teams use the data to design clinical protocols to help patients return home and, ultimately, to full functioning as soon as possible after surgery; to reduce pain and narcotic medication needs; and to start physical therapy immediately after surgery in the inpatient setting in order to create a seamless transition to outpatient rehabilitation. Individual KP surgeons can also use the data to compare their performance to their peers both regionally and nationally. The registry has been a key factor in making KP a global leader in internationally reported outcomes for joint replacement such as 10-year implant survivorship and revision burden.[29]

KP's extensive data on clinical interventions and patient outcomes allows the organization to analyze outcomes at the level of specific population segments, translate that data into meaningful information, and then use that information to stratify for patient risk and to develop customized care pathways for specific population segments and continuously improve them over time. (See Figure 3.3.)

FIGURE 3.3 **Kaiser Permanente translates patient data into meaningful information.**

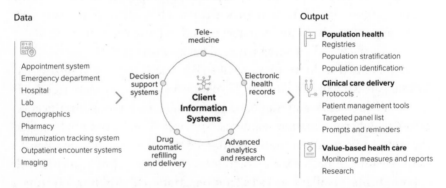

Kaiser Permanente's extensive data on clinical interventions and patient outcomes is a critical support in improving population health, clinical care delivery, and value-based care.

Source: *BCG analysis.*

In 2009, for example, Kaiser Permanente Southern California (KPSC) launched a comprehensive care delivery system known as Complete Care to develop customized, integrated care pathways for three categories of patients: healthy patients, those with chronic conditions, and those with multiple comorbidities. The approach uses existing clinical information and outcomes-registry data to identify high-risk patients, identify gaps in care, and align care with evidence-based guidelines. By 2013, the Complete Care approach had been applied to 26 chronic conditions, as well as to areas of preventive and wellness care and was the catalyst for an improvement in KPSC's scores on 51 HEDIS quality metrics that was nearly three times better than the national HEDIS 50th percentile (13% versus 5.5%).[30]

KP geriatricians have also developed a senior segmentation algorithm that uses administrative and clinical data from KP HealthConnect to categorize each member aged 65 years and older into one of four care groups with similar needs: those without chronic conditions, those with one or more chronic conditions, those with advanced illness or end-organ failure, and those extremely frail or nearing the end of life.[31] The algorithm and categorization are inputs to the care plan for each senior in the KP system, with a focus on slowing progression into the higher-need segments over time.

For terminally ill patients, the system has developed a care pathway based on home-based palliative care in which an interdisciplinary team manages patients' symptoms and pain, provides emotional and spiritual support, and coordinates personal care and physical therapy. In a randomized controlled trial conducted at Kaiser Permanente Colorado and Kaiser Permanente Hawaii, 71% of patients died at home, rather than in the hospital, in accordance with their wishes (versus 51% in standard care).[32] The approach reduced hospitalizations by 39% and cut emergency room visits by 33%, resulting in a 37% reduction in cost of care, or approximately $7,500 per patient. It's important to note that this program did not have a financial objective; it was developed solely to accommodate the preferences of this specific patient group.

As awareness about the critical importance of social determinants of health has grown in recent years, KP has also become a leader in addressing the social needs of its low-income members (about 30% of KP members are considered low-income, as defined by having annual household incomes below a threshold set at 250% of the US federal poverty level; in 2021, that threshold equaled approximately $60,000).[33] In 2016, the company appointed its first chief community health officer to oversee the roughly $2.2 billion the system spends annually on community benefits, including prevention-based community health programs. In 2017, KP's senior leadership developed an initial vision that called for the development of four key capabilities for effectively addressing social determinants of health: a standardized approach to screening for social need and integrating interventions to address those needs into the care process, a social-service resource locator to help local units connect their patients to local community services, partnerships with select community-based social-need providers, and finally, a strategy to evaluate and scale social interventions when they prove effective. That same year, the company created the Social Needs Network for Evaluation and Translation (SONNET) to advance organizational learning about social needs intervention.

For an illustration of KP's approach to the social determinants of health, consider the program developed at Kaiser Permanente Northwest (KPNW), serving some 600,000 members in Oregon and southwest Washington.[34] The organization trained staff across all clinical and operational departments to identify critical social determinants of health in the clinical setting. It also created a new role on the organization's interdisciplinary care teams: nonclinical patient navigators who engage with patients to identify and address social needs. The navigators conduct formal social-needs assessments, document them in KP HealthConnect so they are visible to clinicians, and work alongside nurses, social workers, behavior health specialists, physicians, and other staff to connect patients to needed resources. Between March 2016 and March 2018, KPNW screened more than 11,000 patients, documented nearly 50,000 specific social needs, and made nearly 20,000 community resource referrals to help patients with transportation, food, housing, and the like.

KP's delivery model also puts unusual emphasis on continuous improvement. The organization has more than 130 quality-improvement projects going on at any one time, engages frequently with high-performing teams to identify and share successful projects, and holds an annual quality conference at which clinicians share their experiences with peers. Since 2017, KP has published roughly 50 selected abstracts every year describing the most interesting and potentially useful quality-improvement efforts across the system.[35]

KP's value-based approach to care is a different way of practicing medicine than that found in many traditional provider organizations. The focus on customized care pathways for specific population segments, the team-based approach to care, and the reliance on the intensive analysis of outcomes and other health data to drive continuous improvement all serve to create an organizational context that both demands and encourages different kinds of behavior from clinicians and other health professionals. The result is that everyone is aligned with the goal of providing high-value care as cost-effectively as possible. (See the sidebar "The Importance of Trust.")

The Importance of Trust

In 2015, an interdisciplinary research team of cultural anthropologists and health policy experts conducted a series of focus groups with some 30 physicians who had between 3 and 13 years of experience at Kaiser Permanente.[36] The sessions focused on the differences that the physicians perceived between working at KP and working at their previous employers.

The participants described how working at KP required them to give up a degree of individual autonomy in exchange for being part of a collective, high-powered team in the service of the patient. "There's a thing known as 'KP medicine,' which is value-driven," said one participating physician. "It's got some constraints. [You ask,] 'Who are they to tell me how to practice?' But over time, you get used to it and buy into it. . . . You learn the evidence base behind it, and it's cohesive." "This isn't really *your* patient," said another. "This is Kaiser's patient. And we've got to make sure that we're doing everything efficiently and correctly."

According to physicians in the focus group, one of the benefits of working in the information-rich KP environment is that it encourages greater interaction and collaboration among primary care physicians and specialists. For example, in addition to doing formal referrals, primary care physicians can use KP HealthConnect to consult with on-call specialists, sharing images and discussing the best care strategy for a given patient. "Physicians said they valued the ready availability of specialist advice and noted the contrast with what they experienced elsewhere," wrote the researchers.[37]

One theme in the focus groups, however, surprised the researchers: the degree to which the physicians talked about how they trusted the KP system. "We did not expect to gather data on how the system earned physicians' trust," the researchers wrote. "This trust in the system contrasts with what we have seen in the literature in our previous work in non-integrated settings, where physicians often view the 'system' as something they must work *around* to provide good patient care and where attempts to influence what physicians do are rare and unwelcome when they occur."[38]

In contrast, the focus-group physicians believed that the goals of the organization were aligned with their own professional and clinical goals. What's more, they seemed to recognize that the various elements of KP's value-based approach were allowing them to accomplish goals with their teams and for their patients that would have been impossible in more traditional settings. In an industry that, among other things, is suffering from the severe purpose crisis that we described in Chapter 1, this may be KP's most important achievement of all.

Kaiser Permanente is an admirable provider organization, but it isn't perfect. The regional provider groups in the system have a lot of organizational autonomy, which can stimulate clinical innovation but can also be an obstacle to the dissemination of best practices throughout the entire KP system and to the development of standardized approaches for key patient groups. And while KP has been successful in exporting its care-delivery model to some states outside its California base, it has failed in others, either due to a lack of a critical mass of members or to the lack of cooperation from existing networks of physicians and hospitals in those regions. Meanwhile, other large US provider organizations are moving rapidly to develop their own value-based ecosystems that at some point could end up competing with KP. Will KP's decentralized organization be agile enough to respond? Despite all these challenges, Kaiser Permanente remains perhaps the best example of the kind of integrated, holistic approach to care that a focus on value makes possible.

THE CHANGE CHALLENGE

Most provider organizations, of course, aren't like Martini Klinik, Oak Street, or Kaiser Permanente. In other words, they are not organizations that from their initial conception and launch were designed to deliver patient-centered value-based care. Rather, they are traditional health care organizations with traditional approaches that have developed over years and sometimes even centuries.

For such organizations, the fundamental questions involve: How to transition to a more value-based model of care delivery? And where to begin? Those questions raise an even more fundamental one: How to get people and organizations to change? This is the subject of our next chapter.

Care Delivery: Action Steps

PROVIDERS

1. **Choose your population segments.** Decide where you will focus your efforts and on which diseases, conditions, and population segments.

2. **Use outcomes data to jump-start learning.** Track health outcomes by population segment and use the data to improve outcomes delivered to patients.

3. **Design end-to-end care pathways.** Think in terms of integrated care pathways for your chosen segments. Where will you play in the pathway?

4. **Build multidisciplinary clinical teams.** Encouraging teaming among specialists, and create opportunities for interaction and collaboration along the care pathway.

5. **Integrate prevention and treatment.** Focus on prevention as well as treatment.

6. **Incorporate social and behavioral interventions.** Targeting better patient outcomes requires a holistic perspective on patient needs. Look beyond clinical interventions to incorporate non-clinical interventions that address the social and behavioral determinants of health.

CHAPTER 4
MEETING THE CHANGE CHALLENGE

As the innovators we described in the previous chapter make clear, value-based health care requires clinicians to work together in new and different ways. They need to segment patient groups more comprehensively; track health outcomes more systematically; collaborate in multidisciplinary, team-based approaches to care; and incorporate digital tools and other innovations to continuously improve care delivery.

For leaders of more traditional provider organizations, it is no longer enough simply to manage an institution's existing model of care delivery. Rather, they need to confront what we call the change challenge—that is, to champion the kind of behavior change and changes in clinical practice that value-based care delivery requires. Put another way, every leader needs to be a change leader.

It's not an easy task. There is a common view that the health care provider sector, in general, and the profession of medicine, in particular, are especially resistant to change. Medicine tends to be a risk-averse culture that has—understandably—been shaped by a keen responsibility to "do no harm," often by a commitment to routines and procedures that have developed over decades and sometimes centuries. Dr. Brian Donley, CEO of Cleveland Clinic's new hospital in London put it to us this way: "When you have a patient in front of you, your responsibility is to figure out what is wrong and then propose the safest way to solve the patient's problem."

This conservatism is reinforced by the specialization and fragmentation characterizing most traditional provider organizations and by an operating model that too often discourages cooperation across traditional boundaries. "Most hospital doctors are highly specialized individual contributors," said Donley. "Many have limited time or passion for the long-term engagement necessary for organizational change."

Beyond the innate conservatism of the medical profession, we think there is another reason that helps explain why doctors are so often skeptical about change. For the most part, what passes for change in health care in recent decades has typically focused on activities that are only indirectly connected to the core purpose that brings most clinicians to the profession in the first place: taking care of patients. Change initiatives focused on cost containment, process optimization, or patient satisfaction, however valuable to the organization in their own right, can often seem disconnected from the core task that clinicians engage in every day. Little wonder, then, that many clinicians are skeptical—or even cynical— about the value of such initiatives when it comes to patient care. Too often, they see these changes as imposed on them by management for reasons having little to do with the actual tasks of care delivery and that often disrupt their ability to do the best for their patients.

The kind of change we are talking about in this chapter, however, is different. When change efforts focus on the core purpose of providing better outcomes for patients through the redesign of care delivery, they have the potential to unleash clinician engagement, creativity, and innovation. After all, most highly trained health professionals are open to learning from data and the latest research, keen for innovation that allows them to be better at their jobs, and committed to improve the care they give to patients. If organizations can tap into those values and link operational and organizational changes back to the fundamental purpose of the organization, then clinicians will not only welcome change but also champion it.

That's why it is especially important to focus internal change initiatives on measuring and improving the health outcomes delivered to patients. Outcomes measurement isn't just important in its own right for improving the quality of care. The focus on health outcomes and the debate it sparks—for example, about what outcomes really matter and whether an organization is doing its best to deliver the best outcomes possible—is critical to making a persuasive case for change that speaks to clinicians' deepest values and sense of purpose. A change initiative can, of course, also include other goals: for instance, reducing the cost it takes to deliver quality outcomes or improving the patient experience. But improvements in these dimensions should be a byproduct of the focus on improving health outcomes, not the starting point or main goal.

"Successful change needs to be anchored in meaning and purpose," said Donley. "The key to leading change is to organize it all around improving for the patient. There also needs to be a clear way for clinicians to learn and to grow. If you build that into every change effort, you also strengthen the organization over time and achieve greater commitment and efficiency because the resulting culture drives discretionary effort by the members of your team."

What is the best way to organize such value-based change initiatives? At the risk of oversimplification, there are two basic approaches:

Leaders can choose to take an incremental approach, avoiding big disruptive changes in organizational structure. Incremental change emphasizes pilot initiatives—largely driven from the bottom up, with clinicians taking the lead—and allows the desired changes to emerge organically and accumulate over time. To be sure, such pilots need to be chosen strategically and sequenced, so that the desired changes in clinical practice grow and become embedded over time. But the general principle is perhaps best captured by the old Latin proverb *Festina lente*—"Make haste slowly." This approach to change bears a resemblance to some of the continuous-improvement initiatives at quality registries and at Kaiser Permanente that we described in previous chapters.

Alternatively, leaders can take a more transformational approach, driving the desired changes from the top and making major alterations in the structure of the organization in order to quickly and decisively create a new organizational context that will encourage new behaviors. Perhaps the classic example of this more transformational approach to value-based change is Toby Cosgrove's decision to completely reorganize Cleveland Clinic around patient groups.[1] In 2008, Cosgrove led a major reorganization in which the clinic jettisoned a structure organized around traditional medical disciplines in favor of a new structure based on multidisciplinary institutes organized by disease areas. The patient institutes combine medical and surgical departments for specific diseases. All are required to publish outcomes and measure costs by patient group. The change has allowed Cleveland Clinic to take a more patient-centered approach to care and to achieve the cooperation and alignment necessary to improve outcomes and treatment efficiency by taking a holistic view of costs along each treatment pathway.

Both the incremental and the transformational approaches to change have their advantages but also their distinctive risks. They involve complex trade-offs; there is no single or best model that works for everyone or for every situation. Incremental change, driven by clinicians from the ground up, has the advantage of allowing time for learning and for harnessing growing levels of clinician engagement. The goal is to improve collaboration within the existing organizational structure rather than make radical, and potentially disruptive, changes in roles, reporting relationships, budgets, and the like. In our experience, an organization can make significant progress in identifying the outcomes that matter, redesigning care pathways, involving patients in care decisions, and encouraging cooperation across specialties on multidisciplinary clinical teams without necessarily making changes in the boxes on the organizational chart, or in budgets and reporting relationships.

That said, incremental change always runs the risk of foundering on obstacles built into the traditional way that most health institutions are organized. In many provider environments, the traditional organization structure can be an obstacle to increased cooperation and greater coordination. The ways that budgets, cost accounting, and information systems are all organized can make it difficult to track outcomes and costs across the entire care pathway. Sooner or later, these obstacles will need to be confronted.

That's why, in some situations, it may be necessary—whether because of current organizational dysfunction, financial or competitive threats, or simply the desire to take advantage of new opportunities—to embrace a more transformational approach. Transformation has the advantage of making the transition to value-based care delivery happen faster. Decisive changes in organizational structure, budgets, and reporting relationships can reinforce strategic direction, focus financial and clinical accountability on patient groups, improve operational efficiency, and unleash innovation. But transformative change comes with the risk of turbulence and disruption. And in some situations, it can end up provoking opposition to change that can undermine the change effort.

When considering which change strategy to use, however, leaders need to be careful not to get caught up in either-or thinking. Even the most bottom-up change process requires senior leadership and commitment; in their absence, no change effort, no matter how incremental, will succeed. And even the most transformational initiative needs to focus as much on engaging clinicians on the front lines of care and enlisting them in behavior change as on reorganizing the boxes on the organizational chart. As Dr. Lars Svensson, a Swedish cardiologist who for the past seven years has led the Heart, Vascular and Thoracic Institute at Cleveland Clinic told us: "Organization is important, and I believe in organizing around the patient. But the most important thing is the cultural change that comes from outcomes measurement and transparency, which ensures all members of the institution are focused on patient needs and deliver the best possible outcomes together."

In this chapter, we describe four quite different value-based change initiatives, some that we have supported directly and others that we have observed closely but from the outside.

In the first, we tell the story of the Santeon Group, a consortium of seven independent hospitals in the Netherlands, which formed in 2010 for the explicit purpose of cooperating to improve the quality of care delivered to patients.

In the second, we remain in the Netherlands but travel to a very different setting: Erasmus University Medical Center, one of Europe's most prominent academic medical centers. Both Santeon and Erasmus are classic examples of what we have called incremental value-based change.

In our third example, we look at another European hospital at an academic medical center—Sweden's Karolinska University Hospital—whose leader took a far more transformational approach to change, a decision that has delivered impressive results but that also sparked opposition and provoked considerable public controversy.

Finally, we end by crossing the Atlantic to tell a story of transformational value-based change American-style, describing how a visionary leader, Dr. Marc Harrison, CEO of Intermountain Healthcare, is embracing disruption to position an already successful regional provider organization as a pioneer of value-based health care on a national scale.

"BETTER TOGETHER": THE SANTEON GROUP

Probably the best illustration of what we call the incremental approach to value-based change is the Santeon Group in the Netherlands. Santeon is a cooperative of seven Dutch hospitals that account for about 11% of hospital care volume in the Netherlands, employ approximately 34,000 people, and generate €3 billion in annual revenues. The hospitals are widely dispersed cross the country and do not directly compete with one another. "We are not academic medical centers," Santeon's managing director, Pieter de Bey, told us. "We are hospitals focused on patient care." The hospitals formed the Santeon cooperative in 2010 to work together on quality improvement. From 2015 to 2017, BCG worked with Santeon to develop a comprehensive approach to value-based change at its seven hospitals.[2] The first step was to develop a shared vison that would guide the change effort. The boards and the medical leadership of each of the seven Santeon hospitals defined an ambition to "realize better outcomes for patients faster together" through increased transparency about both the health outcomes delivered to patients and the costs required to deliver them. To emphasize this goal, the group adopted the Dutch tagline "*Samen Beter*"—in English, "Better Together."

Santeon's leadership understood that realizing that vision wouldn't happen overnight; rather, it would take time and probably substantial trial and error. So, they decided to start small with a few carefully chosen pilots involving key patient groups. Then, as the organization experimented and learned from experience, they would ramp up the initiative over time. To emphasize, however, that they were making a long-term commitment, they set a goal of expanding the program to include between 20 and 25 patient groups by 2020. Although the coronavirus pandemic has delayed the rollout, Santeon currently has 16 improvement programs underway. (See Figure 4.1.)

Another key part of the initial vision was to emphasize learning over evaluation. The goal of the project was to help clinicians at the participating hospitals improve their performance, not to punish them for poor performance. So, for example, despite the commitment to transparency, the program built in an initial 18-month phase for each improvement program, during which the results of outcomes measurement at the hospitals would only be shared internally, so that the participants could gain confidence in the quality of the data and the process for comparing outcomes

FIGURE 4.1 Santeon: "Better Together."

Better Together patient groups
Breast cancer
Prostate cancer
Lung cancer
Colorectal cancer
Hip osteoarthritis
Cerebrovascular accident (stroke)
Chronic kidney disease
Pregnancy and birth care
Rheumatoid arthritis
Coronary artery disease
Inflammatory bowel disease
Diabetes
Hip fracture
Knee osteoarthritis
Covid-19
Frail elderly

The Santeon cooperative of seven Dutch hospitals works together to realize better health outcomes for patients than each hospital could achieve on its own. The group currently has continuous-improvement initiatives underway for 16 patient groups.

Source: *Santeon Group.*

and testing improvements. Then, after that initial phase, once they had confidence in the approach, the results for each hospital would be made available to the public. (This process of phased transparency is similar to the evolution at Swedeheart and the US cystic fibrosis registries that we described in Chapter 2.)

Another important element of the vision: the change process would be led by physicians. Multidisciplinary clinical teams would organize the pilots, select the relevant metrics, and orchestrate the dialogue across the hospitals about changes in clinical practice. But because value-based health care puts patient value at the core of decision-making, each team would also include one or two patients to represent the patient perspective and to make sure that all participating health professionals kept that perspective at the center of their efforts. Finally, a small central team consisting of a program manager and a few data analysts would support the local multidisciplinary teams, ensure alignment across the seven hospitals, and provide data, analysis, and quality control.

The initial Santeon pilots were launched in the spring of 2016 and focused on five patient groups: breast cancer, prostate cancer, lung cancer, cerebrovascular accident (CVA), and hip osteoarthritis These were areas where there was clear improvement potential and a fair amount of good data available already, and where there were doctors on staff who were enthusiastic about the change effort and in some cases were already implementing aspects of value-based care delivery. The idea was to give these champions an institutional platform and then use it to generate enthusiasm about the initiative and lay the groundwork for expansion into other disease areas and patient segments.

For each disease area, the seven Santeon hospitals created a local multidisciplinary clinical team that went through the same structured process. First, the teams would work together to develop a shared view on the roughly 15 to 20 metrics that define value for each patient group. The guiding principle was to be pragmatic: to leverage current outcomes measures, existing registries, or standardized metrics such as the ICHOM measurement sets as much as possible, and to identify the biggest cost buckets and most important cost drivers to track.

For example, the breast cancer pilot chose to track health outcomes, such as the unadjusted five-year survival rate, repeat operations after a positive margin (indicating that the surgeon who had performed the initial surgery had been unable to remove the entire tumor), repeat operations after postoperative complications (for instance, wound infections and postoperative bleeding), and PROMs tracking patient quality of life (well-being, functioning, and pain after treatment). As a proxy for costs, the team tracked common cost drivers, such as nursing days per patient, operating room time per patient, and the ratio of single-day versus multiple-day hospital stays. Finally, the list included common process metrics such as time from referral to the first clinic visit, from first clinic visit to diagnosis, from diagnosis to discussion of the treatment plan with the patient, and from discussing the treatment plan to starting treatment.

Once the metrics were agreed upon, the clinical teams at each hospital began a regular cadence of six-month improvement cycles in which they analyzed the data, met to compare results, identified specific clinical practices that seemed associated with better outcomes or lower costs, and launched improvement initiatives. It's important to emphasize that the goal of this process is not necessarily to arrive at statistically significant validation of proposed changes, let alone to do randomized controlled trials. Rather, the approach is to create a foundation for a fact-based discussion of differences in clinical practice, to learn from the best performers, and then to track the impact of changes in practice on subsequent patient outcomes. Much like Martini Klinik, as Santeon collects more and more data in its outcome database, that data can provide researchers with a rich pool of information that they can use for future research, with the aim of publishing scientifically and statistically significant results over time.

The improvement cycles have introduced myriad changes in clinical practice and patient management, including new approaches to the timing of biopsies, new drain protocols and equipment, best practices in patient-flow management to reduce unnecessary preoperative days in the hospital, fewer postoperative X-rays for hip arthroplasty patients, and a new standard practice (proposed by a patient on the prostate cancer team) to invite a family member or caregiver to join prostate cancer patients to a meeting where diagnostic results are discussed.

These changes may seem small, but their cumulative impact has been powerful. The work of the early pilots revealed that the degree of outcomes variation across the seven Santeon hospitals was far greater than participants expected. Depending on the metric, results across the seven hospitals varied by as much as a factor of 4 or 5. But by the end of the third improvement cycle, the various changes in clinical practice served not only to improve the group's average results but also to bring the worst-performing hospitals much closer to the best.

For example, in the breast cancer pilot, the percentage of reoperations due to positive surgical margins declined by 17% across Santeon as a whole, but by 60% at the lowest-performing hospital.[3] Reoperations due to postoperative complications after lumpectomy declined by 27%, on average, but by more than 70% at the worst-performing hospital. And the ratio of single-day to multiple-day hospital stays improved 18% on average but doubled at the lowest-performing hospital. Subsequent pilots have delivered similar results.

Seen from one perspective, the Santeon model is a structured process for outcomes-based continuous improvement. But seen from another angle, it is also a powerful approach to change, a highly effective way to engage clinicians in the challenging task of analyzing their own performance, developing mutual trust, and changing how they work in order to deliver better value to patients. "I definitely see this as a cultural change program," said de Bey. "It is helping us develop the skills that care professionals need to work in a more data-driven environment, as well as from a more patient-centered perspective."

From our interviews over the years with clinicians at the Santeon hospitals, it is clear that the program has had a major impact on how they conceive of their role and their clinical practice. "This is an unbelievably good concept," said Yvonne van Riet, a breast surgeon at Catharina Hospital in Eindhoven. "Although it takes time, it is much more motivating than the other ways we have to look at data and deal with quality indicators. By learning from each other, we can really improve care for our patients."[4]

This emphasis on the advantages of increased teamwork and the value of outcomes transparency was a common theme among Santeon clinicians. "For me, the power of collaboration is in directly getting feedback if something's working or not," said Ron Koelemij, an oncological surgeon at St. Antonius Hospital in Utrecht. "We have a lot more contact with our colleagues about the content of our work. It's a practical way to mold our profession together."

"Transparency is easy when you only get high scores," said Elisabeth Blokhuis, a gynecologist at St. Antonius. "The great thing about our approach is that everyone had the guts to be honest about areas that they did not score as well in. Only then can you maximize the lessons you learn from each other."[5]

The change process at Santeon has become a platform for pursuing other initiatives to improve patient value. For example, although the primary focus of the Santeon pilots has not been cost containment (interestingly, the hospitals' managers have been relatively uninvolved in the pilots), the continuous-improvement process has also led to considerable cost savings. Santeon managing director de Bey gives the example of pharmacy. "The pharmacists saw early that there was a lot of value in working together," he said. "Every year, they develop prioritized prescription guidelines, together with the prescribing physicians, and monitor whether the hospitals are actually prescribing what we have negotiated in terms of volume discounts with suppliers. More intentional prescribing has helped us save in the neighborhood of €20 million per year."

The continuous-improvement cycle has also contributed to a more standardized approach to care, one that combines identified best practices with personalization by means of a growing focus on shared decision-making with patients and attention to patient preferences, informed by outcomes measurement. Outcomes-based dashboards track an individual's disease progression and user-friendly decision-support tools are used during outpatient visits to help inform patient decision-making and personalize their treatment. De Bey compares it to the "mass customization" that one finds in other industries, such as retail or the auto industry.

Finally, Santeon's experience as a pioneer in value-based care has led naturally to other investments in value-based innovation, often in partnership with other industry stakeholders. For example, the group has invested in a health information platform that automates and standardizes outcomes data. It is increasingly working with local primary care practices in its markets to create tighter links between primary and acute care and collaborating with Dutch academic medical centers ("We want to do more research; they want to have more clinical impact," said de Bey). They are investing in the digital transformation of the care pathway through remote patient monitoring and digital health solutions to further improve patient value.

Santeon has also been one of the first provider organizations in the Netherlands to negotiate value-based contracts with Dutch insurance companies for certain conditions such as breast cancer. It has become a preferred partner with leading pharmaceutical companies for value-based contracts in which payment for drugs is partially based on outcomes. Finally, with financial support from two Dutch insurance companies, Santeon is partnering with artificial intelligence firms to use ICU data to develop predictive analytics for determining the optimal time to transfer patients from the ICU.

"In the end, what we want to do is improve patient value," said de Bey. "That's what keeps the group together."

REDESIGNING CARE PATHWAYS AT AN ACADEMIC MEDICAL CENTER: ERASMUS MC

Academic medical centers are especially complex institutions. Because they treat the most unusual and complex medical cases, their clinicians are often among the most specialized in the health system. They also have significant research and teaching commitments, playing a central role in training the next generation of medical professionals. The high degree of specialization and multiple objectives across care, research, and education can make it difficult to create the kind of collaboration for continuous improvement of patient value that we saw at Santeon.

Erasmus University Medical Center, based in Rotterdam and commonly known as Erasmus MC, is the leading academic medical center in the Netherlands, one of the top such institutions in Europe, and an internationally recognized leader in clinical medicine and biomedical science. Since 2013, Erasmus has embarked on an institution-wide effort to define and track key health outcomes and to redesign its care pathways around the patient, and currently has some 30 disease-specific pilots underway.

As was the case at Santeon, one of the early pilots at Erasmus focused on breast cancer care. We spoke to Dr. Linetta Koppert, a breast cancer surgeon at Erasmus, who heads an breast cancer center of excellence that brings together medical oncologists, surgical oncologists, plastic and reconstructive surgeons, radiation oncologists, radiologists and pathologists, nurse practitioners, breast cancer nurses, clinical geneticists, and psychologists. Koppert led the multidisciplinary team that redesigned the hospital's breast cancer care pathway.[6]

Approximately one in seven women in the Netherlands will be diagnosed with breast cancer, Koppert told us, and treatment for the disease is an especially complex care pathway for younger women. Heredity plays a big role in the disease because certain genetic mutations are a strong risk factor, so early genetic analysis is important. There are multiple treatment options: radiation, hormone therapy, chemotherapy, and various types of surgery (for example, more radical breast reconstruction or more conservative breast conservation). As a result, multiple different medical specialties are involved, putting a premium on interdisciplinary collaboration. And because of the variety of treatment options, it's especially important for clinicians to understand patient preferences and help them make informed choices about approaches to treatment.

The breast cancer clinic at Erasmus had the advantage of already being organized as a multidisciplinary center of excellence. Therefore, the primary focus of its continuous-improvement initiative was to define the ideal care pathway—to redesign how they would interact with patients and work together with each other in a multidisciplinary team. When it came to defining the relevant health outcomes to track, a key part of the effort was to incorporate the routine use of patient-reported outcome surveys at various points in the care-delivery process, as a way to bring the voice of the patient into clinical decision-making.[7] A team of doctors and nurses representing the range of specialties at the clinic surveyed patients about the quality-of-life outcomes that were most important to them, and selected PROM surveys that would capture key health outcomes in those areas. In the final outcomes set developed by the team, a full 75% of the metrics are PROMs (the rest are more traditional clinical outcomes). In addition to choosing the specific PROM surveys to use, the team also developed a timeline for when the surveys should be filled out by patients during the course of care.

Tracking the new PROMs was one thing; getting time-starved doctors and nurses to use them in their interactions with patients was another. "When we first started collecting PROMs," said Koppert, "nurses were saying, 'PROMs are great, but our colleagues aren't looking at them!'" The team quickly learned that unless clinicians gave feedback to patients about their results on the surveys, patients were less willing to take the time to fill them out. The team developed an online dashboard that helped clinicians access a patient's survey data, compared to clinic-wide averages, as a way to highlight key issues for discussion with individual patients.

Over time, clinicians began to learn that giving patients feedback about the key issues that emerged from their survey responses could be an extremely useful way to organize the conversation with patients, develop a richer understanding of how they were experiencing treatment, and help patients choose treatment options. One specialist nurse at Erasmus put it this way: "Initially, it was difficult to learn how to use the PROMs selectively, in order to focus on the most important issues and to use the data as prompts for the conversation with the patient. But it has been a huge help in the consulting room. PROMs give you a much clearer picture of an individual patient's needs." The PROM data also helped inform how the clinic deployed its specialist resources. "It helps us decide, for example, when to bring in a psychologist or sexologist," said Koppert.

The focus on patient-reported outcomes has also led to new ideas for innovations in the care pathway that come directly from patients. A 27-year-old patient who happened to be a web designer proposed developing an app to connect patients to their caregivers remotely as a way to manage expectations about wait times for appointments, inform them in advance about the prevalence of potential surgical complications, or provide tailored information on specific treatment options. Koppert asked her to join the pilot core team, and her suggestion led to the creation of Digitally Connected, a digital health app. Another patient, a young mother, kept a diary about her treatment that she shared regularly with her six-year-old daughter. The clinic is now using the diary with other patients who have small children.

"A real transition is happening in our clinical practice," said Koppert. "To be honest, I have become a totally different clinician than I was a decade ago. I never used to ask my patients about how their condition affected their quality of life. Now, I start with that: questions about sexual function, energy level, the impact on their work. There are so many aspects that I talk about openly with my patients today that I never did before. As a result, patients are more in control of their treatment and are taking ownership in many areas."

The focus on PROMs has also opened new lines of clinical research. The breast cancer pilot at Erasmus has gone on to influence how outcomes are tracked and care delivered beyond the hospital itself. Nine other breast cancer centers in the southwest region of the Netherlands have adopted the Erasmus outcomes set, and the hospitals are benchmarking their collective results.[8] Koppert and her colleagues have conducted research comparing the PROM survey findings of breast cancer patients to those in a panel of 9,000 Dutch women without breast cancer. "As a researcher," said Koppert, "I'm eager for us to learn how we might predict outcomes, so that we know which treatments yield the best outcomes in terms of patient quality of life. That will allow us to make targeted decisions, both as a clinical team and with individual patients, and continuously get better at the care we deliver."

Koppert and another member of the Erasmus breast cancer team were also part of the working group that developed the ICHOM outcome-measurement set for breast cancer, which closely tracked the metrics initially developed at Erasmus, and is now in use at more than 40 breast-cancer centers around the world.[9] That measurement set is also the first that ICHOM will use for its global benchmarking platform. So far, five leading university hospitals in the United States, Europe, and the Middle East, including Erasmus, have agreed to participate. The Erasmus breast cancer clinic is also participating in an initiative known as the European University Hospital Alliance, in which nine leading European academic medical centers collaborate to share best practices, and in H2O, a European public-private partnership to establish "health-outcome observatories" in key disease areas, including metastatic breast cancer.[10]

So far, 24 disease-specific teams at Erasmus have put in place a redesigned care and outcomes-measurement pathway, with the ultimate goal of providing care based on outcomes that matters to patients for over 80% of the Dutch disease burden by 2023. Recently, the institution has taken a number of initiatives to institutionalize value-based change at the hospital in an approach that one clinician described as "bottom-up but top-guided." The executive board has made value-based health care the standard for quality at the hospital and has established a dedicated budget for value-based initiatives. A steering committee of senior clinicians coordinates across the growing number of disease-specific pilot projects. There is a dedicated value-based health care project team with a project manager and IT resources to support teams but also to set hospital-wide standards for the change process.

For example, in an initiative to accelerate the use of PROMs at Erasmus, the hospital recently decided to supplement the measures being used by the disease teams with two generic PROM instruments (one for adults and one for children) for use across the entire hospital. The hope is that these generic instruments will accelerate the integration of PROMs into standard clinical practice and reinforce cooperation across all clinical units. "It's a bit like throwing a stone in a pond and watching the ripples expand," said Koppert. "We started small, but the effort has gotten really large. It has taken years, but now it is here to stay."

Of course, numerous challenges remain. Data quality is always a moving target. Erasmus needs to harmonize its generic outcomes measures with those used by the disease-specific teams. For example, 10 oncological units at the hospital (including Linetta Koppert's breast cancer clinic) have recently agreed to adopt a common approach to collecting PROMs and are working with the hospital's IT department to create a common platform to do so. And when it comes to benchmarking across multiple institutions, Koppert said, "We need standardized clinical-data collection, and we are not really close to that. That's the challenge for the future: for everyone to be speaking the same language. The ICHOM standards are an initiative to facilitate that."

Other challenges are organizational. So far, Erasmus has chosen to focus on changing clinician behavior without necessarily changing the traditional organizational structure of an academic medical center based on medical specialties. Although the matrixed center of excellence model works well in some areas such as breast cancer, it works less well in others.

One question the institution will face in the future: Should it let go of its traditional organizational structure and actually reorganize around diseases and patient groups? According to Jan Hazelzet, an intensive-care pediatrician who, until his retirement, led the value-based-health-care effort at Erasmus, "Taking the next step to organize around patients is easier now. But unless integrated practice units have their own budgets, you are relying on goodwill alone and the desire of clinicians to do the right thing. We need to create more formal incentives around collaboration."

Whatever the future of value-based health care at Erasmus, there is little question that the efforts of champions like Hazelzet and Koppert have had an enormous impact, not only at Erasmus but in Dutch health care as a whole. Two signs of that impact: in addition to her role at Erasmus, Koppert was recently appointed the director of the Netherlands' national breast cancer registry. And in January 2022, Ernst Kuipers, CEO of Erasmus since 2013 and longtime supporter of the institution's value-based initiatives, was appointed Minister of Health, Welfare, and Sport in the new government of Prime Minister Mark Rutte.

VALUE-BASED TRANSFORMATION: THE NEW KAROLINSKA UNIVERSITY HOSPITAL

Both Santeon and Erasmus have pursued a strategy of incremental change with senior institutional support but largely driven from the bottom up and allowed to evolve organically over a number of years. That option, however, is not necessarily available to every organization. Whether because of internal organizational problems or external financial or competitive pressures, some may be forced to take a more top-down, disruptive, and transformational approach to change. Such an approach occupies a higher position on the risk-reward curve: it can make change happen faster, putting the organization on a much more positive trajectory, but it is also riskier. Let's consider an example of value-based organizational change that radically shifted both the operational model and organization structure of an entire university hospital. It too is a story of successful value-based change—but change that came with significant controversy and some damage to the progress of value-based health care in Sweden.

The Karolinska University Hospital in Stockholm is one of the most famous and prestigious medical institutions in the world. Founded in the

1940s, it has a storied history of clinical innovation, draws patients not only from throughout Sweden but also from abroad, and is affiliated with the Karolinska Institute, one of the world's leading medical universities and Sweden's single largest center for biomedical research (the Institute also awards the annual Nobel Prize in Physiology and Medicine).

In the early 2000s, Region Stockholm, the government entity responsible for funding health care for the roughly 2.3 million residents of the greater Stockholm metropolitan area, developed a strategic plan to make the Karolinska University Hospital the centerpiece of a world-class cluster for biomedical research and translational science in Stockholm.[11] The idea, in part, was to leverage Sweden's leading position in quality registries and outcomes measurement to position the Stockholm region as a global leader in patient-centered care and precision medicine. As part of this plan, in 2008 the regional government funded the building of a new state-of-the-art hospital known as the New Karolinska University Hospital, replacing one of Karolinska's two campuses in the Stockholm area. A guiding principle for the design of the new building was to facilitate a more patient-centered approach to care by organizing the hospital around multidisciplinary clusters of expertise (which the plan termed patient "themes").

In 2014, the hospital conducted an international search for a new leader to lead the transition to the new hospital, eventually selecting Dr. Melvin Samsom, a professor of gastroenterology who had led a remarkable turnaround in quality care at the Radboud University Hospital in Nijmegen, Netherlands.[12] A Dutch citizen, Samsom was the first non-Nordic national to head a Swedish university hospital (the previous CEO of Karolinska was from Iceland but had trained and spent his entire career in Sweden; all other leaders of the hospital had been Swedish).

Samsom inherited an exciting and ambitious vision for Karolinska's future, but he also inherited an organization facing considerable problems in the present. In 2014, Karolinska was struggling with a series of seemingly intractable performance problems and organizational challenges. Like many hospitals, the organization suffered from a nursing shortage, a problem that had become so acute that a substantial percentage of beds were left unavailable to patients for lack of nurses to staff them. The empty beds were wreaking havoc with the hospital's capacity utilization, causing it to post recurring budget deficits. The hospital had engaged in multiple rounds of belt-tightening and "lean" initiatives to improve process efficiency to get a handle on its utilization and cost problems, but these efforts rarely seemed to have a sustained impact.

What's more, the focus on cost containment and efficiency had resulted in less attention to patient outcomes and to a slow but steady erosion in the quality of care. To be sure, Karolinska had world-class doctors and many areas of genuine clinical excellence; its staff treated some of the most complex cases in modern medicine. But the hospital was finding it more and more difficult to translate that excellence into the consistent delivery of quality health outcomes to broad groups of patients. BCG did an analysis for the hospital based on public data from Sweden's quality registries, comparing Karolinska's performance to its peers on commonly accepted health outcomes in 10 major conditions, ranging from heart disease to diabetes and cancer. In only 1 out of 10 areas was the hospital above the national average in more than half the metrics. And in a comprehensive 2013 national quality ranking, the hospital came in last among Sweden's seven university hospitals.[13]

Like most hospitals affiliated with academic medical centers, Karolinska was primarily organized into departments by medical specialty. Many of these units had strong reputations and therefore a lot of institutional power and professional pride. They controlled their own budgets, managed their own wards, set their own key performance indicators (KPIs), trained their own students, and evaluated and promoted their own personnel. But sometimes this independence came with a degree of isolation from other units, a phenomenon that was made worse by the hospital's budget problems. Given the recurring efforts to increase efficiency, departmental leadership sought to optimize their own department's performance, sometimes at the expense of the hospital as a whole. As one division head put it, "Everyone is focusing on the tents, but nobody is focusing on the circus."

This focus on cost control and the highly siloed nature of the hospital's organization structure also shaped how the individual units were managed. One consequence of the hospital's preoccupation with its financial problems was a proliferation of new guidelines and KPIs designed to help it meet its annual budgets. This led to an overwhelming management focus on process compliance and short-term budget targets—with limited attention to the impact on patients and health outcomes.

Clinicians at Karolinska, of course, cared about doing the best for their patients. But at the end of the day, their managers were judged on whether or not the unit was hitting its budget targets. The overreliance on financial and process metrics helped explain why the hospital's quality of care was not competitive. It also led to considerable tension between managers and clinicians, which contributed to disengagement on the part of clinical staff. This tension was a factor in the high staff turnover the hospital was experiencing, which worsened the hospital's nursing shortage and therefore its capacity-utilization problem.

The independence of the individual units and the historical focus on process compliance and short-term budget targets contributed to cumbersome and ineffective decision-making. Because clinicians in one unit never entirely trusted clinicians in other units to take their interests into account, everyone wanted to be involved in every decision, leading to time-consuming meetings. And because everyone was involved, no one was really accountable—especially when decisions had implications for multiple units. As a result, new initiatives weren't implemented, it was difficult to take a holistic and integrated approach to patient care, and the lack of trust and alignment among the hospital's leaders was an important obstacle to innovation and continuous improvement. When division heads were asked to name their greatest fear as leaders, the most common response was "being accused by peers of having made a mistake."

Faced with the design guidelines for the new building, a tight two-year timeline for the move, and a set of interlocking organizational problems, Samsom decided on a bold stroke. To quickly build a new patient-centered and value-based culture at Karolinska, he decided to completely change the operating model and organizational structure of the hospital. He hired BCG to help design the new organization and help the hospital's clinical units make the transition.

Following the model pioneered by Cleveland Clinic, instead of organizing around medical specialties, the New Karolinska University Hospital would organize primarily around patient groups. Specifically, Karolinska identified a few hundred distinct patient groups based on disease, condition, or risk profile, each with its own characteristic treatment pathway and mix of required specialists and expertise. These groups were aggregated into a smaller number of patient areas characterized by similar treatments and clinical experts, and then further clustered within a handful of broad medical themes (for example, children and women's health, heart and vascular, cancer, or aging). These thematic areas became the main organizational units at the hospital, with accountability for the health outcomes and costs for each of their patient groups.

The new organizational design didn't just define new boxes on the organizational chart, the plan also involved the development of new leaders, new roles, new career paths, and new types of performance evaluation. In a move completely unprecedented in the context of Swedish health care, Samsom announced that the organization's current clinical leaders would have to reapply for their roles, and all appointments would be made from the top down. To animate the new organizational structure, Karolinska also created an important new leadership position: the patient-group manager. These managers were senior clinicians with deep experience in a specific patient pathway (juvenile rheumatoid arthritis, say, or congestive heart failure). They became key leaders in the thematic areas, responsible for designing a holistic, integrated approach to treatment, coordinating the interdisciplinary teams of specialists who care for patients with the particular disease or condition, developing and tracking appropriate outcome metrics, managing resources and budget, and supporting research to drive improvements in value over time.

Since no hospital can be organized entirely around patient segments, the new organizational design also redrew the way that the new patient-group organization interacted with traditional functional units such as the emergency room, perioperative care, the diagnostic laboratory, and the imaging department. Personnel in these support functions continued to report to their functional managers, but within the support functions, clinicians were assigned to work with specific patient-group teams. To encourage productive cooperation in this matrix, the patient-group managers, who were now key actors in multiple treatment pathways, would have a formal say in the performance reviews of support personnel. Similarly, the support functions would have a say in evaluating the performance of the patient-group managers.

Karolinska also developed a balanced scorecard that assessed performance in four key areas: quality of care delivery; productivity and financial performance; research, education, and innovation; and staff engagement and morale (including retention of key personnel). The scorecard was first piloted in the heart and vascular theme, with the goal of rolling it out to other patient groups once IT support for the scorecard was in place. Patient group managers and their teams would track their own performance across all four categories and meet monthly to discuss how they were doing and how they could improve. The model outlined how clinicians and their senior managers would be tracked and evaluated on the same metrics, as an integrated team, with the goal of increasing reciprocity and alignment across the managerial-clinical divide.

Finally, the hospital designed new career paths in which clinical staff would more frequently rotate among different units at various points along the treatment pathway. For example, nurses who traditionally worked exclusively in an inpatient setting would routinely rotate into outpatient settings in order to develop a richer understanding of the challenges facing patients after they leave the hospital and of how decisions made earlier in their care can lead to better outcomes years after treatment.

The organizational design for the New Karolinska University Hospital was a radical change from the traditional organization. But over time, it garnered considerable support, at first from the clinical leaders of the heart and vascular theme, the first unit to make the shift to the new operational model, and then from other clinical leaders. The union representing the hospital's 5,000 nurses also supported the plan because its members saw the advantages of the new design for more patient-centered care and because it provided new opportunities for career development.

But the plan sparked a lot of opposition as well. The new operating model placed new demands on the hospital's clinical leaders, particularly those who had led the large specialist clinics that previously held the lion's share of power. Some spoke out against the change. Others supported it in principle but criticized what they saw as a risky and rushed implementation. And while the nurses' union supported the new plan, the leaders of the Karolinska doctors' union (in Sweden, as in most European countries, doctors belong to a union) came out publicly against it.

BCG worked with some of the first units to move to the new hospital, including heart and vascular and children and women's health, using a change process similar to the one we had developed at Santeon: assembling multidisciplinary clinical teams, identifying the most important health outcomes for patients, and designing integrated care pathways. These two units moved to the new hospital in November 2016 with the patient-centered organizational structure fully in place.

But around the same time, a Stockholm daily newspaper began to publish a series of critical "exposés" about the change effort, which continued over the next three years. In the newspaper's narrative, the initiative represented the unwelcome imposition of American managerial approaches drawn from the private sector on the publicly funded Swedish health system, with BCG cast in the role of the private consulting company making it all happen and profiting from the result.

The media campaign generated considerable public controversy, which proved to be a highly disruptive event in the value-based transformation at Karolinska, as well as in other initiatives for value-based health care in Sweden. The negative media coverage eventually forced the politicians who funded the Stockholm-area health system and had initially supported the transformation to distance themselves from the project. It also created pressures that forced Karolinska to end its contract with BCG in 2017. And after the completion of the final move to the new facility in 2018, Melvin Samsom announced his resignation.

But if the controversy over the Karolinska transformation damaged the reputation of value-based health care in Sweden, it did not reverse the change at the hospital. Samsom's successor, Dr. Björn Zoëga (an Icelandic orthopedic surgeon who was the former director of the National University Hospital of Iceland and who had also led a small Swedish private hospital on value-based principles) was able to calm the controversy. He made some important adjustments to the initial plan that smoothed the transition to the new operating model, but the core principles of the new organization remained largely intact.

In the first two years after the reorganization, the hospital operated without a deficit and improved its ranking on the national quality index from last among all Swedish university hospitals to third. Take the example of Karolinska heart and vascular unit, which was the first to champion the patient-group organization and operating model and to move to the new hospital building. According to Dr. Peter Svenarud, head of thoracic surgery at Karolinska, the hospital's 30-day mortality rate for patients who undergo cardiac surgery has declined by roughly 75%, from 3.9% of all patients in 2014 to just under 1.1% in 2020, despite the fact that the hospital has been seeing increasingly complex cases.[14] This low mortality rate compares favorably with the best heart centers in the world.

These stellar results are partly the result of the Karolinska thoracic surgeons becoming an integrated practice unit similar to that of Martini Klinik. In order to focus volume on fewer operating surgeons, the team reduced its size in half—from 14 surgeons before the transformation to 7. Today, these seven surgeons perform more than a thousand surgeries every year, the most of any thoracic-surgery unit in the country. The high volume not only hones their clinical practice but much like Martini, also allows them to specialize in different aspects of thoracic surgery. And the fact that Karolinska's thoracic surgeons are part of a broader organizational unit covering the entire care pathway for cardiovascular disease makes it easier for them to cooperate with other relevant specialties.

"Today, cardiologists and thoracic surgeons work together in a way that they did not just a few years ago," Svenarud recently told *Dagens Medicin*, a Swedish daily that covers the local health care sector. "With the new organization at Karolinska, we have become . . . a well-functioning heart team that can choose the right surgical method or other intervention for each individual patient. In this way, each patient receives a more individualized and customized treatment."[15]

The operational efficiency, organizational flexibility, and team-based approach to care has also helped Karolinska weather the coronavirus pandemic far better than many other hospitals in Sweden. At the height of the pandemic, the hospital cared for more severely ill Covid-19 inpatients than any other hospital in the country and took the lead in coordinating the medical response to the pandemic in the Stockholm region.[16] At the same time, it served a growing number of patients suffering from other diseases. For example, in 2020, the hospital was able to deliver the same number of heart surgeries as in 2019—and the highest number since 2014. Since the third quarter of 2019, Karolinska has also increased its volume of cancer surgeries by a remarkable 40% compared to the previous three-year average, as stressed hospitals around the country, overwhelmed with the high volume of Covid patients, reduced their elective surgeries and began referring many of their cancer patients to the Stockholm hospital. And yet, waiting times for surgery did not increase. As a result of such achievements, in 2022, Karolinska University Hospital was ranked #8 by an expert panel of medical professionals and medical journalists in *Newsweek*'s international benchmarking of 2,000 hospitals around the world.[17]

Did Melvin Samsom move too quickly to transform Karolinska in the years before the move to the new hospital building? Should he have taken more time, built more support, pursued a more incremental approach? Perhaps. Other European academic medical centers such as Erasmus or Uppsala University Hospital in Sweden have avoided disruptive change, instead allowing each unit to move at its own pace toward a value-based model for care delivery, and relying on horizontal cooperation across traditional specialties to create more integrated care pathways without making major organizational changes. At a minimum, any large change program in a publicly financed health system is likely to face intense and sometimes politicized public scrutiny.

And yet, given the time pressure of the move to the new hospital building and the considerable dysfunction in Karolinska's organizational culture, Samsom's decision to quickly create a new organizational context that would enable new kinds of behaviors and encourage more cooperation among the hospital's various disciplines, may under the circumstances have been the right one. In a time of growing disruption of both health care and the medical profession, some institutions may simply not have the luxury of time.

EMBRACING DISRUPTION: INTERMOUNTAIN HEALTHCARE BUILDS A VALUE-BASED ECOSYSTEM

In the three examples we have discussed so far, value-based change—whether incremental or transformational—has been, for the most part, internally motivated. Whether bottom-up or top-down or some combination of the two, the efforts focus on improving performance at a single hospital or network of hospitals by improving patient outcomes and lowering costs.

But there is another way to think about addressing the change challenge: by emphasizing not only performance improvement but also business model innovation. Such an approach to change is more externally motivated, focusing not just on changing the organization but on changing its competitive position and how it operates in the health system as a whole. And often it embraces disruption, rather than trying to avoid it, as a necessary catalyst to change fundamentally how the system operates.

For an example of this kind of change, we shift our focus from the Netherlands and Sweden to a very different setting, the more commercial and entrepreneurial US health system, to tell a quite different change story: how Dr. Marc Harrison, CEO of Intermountain Healthcare, is pursuing a strategy to transform an already successful provider organization to create a value-based health system on a national scale.[18]

Intermountain Healthcare is a nonprofit health system headquartered in Salt Lake City, Utah, that serves the health care needs of people across the intermountain West region of the United States, primarily in

Utah, Idaho, Nevada, Colorado, Montana, Wyoming, and Kansas. With annual revenue of about $14 billion and nearly 59,000 caregivers, the system comprises a network of 33 hospitals (including a virtual hospital) and 385 outpatient clinics, as well as telehealth services. It has its own medical group, consisting of some 3,800 physicians and advanced practitioners, as well as a network of about 9,300 affiliated physicians. Like Kaiser Permanente, Intermountain also has its own proprietary health insurance plan, known as SelectHealth, with more than one million members. But unlike KP, Intermountain also cares for patients who are not in its health plan and who are insured by other insurers.

When Harrison became CEO of Intermountain in 2016, he inherited a financially robust regional health system with a national and international reputation for providing evidence-based, quality care, which was also recognized as a leader in care process management. Indeed, Intermountain was already doing some of the things that we have described in earlier chapters: organizing multidisciplinary clinical teams around key patient groups, tracking internal quality metrics as a means of continuous improvement, and integrating clinical standards in computer-based information systems.

It would have been easy for the organization to rest on its laurels, maintain the advantages of its strong position in its core markets, and continue business as usual. But Harrison, who was trained as a resident pediatric intensivist at Intermountain and spent much of his career as a senior executive at Cleveland Clinic, where Toby Cosgrove was a mentor, was convinced that business as usual wasn't good enough to position Intermountain in the rapidly changing US health care environment. So instead, he pursued a visionary strategic ambition to take the organization to the next level—in effect, to transform an already good regional health system into a national leader in value-based health care.

Doing so, however, required being honest about some of the limitations of Intermountain's traditional model. For example, despite Intermountain's focus on comparative performance within its network of hospitals, its performance on the national quality benchmarks that were increasingly being used by Medicare to set payment rates was only average. And despite the institution's commitment to process management and continuous improvement, participation was largely voluntary across Intermountain's hospital network and mainly focused on the system's largest and most advanced hospitals.

"Intermountain did a brilliant job at training people about quality and process improvement," Harrison told us, describing the situation when he arrived in 2016. "But our actual health outcomes were only around the median in the country at the time. Despite process maps throughout the organization, care wasn't really standardized across all our hospitals and clinics. We lacked a real operating model for true performance assessment with clear metrics. We didn't have aligned incentives. We were not really a system."

That insight became the catalyst for a series of changes that taken together would represent an innovative new business model for the company. That model emphasizes prevention and early intervention and aims to deliver superior health outcomes as defined by national standards for health care quality. It also embeds that goal in a broader set of systemwide changes in how Intermountain is organized, how financial incentives are designed, how care is delivered, how digital technologies are used to improve access and connect patients to caregivers, and how Intermountain collaborates with partners in a value-based ecosystem.

Harrison's first move was a major reorganization of Intermountain's care network. Before his arrival, Intermountain was organized by region, but Harrison quickly came to the conclusion that the company's regional structure was an obstacle to the development of a genuinely systematic approach to care and systemwide accountability. So in 2017, he combined Intermountain's traditional regional organizations into two main units. One, known as the Community-Based Care group, was a model for primary and ambulatory care that focuses on prevention and outpatient management. The other, known as the Specialty-Based Care group, combined Intermountain's hospitals into a more centrally managed unit for acute care. Harrison calls the former the "keeping people well" business, with the primary goal of keeping people healthy and out of the hospital, and the latter the "taking care of sick people" business, with the goal of providing cost-effective quality care to get patients back into the first group as efficiently and effectively as possible.

Parallel to the organizational change, Harrison also reorganized his leadership team. He brought the CEO of SelectHealth onto his senior executive team so that senior clinical leaders were exposed directly to the financial imperatives shaping Intermountain's insurance offerings. He also included Intermountain's chief nursing executive on the team (more than 10,000 nurses, including about a third of all nurses in the state of

Utah, report to her) because nurses would have a critical frontline role in the new community-care organization. He recruited the head of global consumer insight at The Walt Disney Company to become Intermountain's first chief consumer officer to represent the voice of the customer on the executive board and to lead the shift at Intermountain to a more consumer-friendly approach to care. And he created a new senior vice president for community health, who also joined the leadership team, in response to a growing awareness of the importance of social determinants of health to the company's prevention agenda.

A major advantage of Intermountain's new organizational structure is that it made it easier to align clinician incentives around the specific goals of the two business groups. One example is a 2018 initiative known as Reimagining Primary Care that created a network of clinics exclusively for patients under capitated at-risk insurance contracts, either through Intermountain's own health plan or through contracts that Intermountain has negotiated with private insurers (in Utah, for instance, Intermountain serves as an accountable care organization for United Healthcare's Medicare Advantage patients). By clustering the patients that Intermountain serves under risk-based insurance contracts, Intermountain has been able to redesign clinician incentives in its community-based care group so that multidisciplinary clinical teams spend more time on prevention and on the active management of patients most at risk of becoming seriously ill (for example, those with chronic diseases such as diabetes) in order to slow disease progression and, to the degree possible, keep them out of the hospital. It's an approach similar to that of Oak Street Health, described in Chapter 3. But unlike Oak Street, Intermountain is taking this approach for a far broader range of patients.

In the first year of the new program, the company reported, Intermountain saw a 60% reduction in hospital admissions of its Medicare Advantage members, a 25% reduction in commercial-insurance admissions, and a 20% reduction in per-member, per-month costs.[19] In addition, the company also reported exceeding clinical quality metrics by 120% compared to a control group, improving provider experience of care by 20%, and improving patient experience of care metrics by 3%.

Intermountain's community-based care organization has also developed innovative approaches to addressing the social determinants of health that are so important to long-term prevention. In Utah, for example, the company is collaborating with the state and other providers of social welfare services to pool resources and create one-stop locations in schools and other local-community sites where people can get help in addressing both their health care and social welfare needs.

Finally, a more centralized organization structure has allowed Intermountain to take advantage of economies of scale to lower costs. For example, the system has its own purchasing organization in which supply chain experts work closely with clinicians to influence physicians' choice of medical supplies, allowing Intermountain to negotiate volume-based discounts on pricing. Centralization has facilitated closer links with Intermountain's affiliated physicians (who treat Intermountain patients but are not employees of the Intermountain system)—for example, by providing technology and value-added services to integrate payment and reimbursement.

Parallel to these organizational changes, Intermountain also invested aggressively in digital health services, not only as a way to deliver care more efficiently but also as a way to care for people closer to their homes—an especially important aspect of the patient experience for Intermountain's rural population. Even before the coronavirus pandemic, for example, Intermountain had made major investments in telehealth, including 24-7 digital medical and behavioral-health networks. This digital infrastructure positioned Intermountain to adapt quickly once the pandemic hit, expanding from 830,000 total patient interactions in the five years between 2015 and 2019 (about 454 per day) to nearly 1.5 million (4,300 per day) in 2020 alone.[20]

Intermountain also operates one of the nation's largest virtual hospitals in which patients are cared for at small local hospitals by a geographically dispersed virtual team, including a hospitalist who monitors vital signs around the clock, and at home where nurses and other caregivers do routine rounding. In 2020, the company introduced a personalized digital app known as My Health+ that draws on lessons from more consumer-oriented industries such as travel and banking to create a more seamless experience than that offered by traditional patient portals based on electronic-medical-record (EMR) systems. The new app integrates a wealth of digital health innovations in a single platform, allowing Intermountain patients to book appointments (both physical and virtual), receive reminders about preventive care visits, manage prescriptions, ask questions about routine health issues on their own time that are then reviewed and answered by their PCP, and manage out-of-pocket health-care spending by means of cost-transparency tools that help them know what to expect. The app even includes AI-based symptom checkers that based on predictive analytics can direct an individual to the most efficient site of care.

In a sense, this extensive digital infrastructure is the all-important connective tissue linking the patient to Intermountain and the company's two businesses to each other. It improves patient access to and experience of the system by allowing patients to get care at their convenience in their home or community (connecting remotely when necessary with specialists who previously never would have been able to treat patients in remote areas). It also allows local primary care providers to treat seriously ill or injured patients in lower-cost local hospitals but with the support of virtual consults with specialists at Intermountain's acute-care hospitals.

In an internal review of seven community hospitals, Intermountain's digital critical-care program was associated with a 36.5% reduction in single-year mortality. And a study of 481 people with increased likelihood of colorectal cancer showed that 35.4% of those who had a risk assessment via telehealth with a certified genetic counselor completed a colonoscopy within nine months, compared to 15.7% in the control group.[21]

Finally, when Intermountain's patients in the largely rural areas of the intermountain West have conditions that are serious enough that they need to be admitted at one of Intermountain's acute-care hospitals, they can rely on what Harrison terms an "air force" of helicopters and fixed-wing aircraft at nearly 30 bases to ferry them to the most appropriate care setting. "We are creating a genuine physical-digital ecosystem where people anywhere can receive care in a borderless way," said Harrison, "which is making us a national leader in rural health."

All these organizational changes at Intermountain are in service of a broader transformation strategy: to leverage what the system is learning about providing value-based care to create a comprehensive value-based ecosystem on a national scale through new ventures and strategic partnerships with other industry stakeholders (including some of their competitors). In 2018, for example, Intermountain joined with seven other hospital systems, including Mayo Clinic and HCA Healthcare, to launch Civica Rx, a nonprofit generic-drug manufacturer, in order to ensure that the participating providers have a consistent supply of low-cost generic drugs. By 2022, Civica had grown to include more than 50 health systems, representing approximately one-third of all licensed hospital beds in the United States, and recently announced a plan to begin manufacturing and distributing low-cost insulin. In 2019, Intermountain launched a new company to help providers, payers, and other stakeholders make their own transition to value-based care. Known as Castell, the company offers an IT platform with analytics software and other digital technology, as well as care-management support services, to help other provider networks deliver virtual care, coordinate the patient experience, address social determinants of health, and develop and manage risk-based contracts. Castell positions Intermountain as an orchestrator of value-based integration for other less mature health systems, especially at a time when the coronavirus pandemic has disrupted traditional business models and led many smaller providers to embrace risk-based contracting.

Intermountain has also pursued more traditional paths to creating a value-based health system on a national scale. In April 2022, the company finalized a merger with SCL Health, a Catholic-affiliated health system in Colorado, Montana, and Kansas. Together, the combined entity is the eleventh largest health system in the United States by revenue and extends Intermountain's value-based business model to approximately 1.5 million new patients.

At a time of enormous disruption in the US health care industry, Harrison has clearly chosen to disrupt Intermountain from the inside rather than be disrupted by other players. His approach to change has been more directive and, some might argue, more strategic, focusing on key leverage points in the system—senior leadership, financial incentives, digital infrastructure, and the like—to bring about a decisive shift in how Intermountain delivers high-quality, cost-effective care. In some respects, the approach has upended Intermountain's traditional way of doing things and provoked opposition from some stakeholders. "It's been really hard for the clinical community," says Harrison. "Clinicians, by and large, hate change, and I was the face of it. But I believed in what we were doing. And, over time, people have come around."

FROM ORGANIZATIONAL CHANGE TO HEALTH-SYSTEM TRANSFORMATION

Nearly all the provider organizations we have profiled so far in this book have had the advantage of having visionary leaders and in many cases, favorable circumstances. Not every organization is so fortunate. What's more, even the most innovative value-based providers have confronted a series of obstacles built into the ways most national health systems are organized—obstacles that they have had to overcome to create a more value-based approach to care.

As the Intermountain story begins to suggest, however, the ultimate goal of value-based health care is not just to change individual organizations; it is to transform the entire health system. To drive change across all providers and the system at large will require dismantling systemwide barriers to change—in effect, to transform obstacles into enablers. In our stories of value-based innovation and change, we have already encountered some of the areas where systemwide change is necessary: for example, the need to develop and implement standardized metrics for outcomes measurement; the need for sophisticated information technology platforms to make it easier to collect, share, and analyze such data; the importance of financial incentives that encourage providers and suppliers to invest in prevention and early identification of disease, just to name a few.

To accelerate the transition to value-based health care for all stakeholders in the health care industry, we need to address these systemwide issues that affect every organization because they define the environment in which all health care organizations operate and determine how they develop and evolve. We turn our attention to these system enablers in the subsequent chapters of our book, starting with the issue of value-based payment.

Value-Based Change: Action Steps

PROVIDERS

1. **Link change to purpose.** Unlock clinician engagement by focusing change on providing better care for patients.

2. **Be explicit about your change strategy.** Is it incremental, transformational, or some combination of the two? Be explicit to your people about the strategy and goals of the change effort.

3. **Focus change on improving outcomes delivered to patients.** Make the identification, tracking, and improvement of key health outcomes a central part of the change effort.

4. **Focus on changing behavior, not just changing organizational structure.** Effective value-based change is all about behavior; changes in organizational structure may be required but only when they support necessary changes in behavior and culture.

5. **Know when the time is right to change the organization and operating model.** At a certain point, value-based change must be supported by changes in the operating model, including IT support, an accounting system that enables accurate assessment of costs per patient, patient-centered key performance indicators, and the like. Recognize these needs from start, plan, and resource timely execution.

6. **Drive change top-down and bottom-up.** Even the most incremental change efforts need senior leadership and commitment; even the most transformational need the engagement and participation of clinicians on the front line of care.

CHAPTER 5
PAYING FOR VALUE INSTEAD OF VOLUME

n 2013, our BCG colleagues Bennett Lane, Dave Matheson, Dr. Barry Rosenberg, and David Sadoff were part of a research team led by Dr. Atul Gawande of Harvard Medical School that studied the impact of major surgical complications on the costs and revenues of US hospitals. The team used administrative data from more than 34,000 inpatient surgical procedures at a major US hospital system to analyze the net revenues and costs associated with any medical complications that occurred in the course of the surgeries.

The research, published in the *Journal of the American Medical Association* (*JAMA*), found that the hospital system benefited financially from the occurrence of such complications. Specifically, privately insured surgical patients with one or more complications provided the hospitals with a profit margin that was 330% higher—an additional $39,000 per patient, on average—than the margin from similarly insured patients who had no complications.[1] For patients covered by Medicare (the US federal health insurance program for people 65 years of age or older), the profit margin was lower but still substantial: a 190% higher margin, or an additional $18,000 per patient. In other words, the reimbursement system made it economically irrational to improve health outcomes by striving to mini-mize complications.

We're not suggesting that surgeons were actively neglecting their patients or somehow encouraging complications to pad the hospital system's revenues. What we are suggesting is that the payment model governing how the hospitals were paid for their services was a powerful financial disincentive for improving the outcomes delivered to patients.

It's not a problem limited to the United States. For the most part, health care providers around the world are paid for the activities they perform—irrespective of whether those activities actually contribute to better health outcomes. In many countries, physicians have for decades been paid according to the traditional fee-for-service payment model. And even in many publicly financed health systems where clinicians are salaried, their employers are reimbursed for the number of tests and pro-cedures that their salaried clinicians collectively perform, regardless of the outcomes those activities produce. What's more, in an effort to reduce waiting times, some publicly financed health systems have privatized some areas of care delivery such as elective surgery—with the unintended effect of reinforcing fee-for-service payment and in some cases, leading to overtreatment.

In response to the perverse incentives associated with fee-for-service payment models, an extraordinary amount of experimentation has taken place over the past decade in health systems around the world with so-called value-based payment—that is, payment models designed to cre-ate financial incentives for providers to improve value delivered to patients rather than merely paying them the volume of services provided.

It may seem paradoxical, but the US health system, where the fee-for-service model has long been dominant, is a leader in value-based-payment innovation. As part of the 2010 Affordable Care Act, the US Congress established the Center for Medicare and Medicaid Innovation (CMMI), with the goal, in the words of the agency's enabling legislation, to "reduce program expenditures . . . while preserving or enhancing the quality of care furnished to individuals."[2] CMMI is part of the federal government's Centers for Medicare and Medicaid Services (CMS), which is responsi-ble for overseeing the Medicare and Medicaid insurance programs that together cover about 130 million people, or roughly 40% of the US pop-ulation.[3] By 2019, CMMI had spent approximately $20 billion launching 54 different initiatives in its Alternative Payment Models program, the world's largest initiative to test innovative payment and delivery models, involving nearly 1 million health care providers serving some 26 million patients.[4]

Private US insurers are also innovating new value-based payment models, often in collaboration with CMS through its Medicare Advantage program in which private insurers offer managed-care health insurance plans to Medicare beneficiaries and are paid by Medicare via capitated risk-based contracts. Medicare Advantage enrollment has nearly doubled from 11.1 million participants in 2010 to 22 million in 2019, and today accounts for roughly 40% of all Medicare beneficiaries with enrollment expected to grow to 47% by 2029.[5] In a 2018 survey of US health care executives and clinical leaders, respondents reported that, on average, value-based payments constitute about a quarter of their organization's revenues, and 42% said they believe that value-based payment will eventually become the primary revenue model in US health care.[6]

The United States may have seen the most extensive innovations in value-based payment, but considerable experimentation is going on in other countries as well. In 2019, we studied some 30 value-based payment initiatives around the world.[7] In addition to the many programs in the United States, we found pay-for-performance bonus programs in Estonia, Switzerland, and the United Kingdom; bundled-payment initiatives in the Netherlands, Sweden, and Taiwan; capitation and other forms of risk-based contracting in Spain and the United Kingdom; as well as models that integrate health care and social welfare spending in New Zealand, Singapore, and Sweden. These value-based payment models were initiated by public and private payers covering single provider organizations and multiple organizations, and by governments that are leaders in value-based health care, as well as others that are just beginning to focus on value. (See the sidebar "Varieties of Value-Based Payment.")

Varieties of Value-Based Payment

Although the permutations can get complicated, when you come down to it, there are basically three types of value-based payment models. They can be located on a spectrum defined by the amount of financial risk that providers take on for delivering high-quality care in a cost-effective manner.

Pay-for-Performance Bonuses. The simplest form of value-based payment is to pay a bonus to providers when they achieve a predetermined performance goal—for example, when they meet a defined threshold for quality care, effectively manage costs, follow clinical guidelines, or simply track and report health outcomes. Bonuses can be used to introduce a value-based component to a traditional fee-for-service payment system. They can be used in combination with other value-based payment models. They can be designed as a pure upside incentive to base compensation in order to limit provider risk. Or some portion of that base compensation can be put at risk if providers do not achieve their performance targets.

Bundled Payments. Another value-based payment model that health systems are implementing is to establish a comprehensive fee for a clearly defined episode of care, rather than paying providers for each discrete service delivered in the care cycle. Known as bundled payments, this model also typically makes a portion of provider compensation conditional on the ultimate health outcomes of patients well after the initial surgery or other treatment. This creates incentives for providers to cooperate along the patient care pathway, factor in the downstream effect of their clinical decisions, strive to minimize complications and avoid medically unnecessary care, and make informed trade-offs (such as whether to recommend expensive hospitalization or more cost-effective outpatient care) at various points in the care cycle.

Capitation. Finally, a third value-based payment model pays a predetermined fee to cover all the health needs of each person in a given patient population, an approach typically known as capitation. Capitation gives providers a powerful financial incentive to manage total system costs. In effect, they take on the financial risk of delivering cost-effective care. To the degree that they can keep costs under the capitated payment, providers benefit financially; to the degree that they cannot, providers suffer losses (although most capitated systems insure providers against extreme outlier cases). However, for capitation to be genuinely value based, it needs to be organized around defined patient groups and population segments, adjusted for risk, and linked to an acceptable quality threshold—and, ideally,

transparency around health outcomes. All these features are necessary to avoid inadvertently creating incentives for cherry-picking
healthier patients or for limiting access to required care (so-called
rationing).

It's important to emphasize that these three models are not mutually
exclusive. Indeed, at the boundary, they tend to blur into each other.
For example, many bundled-payment initiatives use some version of
a pay-for-performance bonus. Similarly, bundled payments for discrete episodes of care can be an intermediate step on the road to
adopting capitated payment for specific populations of patients.

Health systems around the world are learning a lot from these experiences and identifying useful innovations. But there has been enormous
variation in the design of various value-based-payment initiatives, and it's
fair to say that the actual results from all this experimentation have, so
far at least, been somewhat mixed. Some value-based-payment initiatives
have improved quality while reducing costs, but others have not.[8]

How to improve the odds that new payment mechanisms deliver
the right kind of incentives to focus providers on value rather than just
volume? Much of the debate about value-based payment focuses on defini-
tional questions (what constitutes a value-based payment) and the relative
merits of various payment models. Do physician bonuses improve quality?
(Yes, at least in some cases.[9]) Are bundled payments better than capitation? (Opinions differ.[10]) Does value-based payment require physicians
and providers to take on risk through some form of risk-based contracting? Does "pay-for-performance" mean actually rewarding providers who
deliver better health outcomes and penalizing those who do not?

All these questions are important, and we'll touch on them in the pages
that follow. But in our experience, the success of any given value-based
payment initiative is not only the product of the design of the particular
payment model but also the result of the organizational context in which
it is implemented. In this respect, value-based payment is no silver bullet.
What's more, value-based payment isn't an end unto itself. Rather, it is a
means to an end: creating a new organizational context in which improving health care value becomes a rational behavior for all stakeholders. The
goal should be creating alignment across providers, payers, and suppliers

so that it is in their interest to deliver high-value care. When it comes to changing behavior, financial incentives certainly matter—but so do business models, organizational cultures, norms, practices, data and analytics, and policy and regulatory frameworks.

Therefore, it is critical not to conceive of value-based payment in isolation but instead to see it as one important element in a broad system transformation that will require long-term institutional commitment, considerable investment, and the development of new kinds of organizational capabilities. If initiatives are conceived narrowly as a way to achieve immediate short-term cost savings or merely to shift risk from payers to providers, they are likely to fail.

How national health systems around the world finance and pay for health care is a devilishly complicated topic. Entire books have been written about it—and we are not going to repeat that exercise here.[11] Rather, in this chapter we want to do three things:

1. Take a step back in order to reflect on the ultimate purpose of any incentive system in health care, whether financial or nonfinancial: changing the behavior of all players in the system.
2. Describe a variety of value-based-payment initiatives involving payers, providers, and suppliers that, we believe, support the right kind of value-based behaviors.
3. Identify the critical success factors for new value-based payment models to actually deliver on their promise of improving patient value.

FIVE BEHAVIORS THAT DRIVE VALUE

The stories of value-based providers told in earlier chapters begin to suggest the kind of behaviors that any incentive system for a value-based health system should encourage. Generalizing from their experience (and at the risk of oversimplification), we think that a genuinely value-based incentive system should be designed so that it becomes in the interest of all health care stakeholders to do five things:

1. Engage with patients so that patients are able to play a more active role in the choices and decisions that shape their health.

2. Prioritize wellness and disease prevention to maximize overall population health and minimize total health system costs.
3. Deliver high-quality, appropriate treatments—with an emphasis on activities with proven value, ideally delivered early to secure better outcomes for the money spent along the care-delivery pathway.
4. Embrace continuous improvement and clinical innovation in care delivery through increased collaboration across the health system and the sharing of best practices.
5. Do all this while taking joint responsibility for managing the total costs of the system.

How these behaviors manifest in any given situation, of course, will vary by patient group. With relatively healthy patients, for instance, the primary emphasis should be on getting individuals to take responsibility for their own health and making prudent lifestyle choices. For the chronically ill, the emphasis will be on early detection and intervention to slow disease progression, avoid the development of acute complications and comorbidities, and thus to the degree possible minimize the long-term costs of treatment. For patients needing an elective procedure or facing an acute illness or condition, a top priority will be to take time to understand the specific health outcomes that matter to the individual, so that those preferences are factored into treatment choices and unwanted (and, potentially, costly) care is avoided. And across all patient groups, providers need to adopt the kind of team-based approach to care that we discussed in Chapter 3, characterized by increased collaboration with other providers in inpatient specialties, such as surgery and oncology, as well as experts in rehabilitation and community and social care, so that clinicians operate at the top of their license in the most cost-efficient way possible.

Finally, providers need to do all this while also paying close attention to managing the total costs to the health system. In an environment characterized by limited budgets, every dollar wasted is a dollar that cannot be spent on helping others in need or on innovations that improve the health outcomes delivered to patients. Therefore, it is critical for a value-based health system to create mechanisms to improve the allocation of scarce resources for a given patient group so that those resources generate the most impact.

This behavioral context helps shed light on the limitations of activity-based payment models such as fee-for-service. It's important to acknowledge that linking payment to specific activities is actually an *improvement* on the undifferentiated global budgets that have typically characterized some publicly financed health systems. Better to link payment to services delivered than simply to set budgets with no relationship to the work actually done. Nevertheless, fee-for-service payment not only creates disincentives for delivering high-value care, as the study of the US hospital system illustrates, but by splitting up payments among multiple clinicians and service providers, it contributes to the fragmentation of care, making it difficult to develop genuinely integrated care pathways. What's more, according to some experts, the way fee-for-service payment schedules are defined and implemented, especially in the United States, has had the unintended consequence of overpaying for expensive procedure-based specialized care and underpaying for the critical upstream tasks of early diagnosis and prevention that typically take place in primary care or in specialties such as geriatrics that focus more on the complex needs of multimorbid populations rather than on clearly defined procedures.[12]

Although it is conceptually easy to define the behaviors of a genuinely value-based health system, it is more difficult to define the details of the appropriate value-payment system for encouraging them—mainly due to the high degree of organizational complexity of the health care sector. Any effective value-based payment system needs to address many different stakeholders: the individual clinicians who provide care; provider institutions who coordinate patient care across multiple individual clinicians; pharmaceutical, medical technology, and other companies that are major suppliers of drugs, medical equipment, and other medical products used by individual clinicians, hospitals, and health systems. What's more, in many countries, any value-based payment system will have to coordinate payments delivered not by a single payer but by multiple payers: national governments, nonprofit sick funds, private insurers (both for-profit and nonprofit), or middle-men organizations such as group-purchasing organizations (GPOs) and pharmacy-benefit managers (PBMs).

The challenge of any value-based payment system is to acknowledge this complexity without becoming a hostage to it. Systems need to be designed according to a few clear goals (for example, encouraging the behaviors described earlier), and stakeholders need access to the right data in support of autonomy and accountability to achieve those goals. And as the work of our colleagues Yves Morieux and Peter Tollman, described in Chapter 1, makes clear, a key mechanism for managing complexity is greater cooperation—for instance, between payers and providers. In the past, most health systems have relied on a typical division of labor. Payers, whether public or private, were responsible for managing the costs of the system, while providers were responsible for the care delivered to patients (although often lacking the information to effectively measure its quality). In contrast, a key principle of value-based payment is that payers and providers should share accountability for and jointly manage both costs and quality.

Whether public or private, health care payers tend to get a bad rap. They are the players in the system who impose bureaucratic constraints on everyone else—for example, limiting patient selection of the doctors they can go to for care or insisting on the compliance of doctors to care guidelines or drug formularies. And yet, in the context of value-based health care, payers are well positioned to help improve health outcomes. They have large comprehensive data sets that can shed light on differences in clinical practice across providers. This data can help increase transparency about health outcomes and inform providers of best practices. More generally, payers can use their unique position within the health care value chain to facilitate optimal treatment decisions and minimize perverse incentives that erode quality and value. Doing so, however, requires payers to shift how they think about their role in the health system—from narrowly focusing on reimbursement and cost administration to becoming an active facilitator of high-value care.

If payers have a key role to play in linking payment to value, so too do providers. Providers are on the front line of care delivery, making the day-to-day decisions that affect patient care and overall system costs. Therefore, they are in the best position not only to make informed trade-offs about how best to deliver quality care in the most cost-effective way, but also, with access to the right data, to innovate clinically so as to transcend those trade-offs and deliver better quality for the money spent.

Let's explore some of the ways that payers, providers, and other industry stakeholders are using value-based payment to achieve some of the desired behaviors we have described in health systems today.

ENCOURAGING PREVENTION AND EARLY INTERVENTION: US MEDICARE ADVANTAGE

For an example of a value-based-payment model that appears to have successfully encouraged a focus on prevention and early intervention, consider the Medicare Advantage program in the United States. Approximately 60% of the Medicare-eligible population see doctors and other providers on a traditional fee-for-service basis, with the costs of the services reimbursed directly by Medicare. About 40%, however, are enrolled in Medicare Advantage health insurance plans provided by private insurers.

Medicare Advantage is a capitated payment model in which Medicare pays the insurer a fixed risk-adjusted payment for the total cost of care for each patient; then it is up to the insurer and its provider partners to figure out the best way to invest that money to provide cost-effective quality care. The program gives insurers an incentive to limit their costs—for example, by developing a selective network of providers, by designing financial incentives that are aligned with clinical best practices, and by investing in active care management that emphasizes prevention in an effort to minimize expensive acute care.

Medicare Advantage also creates financial incentives to improve the quality of care. CMS ranks every Medicare Advantage insurance plan according to a five-star quality rating system that tracks performance against 40 categories for quality and service (using quality rating systems such as HEDIS that we described in Chapter 2). Plans that achieve a four- or five-star rating receive an additional 5% premium on each member's capitated payment.

Since the passage of the 2010 Affordable Care Act, medical-loss-ratio requirements cap an insurer's combined administrative costs and profits at 15% (administrative costs of the program are typically around 10%).[13] Any additional savings must be distributed to beneficiaries (in the form of lower premiums or extra benefits such as dental or vision coverage that are unavailable in traditional fee-for-service Medicare) or to providers (in the form of higher compensation).

The structure of the Medicare Advantage program has a number of features that create incentives for providers to focus on prevention and early intervention. Because the rate that Medicare pays for each beneficiary is risk-adjusted, insurers have a financial incentive to conduct a rigorous diagnostic review for each new member to document his or her medical condition as comprehensively as possible. And because insurers negotiate rates directly with providers, they have the flexibility to define the network of providers for their beneficiaries, steering individuals to doctors and hospitals that are most cost-effective, and to coordinate care to focus on high-value as opposed to low-value care.

Research confirms that Medicare Advantage plans in general are successful at cutting costs compared with fee-for-service medicine. One 2012 study, for example, found that utilization rates in some major categories, including emergency departments and ambulatory surgery or procedures, generally were 20% to 30% lower for patients enrolled in Medicare Advantage HMOs than for those with Medicare fee-for-service coverage.[14]

But what has been the overall impact of such plans on health care quality? In the past, there have been widespread concerns, especially on the part of the general public, that cost savings in capitated payment models came at the expense of quality of care, ultimately limiting access (commonly referred to as rationing). In the 1990s, for example, HMOs received major criticism for denying medically necessary services to patients, ostensibly in order to control costs. And the assumption that higher cost is synonymous with better quality remains widespread.[15]

To better understand the implications of the Medicare Advantage model for quality of care, in 2012 Stefan and our BCG colleagues Jon Kaplan and Jan Willem Kuenen analyzed 2011 claims data and demographic information for some 3 million Medicare patients. Approximately 1.3 million of the patients used providers paid on a traditional fee-for-service basis by Medicare. The remaining 1.7 million patients were enrolled in Medicare Advantage plans offered by private insurers.

We found that on three internationally accepted dimensions of health care quality—single-year mortality, recovery from acute episodes of care requiring hospitalization, and the sustainability of health over time—patients enrolled in Medicare Advantage plans had better outcomes than those participating in Medicare on a traditional fee-for-service basis.[16] The Medicare Advantage patients had lower single-year mortality rates, shorter average hospital stays, and fewer readmissions. They also received higher levels of recommended preventive care such as regular monitoring for diabetes patients and had fewer disease-specific complications.[17]

Our study wasn't peer-reviewed. But at least some of our findings have been confirmed subsequently by the academic literature. For example, a 2021 meta-analysis of 48 studies comparing Medicare Advantage plans to traditional fee-for-service Medicare found that, on average, Medicare Advantage plans made higher use of preventive care visits and had fewer hospital admissions, fewer emergency department visits, shorter hospital and skilled nursing facility lengths of stay, and lower health care costs relative to traditional Medicare.[18]

Humana's Approach to Medicare Advantage

To better understand how Medicare Advantage is transforming how payers pay for care and how providers deliver it, we spoke to Dr. Will Shrank, chief medical officer of Humana, a US health insurer that has about 4.6 million beneficiaries in its Medicare Advantage plans, representing about 20% of the total Medicare Advantage market.[19]

In the context of Medicare Advantage, to call Humana a health insurance company is a bit misleading. Although the company is one of the major US private payers, it also owns its own Medicare Advantage primary care system in south Florida and Texas, known as Conviva, the largest senior-focused health care organization in the country, covering some 220,000 capitated patients, and CenterWell, a network of roughly 70 primary care centers in eight states that accepts patients from all payers, not just those enrolled with Humana. Together, these provider organizations, which report to Shrank, contribute over $3 billion in revenue. Shrank describes the business as "a great lab to innovate" when it comes to designing value-based approaches to care. In this respect, in the domain of primary care, Humana has some similarities to the US integrated payer-providers that we described in previous chapters.

But Humana will never be in a position itself to deliver primary care to all its members across the entire country. So Humana has partnered both with traditional primary care practices and new-style primary care providers such as Oak Street to help them create more value-based delivery models.

"We will always need to have good partners," explained Shrank. "And primary care providers need a partner as well—not just someone who pays them but someone who helps them make the transition to value-based care. The challenge for providers in value-based health care is that you have to build a whole host of new muscles: resources, capabilities, organization, workflows, patient communication. A good Medicare Advantage plan provides data and reporting, supports care management, and surveys all members for their health-related social needs. We have resources to support all these needs, so we can take things off the plate of the provider. We help create a nimble relationship at the local level, so they feel safe taking on risk. We help mitigate the risk in the early years so they can take on more in later years."

A typical first step is to emphasize the position of a chronic-care coordinator, whose role is to be an ongoing contact with patients and serve as a guide to the health system. For provider practices that are new to this role, a Humana employee will often embed in the provider organization to play the role until staff can be trained to take it on over the longer term. The care coordinator role increases the number of contacts with patients, while also decreasing the number of visits with clinicians, since many questions and concerns can be handled by the care coordinator rather than by the physician.

When it comes to physician and provider-group compensation, Humana offers a variety of contractual relationships to its participating practices. At the simplest level, known as "Star Recognition," primary care providers receive an annual bonus payment, conditional on meeting targets in six out of eight quality metrics. Primary care providers that qualify as a "Model Practice" receive quarterly bonuses for meeting a balanced scorecard of quality and outcomes metrics. In addition to receiving a monthly care-coordination payment, model practices also have the potential for shared savings based on how cost-effective their care provision is. Finally, "Full Value" primary care practices take on full accountability for managing patients' conditions and receive a capitated fee to cover each patient—in other words, full risk-based contracting not only for Humana as the payer but also for the provider.

Becoming a Full Value practice is not necessarily the goal for all providers. It depends on a provider organization's appetite for (and ability to effectively manage) risk. But the financial rewards for providers increase as one moves across this spectrum of contractual arrangements because the overall cost savings are greater. Humana estimates that on average, physicians participating in one of these value-based payment models receive 15.6 cents of every health care dollar spent (as opposed to 6.6 cents for those who do not). In other words, they can earn two-and-a-half times more, on average, than they would from the baseline Medicare fee schedule. Those that take on full risk-based contracting can earn, on average, four-and-half times more. "Our message to providers is, 'we will meet you where you are,'" says Shrank, although the expectation is that over time, providers will move toward the Full Value end of the spectrum.

As a result of these mechanisms, Humana estimates that Medicare Advantage beneficiaries who receive care from clinicians in its value-based programs receive preventive screenings for a range of conditions between 8% and 19% more often than those in nonvalue-based care programs. Partly as a result, they have 10% fewer emergency room visits and are admitted to hospital almost 30% less often than those in nonvalue-based programs. All this contributes to what the company estimates as savings of $4 billion that would have been spent if the members in value-based programs were in the original Medicare fee-for-service programs.[20] Recent research also suggests that Humana's Medicare Advantage plans deliver better patient-centered outcomes and lower costs than traditional Medicare in key areas such as post-acute care after hospitalization, home health care, and addressing social determinants of health.[21]

In effect, Humana's intense collaboration with providers around value-based health care and value-based payment is transforming the company from a traditional health-insurance company to a new kind of health company, one that blurs the traditional boundaries between payer and provider. Much like the strategy of Intermountain that we described in Chapter 4, Humana is stitching together a set of strategic assets to build an integrated value-based health care ecosystem—in this case, one that puts primary care at the center of the health system.

In addition to wholly owned subsidiaries, such as Conviva and CenterWell, the company sometimes takes an ownership stake in provider partners, in order to influence or control key decision-points on the total care pathway. The entities in the emerging Humana value-based ecosystem include:

- The primary care startup Heal, with a delivery model that reinvents the traditional house call by emphasizing patient home visits that include a comprehensive assessment of patients' social determinants of health, like food security and social support, as well as their physical health
- Dispatch, a company that strives to "bring the ER into the home" by providing an emergency hotline that patients can call when they need emergency care, so that Dispatch care coordinators can direct people to the most appropriate site of care (which, in many cases, may be a cheaper urgent-care clinic rather than the hospital)
- One Home Care, which coordinates care for hospitalized patients after they leave the hospital

All these assets provide a way for Humana to coordinate care for its Medicare Advantage patients more effectively, steering them to providers who buy in to the insurer's value-based model or providing the care itself. And, of course, the more patient volume that the insurer controls, the better it is able to negotiate prices with hospitals and other providers.

According to Shrank, a major focus of the future will be how Humana measures the results of its Medicare Advantage ecosystem in terms of value to the patient and value to the health system. The CMS five-star ranking system has been criticized for, in effect, making it too easy for Medicare Advantage plans to receive a four- or five-star rating (thus triggering the 5% member-payment-rate premium). In Shrank's view, the star ranking system captures important dimensions of quality care, but he admits, "You can get a perfect score without delivering perfect care." As a result, Humana has been busy supplementing the star metrics with additional internal metrics. The first step was to incorporate more self-reported information from members in order to track member "healthy days" and "mentally healthy days," using metrics developed by the US Centers for Disease Control and Prevention (CDC). More recently, however, the focus has been on the question: "Are we able to actually move the health care system?" Humana has developed composite measures to track health equity, the degree of care integration, the ability to slow disease progression, and quality of care in the home. "These metrics helps us determine whether we and our partners are making a positive contribution to the health system," said Shrank.

We asked Shrank about the potential of ICHOM's comprehensive outcome-measurement sets as a standard for evaluating the performance of Medicare Advantage plans. "What ICHOM is proposing is better," he told us, "but actually doing it would require a lot of resources." Currently, CMS does not require the kind of detailed outcomes measurement that the ICHOM standards represent in its evaluation of Medicare Advantage health plans. For the moment, at least, that represents a major institutional barrier. Because implementing the ICHOM standards has no impact on compensation, it is extremely difficult in the US environment for either payers or providers to justify the necessary investments. "The health system is not oriented today to capture that kind of information," said Shrank. However, he believes that the domain of outcomes measurement is going to continue to evolve and change as more and more data becomes available and as it becomes easier for people to self-report their health status. (We will return to this issue in Chapter 7.)

A Controversial Program

Despite research showing the advantages of the Medicare Advantage pay-ment model and despite the experiences of insurers such as Humana, Medicare Advantage, for some, remains a controversial innovation in the US health system. Pointing to the central role of private insurers and the billions of dollars in venture capital invested in new-style providers such as Oak Street, critics have decried the program as a creeping privatization of Medicare.[22] They also argue that as currently designed, the program encourages overcoding and the gaming of risk adjustment for financial gain, as well as in some cases denying patients necessary care.[23] Finally, they claim that it actually leads to higher costs for the health system as a whole.[24] Critics have argued that CMS should put a brake on the expan-sion of the program.

But such arguments leave a lot out.[25] For one thing, comparisons of the cost of Medicare Advantage to the US health system tend to ignore that Medicare Advantage beneficiaries pay less in out-of-pocket expenses and often receive more benefits than traditional fee-for-service Medi-care beneficiaries. One recent study concluded that the reduced cost sharing and additional benefits for the 22 million Medicare Advantage beneficiaries equaled some $32.5 billion.[26] And whatever the limits of the program's current methodology for risk-adjustment, those methodologies have proven effective in limiting cherry-picking of healthy patients and encouraging the enrollment of the sickest and most socially disadvan-taged patients. Medicare Advantage beneficiaries are proportionally lower income than beneficiaries of fee-for-service Medicare.

Finally, whatever the disagreements and debates about the appro-priate role for private insurers or venture-capital investment in the US health care system, it seems clear that the Medicare Advantage program has unleashed considerable clinical innovation. At least some private US insurers have created an operating model that delivers better care at a lower cost. Their visibility across multiple providers, along with their correspondingly greater scale, broad access to data, and lack of fixed infrastructure (and the corresponding fixed costs that such an infrastruc-ture represents) put them in a position to bring about changes in clinical practice in partnership with the clinical community. From that perspec-tive, the big question for the future of the US health system is how to learn from the best-in-class Medicare Advantage plans and scale up their value-based operational model—not only for the Medicare population, but also for the 60% of Americans who are not covered by Medicare or other publicly financed health insurance.

INTEGRATING PAYMENT ALONG THE CARE PATHWAY

If capitated payment models focus on prevention and early intervention to keep people healthy and therefore minimize the need for expensive hospital-based acute care, other value-based payment models focus on situations where some kind of specialized care such as surgery or other hospital-based clinical intervention is required. Here, the goal should be to encourage the most appropriate and highest-value care takes place at the right time in the right setting, and to make sure that multiple specialists along the care pathway have incentives to work together to produce the best outcomes for a given patient in the most cost-effective way for the health system as a whole.

Take, for example, the approach typically known as bundled payment. Unlike capitation, bundled payments are, in certain respects, activity-based payments like fee-for-service. But instead of paying multiple providers for each discrete service delivered in the care cycle, payment is bundled in a comprehensive fee for a clearly defined episode of care. In the best designed bundled payment plans, a portion of provider compensation is conditional on the ultimate health outcomes of patients well after the initial surgery or treatment.

In recent years, there has been considerable experimentation with bundled payments in health systems around the world. For example, a 2020 study by the Commonwealth Fund reviewed 23 bundled-payment initiatives in eight different health systems: Denmark, Portugal, the Netherlands, New Zealand, Sweden, Taiwan, the United Kingdom, and the United States.[27]

More than half of the initiatives in the Commonwealth study took place in the United States, which reflects the large role that bundled payments have played in the Alternative Payment Model's program sponsored by CMS's Center for Medicare and Medicaid Innovation (CMMI). Currently, CMMI is sponsoring four different bundled-payment models covering a broad cross section of inpatient (and increasingly outpatient) clinical episodes—such as acute myocardial infarction, coronary artery bypass grafting, hip and knee replacements, and some cancers—and involving hundreds of hospitals and physician groups across the country.[28]

Take, for example, the Comprehensive Care for Joint Replacement (CJR) model that was launched in 2016 for hip or knee replacement. In 2013, Medicare covered more than 400,000 such procedures, and the hospital bills alone totaled more than $7 billion. What's more, quality varies widely across providers of these procedures; the rate of complications after surgery can be more than three times higher at some facilities than at others. According to CMS, the CJR program "holds participant hospitals financially accountable for the quality and cost of a CJR episode of care and incentivizes increased coordination of care among hospitals, physicians, and post-acute care providers."[29] Unlike other CMMI bundled-payment models, in which participation is voluntary, in 2018 the CJR model became compulsory in 34 medical service areas covering some 465 hospitals characterized by below-average health outcomes or higher costs.[30]

What has been the impact of these various bundled-payment initiatives? So far, the evidence would appear to be somewhat mixed. The results of the Commonwealth study are generally positive. Thirty-two out of the 35 studies that Commonwealth researchers reviewed evaluated the impact of the model on medical spending, and 20 out of those 32 studies reported either lower medical spending or slower spending growth compared to a control group. And of the 32 studies in the sample that reported on the quality impact, 18 found small quality improvements. The study's authors concluded, "Bundled payments have had a predominantly positive impact on both spending and quality of care, irrespective of country, medical procedure, or condition and applied research methodology" and "have led to closer collaboration among providers, better coordination of care, reduction of low-value care services and overuse of care, and greater use of preventive services."[31]

However, a systematic review of the impact of three of the CMMI bundled-payment programs reached a more equivocal conclusion: only one of the three programs studied, the CJR lower-extremity joint-replacement program, succeeded in lowering costs while also maintaining or improving quality.[32] "The evidence to date suggests that the current bundled payment design is conclusively well suited to only one clinical episode . . . ," the researchers concluded, "and may require changes to produce better value for patients with other conditions." In particular, "Studies have suggested that CMS needs to include more robust risk stratification of patients in bundled payment programs to allow higher payments for more complex patients."

Probably the best designed bundled-payment program that we have studied took place in Sweden. In 2009, the Stockholm regional government (responsible for funding health care for the roughly 2.3 million residents of the greater Stockholm metropolitan area) launched a bundled-payment program for cataract surgery and hip and knee replacement.

This early initiative had a relatively simple design. To minimize the need for risk adjustment, the hip-and-knee-replacement bundle was limited to a narrowly defined group of patients: those without comorbidities that caused functional impairment. The bundle sets a single base price that covers the entire care-delivery value chain, including diagnostics, the cost of the implant, surgery, postoperative care, rehabilitation, and follow-up visits. Patients choose either public or private providers in the region on the basis of publicly available information about waiting times, quality metrics, and health outcomes, all posted on the regional government's website. Providers are financially responsible for the cost of all complications up to two years after surgery, including all diagnostics and any nonacute complications related to the primary surgery. Providers also receive a relatively modest annual bonus (or penalty) of up to 3% of the total bundled-payment reimbursement. The adjustment is based on whether providers meet defined thresholds for reporting health outcomes and for delivering specific outcomes to patients.

The introduction of the new payment model was the catalyst for a shift in patient volumes from acute-care hospitals to less expensive specialty clinics. It has also led to process improvements in hospitals that have resulted in fewer physician visits per case, as well as fewer hospitalizations and inpatient days. Most important, the introduction of the hip-and-knee-replacement bundled payment has had a major positive impact on both health outcomes and costs. In the first two years of the program, complications decreased by 18%, reoperations by 23%, and revisions by 19%. What's more, costs per patient declined by 14% in terms of resources used by providers and 20% in terms of money paid out by the regional government.[33]

In 2013, the success of the hip-and-knee-replacement bundle led the Stockholm regional government to introduce a parallel bundle for spine surgery at the three clinics that provide 70% of all spine care in the Stockholm region. Given the variety of diagnoses and types of spine surgery, the design of the spine surgery bundle is considerably more complex. Working in collaboration with the Swedish Society of Spinal Surgeons and the Swedish digital-health company Ivbar, the government developed a system in which, unlike the joint replacement bundle, the price of the spine bundle varies depending on the specific diagnosis and risk profile of the patient.

The Ivbar digital platform used individual patient health data to create predictive models that set the precise reimbursement level for an individual patient on the basis of the patient's medical history and diagnosis, sociodemographic profile, historical costs per patient, and other factors. The system also made it possible to benchmark outcomes across providers based on case mix.

Like the joint replacement bundle, providers are financially responsible up to two years after surgery, depending on the type of complication under consideration. But a larger portion of the total reimbursement is based on the ultimate health outcomes and includes both upside and downside risk. Finally, the reporting of health outcomes to Sweden's National Quality Registry for Spine Surgery is mandatory for participating providers. If a provider does not report outcomes or reports inaccurate outcomes, they lose half of their pay-for-performance bonus; and if a provider's patients do not report their patient-reported outcome measures (PROMs), that has an impact on the bonus as well.

In the three years after the spine surgery bundle was introduced, the total length of stay for lumbar spinal stenosis (representing about 50% of all spinal surgeries) declined by 28% at participating clinics, compared with only 1% at clinics not participating in the program. And yet, despite this decline in length of stay, reoperation rates also declined by 28%, compared with a 44% increase at nonparticipating clinics in the Stockholm region and an 18% increase in four other Swedish counties with no bundled payment program during that same period. The average cost per episode decreased by 9%, and the average cost per surgery declined by 7%.[34]

The initial success of the Stockholm bundled-payment program helped spark an ambition among the public entities that fund health care in Sweden to launch a national program for value-based performance monitoring and payment (known by the Swedish acronym SVEUS). Inaugurated in

2013, the SVEUS program involved 40 participating organizations in five regions and counties and aspired to provide continuous monitoring of risk-adjusted outcomes and cost data covering 70% of the Swedish population and seven key patient groups: joint replacement, spine surgery, bariatric surgery, birth care, diabetes, stroke, and breast cancer. The data platform developed by Ivbar for risk-adjustment for the spine surgery bundle would form the backbone for risk-adjustment in the other conditions as well.

Unfortunately, the SVEUS initiative has foundered on the same sensitivities in Sweden about public-private partnership in the state-funded health system that contributed to controversy at the Karolinska University Hospital. The fact that Ivbar, a private company, was processing public health data became a step too far for some of the Swedish politicians funding the program, causing them to pull out of the national initiative. A few Swedish regions, Stockholm among them, continue to use bundled payments for some conditions, but in the absence of adequate funding, Ivbar ultimately made the business decision to no longer support the development and maintenance of its innovative data platform. As a result, Sweden has missed an extraordinary opportunity to create the first truly national bundled-payment program in the world. (We will say more about the importance to value-based health care of digital platforms like the one created by Ivbar in Chapter 6.)

Value-Based Payment in Low-Income Countries

Paying for value rather than just volume is important in all societies. But it is especially critical in low- and middle-income countries. Because health care budgets in these countries are often extremely limited, it's imperative to target scarce financial resources in the most cost-effective and highest-value way possible.[35] In Chapter 3, we described MomCare, an approach to reducing high levels of maternal mortality and to improving maternal and newborn health in three African countries: Kenya, Nigeria, and Tanzania. A key part of the MomCare program is an equally innovative approach to payment that uses a variety of different techniques to create a mutually reinforcing value-based payment system.

One of the big problems of traditional payment models for maternal and newborn care in low- and middle-income countries is that they tend to focus on the act of delivery itself to the relative neglect of other important areas such as prenatal care or preventive risk management. Traditional payment can also lead to broken referral chains (due to a hesitancy to refer mothers to other providers), cherry-picking by providers of only the healthiest patients or least complicated cases (to limit the provider's potential costs), and in reaction, a tendency on the part of expectant mothers to seek care at higher-level clinics than is often necessary (leading to higher costs and an overburdened health system).

The MomCare payment model addresses these barriers by creating a series of bundled-payments covering the 130 care steps defined by the World Health Organization for maternal and newborn-child health. Clinics that cover the full WHO cycle of care receive an additional bonus based on individual "patient journey scores" thus creating incentives for clinics to cover the full cycle of care.

The system also takes advantage of the rapid spread of mobile phones in Africa, both to create incentives for patients to seek out the most appropriate types of care and to collect data at very low cost from both providers and patients in order to track health outcomes and estimate likely costs for a given patient based on their risk profile. Each participating patient in the MomCare program receives access to an electronic "health wallet" that they can store on their mobile phone. Unlike a traditional insurance card (which simply covers all treatments), the wallet is loaded with dedicated monetary entitlements, one for each step in the care pathway (up to and including the treatment of complications, such as Caesarean sections, if necessary). The funds are ring-fenced and can only be used for the designated clinical interventions. The amount of the specific payments is initially calculated automatically by MomCare's data platform (based on the patient's risk profile and the program's accumulating data on outcomes and costs). Finally, for the payments to be distributed to the clinics, both providers and patients must continually share data with MomCare, documenting that the patient attended the clinic, received appropriate care with good health outcomes, and was not charged additional fees. These data are then used to monitor outcomes, costs, and utilization at both the patient and clinic level and to continuously adjust the amount in the patient's health wallet as her needs evolve along the care pathway.

The combination of bundled payments and the electronic health wallet create incentives for patients to seek out the right kind of care at the appropriate time and for providers to deliver cost-effective quality care. Expectant mothers know that their full costs of care will be covered, even at the beginning of their pregnancy when the actual costs of care are still uncertain. Providers know that if they deliver cost-effective, quality care, not only is payment guaranteed but they can reinvest any savings in their operations.

Although it is still early days in the program, MomCare's data-driven payment model is one example of how value-based payment can be used to coordinate and expand value-based prenatal care in societies lacking an existing health care infrastructure. Indeed, it may even be relevant to countries with more advanced health systems such as the United States, which suffers from levels of maternal mortality that are several times higher than those of other industrialized nations.

PAYING FOR VALUE FOR DRUGS, DEVICES, AND MEDICAL SUPPLIES

So far, our discussion of value-based payment has focused on how physicians and provider organizations are paid for their services. But roughly 15% to 20% of total health care spending worldwide is on the procurement not of services but of products and supplies ranging from the simplest IV bags and catheters to the most complex drugs and medical technologies. These are all vital inputs to medical care; they also represent significant costs to health systems.

Given the importance of such spending, it should be no surprise that the contracting for such inputs has been another focus of experimentation with value-based payment. Three trends in particular are gaining traction: value-based procurement of basic medical supplies, the use of health technology assessment (HTA) agencies to assess the comparative costs and benefits of new drugs, and value-based contracts for drugs and medical technologies.

Value-Based Procurement

Most hospitals and health systems have traditionally purchased medical products primarily on the basis of up-front purchasing costs. And given the pressures to constrain costs in the industry, most of the focus of negotiation between providers and suppliers has been on getting the best price for a given product. It's understandable, but too narrow a focus on cost containment can often come at the expense of improving health care value.

Take the example of the common surgical glove.[36] Because surgical gloves are critical to maintaining a septic barrier between health professionals and patients, they have become a ubiquitous commodity in any medical setting, purchased at high volume, typically on the basis of price. But the quality of surgical gloves can have an impact on both the cost and quality of care far beyond the price for the gloves themselves. Gloves of poor reliability can lead to tasks being repeated or duplicated, adding cost because of the increase in expensive staff labor time. In addition to their impact on staff productivity, poor-quality gloves can also erode the productivity of expensive fixed assets such as operating rooms. For example, latex proteins can contaminate items in the operating room, requiring a completely new setup before a patient with a latex allergy is operated on— one reason why many hospitals are going latex-free. Pinpricks in gloves of poor quality increase the risk of surgical site infections (SSIs), the most common hospital-acquired infections among surgical patients, as well as a threat to clinicians through exposure to blood-borne pathogens. A recent systematic review of the impact of SSIs on European hospitals estimated that the total medical costs for a patient with an SSI can be up to €30,000 higher than for a noninfected patient.[37] And another review of the costs of needlestick and sharp injuries among health care personnel found that such injuries could cost up to $1,691 per incidence.[38]

Value-based procurement is an attempt to address such trade-offs in order to minimize the total cost of care and maximize patient value. The approach shifts the focus away from exclusively price-based contracts for individual products toward a more holistic assessment of their impact in terms of improving patient health outcomes and reducing the total cost of care. Value-based procurement also often involves a more collaborative, less hands-off approach to negotiation and contracting between providers and suppliers, so they can work together to cocreate innovative solutions that embed a given product in broader changes in clinical practice.

For an example of how the new approach works, let's return to the Erasmus Medical Center in Rotterdam to explore how managers at a new hospital recently organized procurement for another common medical product: hospital beds. Instead of simply buying the lowest-price bed, Erasmus designed the bidding process so that potential suppliers were encouraged to take into account the impact of the beds on the hospital's total cost of care. As a result, the winning bid was an innovative offering for a "digital hospital bed" that actually collects data on patients when they are in bed and feeds it to the hospital information system.

The beds automatically measure patients' weight and alert nurses when patients who should remain in bed are not (perhaps due to a fall or simply to restlessness), so they can check on them. They also collect data that helps reduce the risk of pressure ulcers and infections. In terms of financial savings, an early estimate projects that Erasmus will be able to save €500,000 per year through increased workflow efficiency as a result of the beds. The hospital also expects the beds to contribute to reduced length of stay for some patient groups, thanks to improved weight and fluid monitoring.

To test this assumption, the contract with the supplier also includes a comprehensive service agreement in which the hospital and the supplier will collect and analyze data on hospital-associated infections, the occurrence of pressure ulcers, patient falls, and patient length of stay. This research will be used to assess the impact of the beds on patient health outcomes and to improve both the product and the hospital's processes over time.

The National Health Service (NHS) in Wales has used a similar approach to improve its services for patients who are on blood thinners. NHS Wales conducts nearly 400,000 blood tests every year for such patients. Not only are anticoagulants being used by a growing number of patients for an expanding set of conditions; they are also one of the classes of medicines most frequently identified as causing preventable harm that requires hospital admission.[39]

In the past, the health system purchased the various components of the blood-testing process (devices, consumables, etc.) separately. But in 2017, the agency shifted from contracting for discrete products to contracting for a broader, solution-based offering, including medical devices, diagnostics and consumables, training, software, and care expertise. Today, NHS Wales has a single supplier for anticoagulation point-of-care testing equipment and related consumables, such as test strips and patient self-testing meters, and one IT provider of a comprehensive anticoagulation dosing software system, including device software and mobile applications.

The new approach makes it easier for patients to monitor their own blood levels at home, with online guidance from their provider, which means they no longer have to go to the hospital for the tests. That is not only more convenient for patients; it also frees up care providers to focus on patients with more critical needs, allowing for more rational and cost-efficient resource allocation across the NHS. Finally, the software platform makes it possible to generate consistent data that when added to other health data, can document the impact of this approach on overall patient care and health outcomes (for example, its contribution to avoiding complications and preventable hospitalizations).

Health Technology Assessment

The biggest expense by far in the domain of health care supplies is the cost of drugs and new medical technologies. Pharmaceuticals alone account for roughly 10% to 20% of total health care spending in most OECD countries.[40] And the share of health dollars going to pharmaceuticals is only likely to increase, given the rapid growth in the use of more narrowly targeted (and often more expensive) specialty drugs.

It should be no surprise then that this is another area where value-based criteria are increasingly being used to inform purchasing decisions. A number of European countries are increasingly relying on so-called health technology assessment (HTA) agencies to conduct cost-benefit analyses of recently approved new drugs. Unlike traditional regulatory agencies, which approve drugs based on their demonstrated safety and efficacy as demonstrated in clinical trials, HTAs assess drugs in terms of their comparative cost-effectiveness. Their assessments, based on health-economics analysis of available data, as to whether a given medication delivers results that justify its cost have a major influence on market access and prescription behavior and can often determine the economic success or failure of a new drug.

In the United Kingdom, for example, the National Institute for Health and Clinical Excellence (NICE), an independent HTA organization funded by the Department of Health and Social Care, evaluates drugs in terms of their clinical impact versus the total cost of treatment. Although, in theory, drugs can achieve access to the UK market without NICE approval, the agency's recommendations have a major influence on prescribing behavior; failure to win a NICE endorsement can greatly limit a drug's market penetration. And since 2005, the NHS in England and Wales is legally obliged to make funds available for therapeutics that have been recommended by NICE, following its cost-benefit analysis.[41] Both Italy and Sweden have similar programs for the continuous monitoring of the cost effectiveness of new drugs in the marketplace.

The far more fragmented US health system doesn't have a government-sponsored HTA. But since 2015, the not-for-profit Institute for Clinical and Economic Review (ICER) has issued recommendations about drug cost-effectiveness that are being used by a number of US payers and providers including state Medicaid agencies, the federal Department of Veterans Affairs (or VA, which runs the largest health care system in the United States), and many private insurers and pharmacy benefit managers (PBMs).[42] Despite the fact that ICER's recommendations have no formal regulatory impact, many US payers have vouched for the benefits of independent comparative analysis. According to an account of a collaboration between the VA and ICER written by leaders of the VA health system, "Through this effort the VA has gained an objective, transparent standard to guide its drug price negotiations, and the results have not undermined in any way the clinical focus of the VA drug coverage process."[43]

Value-Based Contracting

Some forward-looking pharmaceutical companies, as well as medical technology companies, are also experimenting with innovative value-based contracts in which the ultimate payment for a drug or device is conditional on its impacts on patient health outcomes and costs. For example, Novartis has signed value-based payment deals with US payers Cigna, Aetna, and Harvard Pilgrim for its heart failure drug, Entresto. The payers receive rebates on the price of the drug if it does not deliver improved health outcomes (for instance, a reduction in hospitalizations for heart failure). Harvard Pilgrim has similar deals with Eli Lilly for Trulicity, its type 2 diabetes drug, and with Amgen for its cholesterol drug, Repatha.

Although the total number of such innovative contracts (or at least those for which information is publicly available) remains quite small, it is growing at double-digit rates. Since 2009, IHS Markit, a London-based research organization, has been tracking publicly announced value-based-contracting agreements in the global pharmaceutical industry. By the third quarter of 2021, there were approximately a thousand such agreements, with the number growing 11% per year, on average. And yet, only 202 of these agreements, about one in five, were directly linked to patient outcomes. This is another area where the lack of standardized outcomes data is hindering broader innovation in the industry.

There are some signs, however, that this may be changing. In the medical technology space, for example, Philips has a project to integrate the ICHOM outcome-measurement sets in its products in order to make it easier to collect outcomes data from remote devices and partner with providers to use the data for continuous improvement.[44] An added benefit would be to generate data demonstrating the impact of the company's products on health outcomes that could be important evidence for value-based pricing. And in the Spanish region of Catalunya, device-maker Medtronic teamed with a health care IT company to integrate remote readings from both Medtronic and non-Medtronic implantable cardiac devices into the hospital's patient monitoring system. Increasingly, these kinds of supplier-provider collaborations are becoming an important factor in provider contracting decisions.

CULTIVATING RESOURCE STEWARDSHIP

The ultimate goal of value-based payment is to create an integrated approach to delivering quality care, while also taking into account the total costs necessary to deliver it. In most provider organizations around the world, however, those who make the clinical decisions have extremely limited access to data on the total cost of care for their patients. But value-based providers tend to be different. In Chapter 3, we described how the US payer-provider Kaiser Permanente has perhaps gone further than any other health care organization to create a genuinely value-based health system. How does the organization encourage that dual focus on quality and costs among its clinicians? And how does payment fit into the organization's value-based model?

When US employers contract with Kaiser Permanente for the provision of care, they pay a capitated global payment meant to cover all required health services. But in its early years, Kaiser Permanente functioned more like, say, the UK's National Health Service—that is, its health plan made direct fee-for-service payments to the organization's network of hospitals, clinics, and physicians. Since the mid-1990s, however, Kaiser Permanente has moved progressively in the direction of value-based payment. Today, each hospital or each segment of the clinical system has value-based-payment mechanisms of some kind.

Individual physicians, for example, are salaried, with performance incentives that can adjust an individual's annual salary by about 10% (either up or down), depending on his or her clinical group's performance against a balanced scorecard of value-based metrics for quality, access, satisfaction, and financial performance. Nurses and other clinical professions are unionized, but they also have the potential for performance bonuses, although they are smaller, in the neighborhood of 3%.

These payment mechanisms are reinforced by a performance-metrics dashboard that provides a comprehensive and integrated view of a unit's performance in six key domains: clinical effectiveness, safety, service, resource stewardship, risk management, and equitable care. The high degree of transparency about health outcomes and the costs required to deliver them encourages physicians and other clinical staff to make trade-offs in the day-to-day provision of care that avoid low-value care.

The combination of value-based payment, a rich information environment that allows clinicians to assess their performance on multiple dimensions, and the climate of trust that Kaiser Permanente has created within its provider organization has contributed to a strong ethic of resource stewardship. In the focus groups with Kaiser Permanente physicians that we described in Chapter 3, participants reflected on that ethic. The doctors described how in previous, more traditional health care settings, what passed for "cost awareness" was really an emphasis on maximizing volume and billing rather than value. But according to the physicians, Kaiser Permanente was fundamentally different: cost awareness meant avoiding low-value care. "When you work in a system like this, all of a sudden [cost] becomes very important," one of the focus-group participants told the researchers. "Looking at it more from the system's point of view, . . . it's so important to you to know we're not paying for procedures that are not necessary or being duplicated or whatever."[45]

At the same time, Kaiser Permanente's value-based payment model and emphasis on resource stewardship also effectively align incentives around patient value. "The common goal is 'take good care of the patient,'" another focus-group participant told the researchers. "Financial motivation is out of the picture." "Previously . . . I was encouraged to see as many [patients] or code as highly as I possibly could, to make money for the group," said another. "[H]ere, we're actually encouraged to give *quality* care."

CREATING A CONTEXT FOR SUCCESS

In every example that we have described in this chapter, value-based payment is just one piece of a mosaic of mutually reinforcing changes that serve to encourage the value-based behaviors we described at the beginning of this chapter and to reorient payers, providers, and suppliers to the delivery of high-quality, cost-effective care. In our work, we have identified six critical levers for leaders to deploy to ensure that value-based-payment initiatives actually achieve their intended goal of improving patient value and are sustainable over the long term.

Link Payment to Outcomes Measurement and Transparency

Because value-based health care is about delivering better health outcomes for the money spent, measuring and reporting health outcomes is a prerequisite for achieving sustainable value-based payment reform. The more payers and providers can track metrics that reflect the actual health outcomes delivered to patients, the more they will be able to link payment to the outcomes that really matter to patients and ensure that new payment models actually improve outcomes (or at a minimum, do not erode them).

Does this mean paying more to providers who deliver better outcomes than their peers? Not necessarily—and, we would argue, never at the level of the individual clinician. Organizations need to be careful that new payment models don't end up creating unintended disincentives to sharing and learning from outcomes data and to cooperation around continuous improvement. As we saw in Chapter 2, the simple act of tracking outcomes data and making it transparent is in itself a strong incentive to change clinician behavior, and no payment system should upset that powerful but delicate dynamic. Therefore, if a health system does choose to reward providers for outcomes delivered, such a bonus should be relatively modest and awarded collectively to a team of providers rather than to individual clinicians—to avoid creating incentives for participants to game the system and undermine the kind of collective learning on which continuous improvement depends.

This is the approach, for example, at Martini Klinik and at Kaiser Permanente. The variable component of each physician's income is determined according to the clinic's overall performance and outcomes, not according to each physician's individual performance. That approach encourages clinicians to support one another in the learning process, allocate patients based on individual capabilities and experience, and engage in continuous improvement together rather than to compete to outperform one another.

Another approach for linking payment to outcomes measurement is to simply pay a bonus or other premium to providers who agree to make their outcomes data transparent. Think of this as "pay-for-participation" rather than "pay-for-performance." This is the approach, for example, that the French cataract outcomes-measurement pilot (described in Chapter 2) is taking. Participating cataract surgeons receive an extra payment for each patient whose outcomes they share with the pilot project. Such a "transparency bonus" has the advantage not only of creating incentives for clinicians to collect and share data, it also communicates that payers consider outcomes measurement to be real work and an essential part of clinical best practice. It can be a useful practice, especially in national health systems where rigorous outcomes measurement is just getting started and where there are no national mandates about collecting outcomes data.

This pay-for-participation approach can also be extended to participation in quality-improvement initiatives and the adoption of new value-based care pathways. A striking example of this approach is the network of 23 collaborative quality initiatives (CQIs) in the state of Michigan, probably the largest collection of multi-hospital quality-improvement programs in the United States.[46] Much like the continuous-improvement efforts at Sweden's quality registries, the CQIs are specialty based and physician led. But Blue Cross Blue Shield of Michigan, by far the state's leading payer (an artifact of the historical dominance of the automobile industry in Michigan) has played a central role. The insurer supports the centralized coordinating centers that lead the CQIs with more than $61 million in annual funding and has created a variety of financial incentives to encourage participation in the improvement initiatives.

For example, in 2018, a CQI program known as the Michigan Opioid Prescribing and Engagement Network developed a postoperative care pathway that minimized the use of highly addictive opioids for managing pain after surgery.[47] Blue Cross Blue Shield modified the fee-for-service payment schedule that allowed for an additional 35% reimbursement for professional fees for surgeons to cover the additional work involved in adopting the new care pathway (which includes extensive counseling of patients on how to minimize opioids in pain management with the goal of reducing inadvertent opioid addiction). The incentive helped stimulate rapid adoption of the program at Michigan hospitals.

Extend the Scope of Payment to the Full Cycle of Care

As payers and providers move toward value-based payment, they also need to manage the tension between comprehensiveness and complexity. On the one hand, many value-based payment initiatives fail because they are focused too narrowly on a single point in the care pathway, and, therefore, do not create incentives for providers to work together to innovate across the full value chain of care delivery or manage the total cost of care. In contrast, successful initiatives extend the scope of value-based payments to the full cycle of care (for example, expanding payments to include diagnostics, surgery, and physical therapy) so that providers have an incentive to share information, cooperate with one another to redesign care pathways, and provide the highest-quality care in the most cost-effective manner. Value-based payment initiatives tend to fail when they are limited to only a subset of the care required to achieve desired patient outcomes.

On the other hand, as payers and providers strive for comprehensiveness, they must also be careful not to exacerbate the very complexity and fragmentation that value-based payment is meant to resolve. The existence of too many different payment models or, as we saw earlier in the discussion of value-based contracting on the part of pharmaceutical companies, of different payment agreements for different providers developed by competing payers, creates transaction costs and coordination problems that will quickly become obstacles to the spread of the new payment models. One of the key learnings to emerge from CMMI's Alternative Payment Model program is to focus on fewer payment models, design them to work together, and invest in a comprehensive approach to design, benchmarking, and metric selection before introducing new models.[48] (We'll say more about the critical role of government and public policy in supporting value-based health care in Chapter 7.)

One particular obstacle to extending the scope of payment to the full cycle of care that is unique to the US health system is the phenomenon of "health insurance churn." Because the US payer landscape is highly fragmented and because health insurance is typically linked to employment status, individuals frequently move from one health insurance plan to another when they change jobs. This regular churn in plan membership creates a strong disincentive for health insurers to invest in early interventions, because the financial payoff (in the form of avoiding relatively expensive acute care later in the disease cycle) typically happens long after the individual has left the insurer's health plan. This is one important reason why some version of Medicare Advantage may make sense for US commercial payers. Requirements to keep members in a Medicare-Advantage-like plan for longer periods of time, and irrespective of their employment status, would allow payers to secure a long-term benefit from early interventions, creating new incentives to focus resources on upstream treatments.

Adjust for Differences in Risk

One of the unintended consequences that designers of value-based payment models need to guard against is inadvertently creating incentives that encourage providers to cherry-pick only the healthiest patients. Effective value-based payment systems include robust risk adjustment to account for patient mix, eliminate adverse selection, and set prices that are fair to all providers, including those managing the most complex and expensive-to-treat cases. The risk-adjustment methodology developed for the Swedish spine surgery bundle illustrates how advances in computing power and the growing availability of large data sets make possible more flexible and sophisticated approaches to risk adjustment.

Getting risk-adjustment right will be especially important to make sure that value-based payment models do not unintentionally exacerbate health inequity by penalizing health systems that serve disadvantaged populations with higher levels of comorbidities and less access to quality care. In this respect, the risk-adjustment mechanisms in the Medicare Advantage plan are a good example of how adjusting payment for risk can become an incentive to better document and address the health status of all social groups, especially the most disadvantaged sectors of the population.

Use Data to Raise Awareness About Quality and Costs

To meet the growing need for more comprehensive tracking of outcomes and costs, to have value-based payments cover the full cycle of care, and to implement value-based payments at scale, both payers and providers are increasingly relying on advanced-analytics platforms. These platforms integrate data from several sources and continuously feed information to all stakeholders on how they are performing on value.

We'll talk more about the promise of advanced analytics in health care in the next chapter. Here, we simply want to make the point that high-quality, transparent data on utilization of resources (and how that utilization affects both costs and outcomes) is a critical resource for getting clinicians to take responsibility for both costs and quality—whether or not organizations have begun to introduce value-based payment.

Build an Environment of Trust

For value-based payment models to drive changes in clinical practice, they need to be introduced in an environment of trust among providers, payers, and patients—the kind of environment that Kaiser Permanente has created. That may sound like a tall order, given the long history of adversarial relations between payers and providers. Still, health systems can take a number of steps to build that trust and ensure sufficient buy-in for value-based payment reform. For example, payers can make clear that the focus of initiatives is not just cost containment but also improvement in outcomes. They can also involve providers in the design, implementation, and refinement of payment models, including defining outcomes and reviewing performance bonus criteria. The more transparent the design of value-based payment models, the more likely they will be accepted by clinicians.

Probably the most important way to build payer-provider trust is for payers to commit to the long-term sharing of the savings that result from more cost-effective care with providers. When value-based payment models are implemented by payers primarily as a means to reduce costs in the face of immediate budget pressure, or if savings are shared in the short term but then become the justification to reduce payment rates in the long term, then it becomes difficult for providers to see a sustainable path to success. As a result, they are likely to resist the transition to value-based payment.

Encourage a Culture of Continuous Improvement

By now, it should be clear to the reader that, in our view, implementing value-based payment is not a one-time event. Rather, it needs to be part of an ongoing transformation of clinical practice and health system management where the goal is not merely to save money but to improve value delivered to the patient. Health systems don't necessarily have to wait until they have advanced-measurement and risk-adjustment systems in place to get started—as long as they adopt a learning mindset in which organizations commit to experimentation, innovation, and continuous improvement over time. Start by using the metrics and methodologies already in place, invest in and learn from pilots, and only implement new payment models systemwide when the key elements for success are tested and in place. In this respect, perhaps one of the most important positive results of CMMI's Alternative Payment Models initiative has been the creation of the Healthcare Payment Learning and Action Network, a nationwide group of public and private health care leaders that supports stakeholders throughout the US health system as they adopt value-based payment models and helps analyze the results.[49]

Once established, a continuous-improvement culture focused on patient value can become a more powerful incentive than value-based payment itself. Take the example of Geisinger Health System, a $6.3 billion US regional payer-provider with an integrated delivery system that has been a pioneer in value-based health care. Over the years, Geisinger has experimented with a variety of alternative payment models. The system is well-known for its groundbreaking bundled-payment program. In 2002, Geisinger became one of the first provider organizations in the United States to tie its physicians' compensation to performance using a set of quality and efficiency measures. Yet in 2016, the company eliminated its pay-for-performance bonus and moved to a pure salary model of physician compensation. The goal of the move was to radically simplify the Geisinger compensation system. "At the end of the day, there's never any perfect system to incent exactly the right things," said Jaewon Ryu, Geisinger's former chief medical officer and, since 2019, its CEO. "You're either missing something that should be in the measurement pool or maybe some things in there aren't exactly the right things."[50]

Instead of relying mainly on financial incentives to drive individual provider behavior, Geisinger chose to rely on the system's strong institutional norms, commitment to outcomes transparency, and physicians' intrinsic motivation to deliver high-value care. The Geisinger culture includes mandatory adherence to a social contract that encourages the best patient care, multidisciplinary collaboration, and innovation. Strong norms allow Geisinger to give physicians the autonomy to make complex care decisions without worrying about how each decision will affect their income and to put their individual autonomy to the service of the shared goal of maximizing value delivered to patients.

The Geisinger story demonstrates that nonfinancial norms and culture can often be more important than financial incentives in encouraging the kind of provider behaviors that are important to value-based health care. It also suggests that the appropriate balance between financial and nonfinancial incentives for value-based health care is likely to evolve over time. In some situations, value-based payments will be the primary catalyst for the long-term reorientation of health systems around value delivered to patients. But as value-based norms and cultures develop in provider organizations, and health systems put in place the analytics to make outcomes and costs transparent, financial incentives may play a less central role.

Value-Based Payment: Action Steps

PAYERS AND PROVIDERS

1. **Link payment to outcomes measurement.** Health outcomes delivered to patients are the ultimate measure of performance. Design payment models to create incentives for tracking and sharing outcomes data.

2. **Extend value-based payment to the full cycle of care.** Design payment models to integrate care delivery and that encourage a holistic tracking of costs per patient along the entire care pathway.

3. **Invest in risk-adjustment.** Adjust payment models for risk to discourage cherry-picking and encourage health equity.

4. **Use data to raise awareness about quality and costs.** Leverage the growing availability of health data to put a spotlight on clinical practices that lead to low-value care.

5. **Build an environment of trust.** Think beyond immediate cost containment to create sustainable payment models with shared savings for all stakeholders.

6. **Encourage a culture of continuous improvement.** Put value-based payment in the context of strong cultural norms for continuous improvement and innovation.

7. **Walk before you run.** Take an evolutionary approach to value-based payment to minimize shocks, manage risks, and avoid resistance. Start by measuring the care delivered (so you know what you are paying for), understand total patient costs per episode of care, and track outcomes in a safe learning environment.

SUPPLIERS *(in particular, pharma and med-tech companies)*

1. **Think "beyond the pill" and "beyond the device."** Offer solutions, not just products, and emphasize how they will improve patient value by delivering better health outcomes, lower total-system costs, or both.

2. **Embrace value-based contracting.** But avoid the proliferation of different models across multiple payers and providers.

3. **Invest in outcomes tracking.** Support the collection of standardized health-outcomes data as a critical evidence base for value-based payments.

4. **Partner with payers and providers.** Create or join emerging value-based ecosystems to jointly develop and test new solutions. Build trusted relationships with shared upside.

POLICYMAKERS

1. **Create policy incentives for payment innovation.** Encourage payment innovation and establish mechanisms to learn from experience.

2. **Avoid complexity.** Define common principles for a limited number of value-based payment models in the national health system.

3. **Encourage payer-provider collaboration.** Through policy and regulation, encourage payers and providers to team up on the design and implementation of value-based payment models that create incentives for moving to a high-value health system.

PATIENTS

1. **Understand how your providers are paid.** Is their compensation linked to value delivered to the patient or primarily to the volume of activities they deliver?

2. **Demand price transparency.** Ask for prices of care and procedures before undergoing treatment.

3. **Factor payment models into your choice of providers.** Consider how payment affects the quality of care delivered.

CHAPTER 6

HARNESSING DIGITAL HEALTH TO IMPROVE PATIENT VALUE

Nearly one third of all the data generated in the world today is created by the health care industry. The total quantity of health-related data is growing faster than that of any other industry, including financial services, roughly doubling every year.[1] According to one estimate, the total universe of available health-related data increased from approximately 153 exabytes in 2013 (an exabyte is 1 billion gigabytes, or 10^{18} bytes) to more than 2,300 exabytes in 2020.[2] In the process, the health care industry has become the world's most data-rich knowledge industry.

What's driving this massive explosion in health data? One factor is the increasing digitization of existing health information. Patient health records previously kept on paper are now stored in digital form in electronic medical records (EMRs). Organizations are digitizing core functions, automating some of the basic tasks related to patient care, administration, and finance. Payers, in particular, are accumulating vast databases of patient information related to payment and reimbursement.

Another factor is the increasing intelligence of traditional medical devices and equipment. For instance, early medical-resonance-imaging machines (MRIs) captured approximately 2,000 images in an average brain scan; today, they capture 20,000, and each of those scans consists of double the resolution images, thus more data.[3]

The desire on the part of consumers both to interact digitally with their caregivers and to track their own vital health statistics is also contributing to the data explosion. The rapid growth in telehealth visits spurred by the coronavirus pandemic has led to the growth in new electronic platforms for patients to interact with caregivers, generating even more data. Or take the example of the rapidly expanding market for health-related wearable technologies (digital earbuds that check our temperature, digital watches that track our cardiac status, and the like), which is growing so fast that it is forecast to become a $20 billion market by 2025.[4] The adjacent mobile-health applications market segment is smaller but expected to grow even faster—to $33 billion by 2025 (there are more than 350,000 health apps on the market today; more than 90,000 of them were added in 2020 alone).[5] And the so-called "connected devices" market—mobile-based remote-monitoring equipment, such as glucometers, wireless scales, blood-pressure monitors, and heart-rate monitors, will grow to be an estimated $88 billion market by 2025 and $268 billion by 2030.[6] So far, the FDA has approved more than 60 digital therapeutic devices that help patients prevent, manage, and treat their own medical conditions, from diabetes and chronic obstructive pulmonary disease to cancer and mental disorders.[7]

Finally, an especially important driver of health care's data explosion is the growing knowledge- and data-intensity of medical practice itself. For example, as our knowledge of human genetics grows, it is becoming possible to customize highly targeted therapies for individuals with specific genetic profiles, an example of precision medicine. But translating genetic information into clinical treatments requires access to vast bodies of data from disparate sources to generate statistically valid recommendations. According to one study, to discover the so-called genetic cancer "drivers" (genetic alterations that contribute to malignant phenotypes) in 2% or more of patients with cancer, researchers would need to analyze the full genetic sequence of more than 100,000 cancers.[8]

The need for such data as evidence to inform cutting-edge clinical practice—as well as the metadata (data about the data) that such research generates—also contributes to the data explosion. And genomics represents only one category of relevant health information. For instance, as payers and providers increasingly focus on the social determinants of health as highly predictive risk factors for chronic disease, data that had rarely been considered as important health information in the past are becoming critical evidence for the development of robust clinical guidelines for effective prevention and treatment.

All these developments have contributed to the creation of a more than $100 billion (in revenue) digital-health market, which is expected to grow at more than 20% per year to more than $600 billion by 2030.[9] Investors are taking notice. With the exception of internet technologies, health tech is the largest sector for venture investment, bigger than consumer goods, finance, energy and utilities, food and beverages, and electronics combined.[10] In 2021, venture investors closed over 700 deals in the United States alone, with funding of nearly $30 billion, more than double the investment of the previous year, and more than four times the total investment in 2019.[11] Although much of this growth has been driven by the pandemic (in particular, the rapid shift to telehealth), and deal funding in the first half of 2022 lagged the previous year's pace, the multiyear growth trajectory also reflects longer-term trends such as the growing focus on health care consumerization and on health equity and associated innovations in community care. Worldwide, there are now more than 70 digital-health unicorns (startups with a market value of more than $1 billion), collectively valued at over $150 billion.[12] Meanwhile, established companies—health care payers and providers, medical technology companies, health-information companies such as the dominant EMR vendors Epic and Cerner, and big-tech platform companies such as Apple, Google, Amazon, and Meta are all positioning themselves to compete in the expanding digital-health market.

We think digital health has the potential to be a critical enabler of value-based health care. Digital technologies, of course, provide new ways to treat patients more cheaply and efficiently—for instance, through digital therapeutics or remote monitoring. And as we saw in the story of Intermountain Healthcare in Chapter 4, they also make it possible to connect patients more seamlessly to their caregivers and to the health system as a whole. Digital technologies are also necessary to automate the routine collection, sharing, and analysis of health outcomes data that we have championed in earlier chapters, reducing the burden of data collection for clinicians.

As important as all these goals are, however, the real opportunity in digital health for improving patient value is in helping clinicians make sense of the vast and growing quantities of health-related data in order to provide ever more targeted and customized treatments for individual patients. In the long term, perhaps the most revolutionary applications in the domain of digital health will involve the use of artificial intelligence (AI), machine learning, and predictive analytics to detect hidden patterns in and generate diagnostic insights from all that data, predict when specific individuals may be susceptible to a given disease, and suggest pathways for prevention or treatment.[13]

According to cardiologist Eric Topol, executive vice president at the San Diego biomedical research institute Scripps Research and former chairman of cardiovascular medicine at Cleveland Clinic, "The promise of artificial intelligence in medicine is to provide composite, panoramic views of individuals' medical data; to improve decision making; to avoid errors such as misdiagnosis and unnecessary procedures; to help in the ordering and interpretation of appropriate tests; and to recommend treatments."[14]

By combining the more systematic collection of standardized health outcomes data with the growing availability of health information of all kinds and the development of sophisticated techniques for predictive analytics founded on AI and machine learning, the health care sector has the potential to build global digital platforms to support continuous learning. Researchers and clinicians could use these platforms to analyze outcomes variation, identify and evaluate the latest clinical innovations, and rapidly translate new insights into continuously improving clinical guidelines and sophisticated software tools for clinical decision support.

Realizing that potential, however, requires acknowledging that so far at least, health care has lagged behind other industries in the development of powerful digital applications such as AI, predictive analytics, and big data. Although the use of digital technologies is growing rapidly, health care invests only about 5% of revenue in information technology, far less than other industries.[15] Even more important, in sectors such as the consumer industry, an already existing infrastructure—bar codes, credit card data that links purchases to the individual, and other standardized data components—makes possible the kind of sophisticated data analysis that leads to new insights into consumer behavior. In manufacturing, clearly defined standards for the internet of things make possible advanced applications such as predictive modeling that anticipates when aircraft engines will require maintenance.

In health care, we are not there yet. The extraordinary complexity of human biology and medical decision-making, combined with the lack of agreed-upon metrics and comprehensive standards for what technologists call *interoperability* (the capacity to easily share and link data from a variety of sources), have so far limited our ability to leverage such techniques to fundamentally improve clinical decision-making. In their absence, the explosion in the availability of health-related information risks simply to overwhelm clinicians and patients with new degrees of information complexity.

What will it take to overcome these obstacles? The short answer is: better cybersecurity to protect patient data and privacy, while enabling data sharing and analytics; shared technical standards to ensure seamless interoperability among health-information systems; and new practices, rules, and regulations to integrate new technologies into clinical practice, and to balance data privacy and data transparency. It will also require the more systematic collection of standardized health-outcomes data as a critical foundation enabling researchers to "train" the machine-learning algorithms of the future, validate their performance, and use them to improve patient value over time.

But before addressing these challenges in detail, let's first dig deeper into what is happening in digital health today and what, if we get it right, digital health can make possible in the future.

DIGITAL HEALTH: FROM AUTOMATION TO TRANSFORMATION

In 1990, during the height of the reengineering fad in business, *Harvard Business Review* published an article entitled "Reengineer: Don't Automate, Obliterate."[16] It was a provocative title for an article that made a commonsense observation: it's one thing to use information technology simply to automate existing business processes, but it is quite another to use information technology to fundamentally transform how work is done. Focus on the latter, not the former, was the article's message.

The health care industry is poised between these two options today. Many of the applications of digital technology in health care, especially at established provider organizations, automate existing processes and practices—for example, for filling out of forms and other operational tasks or for eliminating the duplication of services through online databases for lab work or imaging.[17]

Such uses can make existing processes more efficient and save costs, eliminate waste, or replace specific tasks or steps in the diagnostic or therapeutic pathway, but they typically don't lead to the fundamental transformation of clinical practice. What's more, most digital-health systems and applications today, especially at traditional provider organizations, still exist in siloes, locked away in the legacy systems of different departments or units, using different frameworks and standards, which makes it difficult to share and aggregate data.

Even enterprise-wide applications can suffer from similar problems. For example, one of the limitations of today's dominant EMR systems is that depending on the specific EMR vendor and the degree of customization done for a given hospital system, the data captured in the EMR system of one hospital is often uninterpretable by the EMR system of another. What's more, because these systems were initially designed primarily as documentation systems to support reimbursement in a fee-for-service market, they have proven to be a relatively poor foundation for the development of the kind of advanced analytics that are critical for precision medicine and value-based health care.

Other applications, however, are having a more profound impact. For example, new consumer-facing applications are helping patients answer immediate health questions online without necessarily speaking to a doctor or nurse, talk to a provider through telemedicine without having to visit the office, or when urgent care is required, guide them to appropriate and less costly sites of care, such as an urgent care clinic rather than the emergency room. As the experience during Covid has made clear, many patients like this way of connecting to the health system, and some providers like Intermountain are investing heavily in consumer-facing digital-health applications to help improve access to the health system.

More and more health care institutions are also finding ways to use big data and advanced analytics to combine diverse data sources—including patient records, clinical trials, insurance claims, government records, registries, wearable devices, and even social media—to analyze care delivery in a truly value-oriented way. Interestingly, this trend is often being pioneered by payers.

Consider, for example, how VGZ, one of the largest nonprofit health insurers in the Netherlands, leveraged the massive data it has accumulated about its clients' interactions with the health system to identify opportunities for saving an estimated 5% of health care spending without negatively impacting health outcomes delivered to patients.[18]

One area the company has focused on is physician prescribing behavior (medications represent about 15% of the insurer's total costs)—in particular, their prescribing of generic versus branded drugs. In the Netherlands, as in most countries, once a drug goes off patent and generic alternatives become available, pharmacies are obliged to use the generic alternative because they typically cost less than a tenth of the price of branded medicines.

Doctors, however, can override the recommendation by declaring that medical necessity requires the patient to receive the expensive branded drug instead. Since the active ingredient in generics is the same as in branded drugs, however, prescriptions for a branded drug on the grounds of medical necessity should be rare—less than 5% of prescriptions, according to calculations based on best practices.

An in-depth analysis of the prescriptions paid for by VGZ, however, found that for a number of important drugs, the expensive branded version accounted for approximately 30% of prescriptions. The initial analysis showed, for example, that switching those clients who had been prescribed a branded anticholesterol drug to generics would save more than €30 million. So in an effort to increase the rate of generic adoption among doctors, VGZ decided to use its own records to pinpoint exactly who appeared to be overprescribing branded drugs.

The company looked, in particular, for anomalies and outliers that indicated overprescribing behavior by specific doctors and groups and unusual combinations of prescribers and prescriptions. The analysis focused on the top 25 medicines with the greatest potential for reducing prescription drug costs. A compelling visualization showed the prescribing behavior of groups of doctors and, when required, the prescribing behavior of individual doctors as well. (See Figure 6.1.) For the first time, VGZ could show physician groups how their behavior compared with best practices. Extreme outliers were highly visible.

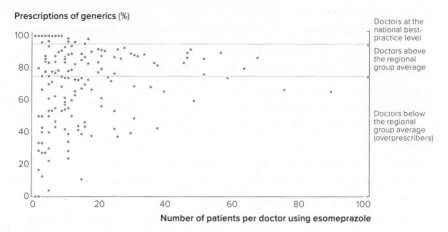

FIGURE 6.1 Dutch insurer VGZ uses big data to influence physician prescribing behavior.

The chart plots a subset of approximately 160 Dutch physicians based on the degree to which they prescribe the generic version of the drug esomeprazole (used to treat excess stomach acid). The data allows the insurer to identify who is oversubscribing higher-priced branded versions of the drug.

Source: *BCG analysis.*

By putting a spotlight on prescribing behavior, the data visualization became an opportunity for VGZ to have constructive discussions with providers about the financial impact of their (sometimes, inadvertent) choices. As a result, VGZ was able to bring down the rate of branded-drug prescriptions to below 5% for nearly all the drugs studied, saving the insurer more than 10% of its total pharmaceutical costs. Similar bench-marking analyses have since been used in other areas such as diagnostics, hospital contracting, and claims verification. For instance, VGZ has developed advanced analytic algorithms to automatically analyze millions of lines of data across different areas of care in order to highlight suspicious combinations of treatments and instances where medical specialists seem to routinely choose the most complex and expensive treatments.

In Australia, the department of health in the state of Victoria used similar techniques to analyze resource utilization in the regional health system.[19] Federal and state governments in Australia, along with private insurers, each pay roughly one-third of all health care spending that is not covered by patients' out-of-pocket fees. But institutional payers have little visibility into—and no control over—one another's expenditures, which contributes both to duplication and to gaps in services.

The health department wanted to create an integrated picture of health care across the state by combining data about health needs from population surveys with information about services paid for by each of the responsible payers and with outcomes data from patient, population, and clinical sources. Even though all this data had been collected for some time, the complexities of aggregating and interpreting it had discouraged earlier efforts to analyze the combined data.

The health department developed a model of the natural progression of chronic diseases in order to organize the more than 400 health-related measures gathered. The analysis was conducted across some 200 geographic units, each with a population of roughly 25,000 people. The approach allowed the department to pinpoint specific needs, identify areas of over- and undersupply, and assess the effectiveness of health services received, while still maintaining individual privacy.

For example, the analysis looked at the rate of hospitalizations for ambulatory-care-sensitive conditions—which include illnesses such as diabetes, asthma, and chronic obstructive pulmonary disease—because hospitalization rates are often inversely correlated to patient access to primary care. The department learned that while primary-care providers were quite effective in managing chronic diseases in more affluent communities, they were relatively ineffective in low-income communities, resulting in higher hospitalization rates, mortality levels, and costs. The department estimated that even a modest reduction in avoidable hospital admissions through better primary care would save health care payers an estimated A$60 million per year.

Such uses of big data to improve health-care value are exciting and will grow in importance as more and better data become available for analysis. But the digital-health applications with, perhaps, the most potential to genuinely transform clinical practice use cutting-edge techniques from AI and machine learning at scale. With enough access to high-quality data, such applications will be able to predict the likely health outcomes for patients with a given profile, disease, or condition, allowing clinicians to identify at-risk individuals early and recommend appropriate clinical interventions at the right time.

Because of the early adoption of international data standards for image analysis, AI and machine learning are already transforming

medical specialties such as radiology and pathology by radically shorten-
ing analysis time, cutting costs, and supplementing the human judgment
of radiologists and pathologists.[20] Automated transcription from voice to
text and natural language processing are helping extract data from EMR
notes. And we saw in Chapter 3 how Oak Street Health is using machine
learning and predictive analytics to categorize patient health needs more
precisely so as to focus resources on those with the highest health risks.

Within relatively narrow and well-defined domains, clinical researchers
are also using such techniques to generate important insights for clinical
care. For example, one team of researchers has developed a dynamic prediction system for renal transplant survival, using AI analysis of clinical,
histological, and immunological data from 18 academic transplant centers across Europe, the United States, and South America.[21] Another has
used data on Covid-19 patients drawn from some 20 health care institutions around the globe to train an AI system to predict the future oxygen
requirements and clinical outcomes for symptomatic patients, based on
inputs such as vital signs, laboratory data, and chest X-rays.[22]

Entire companies are emerging to do this kind of predictive analysis
at an industrial scale. Take, for example, the Chicago-based health-data
company Tempus, which has assembled the world's largest library of clinical and molecular data on patients suffering from a variety of diseases.
The company has analyzed clinical notes, lab reports, pathology images,
and radiology scans and combining it with DNA, RNA, and proteomic
data on the molecular structure of tumors for nearly a third of all US cancer patients. The Tempus operating system uses advanced analytics and
machine learning algorithms to structure the data, analyze thousands of
clinical and molecular data points, and identify meaningful population
segments.

So far, Tempus has mainly used its analytical engine and databases to
help pharmaceutical companies accelerate R&D, for example, by providing real-world comparative data for clinical trial design. But in theory,
the approach could be used to develop distinctive therapeutic options that
help physicians deliver highly personalized patient care. A team of Tempus data scientists recently worked with clinicians at Geisinger Health
System in Pennsylvania to use AI to predict patients' risk of developing atrial fibrillation (AFib) and AFib-related stroke. The team used 1.6
million electrocardiograms (ECGs) to train a deep neural network to
predict who among a population of people without a previous history of

AFib would develop the condition in the future. The model successfully predicted high risk for new-onset AFib in 62% of those patients in the sample who went on have an AFib-related stroke within three years of the index ECG.[23] The result led the FDA to award Tempus's AFib prediction model with its "breakthrough device" designation for clinically useful AI applications.

TOWARD DIGITAL LEARNING PLATFORMS ON A GLOBAL SCALE

Such pioneering efforts point the way to the ultimate promise of digital health: the development of digital learning platforms on a global scale. Such platforms will help clinical researchers generate new scientific evidence and clinical insights from the rapidly accumulating universe of digitized health data about what Nicholas Schork, director of human biology at the J. Craig Venter Institute, has described as "the myriad factors . . . that shape a person's response to a particular treatment."[24] Those insights can then be used to inform decision-support systems that guide clinicians in ever more refined and personalized clinical interventions, delivering the right interventions at the right time to each individual patient.

It's always difficult to describe a future that doesn't exist yet. But imagine a world where standardized health outcomes data of the kind we have argued for throughout this book are routinely collected by national health systems and, with appropriate adjustment for patient risk factors and provider case mix, are made routinely available for aggregation and analysis on a global scale. (See Figure 6.2.)

Researchers would be able to combine this standardized outcomes data with other health data from a broad variety of sources—quality registries, provider networks, hospitals, biobanks, genetic databases, government population statistics, and the like—to compare comprehensive anonymized patient profiles and identify relevant variations in outcomes across providers, regions, and nations or within a defined population of patients across all institutions and geographies. When that happens, the phenomenon of outcomes variation ceases to be merely a problem to solve; it becomes an asset from which health systems can learn.

In some situations, the most likely explanation for differences in outcomes among comparable populations of patients may be meaningful

FIGURE 6.2 A conceptual model of global digital learning platforms.

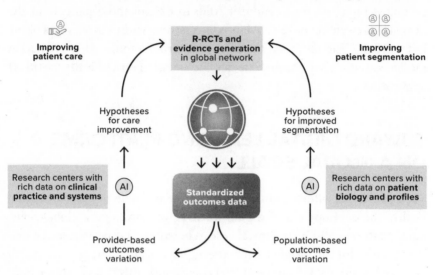

The aggregation of standardized outcomes data on a global scale will allow researchers to detect patterns and develop hypotheses about the sources of outcomes variation, generating new scientific evidence to incorporate in clinical decision-support systems.

Source: *BCG analysis.*

differences in clinical practice across providers—for example, differences in how they organize care pathways or use clinical guidelines, in the use of specific clinical interventions, in the distinctive capabilities of their clinicians, or in the degree of patient engagement in treatment. Here the goal of comparative research would be to correlate outcome variations to these factors and develop hypotheses about the link between specific types of interventions and the health outcomes ultimately achieved.

In other situations, however, the differences in outcomes may have less to do with differences in clinical practice. Rather, they may signal important differences among various subsegments in what clinical researchers had previously understood as a single undifferentiated patient population (for example, differences in genetic profiles or gene expression, in behavior profiles and habits, in medical history, or other factors). Here, the goal of comparative research will be to develop hypotheses about the links between personal traits and the health outcomes ultimately achieved, thus refining the diagnostic precision of patient-segmentation categories with the goal of further customizing treatment for each subsegment.

Given the complexity of modern medicine, the number of variables and potential causal factors for any given pattern of outcomes variation will be extremely large. Therefore, much of the initial pattern recognition to identify the most plausible explanatory hypotheses will be done by applications using AI and machine learning that roam this vast universe of standardized data. Such applications will be able to analyze a broad range of variables across large data sets, detecting patterns and generating insights about what might most plausibly explain the observable variations in health outcomes. For example, AI is already being used to increase diagnostic precision by helping clinicians distinguish between high- and low-risk patients for a given condition and to address the problem of diagnostic overuse (and underuse) by targeting expensive diagnostic tests on those most in need.[25]

Of course, such AI-generated hypotheses will have to be validated and, in many cases, tested in prospective randomized clinical trials on new patient populations to confirm the causal relationships between specific clinical interventions and outcomes achieved or the predictive value of a specific patient characteristic or segment. Here the model should be the registry-based randomized controlled trials (R-RCTs) pioneered at quality registries such as Swedeheart that we described in Chapter 2. The design of large trials, using real-world clinical evidence from populations of patients at clinical centers around the world and assembled rapidly across the international network engaged in shared outcomes measurement, would enable much faster cycle times of evidence generation and contribute to both the identification of ways to improve care for a given population of patients and to find meaningful differences within today's population segments that improve diagnostic precision.

The ultimate goal, however, will be to integrate these new insights about diagnosis and treatment into new clinical guidelines and AI-based analytical tools in clinical decision-support systems. Such systems would help clinicians on the front line of care navigate the daunting complexity of health information, and translate that information into strategies of care for specific patients (based on their profile, risk category, and membership in a given population segment or disease group)—for example, allowing clinicians to get upstream of disease risk, to highlight and manage critical gaps in care, or to identify social and other determinants of health that are root causes of a patient's current condition.[26]

Such tools must also be tested and validated through prospective randomized trials to assess their safety and efficacy, to uncover and address any unknown biases in the resulting algorithms, and ultimately to win the trust of the global clinical community in their accuracy and efficacy.[27] And once integrated into care delivery workflow software, they will be continuously evaluated for their real-world impact on patient health outcomes, and regularly upgraded as new evidence comes to light.[28]

In summary, global digital-health platforms would take the capabilities for learning, continuous improvement, and clinical innovation at the national quality registries described in Chapter 2 to an entirely new level. Indeed, it would be systematic clinical research and innovation at an industrial scale. What's more, the combination of precision diagnostics and more customized clinical interventions would finally realize the decades-long promise of precision medicine.

Of course, the kind of digital learning networks that we envision don't exist in full-fledged form yet. But in bits and pieces, they are starting to emerge. Consider, for example, the Community in Oncology for Rapid Learning, known by the acronym CORAL. CORAL is a global community of partners from the academic and clinical worlds with the common goal of sharing routine cancer data and using AI methods to generate new knowledge and insights from the data. Formed at the 2016 conference of the European Society for Radiotherapy and Oncology, the group now consists of some 50 participating institutions across 16 countries, including the Princess Margaret Cancer Centre in Toronto, Canada; the Moffitt Cancer Center in Tampa, Florida; the Christie and Cambridge NHS trusts in the United Kingdom; the Tata Memorial Hospital in Mumbai, India; Erasmus Medical Center in the Netherlands, and Shanghai Medical College at Fudan University in China. (See Figure 6.3.)

In the first five years of its existence, CORAL researchers have analyzed more than 23,000 lung-cancer patients across eight health care institutions in five countries to develop a validated model predicting post-treatment two-year survival.[29] Another focus of the consortium is rare diseases, such as anal cancer, in which 18 participating institutions from Europe, Australia, Canada, and the United Kingdom are creating the largest distributed data set for this rare cancer and developing outcome prediction models.

FIGURE 6.3 **CORAL is an international network of 50 clinical and research institutions.**

The Community in Oncology for Rapid Learning (CORAL) is a global community of partners in 16 countries with the common goal of sharing routine cancer data and using AI methods to generate new knowledge and insights from the data.

Source: *Andre Dekker, Maastricht University, Netherlands*

CORAL is still in its early stages. According to Andre Dekker, professor of clinical data science and a board-certified medical physicist at the MAASTRO Clinic at Maastricht University in the Netherlands, who leads the initiative, there are still many problems to solve. "Challenges do exist," Dekker told us. "Data quality varies across institutions. And there are differences across countries and institutions in the ways patients are treated and data is recorded. But by establishing trust, building a community, and sharing our data, these challenges are being addressed. Our goal is to ask research questions on a global scale and, ultimately, to create value from big data in a responsible and equitable manner, and to use AI to provide value through clinical-decision support for our cancer patients."

CORAL provides a glimpse of how digital health can transform patient value. Now, let's turn to the challenges that the industry needs to address to make that desired future a reality.

PROTECTING DATA SECURITY AND PATIENT PRIVACY

Achieving the goal of using the growing quantity of health data to improve health outcomes requires addressing an unavoidable tension: on the one hand, patients and clinicians need to be encouraged to share their data for the purposes of benchmarking and research; on the other, health-related data is some of the most personal and private information about individuals that it is possible to collect. People whose credit card information has been hacked can always block their account and replace their card. But an individual's genetic information can never be changed—once it has been stolen, one's privacy is lost forever. It should be no surprise, then, that stolen patient records sell on the dark web for anywhere between 10 and 30 times the price of a stolen credit card number.[30] It is essential, therefore, for any digital platform for health data to have stringent data security and patient privacy protections.

The good news: many countries around the world have longstanding norms about using patient data for research purposes, and most patients are quite willing to share their data for such purposes, as well as to improve the overall health system. For example, a 2016 review of a large number of independent studies found that with appropriate safety cautions, roughly two-thirds of US patients were willing to allow their tissue samples, genomic data, and other health information to be retained and used in future research found acceptable by recognized oversight bodies.[31] A survey of 771 US patients who had participated in clinical trials found that 93% were either very likely or somewhat likely to allow their data to be shared with researchers, and 82% were very or somewhat likely to share it with for-profit companies.[32] Fewer than 8% felt that the negative potential consequences of sharing data outweighed the cost.

The bad news: despite increasingly stringent regulations and laws to protect the integrity of patient health information such as the US Health Insurance Portability & Accountability Act (HIPAA) and the European Union's General Data Protection Regulation (GDPR), data security breaches in health care are growing at a rate faster than even in the financial services industry—with devastating consequences both for health care institutions and the patients they serve.[33]

In May 2017, National Health Service hospitals in England were attacked by the global virus WannaCry and forced to pay a ransom to remove the imposed encryption of the hospitals' information systems by the virus. In January 2018, the South-Eastern Norway Regional Health Authority, responsible for health services for some 2.8 million people, representing more than half of Norway's population, announced a cyber-security breach of protected patient health information. And in 2020, the University of California San Francisco (UCSF) health network was hacked by the cybercrime group Netwalker and was forced to pay a ransom of $1.14 million to prevent the leaking of confidential patient information.[34]

The problem appears to be getting worse. The US Department of Health and Human Services collects and publishes data on breaches of protected health information at US health care institutions that affect more than 500 people. The number of such breaches in 2021 occurred at more than double the rate of 2020—650 compared to 300, or nearly 2 a day.[35]

Why do health information systems seem to be particularly vulnerable to security breaches? The fragmentation of health care—the fact that there are so many different sources of data and multiple information systems existing in separate silos—is a big part of the problem. Most sensitive patient data is captured at the point of care. Doctors enter data into EMRs, but a great deal of information is captured in separate lab systems, radiology equipment, and other medical devices used for diagnostic or therapeutic purposes. As home care becomes more important, a growing share of this data is captured outside institutional firewalls. A typical hospital can have literally thousands of interconnected medical devices introducing numerous cybersecurity risks. What's more, in many provider organizations staff can bring their own devices—digital phones, iPads, and so on—and connect them to the hospital network. The more sources of data, the more access points for bad actors to acquire it, and the more customization required to prevent them from doing so.

Poor cybersecurity capabilities also contribute to the problem. In contrast to, say, the financial sector, health care organizations have systematically underinvested in cybersecurity. In an environment of cost constraint, IT security is invariably one of the areas where necessary investments have been neglected, leading to a severe lack of qualified human resources, inadequately updated technological protection, and limited understanding of cybersecurity among clinical staff.

Within the industry, there is broad agreement about the scope of the problem.[36] But the existing fragmentation of the industry and the misalignment of incentives that this fragmentation brings have made it difficult to devise a holistic solution. This is one other area where a whole-of-industry initiative is critical. Until the vulnerability of health information systems is addressed, it will be challenging—if not impossible—to get support for large-scale studies on multinational health data either because patients will withhold consent or organizations with critical data assets will refrain from participating because of the risks involved.

ENSURING INTEROPERABILITY

Another critical challenge is to ensure the seamless interoperability of health-information systems across multiple institutions. Put simply, interoperability is the ability of two or more information systems to exchange and use data with each other. While it may seem like a narrow technical subject, it actually has enormous practical impact on the world we live in. Every time an individual books an airline ticket, transfers money from one bank to another, or buys a product from an online marketplace, he or she is relying on the seamless interactions among a variety of fully interoperable information systems.

In health care, however, interoperability lags far behind what one finds in other industries. Partly, this lag is due to the extraordinary complexity of health information, a result of the rapidly expanding quantity of biomedical information and the diversity of diagnostic and treatment options available. Partly, it is the result of the concerns we just discussed about patient privacy and data security about what is among the most sensitive categories of personal information. But it is also the product of self-interest—for instance, the desire of providers to hold on to patient-generated data because they see it as a potential source of future revenues and competitive advantage, or the desire of dominant EMR vendors to maintain "vendor lock" on the vast quantities of patient data collected in their proprietary EMR systems.

All these factors have delayed the development of the kind of common technical standards that would make interoperability routine and ubiquitous in health care. What's more, the lack of standards limits the development of health-related AI applications because the development of such applications relies on the availability of massive volumes of heterogenous but standardized data—to "train" machine learning algorithms, validate their performance, and improve them over time. In the absence of standardized data, the challenges involved in assembling the requisite data remain a formidable barrier to the development of genuinely transformative AI-based applications. On AI projects, the vast majority of time—up to 80%, according to one estimate—is spent on the data collection, cleaning, preparation, and labeling phases so that the system can use its machine-learning capabilities to process, understand, and learn from input patterns.[37]

Fortunately, considerable progress has been made in recent years in defining the key standards in three critical areas: what data to collect, how to share it, and how to access and use it.[38]

What to Collect: A Library of Core Data

Health systems around the world are routinely collecting more and more data. But many types of data relevant to the mission of improving patient value are not necessarily being recorded on a systematic basis or in a standard fashion. To address such gaps requires standards for data capture.

Think of the standards for data capture as a kind of library in which the books are all of the standard data that should be routinely collected for every patient. Examples include basic patient information (medical and diagnostic history, genetic and behavioral profiles, and demographic and socioeconomic information); the range of clinical and nonclinical interventions taken to address a patient's condition (medications, surgeries, social and environmental interventions, and the like); and especially important, the *results* of the interventions and therapies such as the all-important health-outcomes measures described in Chapter 2.

In addition to the specific data categories, technical standards are necessary for a particular type of metadata: contextual information that travels with a given piece of data and provides important information about it. Some metadata categories are necessary to link data from different data sources—for example, a standardized time concept, a patient identifier that allows the linkage of data about the same patient from different institutions, or a license governing patient consent for use of the data for research purposes and access permissions for specific researchers to use the data. Capturing this kind of metadata is critical because it provides information about whether the data in question is "fit for purpose" for the clinician or researcher who wants to use it.

Probably the most widely used data standard today is the system known as the International Classification of Disease (ICD), which includes tens of thousands of data categories that define diseases, pathogens, symptoms, and developmental anomalies, and is used by more than a hundred nations.[39] First developed by the World Health Organization (WHO) in 1977, the eleventh generation of the standard, known as ICD-11, was released in January 2022. Another example is the United States Core Data Interoperability (USCDI) standard, adopted by the US Department of Health and Human Services as part of the final rule defining regulations for the implementation of the 2016 21st Century Cures Act. USCDI defines a standardized set of health data classes and constituent data elements that all health care institutions must use for nationwide, interoperable health-information exchange.[40] (We'll say more about the evolution of interoperability in the US health system later in this chapter.)

How to Share: Creating a Common Vocabulary

In addition to standards for what data to collect, technical protocols must also be developed so the data can be converted to standardized terms and formats so as to be "machine readable"—that is, able to be understood by different information systems so that disparate data sources can communicate with each other. Here, two types of standards are especially important.

The first is a common data model (CDM) that allows data to be extracted from disparate vendor systems and mapped to a common template. A CDM makes it possible to capture and combine data from different sources in a consistent, logical manner. It organizes and defines the properties of individual data and metadata and sets standards for how they relate to one another.

The second is a semantic model (often known as semantic interoperability) that allows data collected using a variety of terminologies and coding systems to be mapped to a single common language so that terms can be understood in the same way by different systems. When data comes from a wide variety of sources, it is typically collected and organized according to different categorization systems. The situation is akin to communication among a group of people who all speak different languages. Before they can understand each other, they need to translate what they have to say into a common shared language. The semantic model provides the rules for translating data from different data sets into a common language for analysis. The challenge, of course, in creating such a common language is to find the right level of granularity so that important information is not "lost in translation" but without adding too much complexity.

There are several CDMs in use across the industry today. For example, Observable Medical Outcomes Partnership (OMOP) makes possible the systematic analysis of disparate observational databases by transforming the data contained in them into a common format and representation (including terminologies, vocabularies, and coding schemes), and then performing systematic analyses using a library of standard analytic routines.

The nonprofit Health Level Seven International, commonly known as HL7, has since the 1980s been developing a comprehensive framework that describes data formats, components (resources), and application programming interfaces (APIs). Today HL7 is the most widely used health-care interoperability standard in the world, supported by more than 1,600 participating organizations in over 50 countries.

More recently, an open-source standard known as FHIR (Fast Healthcare Interoperability Resources, pronounced "fire") has been developed on top of the existing HL7 platform. FHIR is the first truly open-source standard for electronic information sharing in health care and is designed to be easier to implement, more open, and more extensible than the current HL7 family of standards. With its dynamic characteristics, FHIR is rapidly gaining popularity and has a good chance to become the de facto standard for clinical information exchange and the lingua franca needed to translate health data from one system to another.[41] Many analysts have argued that the FHIR standard will be especially critical for the implementation of AI technologies in health care.[42]

When it comes to semantic interoperability, SNOMED-CT (Systematized Nomenclature of Medicine—Clinical Terms) defines a standardized vocabulary of clinical terminology that is used by doctors and other health care providers for the electronic exchange of clinical health information and is widely considered to be the most comprehensive, multilingual clinical health care terminology in the world. Initially a product of an initiative combining US and UK clinical terms, the standard has been translated into 11 languages and is now used in more than 80 nations.[43]

How to Use: Balancing Access, Privacy, and Security

As the health care industry makes progress in developing standards for categorizing and sharing health information, additional standards will be necessary for how patient health data is accessed and used. For example, the prospect of a broad sharing of data across multiple institutions raises additional data security and data privacy issues beyond basic cybersecurity. It will be important to develop secure automated procedures for garnering patient consent for use of personal health data, verifying permission to access and use data, and generating an audit trail recording every access and use of such data.

One area in this domain that has seen considerable recent progress is new approaches to data access. Traditionally, most techniques for data access followed some version of a centralized model. Data is stored in centralized data warehouses; to access specific data, the data needs to be transferred to the user's own warehouse. For example, most quality registries that track health outcomes have created their own centralized data warehouses, which are entirely separate from the data captured in hospital information systems.

There is growing recognition among data scientists, however, that centralization has its limits. For one thing, it is not easy to scale. The large amounts of data necessary to get statistically significant results in precision medicine very quickly encounter storage constraints. The concentration of patient data in centralized data warehouses also creates a single point of failure that makes data more vulnerable to hacking. Finally, exchanging data across jurisdictions adds another level of regulatory complexity and risks to data-sharing efforts.

For all these reasons, recent approaches are moving away from centralized data storage and access toward more distributed models (an approach sometimes categorized as "federated" or "swarm" learning).[44] In a distributed model, analytical software and algorithms travel to the data rather than the other way around. Because data always remains behind each institution's firewall, distribution also has real privacy benefits, because no individual's entire data is stored within one single place or moves from where it is stored.

The CORAL consortium, described earlier, has adopted one version of this decentralized approach known as the "Personal Health Train." As the name suggests, the approach can be likened to a traditional railway network. In this analogy, every participating institution has a dedicated data station with which researchers, clinicians, and other data users communicate to get access to data following specific rules. The analytical tools or algorithms developed by researchers and other medical specialists—the equivalent of trains in the railway analogy—travel to the data stations and gain access to data for analytical purposes and develop insights from it but without extracting any patient data or transferring it beyond each institution's firewall. There is also a linking infrastructure—the tracks—over which the algorithms move, regulating access and providing data security.[45]

All these developments represent important progress in ensuring the interoperability of health systems in recent years and are reasons for growing optimism. Nevertheless, critical gaps and obstacles remain. For example, the lack of adequate financing of standard-setting initiatives is a consistent shortcoming. So is the fact that some leading standards—for example, SNOMED—are proprietary, not open source, and require a licensing fee. There is also considerable work to be done to harmonize across different standards to make sure they are compatible with each other.

But perhaps the greatest challenge to effective interoperability is not so much the development of technical standards, as important as they are. Rather, it is what specialists call human and institutional interoperability: the development of new practices, norms, rules, and regulations to integrate the increasing availability of health-related data into clinical practice and translate it into sustainable clinical innovation.

BUILDING A SUSTAINABLE INNOVATION SYSTEM

Even when health information systems can collect, share, and analyze large quantities of data, it will be of little consequence unless clinicians find it easy to use in their daily clinical practice to continuously improve patient value. Health care provider organizations need to work closely with technology developers to facilitate the optimal integration of new digital tools. Only then will advanced analytics based on large data sets be used in the right way and in the right context to benefit human health. "This human side of interoperability is the most challenging, and where we have the most work left to do," Dr. Stanley Huff, clinical professor in the University of Utah's department of biomedical informatics and former chief medical informatics officer of Intermountain Healthcare, told us.

"As various standard terms become codified," Huff explained, "they will need to be combined and translated into relevant knowledge. For example, what combination of objective measures and observations adds up to a standardized definition of diabetes? What is the standardized process for how to diagnose and treat it? What in the data qualifies as a more important or relevant clinical observation for a given type of patient? What we need is a clearly defined knowledge base of objective algorithms for diagnosing the full range of diseases and conditions. Through a process of inference based on reproducible observations, the rules of such algorithms would define an objective, computable way to determine when a given medical condition exists and when it doesn't."

What Huff is describing is AI-based clinical decision support systems that use the growing body of health information and sophisticated techniques of predictive analytics to inform and support clinicians in their day-to-day decision-making. Ideally, the analyses of these new-style clinical decision-support systems should automatically generate actions along the clinical workflow. For example, if the systems determine that a given patient is at high risk for developing sepsis, a set of orders and actions—drawing a blood sample to analyze white blood count, lactic acid, and electrolytes; starting an IV; measuring vital signs at 15-minute intervals, and the like—would automatically be generated so that the clinician can quickly review and activate them with a single click. "It would be more accurate than clinician memory, and it would save time and reduce the clinical burden," said Huff.

Creating more powerful and more user-friendly clinical decision support systems will also require more participatory and agile approaches to technology design. Consider, by way of contrast, the typical experience of clinicians with today's EMR systems. In most of the current systems on the market, care pathways are hard-coded. Making any changes depends on the support of programmers who, in many organizations, are in short supply. What's more, reporting requirements put the onus for data-gathering on already overloaded doctors. As a result, many clinicians complain that using EMRs takes too much time away from interaction with patients and ends up disrupting rather than supporting the clinical workflow. The health care sector needs a major shift in its approach to technology design equivalent to the transition from traditional mobile phones to smart phones or the shift from traditional hierarchical programming models to agile software development. Making that shift happen is primarily a function of designing incentives so that clinicians have the time and the motivation to engage in this important work.

Other challenges in building a sustainable digital clinical innovation system have to do with the development of new institutional norms and regulatory rules. To understand what's at stake, let's return to the example of AI. The development of new applications based on machine learning and predictive analytics depends on access to massive quantities of patient data in order to train the systems and to detect clinically relevant patterns in the data and make reliable predictions. To that end, a number of leading providers are cutting licensing deals with health technology companies and startups in which they provide de-identified patient data to train AI-based applications without informing patients that their data is being used. Academic medical centers, in particular, are participating in what one journalist describes as "a vast marketplace in which data and biological specimens are shared with digital startups and large technology companies such as Google, Microsoft, Amazon, and IBM."[46]

The lack of clear norms, rules, and regulations for this emerging marketplace raises fundamental privacy and ethical issues.[47] For example, many critics have raised concerns that if the de-identified data is combined with other data sets (for example, consumer data), patients risk being identified, violating their privacy. And even beyond basic privacy concerns, should patients have the right to opt out of such data deals? Should they have the right to some kind of financial compensation if the applications created through analysis of their health data prove successful in the marketplace? And what about commercial conflicts of interest? Memorial Sloan Kettering Cancer Center granted access to 25 million pathology slides to an AI company in which the hospital and several of its clinicians and board members had financial stakes, and Ascension Health gave Google widespread access to identifiable patient data without informing either doctors or patients, leading to a federal inquiry.[48]

Currently, there is no consensus around these issues. Different institutions have different guidelines, and many institutions are currently reviewing their approaches. For example, Michigan Medicine, an academic medical center based at the University of Michigan and one of the largest biomedical research communities in the United States, has recently outlined a formal process for giving patients a choice whether to permit secondary uses of their data that attempts to achieve an appropriate balance between risk to individual participants and benefit to medical centers and to society, and that in many respects is more stringent than existing federal regulatory requirements.[49] But, of course, Michigan Medicine is only one institution. We need to develop industrywide standards, preferably on a global scale. (See the sidebar "A Digital-Health Patient Bill of Rights.")

A Digital-Health Patient Bill of Rights

Since value-based health care puts the patient and value delivered to patients at the very center of the health system, digital-health standards designed to improve health care value need to put the health interests and trust of patients at the center of the standard-setting effort. One way to achieve this goal is for industry stakeholders and the world's governments to commit to a digital-health patient bill of rights. The bill of rights would define foundational principles that inform individual rights of access to personal health data and that govern the use of that health data in research and clinical decision-making.

In 2018, BCG worked with some 30 health technology experts under the auspices of the Value in Health Care project of the World Economic Forum to develop the outlines of such a proposal.[50] We identified five basic principles that any digital-health bill of rights should include:

1. Individuals should have access to their health data in a standardized computable format, irrespective of source, through an individualized point of access.

2. Individuals should be informed about how their health data is used, and in situations in which the sharing of their personal health data is voluntary, they should be able to provide or withdraw consent for the use of their data.

3. Individuals and the organizations that have access to their data should be able to use the data to inform care decisions, improve

operations, deliver personalized high-value care, and advance research.

4. Individuals should be able to seamlessly grant access to their data to relevant individuals and institutions.

5. Individuals and organizations should have access to information based on anonymized health outcomes and other relevant health data to ensure transparency, enhance accountability, enable choices about providers and treatments, and improve public health.

The goal of developing a digital health bill of rights is to provide a general framework for the creation of digital-health standards and support the objective of producing secure and truly interoperable health information systems. International agencies can use these principles to set the global agenda for standardization. Patients and patient advocacy groups can use them to create awareness among their constituents and to advocate for governments to include these rights in the legal and policy framework for the national health system. And providers, payers, and pharma, med-tech, health information, and life science companies can use them to design new informatics initiatives.

Some countries are already building health information systems informed by, at least, some of these principles. In Estonia, for example, it is a legal requirement for all personal health information to be stored in a machine-readable common format within one to five days of service delivery. The health informatics system links data from different providers and ancillary stakeholders such as ambulance services. Individuals have access to their data through a single point of access. Providers also have access to aggregated data for clinical and research purposes, although patients have the right to restrict access in specific situations.[51]

Another key area where new rules and norms are required is algorithmic transparency. AI and machine learning may make it possible to create the new clinical decision support tools that Stan Huff envisions based on algorithms that extract clinical insight from large data sets. But if clinicians cannot understand the underlying analytics that inform the diagnostic and therapeutic recommendations made by the algorithms, they are unlikely to put their trust in them. Therefore, transparency around how data is being accessed and used by analytical tools is critical in gaining the trust of clinicians for widespread adoption.

Currently, health-related AI applications suffer their own version of the evidence crisis we described in Chapter 1. Randomized clinical trials (RCTs) may be the much-cited "gold standard" for determining whether a new diagnostic or treatment is superior to prior standards. And yet, digital-health applications almost never undergo a rigorous scientific assessment of their efficacy and safety that, say, a typical drug or medical device does. This has created a disconnect between the developers of digital-health technologies and clinical practitioners. In the words of two medical experts, "On one hand, the rapidly moving health technology companies have largely avoided performing formal scientific efficacy testing, citing impracticalities in cost and the time they require. On the other, clinicians and health insurers have often ignored new IT solutions, citing lack of proven benefit."[52]

Eventually this disconnect will have to be addressed. So far, regulatory agencies such as the FDA have allowed digital-health innovators and entrepreneurs a large degree of freedom, primarily delegating to them the oversight of new digital-health applications.[53] While this has encouraged innovation, it is unlikely to be a sustainable long-term strategy. At the August 2021 global meeting of the Health Information and Management Systems Society (HIMSS), Dr. John Halamka, president of Mayo Clinical Platform, the digital-health unit of Mayo Clinic, proposed a public-private collaboration of government, academia, and industry to address the challenge of transparency in machine learning.[54] "[O]ptimism for AI is justified, but there are caveats," Halamka told the audience. "We need, as a society, to define transparency of communication: to define how we evaluate an algorithm's fitness for purpose." Halamka called for the development of the equivalent of a "nutrition label" for health-related AI algorithms that would make publicly available information such as the type of algorithm deployed and the composition of the sample population on which it was trained.[55]

A PUBLIC-PRIVATE PARTNERSHIP FOR DIGITAL-HEALTH TRANSFORMATION

Protecting patient privacy, ensuring interoperability, building a sustainable innovation system—this is a broad and multifaceted agenda that will evolve not over the next year or multiple years but over the next decade or more. All the more reason to start now. We agree with Halamka that guiding that agenda will require industry stakeholders and the world's governments to come together in a public-private partnership, ideally on a global scale.

For an example of what we mean, consider the story of the establishment of the TCP/IP networking standard, which laid the foundation for the modern internet. The development and dissemination of the TCP/IP protocol is the story of a dynamic public-private partnership in which key institutions in government, academia, and private industry worked together to create technical standards that had a transformative impact.

The development of the TCP/IP standard in the 1970s was funded by government—specifically, the Defense Advanced Research Projects Agency (DARPA) of the US Department of Defense—and first used in ARPANET, the first public packet-switched computer network. The initial working group included university researchers from Stanford and industry experts from Xerox's Palo Alto Research Center. Operational models of the protocol, which allowed it to run on different computing platforms, were developed by the private contract-research firm Bolt, Beranek and Newman, in collaboration with Stanford and University College London.

Once the standard was developed, the US government played a key role in accelerating its adoption when, in 1982, the Department of Defense made TCP/IP the standard for all military computing. In 1985, the National Science Foundation chose the standard for the design of NSFNET, the wide-area network that handled the bulk of early internet traffic and which became the general networking infrastructure for roughly 2,000 institutions of higher learning and leading high-tech companies. Soon after, major computer companies such as IBM, AT&T, and DEC adopted the standard, and smaller companies began including it in DOS and Windows, which would become the key operating software for the then-emerging personal computer. A key step in the dissemination of TCP/IP occurred in 1989 when AT&T agreed to place its TCP/IP code for the popular UNIX operating system in the public domain.

Once the TCP/IP standard was established, it then became a platform on which industry players worldwide could innovate, producing fundamental game changers such as Tim Berners-Lee's concept of the hypertext-based "worldwide web," developed in the early 1990s at the

European Council of Nuclear Research (CERN), based in Geneva, which led to the first hypertext web browser.

Can a similar scenario take off in health care to create the digital learning platforms of the future? According to Micky Tripathi, it is happening already. Tripathi is the Biden administration's head of the US Office of the National Coordinator for Health Information Technology (typically abbreviated as ONC) in the Department of Health and Human Services. Established in 2004, ONC is the principal federal entity charged with coordinating nationwide efforts to implement and use the most advanced health-information technology and the electronic exchange of health information. Tripathi walked us through the recent history of health technology standards development and what he described as a "fundamental paradigm shift" in how ONC is approaching the development of interoperability standards for health-information systems.

Ever since the passage of the Health Insurance Portability and Accountability Act (HIPAA) in 1996, Tripathi explained, health care organizations have been allowed to share patient health information between institutions. But they were not required to do so. And there were no standards in place to do so electronically.

The 2009 Health Information Technology for Economic and Clinical Health (HITECH) Act set aside $27 billion in incentives (the amount eventually increased to more than $35 billion) to support the adoption and "meaningful use" of EMRs, a key step in building out a digital infrastructure for information exchange. Research suggests that the program helped boost EMR adoption at eligible hospitals and office-based physicians from 16% and 28%, respectively, in 2010 to 96% and 72% in 2019.[56] But according to Tripathi, while ONC acknowledged at the time that interoperability was an important issue, "it also recognized that it would require tremendous coordination in the highly fragmented US health-care market, and that technical standards were simply not yet mature enough." So the EMR initiative focused primarily on creating the infrastructure for the digitization of existing patient records. As a result, the systems created, both by the dominant EMR vendors and by open-source vendors, had major issues of compatibility—across systems from different vendors and even across systems from the same vendor that had been customized for different institutions.

A major change came with the passage of the 21st Century Cures Act in 2016. "For the first time," according to Tripathi, "the federal government said not only that health institutions had permission to share health data, but also that they were *obliged* to do so and to share that data in the appropriate electronic form."

In 2020, ONC published the "final rule" outlining the key regulations for implementing that new legal requirement.[57] The new rule does three things. First, it spells out enforcement mechanisms to prevent information blocking (including financial penalties of up to $1 million in fines per incident). Second, for the first time in ONC's history, it designates a specific data-sharing standard—the open-source FHIR standard described earlier—for the application programming interfaces (APIs) that all health IT developers must include in their systems and applications so that they can communicate with each other. Finally, it defines a common legal agreement and technical standards for health-information networks to connect more easily with each other. "Each of these provisions will allow scalability across the entire industry," said Tripathi.

Another key part of the paradigm shift has to do with the best way to approach the task of standard development. According to Tripathi, the traditional approach to interoperability tended to focus exclusively on the definition of standardized data that resulted from many years of consultation by multistakeholder committees. In contrast, the Cures Act and the subsequent ONC rule cover both standardized and nonstandardized data (for example, unstructured physician notes and transcriptions). Focusing on standardized data alone, Tripathi explained, allows the sometimes-cumbersome standard-setting process to become a brake on progress. Meanwhile, advances in analytics, machine learning, and natural-language processing now make it possible to develop insights from unstructured data. Insisting on the sharing of both types of data as part of interoperability requirements should speed up the innovation process. "We'll continue to support standardization to improve data quality," said Tripathi. "But we are not going to limit ourselves to the traditional standard-setting process. We are not trying to define the solutions of the future. Rather, we are creating an open architecture so that innovators can create the solutions of the future. Our role is to create the floor."

ONC's entrepreneurial approach has been the catalyst for many industry stakeholders to champion greater interoperability. For example, ONC was instrumental in initially developing the eHealth Exchange, a nationwide, public-private health information network supporting more than 120 million patients. It is one of a number of health-information-exchange networks that currently broker roughly 50 million health-care interactions every day (more than the number of financial transactions handled globally by the SWIFT banking network). In 2012, the agency spun out the day-to-day management of the eHealth Exchange network to the nonprofit Sequoia Project, an industry consortium created by the American Medical Association, Kaiser Permanente, Humana, and EMR vendors Cerner and Epic to advance the implementation of secure, interoperable nationwide health information exchange. Apple is implementing ONC's USCDI and FHIR standards in the Apple health record. "Far better than merely defining a standard," said Tripathi, "is to actually get it incorporated into the operating system of the iPhone!"

Another major ONC focus is to coordinate across multiple federal government agencies to bring their resources to bear on accelerating interoperability. "The federal government in health care IT does not use even a fraction of its regulatory and purchasing power," said Tripathi. "One card we have to play is that ONC is responsible for certifying how various players implement the new regulations," he said. "Although the process is voluntary, the major EMR vendors all participate because CMS payment programs require certification."

Of course, the United States is only one (albeit, large) country. In a genuinely value-based health care industry, digital-health standards, just like those of the internet, would be global in scope. Tripathi's office has the chance to influence global developments. ONC represents the US government at the Global Digital Health Partnership, a collaboration of 30 countries and territories and the World Health Organization to support the effective implementation of digital health. "Some of the loudest voices for international operability standards," said Tripathi, "are the US EMR vendors who are looking to sell their systems to a global market."

SCALING UP

In summary, the full interoperability of health information systems may finally be achieving liftoff. But to realize the vision of digital learning platforms for value-based health care, much more still needs to be done. In particular, the scale of funding is key. To give one point of comparison, the fiscal year 2022 budget request for ONC from the Biden administration to

Congress is $86.6 million.[58] In contrast, DARPA has a budget of roughly $3 billion and employs 200 people.

Accelerating the development of safe and secure standards for digital health is just one example of the activist and enabling role that the world's governments need to play in value-based health care across multiple fronts. In the next chapter, we will explore that role in more detail.

Digital Health: Action Steps

POLICYMAKERS

1. **Enact a digital-health patient bill of rights.** Patient data should be owned by patients, not institutions. Patient information should remain available for care and clinical research, but in particular circumstances, patients should have the right to opt out.

2. **Take ownership of health data out of competition.** Create incentives for stakeholders to invest in interoperability, including penalties for information blocking. Focus competition on innovative uses of data, not control of the data itself.

3. **Make digital-health standards open source.** In most industries, the era of proprietary information standards is over. Standards and platforms are open source. Encourage health care to follow the same trajectory.

4. **Encourage technical standards for outcomes measurement.** Promote and fund the establishment of a national IT platform for outcomes data, based on leading international standards, and require use of standards as base for registry funding.

5. **Fund the development of best-in-class cybersecurity and interoperability standards.** Make both criteria for certification of all medical information systems, software, and smart devices—including med-tech products and wearables.

6. **Look beyond the national health system.** Require that digital-health applications and national digital-health platforms comply with international standards to encourage international sharing of health data.

PROVIDERS

1. **Insist that technology vendors support interoperability.** Make interoperability a key selection criterion in purchasing decisions—for example, for EMRs or other major digital-health investments.

2. **Form alliances for open standards with other providers.** Team up with other providers to demand integration of outcomes measurement standards into software and development of solutions to facilitate analysis and benchmarking of the results. Support shared standards for patient privacy and informed consent.

3. **Engage in participatory technology design.** Partner with technology vendors to make sure systems are agile and fit for use by clinicians.

PAYERS

1. **Pay for interoperability.** Develop financial incentives that encourage providers and technology suppliers to use interoperable systems.

2. **Help to fund cybersecurity initiatives.** Develop robust cybersecurity standards adequate to the unique sensitivity and data-security needs of individual health data.

3. **Pay for data collection in addition to care.** Create financial incentives for data capture by patients and providers.

SUPPLIERS (in particular, health technology companies)

1. **Commit to interoperability.** Develop all solutions based on international health interoperability standards.

2. **Embrace outcomes measurement.** Integrate national—and, where possible, international—standards for outcomes measurement in the design and testing of applications.

PATIENTS

1. **Insist on ownership.** Your health data should belong to you. Support initiatives such as the digital-health patient bill of rights.

2. **Opt in.** Allow your health data to be used for approved research and clinical-improvement initiatives.

CHAPTER 7

A MOONSHOT FOR VALUE-BASED TRANSFORMATION

I n nearly every nation in the world, national and regional governments play a central and multifaceted role in the regulation and governance of the national health system. Government is typically the primary (and in many countries, the sole) payer for health care services.[1] And whether it involves assessing the safety and efficacy of new drugs and devices or licensing health care professionals and clinical facilities, government agencies are also the paramount regulator of what is, by necessity, a highly regulated industry. Given the importance of population health to social stability and prosperity, and to national competitiveness—and given that the people who are ill are in a position of unique vulnerability when they encounter the health system—there are overwhelming political, ethical, and moral reasons for this role.

Finally, because of its outsized role as payer and regulator, there is a third important role that government plays in health care, whether government officials consciously embrace that role or not: as a convenor of and mediator among the many stakeholders and interest groups in the industry. Only government can bring all the stakeholders to the table and set the "rules of the game" for interest group competition and cooperation.

For all these reasons, government will be at the very center of any plan for the value-based transformation of the world's health systems. The laws, policies, and regulations governing the health care sector can either enable or hinder the transition to value-based health care. To support and accelerate the changes we have discussed in previous chapters, we believe the world's governments should play a more active role in encouraging value-based transformation. They need to create new rules that realign the goals of industry stakeholders around improving the health outcomes delivered to their citizens, and start assessing the performance of the national health system based on the actual results delivered to patients.

In her book *Mission Economy: A Moonshot Guide to Changing Capitalism*, economist Mariana Mazzucato calls for governments to play an activist role in shaping markets so that society can achieve its most ambitious goals, "the ones that really matter to people and to the planet."[2] Mazzucato's moonshot analogy is to President John F. Kennedy's 1962 decision to put the full weight of the US government behind the goal of landing a man on the moon by the end of the decade. The Apollo program cost the US government the equivalent of $283 billion in 2020 dollars, represented about 4% of the federal budget at the time, and employed some 400,000 workers, both at the National Aeronautic and Space Administration (NASA) and at private contractors.

In addition to achieving its goal by 1969, the investments in the Apollo program also had important spillover effects for society and the economy. For example, it helped jump-start the computer revolution. The guidance computer for the Apollo spacecraft was, in effect, the world's first portable computer. At the peak of the space program, MIT, a major Apollo contractor, was buying 60% of all silicon chips manufactured in the United States.

The moonshot analogy has become something of a go-to term to describe any ambitious public or private project. The US government's current program to accelerate scientific understanding, diagnosis, and treatment of cancer is known as the "Cancer Moonshot."[3] And the recent book by Pfizer CEO Albert Bourla describing the company's nine-month effort to rapidly develop its mRNA coronavirus vaccine is titled simply *Moonshot*.[4] But Mazzucato's use of the term highlights the need to resurrect ambition and vision in government policymaking and to return to "using the idea of public purpose to guide policy and business activity."

Although there are many candidates for a twenty-first-century moonshot—combatting climate change or ending world poverty immediately come to mind—the future of the global health care system should be on anyone's short list of objectives that "really matter to people and to the planet." It is an example of what Mazzucato calls a "wicked problem" that is "huge, complex, and resistant to simple solutions." For such society-wide challenges, only governments have the capacity to steer the transformation on the scale needed—in Mazzucato's words, "focusing policymaking on outcomes" and enabling "the public and private sectors to truly collaborate on investing in solutions, having a long-run view, and governing the process to make sure it is done in the public interest."[5]

In this chapter, we define the ambition for a government moonshot designed to accelerate the transformation of the world's health systems so that they provide better value to patients. We argue that such a mission should be embraced by the world's governments, no matter what economic model they follow and irrespective of whether their national health system is primarily public or market-based. (See the sidebar "Moving Beyond the Public-Versus-Private Debate.") Drawing on Mazzucato's book, we emphasize three critical roles for government in any moonshot-like mission for value-based health care: defining a clear mission, shaping the market, and placing game-changing bets. In the following sections, we describe each of these roles in turn, interspersed with case studies of governments that are putting various aspects of this model into practice.

Moving Beyond the Public-Versus-Private Debate

There has been a decades-long debate about whether health care should be a public good or, alternatively, can benefit from the introduction of competitive, market-based mechanisms. The United States is an exception in the degree to which the health system relies on the private marketplace. But even in countries where health care has traditionally been part of the public sector, many have been exploring various forms of privatization in the hope that introducing market mechanisms into the health system will promote efficiency and a more rational use of resources. What's more, in many low-income countries, health systems also suffer from critical infrastructure and capacity gaps that the government lacks the resources to address adequately. In such situations, the private sector can be an important source of investment to build capacity and fill gaps that the publicly owned health system cannot or chooses not to make a priority.

Champions of privatization tend to emphasize how market mechanisms, competition, and increased patient choice can counter bureaucracy and fuel innovation in the organization and delivery of health services. Critics, meanwhile, emphasize the universal coverage and broad social equity of publicly financed (and in some cases, publicly delivered) health systems and point to the high costs, extensive overtreatment, investor profit taking, and lack of universal coverage of the more commercially driven US health system.

To be honest, we don't have a dog in this particular fight. In our work with health systems around the world, we have advised public-sector and private-sector, nonprofit and for-profit, tightly regulated and more purely market-driven (or some combination of the two) organizations.

What we observe is that while there are advantages and disadvantages to any organizational model, nowhere in the world—including in the United States—does the health sector rely on truly free markets that allocate resources efficiently. Nowhere is the full range of health care services transacted at publicly known prices or with transparent outcomes. What's more, because so much of care provision is local, and patients are often frail or vulnerable, and suffer from extreme asymmetries of information, market competition alone is an inadequate organizing mechanism for care delivery. As a result, most health systems are converging on some kind of hybrid public-private model.

It's also important to realize that privatization and market-based competition don't automatically lead to improved health care value. As Michael Porter and Elizabeth Teisberg made clear in their classic, *Redefining Health Care,* the impact of market mechanisms in any market depends on the design of the rules governing market competition.[6] In all countries, governments need to design the rules for competition so that all stakeholders—public and private—have incentives to compete on value and so that the health system rewards participants that deliver the highest-quality outcomes in the most cost-effective way.

In other words, the fundamental question is not whether government should be involved in health care. Rather, it is: What should government's role be? Value-based health care should not be an ideological or partisan question. As previous chapters have made clear, we have found important value-based innovations in both mainly public and mainly commercial health systems. What the world's health systems really need is a set of general principles for health system governance that transcend the ideological debate and that all citizens, stakeholders, and political parties can get behind.

DEFINING A CLEAR MISSION

The first role of government in value-based health-system transformation is to define a clear mission by setting a strategic goal and direction, but without micromanaging or becoming too prescriptive about how stakeholders actually achieve it. Defining a clear mission needs to combine an explicit articulation of the desired results with the creation of an environment that aligns the incentives of various stakeholders, fosters experimentation and innovation, and encourages collaborative public-private partnerships to achieve those results.

How close are the nations of the world to articulating a value-based mission for health care today? In a recent milestone, one of the 17 Sustainable Development Goals (SDGs) developed by the United Nations concerns "Good Health and Well-Being," defined as "ensur[ing] healthy lives and promot[ing] well-being for all at all ages."[7] The SDGs define nine specific targets to achieve this goal, ranging from reducing maternal mortality and ending preventable newborn and child deaths to ensuring universal access to sexual and reproductive health services and strengthening prevention and treatment of substance abuse.

Other initiatives take a more focused, disease-based approach. One of the five missions of the European Union's Horizon Program, for instance, focuses specifically on cancer. The goal: to avert more than 3 million additional premature deaths between 2021 and 2030 by accelerating progress in cancer prevention and treatment, including creating more equitable access to cancer care.[8] As mentioned previously, the US government has funded a "Cancer Moonshot" that aims "to make more therapies available to more patients, while also improving our ability to prevent cancer and detect it at an early stage."[9] One of the four areas of focus in the UK government's recently published industrial strategy focuses on the health needs of a specific population segment: the elderly. The "Healthy Ageing" program aims "to enhance capabilities and quality of life across the course of our increasingly longer lives"—in part, by leveraging very large data sets collected by the UK's National Health Service to improve health outcomes by diagnosing and treating illnesses earlier, an initiative known as "data to early diagnostics and precision medicine."[10]

Goals of this kind that articulate improvements in health outcomes for specific population segments or diseases are a good first step. What such high-level goals typically lack, however, is a clear pathway for the structural changes in health systems necessary to achieve these goals. For example, there is growing evidence that tracking progress against the SDG goals for population health is already forcing nations to confront major gaps in the collection of health information and data to measure progress against the goals.[11] And a recent commentary by participants in the US Cancer Moonshot argues that while the initiative has led to exciting new approaches to fighting the disease, future progress depends on government leadership and investment in key capabilities and infrastructure "to establish cloud-based repositories, set data standards, ensure privacy protection, and incentivise data sharing."[12]

This is where other efforts to define a clear mission strike us as more promising. In recent years, a number of national and regional governments have made explicit commitments to reorient their health systems around four critical components of a value-based health system that we have described in previous chapters: systematic outcomes measurement; more integrated and patient-focused care delivery; digital platforms to collect, share, and analyze health data for continuous improvement; and new models of value-based payment. Consider the example of the Netherlands.

TOWARD A NATIONAL STRATEGY FOR VALUE-BASED TRANSFORMATION: NETHERLANDS

In October 2017, about a hundred Dutch health care leaders attended a meeting at the Dutch embassy on Linnean Avenue in northwest

Washington, DC. The participants, in Washington to attend the annual conference of the International Consortium for Health Outcomes Measurement (ICHOM), represented a cross-section of the major stakeholders in the Dutch health system. They included professors from the country's leading academic medical centers; board members of Dutch health care companies; medical directors from leading hospitals; senior executives from private insurance companies; country managers of global pharmaceutical and med-tech companies; physician-scientists from the top biomedical research institutes; representatives from medical professional societies, the Dutch Hospital Association, and the national patient federation; directors of national quality registries; and government policymakers.

Convened by the Dutch Ministry of Health, Welfare, and Sport, the purpose of the meeting was to brainstorm how to advance the adoption of value-based health care in the Dutch health system. As one participant put it, reflecting on the presentations and discussions at the ICHOM meeting, "This all sounds great. But how do we make it real in the Dutch context? We're all believers, but how do we convince the others?"

The meeting of what came to be known as the Linnean Group was a key event in the development of a five-year Plan for Outcome-Based Healthcare, announced by the Dutch government in 2018, the first step in developing a national strategy for the value-based system transformation of the Dutch health system.[13]

In retrospect, it should be no surprise that the Netherlands would be one of the first countries to embrace value-based health care at the national level. Like Sweden, the country has an extensive network of quality registries. Dutch clinicians have been active participants in international outcomes-measurement initiatives such as ICHOM (the Dutch delegation was the largest national group at that ICHOM conference). As we have seen in previous chapters, Dutch provider institutions such as Diabeter, Santeon, and Erasmus MC have been leaders in redesigning care delivery on value-based principles. And the nation's private insurers have introduced value-based payment pilots for some key procedures and conditions.

The Netherlands also benefits from what the Dutch call the country's "polder culture." The term refers to the distinctive civic culture that emerged from the centuries-long efforts to build and maintain the dikes that preserve the land that the Dutch have reclaimed from the North Sea. That culture emphasizes involving all social groups in major decisions and encouraging frank discussion in the service of building broad national consensus. The cooperation around value-based health care is very much part of this national tradition.

Finally, there's the fact that the Netherlands is a relatively small country of some 17 million people. The key decision makers for the health system probably number a few hundred people. If that group can forge an agreement about what ought to be done, it's likely to happen.

The five-year program's €70 million budget was a relatively modest investment, representing only about 0.1% of the approximately €70 billion that the Netherlands spends on health care in a single year. It supported four main goals:

1. To reach a consensus among key stakeholders by 2022 on the outcomes to be measured for conditions representing 50% of the total disease burden, both by adapting international standards for use in the Netherlands and by developing new metrics
2. To support shared decision-making on treatment choices between providers and patients, by making health information more understandable for patients, and by equipping health professionals with the necessary skills and information to have meaningful conversations about treatment choices with their patients
3. To promote the outcome-based reorganization of care delivery and reimbursement through the sharing of best practices, the development of more integrated care chains, and the encouragement of more outcome-based contracts between insurers and providers
4. To facilitate better access to relevant and up-to-date outcome information, through the development of a state-of-the-art health informatics infrastructure, with the goal of making it easy for patients to report data, ensuring that data is well-organized and scalable, promoting access for all relevant parties for the purposes of benchmarking and research, and maintaining privacy and security

Although the coronavirus pandemic has delayed the achievement of these goals and led to the extension of the original five-year time frame through 2023, the country has made considerable progress. For example, national outcome measures have been defined for an initial four conditions—knee osteoarthritis, chronic kidney disease, pancreatic cancer, and inflammatory bowel disease—and a proof-of-concept field test began for them in November 2021. Meanwhile, working groups for eight additional conditions began work in April 2021, with a second set of eight launched in September 2021. Once these outcome sets are tested and validated in the field and formally launched, Dutch law will mandate that all Dutch health care providers measure and publicly report the health outcomes they deliver to patients.

Another area where the Dutch government has played an active role is in the development of new legal and technical standards to support the sharing of health information across the national health system. Roughly 20% of the funding for the five-year plan has been targeted toward the development of tools and processes for data management to facilitate the collection of patient-reported health outcomes, the secure exchange of health information, and access to aggregated outcomes data on a national level. A framework law mandating the creation of interoperable systems for health information exchange was introduced to the Dutch legislature in May 2021 and is nearing final passage. And a so-called Dutch Interoperability Maturity Model has been developed to define what providers must do to comply with the new law. Discussions are also underway on regulations to ensure vendor compliance. The maturity model is currently being piloted for the exchange of patient summaries and diagnostic images to assess the readiness of providers for implementing the new standards.

As we saw at Santeon and Erasmus MC, shared decision-making has also become a dominant theme at many Dutch provider organizations. While the development of national outcome measures will certainly play a critical role in that effort by providing the necessary data for different treatment options, the government's approach in this area has been to let providers and patient organizations take the lead. Rather than issuing directives mandating any particular approach, the government has played more of a support role. For example, it has funded the development of decision-support tools that can be used in conversations to review basic facts and risk factors about different treatment options, competency sets (including training materials) that define the skills that clinicians need to develop to guide effective conversations with patients, and patient education programs to help hospitals engage with patients with limited health literacy.

The government has taken a similar approach to value-based payments: convening stakeholders, funding local initiatives, sharing information and best practices, but without creating guidelines or mandating anything. The attitude has been to play a supporting role but to let industry stakeholders and the market iron out the details. This may be due to the fact that among the goals of the five-year plan, outcomes-based payment has been the most controversial with some Dutch medical-specialty societies opposing the idea out of concerns that it will lead to cuts in health care budgets.

Interestingly, in our interviews with leaders in the Dutch health sector, we heard some complaints that the Dutch government has, perhaps, not been directive enough. In an environment where different stakeholders often have conflicting interests, sometimes it is necessary for strong leadership to set a clear context for multistakeholder cooperation. "Without stronger guidance, we can't really move very far," one participant in the Dutch debates around value-based health care told us. "If you want to make big changes, you need stronger coordination."

Whether or not one agrees with this criticism, it seems clear that the Netherlands is confronting, at the national level, the same set of strategic choices about bottom-up versus top-down change that individual health care organizations face. The country has developed a rich network of bottom-up initiatives to support value-based transformation of the national health system. To cite just one example, the Linnean Group has gone on to play a key role in convening health care providers and representatives of patient, professional, and government organizations to accelerate the implementation of value-based health care in the Netherlands. Time will tell whether the appointment of former Erasmus CEO Ernst Kuipers as minister of health in the new Dutch government will complement such bottom-up initiatives with more top-down strategic direction. (See the sidebar "Additional Governments Pursuing a Value-Based Strategy for Health Care.")

Additional Governments Pursuing a Value-Based Strategy for Health Care

Other governments besides the Netherlands are embracing aspects of value-based health-system transformation. Consider the following three examples:

Denmark. Much as in Sweden, the provision of health care in Denmark is primarily the responsibility of the country's five regional governments, with the central government playing a coordinating and regulatory role. In 2015, the association of regional governments launched a project to develop and test new governance and payment models based on patient-centered treatment outcomes for targeted patient groups. Between 2016 and 2019 the association also sponsored a national Value-Based Health Care project that studied value-based models for diseases such as hip and knee replacement, diabetes, stroke, prostate cancer, epilepsy, ischemic heart disease, and anxiety and depression.[14]

Wales. The National Health Service in Wales has been developing a robust value-based strategy since 2014. In 2015, the Aneurin Bevan University Health Board in southeast Wales formed a strategic partnership with ICHOM around Parkinson's disease, a collaboration which was the catalyst for a region-wide strategic partnership between NHS Wales and ICHOM focused on implementing outcomes measurement for a variety of conditions, including heart failure, dementia, lung cancer, prostate cancer, and cataracts. These and other initiatives culminated in the publication in 2019 of a three-year action plan by the Welsh government and NHS Wales that focuses on three critical components of value-based transformation: systematic measurement of both clinical and patient-reported health outcomes, a national program to track activity-based costing to support decision-making about resource allocation, and the development of a digital infrastructure for electronic communication between patients and providers with a goal of furthering digital inclusion and citizen engagement.[15]

New South Wales. In Australia, the state government of New South Wales launched its "Leading Better Value Care" program in 2016.[16] The program involves clinicians, provider networks, and other health care organizations in high-impact initiatives to improve health outcomes and the patient experience for people with a variety of conditions.[17] The state government has also invested in the development of a "Health Outcomes and Patient Experience" (HOPE) IT platform for the collection of real-time patient-reported health outcomes data to support shared decision-making about care.[18]

SHAPING THE MARKET

According to Mazzucato, one of the roles of government in the mission economy is to shift its focus from merely fixing market failures to actively shaping the market, including creating new markets that didn't exist before but that are necessary to achieve a given mission. Public interventions, including strategic investments, early in the innovation process can absorb and manage major uncertainties and long-term risks that private investors are reluctant to take on but that are in the public interest.

We recommend three basic market-shaping moves to reorient health systems around value: mandate comprehensive outcomes measurement, invest in the creation of digital platforms for continuous improvement, and design new incentives for the better allocation of resources.

Mandate Comprehensive Outcomes Measurement

To establish a baseline against which systems can assess their performance, governments should support—and where necessary mandate—the collection of comprehensive health outcomes measures by disease and population segment according to agreed-upon global standards. Just as every public company needs to report standardized data about its financial performance, every health care provider should have to report standardized data about the health outcomes it delivers to patients.

Such a reporting system would have multiple benefits. As discussed in earlier chapters, it would be a stimulus to organizational learning and continuous improvement. What's more, by making the measurement of outcomes, including those directly affecting the quality of life of patients, routinely transparent to the public, it would also arm consumers with the information they need to make informed choices among different providers and different treatment options. Finally, as Michael Porter and Elizabeth Teisberg first argued some 15 years ago, it would be a fundamental market-shaping intervention that would orient competition in the industry around value delivered to patients, creating the right kind of selection pressure on providers and all other contributors in the system, promoting meaningful innovation, and introducing a powerful stimulus to value-based transformation.[19]

All nations already mandate at least some reporting of health outcomes—for example, basic mortality statistics, hospital infection rates or accidents, pharmaceutical side effects, and the like. But these reporting systems typically focus narrowly on patient safety and medical errors; they need to broaden to include the kind of positive health outcomes (including patient-reported outcomes) that ICHOM is capturing in its outcome measures. And outcomes reporting needs to be fully integrated into standard clinical practice and electronic health records.

As we have seen throughout this book, many providers, regional health systems, and national quality registries have already taken substantial steps in this direction. In our interviews with leading clinicians, however, we were struck by how many argued for the importance of government standards and requirements to accelerate the routine use of comprehensive outcomes measurement and to increase transparency in sharing outcomes with the general public. They all believed that clinicians need to drive the process and define the metrics, but they saw an important role for government in setting the basic expectation that all provider organizations need to track and report their outcomes. A national approach to implementing standardized outcome metrics should follow the phased approach that we have observed at some quality registries and provider organizations: first, define the standards that all providers should track; second, test and validate these metrics in clinical settings; third, encourage clinicians within individual institutions to use metrics for internal benchmarking; and, finally, once confidence builds in the clinical community, start making the outcomes delivered by providers transparent to the public and use them for benchmarking across provider institutions.

Create Digital Platforms for Continuous Learning and Improvement

So as not to overburden providers and to ensure that health systems reap the full benefit of accumulating outcomes data, governments should also invest in next-generation digital platforms that ensure the efficient and secure collection, sharing, and analysis of outcomes and other health data. As we argued in Chapter 6, the development of such platforms are essential not only to automate the collection of health information but to allow clinicians to learn faster from clinical experience and to benefit from continuously improving decision-support tools.

By establishing robust standards for interoperability and cybersecurity, governments can facilitate the collection, sharing, and analysis of health outcomes data and the transparent reporting of health outcomes to the public. They can also jump-start a dynamic new innovation market in which health technology companies collaborate with clinical researchers, providers, and drug and med-tech companies to reinvent clinical research and trials, and deliver better evidence for clinical guidelines. This is, essentially, the approach that the ONC is taking in the United States.

Creating global standards for these digital platforms is one area where international cooperation could have a major payoff. By cooperating to create such standards in order to enable secure data collection, sharing, and analysis, governments can greatly accelerate current efforts at national and international benchmarking and research.

Design New Incentives for Better Allocation of Resources

Governments should leverage their role as the primary (and often the sole) payer in national health systems to redefine payments in order to promote high-value care. Health care budgets and payment models need to steer investment to prevention and early intervention, encourage the development of fully integrated care pathways, and create incentives for informed patient choice of both providers and interventions. And outcomes measurement and pay-for-performance models should be integrated into procurement guidelines used by hospitals for the purchase of health care products.

As part of a new incentive system that emphasizes prevention and continuous improvement in health outcomes, governments should also pursue a more integrated approach to health and social welfare budgeting and planning. When most people think about health care, they tend to focus on the treatment of disease and on the complex network of providers, drug companies, and medical device makers responsible for delivering treatment to patients. In a world where major chronic diseases are becoming increasingly prevalent and now account for a major portion of health care costs, preventing disease is as important as treating it.

Many important interventions to prevent disease, however, are not typically viewed as being integral to medical care or in some cases, even part of the health system. Examples include efforts to address socioeconomic determinants of health or patient lifestyle choices. Too often, budgets for preventive activities stretch across multiple government agencies, creating obstacles to coordination, planning, and more rational resource use. The result is systematic underinvestment in prevention and public health.

In their role as the main financer of the health system, governments should strive to take a more holistic and integrated approach to budgeting for health care and social welfare, because social welfare spending is critical to addressing the social and behavioral determinants of health. (See the sidebar "Integrating Health Care and Social Welfare Services.")

Integrating Health Care and Social Welfare Services

In earlier chapters, we described how value-based innovators such as Kaiser Permanente, Intermountain Healthcare, Oak Street Health, and Humana are integrating clinical interventions with social welfare interventions to improve health equity and address the social determinants of health.[20] Some governments are also taking a more integrated approach to the financing of clinical care and social welfare services.

In January 2020, the Oregon Health Authority, the state agency that administers Oregon's Medicaid program, signed a contract with 15 coordinated-care organizations (CCOs) that provide care to the nearly 1 million low-income Oregon residents who receive Medicaid. The $6 billion contract (the largest in the state's history) sets new requirements for CCOs to improve the care delivered to Medicaid participants and thereby slow the growth in program costs.[21]

The plan also includes new provisions to reduce health disparities, address the social determinants of health, and promote health equity. For example, it requires CCOs to assess annually the health status and needs of the full population (not just the CCO's members) within its service area and to define a Community Health Improvement Plan in collaboration with mental, physical, and oral health care providers and related agencies such as community partners and local and regional governments.[22]

Ultimately, however, effectively addressing the social determinants of health and other health-equity issues will probably require a tighter integration not only of health care and social welfare budgets but also of clinical and social service provision. Take, for example, the innovative approach taken by the municipality of Norrtälje, north of Stockholm, in Sweden.

As discussed earlier, health care in Sweden is financed and managed by each of the country's 21 regional counties. Social welfare services, however, are financed and managed separately by each local municipality (there are 290 in total). Different administrative systems and service-delivery infrastructures can make it difficult to coordinate care across the boundary between the two systems, especially for elderly patients whose needs are more complex and who use a higher share of both services compared to the normal population. The result: higher total costs and poorer outcomes.

The municipality of Norrtälje has the highest portion of elderly residents over the age of 65 and over the age of 80 in the Stockholm region, an average income 15% below the regional median, and among its still-employed residents, a sick-leave rate that is 18% higher than the Swedish average. In 2006, as part of an effort to customize and integrate care in order to address the special needs of its elderly and relatively low-income population, the municipal government and the regional Stockholm County government joined together to create a new company known as Tiohundra to serve as a single public provider of both health care and social-welfare services.[23]

The company operates an emergency hospital, six primary health care clinics, and a home health care unit for patients who are unable to travel to obtain care. It also runs nursing homes and nursing centers; coordinates post-hospital rehabilitation in both primary care centers and in patients' homes; offers personal assistance and support at home for people with disabilities; and manages homes for children and adults who are unable to live independently. It even runs a preschool.

Tiohundra receives a single pool of funding from both municipal and county taxes. And the company combines caregivers from both the county and the municipality in multidisciplinary teams that address the full breadth of needs of the municipality's citizens. Taking an integrated approach to primary care and social services has contributed to a significantly lower increase in the cost for elderly care in Norrtälje than in the Stockholm region as a whole or in other parts of Sweden. And when patients do require acute care, they tend to spend less time in hospital because of Tiohundra's extensive network of home care and rehabilitation services. For example, Tiohundra patients hospitalized for chronic obstructive pulmonary disease (COPD) or heart failure have a shorter average length of stay in hospital than the Swedish average. Total health-care and social-service costs in Norrtälje are roughly equal to the Swedish average, but given the relatively heavy health care and social service needs of its elderly citizens, this is actually a considerable achievement.

This is an ambitious agenda. And no single country has put all these elements into place in a comprehensive fashion. But some governments are moving in this direction. Consider the example of Singapore.

MARKET-SHAPING TRANSFORMATION: SINGAPORE

The nation of Singapore has the second highest health-adjusted life expectancy in the world (second only to Japan), even as it spends only about 40% per capita on health care that the United States does.[24] Like the Netherlands, Singapore has made value-based health care a cornerstone of its strategy for the national health system. But unlike the Netherlands, the Singapore government has been far more directive in shaping the market for health services and influencing the behavior of both industry stakeholders and citizens when it comes to population health. In 2016, the Ministry of Health announced a strategy for the national health system known colloquially as the "Three Beyonds": beyond health care to health, beyond hospital to community, and beyond quality to value.

Beyond Health Care to Health

Singapore's strategy starts from a holistic perspective on the place of health care in the broader society and its role in encouraging human potential and national social and economic development. For example, a prominent theme of the current five-year Research, Innovation, and Enterprise plan of Singapore's National Research Foundation is "Human Health and Potential." The plan puts a premium on improving population health to support a strong economy, stating that "human capital is our principal and most valuable resource" and pledging to invest in R&D and other activities "to support improvements in health, productivity, and learning capacity across an individual's life course."[25]

The broad emphasis on improving population health and well-being has a number of implications. For one, it has led Singapore to invest significantly in screening, health promotion, and other preventive services. Nearly 6% of the government's non-Covid health care budget is devoted to health promotion and preventive health programs.

It has also led the government to think strategically and creatively about population segmentation, defining critical population segments in terms of pivotal stages in life when an intervention can have a significant positive impact on the individual. For example, as early as 2009, the government funded a birth cohort study called "Growing Up in Singapore Towards Healthy Outcomes (GUSTO)." The study enrolled some 1,200 pregnant women and has been systematically tracking their health outcomes through pregnancy, as well as the development of their children over time. Insights from GUSTO data have led to a variety of health policy changes. For instance, after approximately 20% of the pregnant women in the study were observed to suffer from gestational diabetes, the country implemented universal screening for the condition. The children in the GUSTO study are currently being followed into adolescence to identify associations between early development and subsequent cognitive development, growth, and executive function.

Another key theme of the strategic focus on value is to encourage citizens to develop a sense of personal responsibility for their health and their use of the health system. This is reflected in aspects of how Singapore finances its health system. In addition to universal basic health insurance and safety-net catastrophic coverage, Singapore uses a program known as MediSave, a compulsory health savings plan, to increase individual accountability. Under the plan, all employees contribute a percentage of their wages to their MediSave accounts, alongside employer contributions. Meanwhile, the government incentivizes the right behavior by continually adjusting how the funds can be used. Medisave withdrawals account for about 5% of national health expenditures.

Beyond Hospital to Community

The holistic focus on improving overall population health has also led to the creation of more integrated care pathways, both inside the traditional health sector and between it and other sectors of the economy. In 2017, the nation's health system was reorganized into three integrated regional clusters, with services that span the care continuum from primary care clinics to national specialty centers. In 2018, a pilot program known as "Integrated General Hospital" was launched by the Ministry of Health's Office of Healthcare Transformation. The program focuses on streamlining patient transitions back to the community, including a "hospital at home" option supported by community medical partners. An initiative, known as "Future Primary Care," emphasizes improving patient self-management of chronic conditions in partnership with primary care providers—for example, through the increased use of remote monitoring and diagnostics.

Another community-based strategy is to support grassroots community action to make it easier for people to adopt healthy behaviors. For example, the Ministry of Health has developed and tested a "Healthy Precinct" concept for assisting non-health-related government agencies to adopt health-promoting policies and approaches in their projects. Other initiatives assist community organizations to develop programs that encourage healthy behaviors and reinforce citizen health. Throughout the Singapore health system, one can find myriad programs aimed at encouraging healthier behaviors and linking clinical care to everyday social interventions. Examples include: urban neighborhoods designed to encourage exercise, a "Healthier Dining Program" in which restaurants commit to reduce saturated fat content and increase the use of whole grains (by March 2021, some 40% of commercial establishments had joined); healthy aging programs that design jobs around the needs of older adults, support senior-friendly transportation, and encourage social connection; even the creation of "dementia-friendly" communities where residents are trained in simple interventions to assist people with dementia.

Beyond Quality to Value

Finally, Singapore's strategy for health-system transformation embraces the focus on outcomes measurement that has been a major theme of this book. In 2017, the Ministry of Health identified 17 highly prevalent and costly medical conditions, including total hip replacement, spinal fusion, and congestive heart failure, and began working with clinical teams to standardize outcome and cost measures in order to benchmark performance across institutions. In 2019, the National University Hospital announced that its own continuous improvement initiative had improved quality and lowered cost in 27 out of 34 conditions. Efforts are also underway to develop comprehensive outcomes measurement for patients with multiple comorbidities to reinforce a more integrated approach to care.

The one area where Singapore has made less progress, however, is in the digitization of health information. Although the country deployed a national electronic health record in 2011 to provide longitudinal patient data to all authorized health care professionals, so far, the bulk of the data comes from public institutions, with only 3% of the more than 4,000 private health care providers contributing data. The fact that roughly 20% of private general practitioners in Singapore still use paper-based medical records is one obstacle to the universal use of the electronic health record. So are concerns about data security (in 2018, a cyberattack caused a data breach at Singhealth, Singapore's largest provider, that affected the data of some 1.5 million patients). To increase provider adoption and facilitate secure data sharing, the Singapore government is developing health-information legislation that should be put in place in the near future.

Shaping the Market to Compete on Value

Singapore's national health care strategy is highly directive. But that's not to say it is bureaucratic or opposed to the introduction of market-based mechanisms in the health sector. Rather, the goal is to encourage competition and to steer it so that providers compete on value delivered to patients in the form of cost-effective high-quality care. For example, the Singapore public hospital system has been restructured to provide hospitals with more autonomy, enabling competition to achieve higher quality at lower costs and providing a viable alternative to private hospitals.

"Health care systems tend to be hyperlocal, and care is generally delivered by teams who value their autonomy greatly," explained Dr. Chorh-Chuan Tan, former president of the National University of Singapore and currently chief health scientist of the Singapore Ministry of Health. "Most providers want to do better for their patients. We try to tap into this positive energy by removing barriers to change and supporting care-model transformation at scale. Then, we gain support for reforms by demonstrating the success and impact of our programs."

At the same time, the policymakers guiding the national strategy for the health sector recognize that health care is an imperfect market. They have taken multiple measures to shape that market toward maximum value. They control the number of hospitals and specialists in order to guard against supplier-induced low-value care. In 2015, they established the Agency for Care Effectiveness to conduct value-based pricing negotiations with drug and med-tech manufacturers to ensure pricing aligned with outcomes for patients, provide evidence-based appropriate-care guidelines, and support professional and consumer education to enable shared decision-making in treatment. Like other nations, Singapore is actively embracing value-based payment. In March 2022, the Ministry of Health announced that the nation's three publicly financed health clusters would transition from a traditional fee-for-service payment model to a population-based capitated payment model.[26]

MAKING GAME-CHANGING BETS

As part of a broad market-shaping mission, governments should also consider making strategic investments to jump-start key infrastructure for a value-based health system. Mazzucato points out that parallel to the creation of NASA in 1958, the US Department of Defense created the Defense Advanced Research Projects Agency (DARPA). DARPA is famous for the strategic investments it made in ARPANET, which (as described in Chapter 6) led to the basic technologies and technical standards that made possible the internet. More recently, DARPA funded early R&D at two pharmaceutical companies, Moderna and Inovio, which led to the creation of mRNA vaccines such as the Covid-19 vaccines that are protecting more and more people around the world from the ravages of the pandemic.

Other examples of mission-related strategic public investments include the South Korean government's initiative to make South Korea a leader in HDTV technology and the $465 million loan made by the US Department of Energy in 2010 to Tesla Motors to produce all-electric plug-in vehicles. These are all examples of how, during periods of rapid technological change, governments have often played a critical role in making strategic investments to jump-start new markets.

Precisely how governments organize these investments is critical. The goal should be not so much "picking winners" in the sense of championing specific companies or organizations (a common criticism of government strategic investments). Rather, it should be creating the right kind of environment for successful value-based innovations to emerge. As Mazzucato puts it, in order to effectively drive a society-wide mission, government "must transform itself into an innovating organization with the capacity and capability to energize and catalyze the economy to be more purpose-driven."[27]

The Apollo program, for example, combined centralized top-down strategy, planning, and monitoring with highly decentralized project execution. The approach to creating value-based health systems should be the same: top-down alignment around shared goals with common standards that all stakeholders must follow, but with a high degree of autonomy, allowing stakeholders the organizational flexibility to innovate and adapt to changing conditions. Interestingly, a key component of the approach used in the Apollo program was so-called outcomes-based budgeting. In this approach, the outcomes for a particular project or initiative were clearly defined, but contracting organizations had a large measure of autonomy in terms of how to organize to achieve those outcomes, leaving room for innovation and new thinking.

As we have seen, some governments are making relatively modest investments in the creation of a value-based infrastructure for the health system. Examples include Sweden's program in the mid-2010s to expand that country's network of quality registries (described in Chapter 2) or the Netherlands' five-year plan for outcomes-based health care, described earlier in this chapter. But a true moonshot will require a higher level of ambition and significantly more investment.

What might such strategic investments look like? Let's consider one last country example: the United States.

HOW STRATEGIC INVESTMENTS COULD CHANGE THE GAME: UNITED STATES

The Netherlands and Singapore are small countries with populations of approximately 17.5 million and 6 million people, respectively. A moonshot transformation of the world's health systems won't really take off until the governments of much larger countries commit to the value-based transformation of their national health systems. And given the size and sophistication of its health care sector and its dominant role in the funding of biomedical research, future developments in the United States will probably be a key driver in the evolution of value-based health care.

At first glance, it might seem unlikely that the US health system could play a leadership role in the value-based transformation of the world's health systems. The system is highly fragmented (indeed, some argue that the country does not have a truly national health system at all, but rather a collection of regional and local systems). Despite years of trying to address the problem, US health care still struggles with the persistence of high-cost low-value care. Among the world's countries, the United States spends the most on health care per capita and yet delivers health outcomes that in many areas lag those of its peer nations. As Elizabeth Bradley and Lauren Taylor point out in their book, *The American Health Care Paradox*, the United States spends considerably less on social welfare than many peer countries, despite the fact that more and more evidence demonstrates the centrality of social-welfare programs to population health.[28]

And yet, as we have seen in previous chapters, there is a remarkable amount of value-based innovation taking place in the US health system today. And the US government, through its role as funder of the Medicare and Medicaid public-insurance programs, has played a leadership role and invested considerable public resources—for example, $20 billion to launch the value-based payment initiatives in the Alternative Payment Models program and nearly $40 billion to jump-start the widespread adoption of electronic medical records, the first step in what has become a growing government focus on health information interoperability. And, of course, about 40% of Medicare's spending for health services (roughly

$350 billion per year) is funneled through Medicare Advantage plans that, as we discussed in Chapter 5, have been an engine for innovation in value-based payment and value-based care delivery.

What would it take for the US government to go to the next level in the value-based transformation of the US health system? Consider the following scenario. The United States spends roughly $4 trillion on health care every year. Imagine if 1% of that amount, $40 billion per year, or $400 billion over a 10-year period, were set aside in a value-based health care public investment fund. That may sound like a great deal of money, and it is. But the annual cost is only about 4% to 5% of the estimated $760 billion to $935 billion that the United States wastes every year on unnecessary or medically inappropriate health care spending.

Building on the progress already made by initiatives such as Alternative Payment Models program, Medicare Advantage, and ONC's interoperability agenda, such an investment fund could be used to:

- Create a national resource center for patient-value improvement
  - Develop and validate standardized outcomes measures in cooperation with the Centers for Medicare and Medicaid Services (CMS), the National Quality Forum (NQF), and private payers
  - Establish a national network for conducting prospective registry-based randomized clinical trials (R-RCTs) to evaluate drugs, devices, and decision-support tools together with the FDA and other regulatory bodies.
- Accelerate the development and implementation of health-information technical standards
  - Set health-care-specific standards for cybersecurity to improve protection of patient data while enabling relevant data sharing
  - Adequately finance the development of current and next-generation interoperability standards
  - Establish a national platform for the distributed analysis of health data
  - Collaborate with other nations to develop and endorse international interoperability standards
- Create a regulatory framework and system of incentives for health-system innovation
  - Design a legal framework to regulate the use of patient health data

- ○ Require all digital-health devices to comply with international cybersecurity and interoperability standards
- ○ Strengthen regulatory requirements for evidence generation—for example, by publicly funding or requiring pharmaceutical and medical technology companies to fund comparative-effectiveness research
- ○ Define a national framework for value-based payment models to reduce complexity and align all health care stakeholders around improved patient value

Finally, some portion of this budget—say, 10% or about $4 billion per year (roughly equivalent to DARPA's annual budget)—could be used to fund adequately the new Advanced Research Projects Agency for Health (ARPA-H), proposed by the Biden administration and authorized by the US Congress in March 2022. The funding could focus the new agency's mission on supporting cutting-edge public-private research initiatives on the future digital learning platforms for clinical research, evidence generation, and innovation in support of value-based care delivery and precision medicine.[29]

Such an ambitious agenda would begin to reach genuine moonshot territory. It would also be of the order of magnitude necessary to build on the existing islands of innovation in the US health system and decisively reorient the trajectory of the entire sector toward cost-effective high-value care. Even more important, it would put down a marker for the world and, we hope, stimulate similar investments from other large countries in Europe and Asia.

WHICH GOVERNMENTS WILL TAKE THE LEAD?

At this stage, it is unclear which governments or governmental agencies, let alone which political leaders or policymakers, will play the role in the value-based transformation of the world's health systems that John F. Kennedy and the US government played in the space race. The different approaches to health care in various parts of the world all have their strengths and weaknesses—which is to say that no single nation has all the answers, and everybody has something to learn from everyone else.

Europe, with its publicly financed health systems, has a strong focus on universal access and overall public health, a balanced and complementary approach to health and social welfare spending, and many nations with robust national systems for the collection of health data, including outcomes data. And yet, recent trends toward geographic fragmentation exemplified by Brexit and differential responses to the coronavirus pandemic may hinder the continent's effort to take an integrated approach to value-based transformation. For example, so far, the European Union's approach to setting standards for the interoperability of digital-health information has been highly fragmented.

The US health system, by contrast, benefits from American society's embrace of innovation, making it a leader in some areas of value-based health care, including risk-based contracting and other forms of value-based payment. Digital-health interoperability is now very much on the agenda of government policy makers. But the US system's Achilles heel is the lack of universal coverage and unequal access to care, the high costs and excessive fragmentation of the national health system, and a relatively unsystematic approach (compared to European countries) to tracking health outcomes. What's more, the relative weakness of the federal government in driving strategic change and the power of deeply entrenched vested interests are also potential obstacles to system transformation.

In the early days of the coronavirus pandemic, some Asian governments demonstrated the capacity to respond rapidly and coherently to the crisis and to develop holistic "whole-of-government" strategies and solutions.[30] They, as well as many low-and middle-income countries, also have the advantage of being less burdened by traditional legacy health systems and are, therefore, in a position to make important strategic investments in value-based health infrastructure that will allow them to leapfrog the systems in more high-income nations. For example, it may well be that, years from now, China's current massive investments in artificial intelligence will prove to be a competitive advantage in that country's capacity to deliver high-value care to its population.

Or, alternatively, is there an opportunity for a genuinely global effort, in which the world puts national prestige and geopolitical differences aside to cooperate and learn from the extraordinary variety of the global population and from the diversity of its health systems and clinical practices? During this period of mounting international competition and conflict, it may seem unlikely. But as our experience of the pandemic has made painfully clear, protecting and improving population health, much like efforts to fight climate change, will only be effective if they take place on a global scale. Such an international effort could build on the experience of the pandemic and recognize the importance of learning from each other and developing joint standards, whether it is for pandemic monitoring and response, or for better managing other major conditions such as diabetes or bipolar disease. The independent commission established by the World Health Organization (WHO) to assess the world's response to the pandemic has recommended the creation of a supranational body, under the auspices of the United Nations, to oversee the development of the most critical global standards to ensure we never experience so devastating a global health emergency again.[31] One could imagine the same or a similar body to oversee the development of global standards (both medical and technical) to enable global cooperation on the targeted value-based interventions that we have described in this book.

A national or international mission for the value-based transformation of the world's health systems will face inevitable challenges. How to balance the priority of building better, more cost-effective health systems against other urgent global priorities? How to allocate society's limited health care dollars across different patient groups (for instance, the young versus the elderly, or sufferers of acute diseases versus sufferers of chronic diseases)? How to get political leaders with radically different ideological preferences to agree on the steps necessary to achieve the shared goal of improving health outcomes for the population? How to persuade various stakeholders, often with conflicting interests and some of whom have lived well off the dysfunctionalities of the current system, to sign on to the change journey, especially if they run the risk of being harmed economically? These are tough—or as Mazzucato says, "wicked"—problems, and while we have described a broad range of promising initiatives, we don't have all the answers.

But that's not a reason not to get started. As John F. Kennedy said when announcing the moonshot in 1962: "We choose to go to the moon in this decade and do the other things, not because they are easy, but because they are hard, because that goal will serve to organize and measure the best of our energies and skills, because that challenge is one that we are willing to accept, one we are unwilling to postpone, and one which we intend to win."[32]

As a leadership vision, the world's health care sector—and the world's population—deserve nothing less.

Value-Based Transformation of National Health Systems: Action Steps

POLITICIANS AND POLICYMAKERS

1. **Be strategic.** Plan for the national health system of the future, not the health system of today.

2. **Mandate comprehensive outcomes measurement and transparency.** While the timing of the transition may vary, every country should embrace the goal of comprehensive health-outcomes measurement, transparent to the public.

3. **Design new incentives for more effective resource allocation.** Steer investment to prevention and early intervention; encourage the development of fully integrated care pathways; integrate outcomes measurement and pay-for-performance into procurement guidelines for hospital and health care products.

4. **Invest in a value-based digital infrastructure.** Establish standards for digital interoperability and cybersecurity. And insist that providers and technology vendors incorporate them.

5. **Focus on health, not just health care.** Take a holistic approach to health care and social welfare spending to address issues of social equity and effectively address the social determinants of health.

6. **Regulate to innovate, not just to avoid risk.** Managing risk is important, but too much emphasis on avoiding risk can hinder innovation. Strike a balance between these two goals.

CHAPTER 8
THE VALUE LEADERSHIP AGENDA

n previous chapters, we have described a road map for transforming the world's health systems to align all stakeholders around the shared goal of delivering better health to defined patient groups and population segments.

We have told the stories of pioneering organizations that are driving the transition to value-based health care and delivering exceptional results. We've also described the many systemwide changes that are necessary to accelerate that transition: changes in how health systems measure performance and define success, how they organize care delivery, how they pay providers and suppliers, and how they use digital technologies to leverage the rapidly expanding quantities of health information to improve clinical practice. We've also argued that the world's governments need to embrace a clear strategic agenda for the transformation of their national health systems, including focused but firm guidance on the part of policymakers and regulators. Finally, we have made the case for more international cooperation to reap the benefits of global scale.

In this final chapter, we focus on the responsibilities of health care leaders, both to prepare their organizations to thrive in an increasingly value-based world and to work together, across the various sectors of the industry, to bring about the system changes necessary to make value-based health care the organizing principle of the world's health systems.

In particular, we believe that successful health care leaders must embrace three distinctive leadership tasks:

1. *Strategic* leadership: defining how their organizations are going to survive, thrive, and compete in a value-based world
2. *Transformational* leadership: engaging their people in the hard work of becoming a value-based organization
3. *System* leadership: looking beyond the immediate interests of their own organizations to become champions of the broad changes necessary to ensure the long-term sustainability of the health care industry as a whole, on which their own success ultimately depends

STRATEGIC LEADERSHIP

In any industry that is experiencing rapid change, leaders of established institutions face a fundamental strategic dilemma: Do they embrace change and move quickly to take advantage of the latest developments? Or do they wait until the new landscape is firmly established and better understood, protecting their current sources of strength and competitive advantage as long as possible?

Some readers may be uncomfortable with our applying the language of competitive advantage to health care. Health care isn't, or shouldn't be, a business, they may be thinking; it's a public service. And there shouldn't be room for competition—and therefore the discussion of competitive dynamics—in the health sector. Yet the reality is that there have always been varieties of competition in health care. For one, large portions of the global health care industry—in particular, the pharmaceutical and med-tech sectors—are organized as highly competitive (albeit, regulated) for-profit businesses. In the United States, providers are typically non-profit, and while private insurers are for-profit, they are heavily regulated. They often compete with each other—for example, for access to patients or for market power in local markets so they can influence negotiations over pricing. Even in the publicly financed health systems of western Europe, new varieties of competition are emerging. When Swiss payers start sending their prostate cancer patients to Martini Klinik in Germany, as we described in Chapter 3, that puts Swiss prostate cancer surgeons in competition with German prostate cancer surgeons for patient volume.

In our view, the goal should not be to eliminate all forms of competition but rather to *harness* it so that it contributes to improvement in the value delivered to patients. Although some health care leaders may think they have the luxury to wait and see how the various trends described in this book play themselves out, the fact is, the shift to value-based health care is already changing the terms of competition in the health care sector.

A number of powerful forces are converging to reshape industry competitive dynamics around value. The value-based innovators whose rise we have chronicled in this book are developing powerful new business models for delivering better care at lower cost from which other players can learn and to which they must respond.

What's more, large established players, especially in the pharmaceutical and med-tech sector, are increasingly making big strategic bets to take advantage of the trends discussed in this book. To cite one example: in the last decade, Philips has reshaped itself from a multibusiness conglomerate into a focused provider of value-based med-tech products, solutions, and services—including embarking on a number of serial acquisitions to better position itself to compete in a more integrated, outcomes-based digital-health environment. Among the acquisitions the company has made to build out its value-based capabilities: Wellcentive, a digital-health platform that supports the management of high-risk, high-cost patients; Forcare, which specializes in interoperability software solutions to support data exchange between medical systems; VitalHealth, which provides tools for outcomes measurement, patient engagement, and care coordination; Medumo, a patient-engagement startup to support communication with patients outside of the hospital in an effort to increase pre-exam instruction adherence; and Capsule Technologies, a device-information platform that integrates digitized information from medical devices into patient EMRs. And as we discussed in Chapter 6, the big digital platform companies are also beginning to reshape the health care marketplace, much as they have other sectors of the economy.

Venture capital and private equity are also getting into the act. Value-based health care is becoming a growing niche for venture and private-equity investment in companies that are reinventing US primary care, creating new digital-health solutions, or otherwise pursuing value-based strategies. Major venture-capital and private-equity firms such as Blackstone, KKR, Carlyle, General Atlantic, and Warburg are not only investing in existing health-care businesses but also launching growth-equity funds to invest in early-stage ventures in the provider space. For example, General Atlantic, with nearly $80 billion under investment, was an early investor in Oak Street Health. Nor is growing investor interest in value-based health care purely an American phenomenon. The Swedish investment firm Kinnevik (with a net asset value of 75.8 billion Swedish kronor, or more than $8 billion) is focusing on companies that are using digital technology to redefine care delivery, transform care management for chronic conditions, improve the health of underserved populations, and scale the delivery of high-quality, value-based care.

Finally, as we saw in the previous chapter, many governments from the Netherlands to Wales to Singapore to the United States are beginning to reshape the policy and regulatory environment in which health care companies operate to encourage value-based models of care. All these forces are changing the landscape and decisively shifting competitive dynamics in health care.

What will characterize the new environment in an increasingly value-based health sector? We see three fundamental megatrends.

1. **Increasing transparency of outcomes and costs.** First, health care organizations will increasingly operate in an environment characterized by transparency of and accountability for the specific health outcomes delivered to patients, as well as the costs to the health system for delivering those outcomes. As Intermountain's Marc Harrison told us: "Unless an organization is transparent about its costs of care and what it is charging people, it can't really say it is a value-based organization."

   Hospitals, primary care organizations, drug companies, and device makers that cannot demonstrate that their procedures, medications, and products genuinely add value to patients and to the health system are likely to suffer. It will no longer be enough for organizations to rely on a historical brand to promote the quality of the care they deliver. They will have to demonstrate that quality by means of the documented superiority of the health outcomes they deliver—for example, through better access to and analysis of clinical data; deeper insight about how to improve outcomes; and more effective collaborations and partnerships to develop new value-based innovations and business models.

2. **Growing integration and consolidation of care pathways.** Patient care pathways will become more integrated and more networked. Traditional boundaries will become increasingly blurred as players try to provide end-to-end solutions for specific patient segments or population groups.

One form this integration will take is the progressive blending of physical and digital infrastructure, creating what our colleagues at the BCG Henderson Institute call the "bionic" organization.[1] New digital-health applications will not so much replace doctors and other clinical staff, but rather support them in their decision-making and clinical interventions. But organizations are going to have to learn how to seamlessly integrate such applications into the clinical workflow.

Another dimension of this trend will be growing payer-provider integration as payers introduce new value-based payment models and leverage their vast databases about their members to contribute to, and in some cases fundamentally shape, the coordination of patient care and to help providers manage risk in a world of risk-based contracting.

3. **The rise of multipartner health ecosystems.** As health systems increasingly focus on comprehensive solutions, incorporating multiple factors that affect health outcomes—drugs, medical technology, health information, care management, new types of clinical and socioeconomic interventions—the role of orchestrating and managing all these inputs will grow in importance.

In most situations, it is highly unlikely that any one organization will control every input along more integrated care pathways. Rather we are seeing the emergence of complex health ecosystems in which different players will compete in some situations and collaborate in others.[2] In the late 1990s, Adam Brandenburger and Barry Nalebuff coined the term *coopetition*—the combination of competition and cooperation—to describe this increasingly common competitive dynamic.[3] It is highly applicable to the emergent value-based health care sector today.

A key open question for the future is: Which institutions will play the lead role in orchestrating these health ecosystems? At first glance, it would seem that providers are well positioned to do so. After all, they control the decision-making along the treatment pathway. But if provider organizations don't move fast, they risk playing a subordinate role, while more dynamic payers, suppliers, or new network integrators take on the system-integration role and overlay their services and products to deliver value to a customer—the patient—whom the provider sees but doesn't actually "own."[4]

All these trends will confront health care leaders with complex strategic questions. Throughout our book, we have provided readers with detailed action steps, organized by stakeholder, for transitioning to value-based health care. But such actions will only make sense if they are embedded in a coherent value-based strategy.

Providers

Do leaders at provider organizations embrace outcomes transparency and use it to drive continuous improvement to position their organizations favorably to payers and prospective patients and to attract the best clinical talent? If so, they will need to engage their clinical teams in the task of tracking and learning from standardized outcome metrics.

Do they aspire to become a leader in a specific disease area as Martini Klinik has done in prostate cancer, or to serve the full range of health needs for a specific population segment like Oak Street is doing for the low-income elderly? If so, they will need to learn how to leverage the collection of outcomes data to move faster down the experience curve than rivals, providing levels of quality that are demonstrably better than their peers.

Or are they in a position to become integrated full-service providers that manage a broad-based population for maximum health care value via their own integrated care chains, much like Kaiser Permanente? And if so, to what degree should they build the necessary capabilities internally or instead act as brokers, helping their patients navigate to the best independent providers, which align their approaches with the integrated provider's systems and have unique capabilities?

Finally, can they assemble a full-fledged value-based ecosystem such as Intermountain Health is doing that can deliver quality care on a national or even international scale?

Given their complex multifaceted missions, combining care delivery with research and education, traditional academic medical centers will face unique strategic challenges. What is the right balance between increased specialization (and often high-cost care) and team-based disease-focused care delivery? What are the opportunities to become a global center of excellence for clinical research and practice in value-based care (akin to the approach that Erasmus MC is taking in the Netherlands)? What would it take to become a leader in the kind of global learning networks described in Chapter 6 to drive faster evidence generation in the service of improving clinical guidelines?[5]

Payers

As new approaches to value-based payment make value a major criterion for reimbursement and push financial risk to both providers and suppliers, payers are in a position to play an increasingly central role in the coordination of care. As a result, they have a major responsibility to make sure that the health care market is designed so that outcomes-based competition leads to increased innovation, better quality care, and lower costs.

In countries where health care markets are highly fragmented, such as the United States, there will be increased pressure to rationalize the system. This trend will create opportunities for private insurers that are able to improve outcomes by coordinating care and making better use of clinical information—as we saw in the Humana example in Chapter 5.

Value-based health care will also likely drive payer consolidation to address issues such as health insurance churn (in which individuals move frequently from one health insurance plan to another) that we described in Chapter 5. The ultimate success of value-based payment models will require either fewer payers, with longer-lasting relationships between an individual payer and insured individual, or stronger guidance from government regulators (for instance, requirements to invest in a multipayer fund covering investments in prevention or to participate in a relatively small set of standardized value-based payment models).

Meanwhile, the leaders of government-funded health systems that are already highly integrated have to be careful not to allow too-narrow a view of market competition to fragment what is already a relatively integrated health care environment. In Sweden, for example, recent privatization reforms to encourage patient choice and reduce waiting times for elective procedures has had two contradictory impacts. In some situations, it has led to the development of some of the most successful value-based payment models we have seen. In others, however, it has reinforced the traditional fee-for-service payment model that, in other countries, has been a major obstacle to the delivery of integrated value-based care.

Pharma and Med-Tech Companies

To remain competitive, med-tech and pharmaceutical companies will need to "think beyond the device" and "beyond the pill." For example, they may seek to do what Medtronic is attempting for diabetes care through its acquisition of Diabeter: integrate downstream and build a fully integrated supplier and care-provision franchise in a specific disease area. Their access to data from patient populations on a global scale may provide a strong competitive advantage, especially in new and rapidly evolving therapeutic areas. (For more on the strategic challenges and opportunities that value-based health care poses for the pharmaceutical industry in particular, see the sidebar "What Value-Based Health Care Means for Pharma.")

What Value-Based Health Care Means for Pharma

The global pharmaceutical sector is one of the most profitable industries there is, so it would seem that the sector would have little to worry about in the development of value-based health care. And yet, the trends we have described in this book—in particular, increasing transparency about health outcomes—are likely to have a major impact on the traditional sources of competitive advantage in the industry.

For years, pharma companies have competed on the basis of the medical differentiation of their products and the sophistication of their marketing and sales activities. The former has put a premium on a strong R&D organization able to design new drugs that address unmet medical needs. The latter has increasingly focused on engaging with a broad range of influencers—payers, patients, and individual clinicians who prescribe a company's drugs. Both these areas of strength risk being eroded by value-based health care.

The number of criteria determining the success of a new drug is expanding, and commercial access is increasingly linked to the post-registration performance of the drug. Where market access traditionally focused on efficacy, safety, and whether the new drug addressed an unmet medical need, both public and private payers are increasingly evaluating new drugs in terms of their comparative effectiveness and cost-effectiveness based on real-world evidence (that is, data from the use of the drug in an uncontrolled patient population in normal clinical practice). Failure to meet these new criteria can lead to lower levels of reimbursement, outright exclusion from a payer's benefits package, or even the withdrawal of regulatory approval. As one pharma sales executive told us, "We need to move from 'price per tablet' to 'price per outcome.'"

In many respects, however, pharma companies are actually well-placed to play a dynamic role in a health care environment increasingly organized around the delivery of superior health outcomes to patient segments defined by disease. They possess strong disease-based clinical knowledge, which could provide the foundation of new approaches for improving health outcomes in key diseases. Their global reach positions them better than national or regional payers and providers to identify and disseminate excellent clinical practice. And they have developed considerable expertise in managing stakeholder relations with both public and private payers, as well as, in some cases, with providers), enabling them to play an orchestrator role among clinicians and suppliers.

To take advantage of such opportunities, however, pharma company leaders need to be exploring basic strategic questions such as: How far should a company expand from a traditional focus on providing therapeutic interventions—whether going upstream into diagnosis and prevention and wellness activities, or downstream into treatment monitoring and follow-up? Should it consider offering data and health-information services in addition to drugs? What about care-management or care-delivery expertise? Where on the spectrum from drug supplier to complete health-solution provider should a company operate—and in what specific therapeutic or disease areas?

New value-based strategies will also force companies to greatly increase collaboration, both internally between the R&D and commercial sides of the business and externally with innovative clinical centers around the world. Such imperatives pose additional strategic questions: How to encourage more multifunctional cooperation across traditionally separate silos in the organization? And how to build trust with other stakeholders to work together to cocreate the innovative solutions of the future?

Politicians and Policymakers

The government decision makers who set the rules of the game for the health sector also face fundamental strategic choices. Their decisions shape the environment in which other stakeholders operate. Whether they see health care as a public service or a regulated private market or some combination of the two, they need to make sure that the rules and regulations they develop—for payment, pricing, drug-and-device regulation, and the acceptable uses of health information—combine in a coherent policy framework that encourages better value for patients and improved public health.

Identifying New Capabilities

For all stakeholders, strategic leadership includes identifying the new capabilities needed to effectively execute the desired strategy and planning to develop or acquire them. For provider organizations, for instance, the capacity to collect and analyze outcomes and cost data at the patient group level will be critical, not only for driving performance improvement but also for responding appropriately to payers' demands that both providers and suppliers take on more risk. Provider organizations will also need to beef up their capabilities in procurement to evaluate suppliers' offerings in terms of their impact on patient outcomes and the total cost of care. Finally, in a world increasingly defined by value-based ecosystems, the ability to forge trusted partnerships and close collaborations with other organizations will be an increasingly important capability.

TRANSFORMATIONAL LEADERSHIP

For many organizations, the transition to value-based health care will be disruptive. New clinical practices, care pathways, and modes of value-based payment will shift the balance of power in organizations. It will also make new demands on organizations to work in a more team-based and agile fashion. Such changes will inevitably provoke resistance from some parts of the organization, even as others welcome the change.

Getting organizations to move quickly to embrace a more value-based model will require transformational leadership: the ability of leaders to engage with key interest groups, to set a clear value-based mission that is tied to the fundamental purpose of the organization and make clear why achieving it is essential, to bring their organization along in a way that combines autonomy with accountability, and to persist in the face of doubt, criticism, and opposition.

Fortunately, they have the examples of the pioneers whom we have profiled throughout this book to learn from. In previous chapters, we have encountered committed leaders who with vision and persistence are fundamentally reinventing how health care works. Reflecting on their example, we have identified six basic characteristics of transformational leadership that we believe all health care leaders need to cultivate.

1. **Set the goal beyond the grasp.** The first trait is to set ambitious and—what to many may appear to be—impossible goals. That's what Michael Porter and Elizabeth Teisberg did in their 2006 book, calling for a fundamental redefinition of health care by putting the outcomes delivered to patients for a given cost at the center of how the sector measures and assesses performance. Neither was a health professional, and industry insiders criticized their proposal to define and track the outcomes that matter to patients as "utopian."[6] Yet, 15 years later, their work has inspired a global movement. A thousand clinicians and patient representatives from around the world have dedicated enormous amounts of time to establishing, testing, and validating the ICHOM outcome-measurement sets; thousands more are using them in clinical sites. And Porter and Teisberg (who now has a dual appointment in the medical and business schools at the University of Texas, where she leads the Value Institute for Health and Care) are training the next generation of clinical leaders and health care managers.

Or take Mike Pykosz and his colleagues at Oak Street Health. They created the organization because they wanted to do the right thing for an underserved population, the low-income elderly, and because they saw an opportunity to use the emerging Medicare Advantage payment model to rethink the delivery of primary care. They set an extraordinarily ambitious goal and took risks in an environment where there were no guarantees. Ten years later, their company is serving 150,000 people in 20 states.

2. **Surround yourself with people who are more capable than you.** Of course, no leader can transform an organization on his or her own. The best leaders make sure to surround themselves with people who bring unique skills, capabilities, and a sense of commitment to the mission. This is what Hartwig Huland did when he decided to change the rigidly hierarchical structure of the traditional German urology clinic to create a flatter, more equal, and more collegial team structure for Martini Klinik's faculty. It is also what Marc Harrison did when he appointed the head of Intermountain's nursing organization to his executive team and recruited Disney's head of global consumer insight to become Intermountain's first chief consumer officer. And it is what Ernst Kuipers did at Erasmus MC when he empowered first-rate clinicians like Linetta Koppert to redesign the institution's care pathways.

3. **Put mission ahead of self.** Change can put an organization under considerable strain, especially in large provider organizations. Sometimes that requires leaders to take risks, including putting their own careers on the line. For example, Melvin Samsom stayed true to his mission of transforming the organizational and operating model of the Karolinska University Hospital, despite considerable opposition, both inside and outside the hospital—opposition that eventually contributed to his resignation. Yet four years later, the core principles of Samsom's value-based operating model for the hospital remain in place, and the organization is delivering remarkable results.

4. **Combine authority with humility.** Transformational leaders need to be strong, even stubborn, in the face of opposition. But they also need to be humble. When Hartwig Huland joined forces with Markus Graefen to establish Martini Klinik, he was a world-leading urologist at the apex of the professional pyramid in academic medicine.

Yet when the clinic's outcomes data showed that a young surgeon had better results than Huland, his immediate response was: "You're better than me. When you do your next surgery, I want to observe and learn from you." The complexity of medicine and the enormous opportunities to further improve patient health requires just that kind of humility and openness to learning from what experience and the data have to teach.

5. **Establish common standards, and insist on the discipline of following them.** Improving performance depends on the establishment of shared standards and the commitment of the organization to live by them. The founders of leading quality registries—for example, Lars Wallentin at Swedeheart and Warren Warwick at the US cystic fibrosis registry—realized the importance of enforcing standards to be able to use high-quality data to learn from experience. It took several years of hard work to get alignment from peers and different clinical centers, and then to convince colleagues across each nation to gather and share their data, including with the general public. Wallentin, Warwick, and numerous other registry leaders unmentioned in this book have demonstrated that outcomes measurement can transform health care and inaugurate a new era of faster evidence generation and clinical innovation, resulting in better care for patients.

6. **Lead from the front.** Finally, transformational leaders can't be distant from the organization. They need to be present, visible, continuously interacting with people, constantly communicating the goals of the organization and the payoff that will eventually come from changing how everyone works together. We saw how Marc Harrison has led this way at Intermountain, driving change through the organization, even in the face of initial skepticism. But so have other health care CEOs—for example, Frans van Houten at Philips and Bruce Broussard at Humana.

As the health care environment continues to evolve under the impact of the trends described in this book, such transformational leadership traits will become increasingly important. Health care no longer needs leaders who simply maintain the status quo. It needs transformational leaders. (See the sidebar "A Venture Capitalist's View on Health Care Leadership.")

A Venture Capitalist's View on Health Care Leadership

To get a venture capitalist's perspective on the kind of qualities that health care leaders need to succeed in a value-based environment, we talked to Trevor Price, founder and CEO of Oxeon Partners.

Price founded Oxeon in 2011 as an executive search firm focused on recruiting talent and building leadership teams for companies with a mission to transform health care. Over the past decade, he has leveraged his relationships with literally thousands of health care entrepreneurs to expand his business into value-based investing, taking positions in startups that are addressing major gaps in the US health system. Oxeon was an early investor in new-style primary care companies such as Landmark Health, Iora Health, VillageMD, and Oak Street Health. (In 2018, Price cofounded Town Hall Ventures, an institutional venture-capital firm, with Andy Slavitt, the former acting administrator of the Centers for Medicare and Medicaid Services in the Obama Administration.)

Price believes these companies are on the leading edge of a major transition in the US health care industry. "The entire hierarchy of power on the clinical side is shifting," he said. "Traditionally, the specialists have been the alphas in health care. They made the most money and had the most prestige. But they are being disintermediated. In the future, it will be the primary care providers and the mental and behavioral health specialists who will be the quarterbacks of the system, distributing the patients to the most appropriate sites of care."

Such companies also represent a general transition in health care leadership. "A decade ago, when we started Oxeon, I used to hear frequently, 'There is no great leadership talent in health care.' The core leaders, especially at the big hospital systems, were typically in their 70s—and they are even older now." But according to Price, the situation has changed dramatically in the past 10 years. "The industry has woken up to entrepreneurship. There has been a dramatic demographic shift in terms of leadership. The companies we are recruiting for and investing in are all started by 35-year-olds. They have a different, less conflictual, view of payers than traditional providers do and are far more willing to partner with them. They have a different view of technology. Most of all, they have a completely different view of the 'product'—by which I mean how they think about how patients interact with the health system."

When recruiting for leadership roles at value-based health care companies, Price looks for people who are willing to engage in the hard work of designing and building the business (what he calls a "take out the trash" mentality) and who can cooperate and enable others. "Do they describe their peers with respect, or do they see them as competitors?" explained Price. "The biggest red flag for me when I speak to a potential recruit is when they start describing the number of people who report to them and how big their budget is. Relying solely on a traditional functional skill set or the ability to operate a business at a large scale is a recipe for failure in a new venture."

Price, who also serves on the boards of some hospitals, is worried that as the trends toward value-based health care accelerate, traditional provider institutions will find it increasingly difficult to attract the best talent to their leadership roles. "Everyone in health care is mission driven," he said. "That's true whether a business is not-for-profit or for-profit, an established big institution or a disruptive startup. Why in the world would you want to apply your talents in a large, bureaucratic, slow-moving organization?" In a fast-moving entrepreneurial environment, there is more room to have a major impact, to really transform how care is delivered. What's more, there is the opportunity to take an equity stake in the business. "It's a really tall challenge for a traditional hospital system to compete with that."

But Price also acknowledges that there are great leaders at established provider organizations. "At Intermountain, Marc Harrison has figured out how to marry the old culture with a new faster-moving leadership culture. But it's not easy. It requires drive, passion, and vision. And the organization has to embrace the new style and new ways of doing things."

SYSTEM LEADERSHIP

In addition to helping their own organizations navigate the demands of an increasingly value-based industry, health care leaders face a third leadership challenge. They need to look beyond the interests of their organizations to become stewards of value-based transformation in the health care sector as a whole. That is, they have a collective responsibility to accelerate and manage the transition to a more sustainable value-based health system on which the success of their own institutions ultimately depends.

The analogy here is to the emerging public-private partnerships to combat climate change. Partnerships consisting of businesses, investors, startups, governments, and universities and other research institutions are essential to accelerating the pace of green innovation through the development of infrastructure and capabilities (for example, a common charging infrastructure and related grid reinforcements required for electric vehicles) that will benefit everyone.[7]

So too in health care. Leaders need to encourage collective action on the part of all stakeholders in the industry to accelerate the development of the critical components of a value-based infrastructure—standardized outcomes measurement, value-based payment models, digital standards and platforms, new regulatory approaches, and the like—that we have described in previous chapters. In the past two years, it has been inspiring to witness how the immediate emergency of the coronavirus pandemic created a sense of urgency that pushed stakeholders to be pragmatic, work together, go the extra mile, and innovate. But unlike the coronavirus pandemic (and similar to the fight against climate change), the transition to value-based health care will play out over a far longer period of time. Therefore, the response will require consistent system leadership.

This system-level leadership takes a variety of forms. In some cases, institutions are partnering across sector boundaries to improve health outcomes at the regional or national level. We mentioned one such effort in Chapter 5: the payer-provider partnership that fuels the collaborative quality initiatives (CQIs) in the state of Michigan.

In other situations, organizations are working through their industry trade associations to accelerate the development of the critical enablers for a value-based health system. For example, MedTech Europe, a European trade association representing medical technology companies, has been instrumental in developing a value-based purchasing framework for medical technologies.

In still other cases, governments are taking the lead. For example, the European Union has recently passed legislation authorizing a €2.4 billion Innovative Health Initiative (IHI), a public-private partnership that brings together the EU Commission and a network of industry stakeholders to facilitate innovation in areas of unmet health-care need.[8] One IHI focus is the Health Outcomes Observatory (H2O), a collaboration between patients, clinicians, regulators, and the industry to develop a governance model for incorporating health outcomes, including patient-reported outcomes, into health care decision-making across Europe.[9] Initially focusing on diabetes, inflammatory bowel disease, and oncology, H2O is establishing standardized outcome metrics mainly based on the ICHOM measurement sets as the foundation of a multicountry network for data collection, management, and analysis with patient autonomy over data sources. H2O targets large-scale implementation and will launch in Austria, Germany, the Netherlands, and Spain by December 2022, with a plan eventually to expand to more conditions and more countries.

The next frontier for this kind of multistakeholder collaboration to accelerate value-based health care will be to extend cooperation to the global level. Emerging international registry networks such as EUREQUO and ISAR (described in Chapter 2) are one example of this trend. ICHOM is another. But perhaps the most far-reaching initiative of system leadership at the global level that we have been involved in has been under the auspices of the World Economic Forum and is known as the Global Coalition for Value in Healthcare.

"OUR WORK HAS ONLY JUST BEGUN"

It's easy, too easy, to make fun of the World Economic Forum. Critics pan its annual January meeting where billionaires, CEOs, government ministers, and consultants converge on Davos, Switzerland, to discuss global problems and network with each other.[10] And yet the Forum, perhaps more than any other organization in the world, convenes senior global leaders from the private and public sector to address precisely the kind of "wicked" problems that Mariana Mazzucato writes about. And behind the scenes of the highly visible annual Davos meeting, the Forum does valuable work in convening the kind of multistakeholder constituencies necessary to effectively address such problems.[11]

In 2016, we received a request for a proposal from the senior committee of private and public sector leaders overseeing the Forum's Health and Healthcare topic. Led by Medtronic's then CEO Omar Ishrak and Christophe Weber, the French CEO of the Japanese pharmaceutical company Takeda, the group wanted help in exploring value-based health care as a potential solution to what its members worried was the growing dysfunctionality and lack of financial sustainability of the world's health systems.

That initial RFP led to a three-year engagement between BCG and the Forum on what became known as the Value in Healthcare project. The project's executive committee brought together leaders from across the industry and around the globe, many of them innovators in value-based health care. In addition to Ishrak and Weber, for example, its members included provider CEOs such as the late Bernard Tyson of Kaiser Permanente (and his successor Greg Adams) and Marc Harrison of Intermountain Healthcare; government officials such as Edith Schippers, then Minister of Health, Welfare, and Sport from the Netherlands (and her successor Bruno Bruins); and Simon Stevens, then CEO of the UK's National Health Service; pharma and med-tech executives such as Joe Jimenez, then CEO of Novartis (and subsequently, his successor Vasant Narasimhan) and Philips CEO Frans van Houten; and health IT executives such as Rick Valencia, president of Qualcomm Life. Michael Porter also participated as an academic member of the executive board.

From 2016 through 2018, the team interacted with literally hundreds of stakeholders in the global health care industry, holding major workshops and giving presentations at events such as the ICHOM annual meeting, global summits of health insurance and hospital leaders, and the annual World Health Summit. We launched pilots that brought together local coalitions of public and private industry stakeholders to develop value-based approaches to specific diseases in their communities—for example, a pilot focused on congestive heart failure in the city of Atlanta and one on type 2 diabetes in the Canadian province of Ontario. And we convened a working group of more than 30 leaders from government, NGOs, academia, payers, providers, digital platform companies, and patient advocacy organizations to create a road map for the creation of digital-health standards. Finally, we developed the conceptual model for a genuinely value-based health system that we introduced in Chapter 1 and that in large part has defined the structure of this book. (See Figure 8.1.)

FIGURE 8.1   **A conceptual model of a value-based health system.**

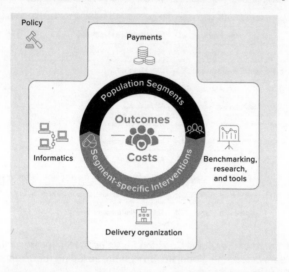

The model portrays the building blocks of a health system designed to improve patient value. At the core is the systematic measurement of outcomes and costs for defined population segments, supported by complementary enablers.

Source: *World Economic Forum*.

After all this work and the publication of three major reports, the Value in Healthcare project ended as planned. But the strong message from our executive committee was, in effect, "Our work has only just begun." In their view, the global health care community needed an ongoing organization to function as a convener of the expanding global value-based health care community and as a clearinghouse for information about best practices.

So in 2019, the members of the executive committee decided to create the Global Coalition for Value in Healthcare.[12] The coalition is a public-private partnership that brings together leading CEOs, government ministers, and other health care leaders to advocate for the value-based transformation of the world's health systems. (For a list of the current members of the Coalition's executive board, see Table 8.1.)

TABLE 8.1   **Global Coalition for Value in Healthcare Executive Board**

Nancy Brown, CEO	**American Heart Association**
Hans-Paul Bürkner, Global Chair Emeritus	**Boston Consulting Group**
Margaret Chan, Founding Dean	**Vanke School of Public Health, Tsinghua University, China**
Francesca Colombo, Head of Health Division	**Organisation for Economic Co-operation and Development (OECD)**
Marc Harrison, CEO	**Intermountain Healthcare**
Frans Van Houten, CEO	**Philips**
Karen Lynch, President and CEO	**CVS Health**
Geoff Martha, CEO	**Medtronic**
Vasant Narasimhan, CEO	**Novartis AG**
Michael Porter, Bishop Lawrence University Professor	**Harvard Business School**
Budi Gunadi Sadikin, Minister of Health	**Republic of Indonesia**
Pascal Soriot, CEO	**AstraZeneca**
Chorh Chuah Tan, Executive Director	**Office for Healthcare Transformation, Ministry of Health, Singapore**
Elizabeth Teisberg, Professor	**Dell Medical School, University of Texas at Austin**
Christophe Weber, CEO	**Takeda Pharmaceuticals**

The executive board of the Global Coalition for Value in Healthcare includes leaders from stakeholders across the global health system, including representatives from both the public and private sector.

Source: *World Economic Forum (*https://www.weforum.org/global-coalition-for-value -in-healthcare/leadership*)*

Since then, the Coalition has been identifying a series of "global innovation hubs" that it considers to be best-practice examples of value-based models of care. The first hubs, announced in March 2021, include the Diabeter model for type 1 diabetes care; Health Cluster Portugal, a public-private partnership implementing a value-based model of care delivery for cataracts in that country; NHS Wales which has developed a whole-of-system approach to value-based health care; and the Steno Diabetes Center in Copenhagen, Denmark, a hospital with an integrated approach to treatment, prevention, and patient education that has significantly improved the prognosis for patients with that chronic disease. The Coalition is also expanding its focus to include cataloging best practices for the enablers of value-based health care. An initial working group, focused on the theme of value-based payments, was launched in 2021. The plan is that these initiatives will become nodes in a global collaboration network that will accelerate the value-based transformation of the world's health systems by identifying and sharing best practices among its participants.

IN IT TOGETHER

Playing an active leadership role in multistakeholder initiatives such as ICHOM or the Global Coalition for Value in Healthcare will become an increasingly important part of the responsibilities of health care leaders as the sector moves rapidly into the value-based future. No single institution can make value-based health care happen on its own. The deficiencies of global health systems are a systemic problem, and addressing them will require concerted collective action.

The English poet John Donne famously wrote, "No man is an island." The same is true for the myriad organizations of the global health sector. When it comes to the ongoing value-based transformation of health care, we are all in it together.

ACKNOWLEDGMENTS

This book is the product of more than a decade of client work, research, and thinking at Boston Consulting Group and with academic and health care organizations around the world. As a result, there are a great many people we wish to thank.

We start with the many BCG leaders who have been unstinting in their support of BCG's value-based health care work and pro bono collaborations with nonprofit health-care institutions.

Hans-Paul Bürkner (CEO from 2004 to 2012 and currently global chairman emeritus) supported our early work in value-based health care and had the vision to put BCG's institutional support behind the creation of the International Consortium for Health Outcomes Measurement (ICHOM). What's more, Hans-Paul's personal commitment to our book project was instrumental in making it possible.

Rich Lesser (CEO from 2013 to 2021 and currently global chair), in addition to being a longtime colleague in BCG's Health Care practice, is someone who understands just how critical it is for the public and private sector to work together to solve the world's biggest problems. We thank Rich for his ongoing support of our project and for maintaining BCG's institutional commitment to ICHOM, including during a difficult period when the future of the organization was in doubt.

We also want to thank BCG's current CEO, Christoph Schweizer, who in addition to being a former global leader of the firm's Health Care practice has been a coauthor with us on early publications about value-based health care.

Other BCG leaders have supported our work over the years and have been instrumental in developing some of the ideas in our book. We would like to thank Adam Farber and Torben Danger, the former and current leader, respectively, of BCG's Health Care practice; Larry Kamener and Vincent Chin, former leaders of BCG's Public Sector practice; Sharon Marcil, until recently head of Global Marketing at BCG; and Martin Reeves, founder and chairman of the BCG Henderson Institute (BHI), the firm's innovative think tank and home of the BCG Fellows program, of which Stefan was an early member.

A great many current and former BCGers have contributed to the ideas in this book through many years of working together and long hours of conversation. In Sweden, Johan Öberg helped launch our very first project in value-based health care and has continued to be among our strongest supporters and a true friend. In the United States, Pete Lawyer was an early collaborator and coauthor of our first peer-reviewed publication on the subject.

Daniel Gorlin and Jon Kaplan in Chicago alerted us to the innovative potential of Medicare Advantage as a model for value-based payment. Jan-Willem Kuenen, Jaap Schreurs, and Wouter van Leeuwen in Amsterdam helped shape our thinking on the evolution of value-based health care in the Netherlands. Yves Morieux and Peter Tollman profoundly influenced our views on organizational change in complex work environments such as health care. Satty Chandrashekhar, Steve Filler, André Heeg, Ania Labno, Michael Ruhl, and Gunnar Trommer helped us navigate the complexities of digital health and opened our eyes to its enormous potential. Adina Symreng, who has contributed to our value-based health care work from her first months with BCG, kept us up to date with the latest developments in Sweden and the wider Nordic region. And Mathieu Lamiaux taught us about the opportunities for value-based health care in low- and middle-income countries.

A core group of BCG colleagues also read earlier versions of our manuscript and provided valuable input. We should like to thank Nate Beyor, Jad Bitar, Ben Horner, Ben Keneally, Jan-Willem Kuenen, Paul Michelman, and Adina Symreng.

Numerous other BCG colleagues have shared our passion for value-based health care and worked with us on projects over the years. We want to thank Jess Aisenbrey, Matthias Becker, Pieter de Bey, Mathias Blom, Priya Chandran, Karalee Close, Andre Dias, Heike Dorninger, Philip Evans, Nadine Gerson Flam, Chloe Flutter, Stuart Gander, Goetz Gerecke, Marty Gilbert, Paulo Gonçalves, John Gooch, Jens Grueger, Elisabeth Hansson, Taneli Hirvola, Sultan Hochweiss, Thomas Jensen, Tommi Kainu, Iiro Kauma, James Kent, Mark Khayat, Arne Koehler, Nick Kransz, Bennett Lane, María Lopez, Mark Lubkeman, John Luijs, Dave Matheson, Maria Nidefelt, Hanna Nyström, David Pérez, Romney Resney, Barry Rosenberg, David Sadoff, Emile Salhab, Sanjay Saxena, Josefine Sellman, Neil Soderlund, Brett Spencer, Jean Stoefs, and Srikant Vaidyanathan. Needless to say, none of them are responsible for any errors of fact or interpretation in our book, which are our own.

In addition to our current and former BCG colleagues, we should also like to thank the many health care CEOs, clinical leaders, researchers, patient representatives, policy makers, and investors with whom we have had valuable discussions over the years and many of whom we have interviewed for this book. Although some of them are quoted in these pages, many are not; nevertheless, they all made important contributions to our thinking and to the stories we tell.

We would like to thank Pieter de Bey, Maria Björkander, Willem Jan Bos, Francesca Colombo, Kalle Conneryd, Patrick Conway, Andre Dekker, Brian Donley, Anders Ekblom, Sofia Ernestam, Günter Feick, Barbro Fridén, Göran Garellick, Markus Graefen, Peter Graf, Ralph Graichen, Marc Harrison, Jan Hazelzet, Rob ten Hoedt, Stan Huff, Hartwig Huland, Stefan James, Tomas Jernberg, Gregory Katz, Morten Kildal, Jan Kimpen, Lars Klareskog, Linetta Koppert, Ernst Kuipers, Jasmine Lau, Tom Lee, Sally Lewis, Bertil Lindahl, Jacob Lippa, Shanleigh Lount, Mats Lundström, Kees Molenaar, Barend Mons, Tobias Nilsson, Shoni Philpot, Trevor Price, Marc Probst, Mike Pykosz, Ola Rolfsson, John Rumsfeld, Dana Safran, Melvin Samsom, Will Shrank, Nicole Spieker, Holger Stalberg, Caleb Stowell, Lars Svensson, Chorh-Chuan Tan, Vivian Tan, Elizabeth Teisberg, Micky Tripathi, Andreas Ringman Uggla, Mark van der Graaf, Dennis van Veghel, Robert Vorhoff, and Björn Zoëga.

Our colleagues at ICHOM have been important partners in our decade-long journey. We would like to thank ICHOM cofounders Michael Porter and Martin Ingvar, as well as Swedish philanthropist Carl Bennet who played a critical role in financially supporting ICHOM in its early years.

We would also like to thank ICHOM's newest board members, Jamie Heywood and Daphne Psacharapoulus.

We would especially like to acknowledge three ICHOM leaders who were instrumental in guiding the organization through its first decade. Jens Deerberg-Wittram moved his family from Germany to Cambridge, Massachusetts, to take the role of ICHOM's first CEO at a time when the organization existed only on paper. A giant in the field of value-based health care, Jens laid the foundation for all that would follow.

In addition to being the person who first opened Stefan's eyes to the power of outcomes research and quality registries more than 15 years ago, Christina Rångemark Åkerman succeeded Jens in 2014 and became ICHOM's longest-serving CEO. She was instrumental in scaling up the organization, forging strategic partnerships with key international organizations such as the OECD, and establishing its global brand.

Finally, current ICHOM president Suzanne Gaunt has led the organization with aplomb, including during a period of financial difficulty, and has formed an outstanding team to take the organization into its second decade.

Our work in support of the World Economic Forum's Value in Healthcare project was instrumental in shaping our perspective on health-system transformation. We want to thank the leaders of the Forum's Health and Healthcare team: Sofiat Akinola, Arnaud Bernaert, Vanessa Candeias, Genya Dana, Utako Katano, Kelly McCain, Shirali Mewara, Olivier Oullier, and Lucas Scherdel. A special thank-you to the three BCG secondees to the Forum who served as project leaders on the three reports that we wrote for the Value in Healthcare project: Ovid Amadi, Jonathan Lim, and Gabriel Seidman.

Michael Porter's Institute for Strategy and Competitiveness at the Harvard Business School has been a global center for research and thinking about value-based health care, and we have had the privilege of a close and fruitful collaboration with the Institute over the years. We would like to thank Michael and his colleagues Tom Feeley, Caleb Stowell, and Mary Witkowski.

A great many BCG people helped us in the research and writing of this book. Rose-Marie Mesias, Emelie Nybom, and Eduardo Garcia provided valuable administrative support. Matti Heikonen helped design our figures. Julia Baker, Andrea Ceballos, Joachim Engelhard, Julia Eleuteri, Lauren Gargan, Nayel Hakim, Laura Lüdtke, Gabriel Osterdahl, Shalini

Pammal, Juho Pirhonen, Irina Stati, Marcus Torelm, and Jessica Ye assisted with a wide variety of research tasks. And a special thank-you to Azraa Chaudhury, who was the lead researcher on our book project—even as she was completing her second year of medical school at Northwestern University's Feinberg School of Medicine.

We owe a special debt of gratitude to our collaborating writer, Robert Howard. For more than a decade, Bob has been an invaluable thought partner in our work on value-based health care, always pushing our thinking, helping us crystallize what we are learning, and communicating it with clarity, without neglecting the necessary complexity of the subject. We could not have written this book without him.

Publishing this book with McGraw Hill has been a pleasure. We cannot think of a better editor to work with than Casey Ebro, whose sure guidance has been everything that authors could ask for: authoritative, pragmatic, and responsive. We would also like to thank Pattie Amoroso, Maureen Harper, and Scott Sewell at McGraw Hill and Steve Straus and his team at THINK Book Works—in particular, copyeditor Richard Camp—for their assistance in production and marketing.

Last, but far from least, we would like to thank our families to whom we have dedicated this book. Their support has been unwavering during the two years that we have been working on this project, even as all our lives, like everyone else's, have been disrupted by the extraordinary turmoil of the coronavirus pandemic. We can't thank them enough.

Stefan also has one other person he would like to acknowledge: Inez Sutton (1917–2014), biology teacher at Sturgis High School, in Sturgis, Michigan, and Stefan's teacher during the 1976–1977 academic year when he attended as a foreign exchange student from Sweden. Mrs. Sutton helped plant the seed of his passion for research and medicine.

NOTES

PREFACE

1. See, for example, Marshall H. Chin, "Uncomfortable Truths—What Covid-19 Has Revealed About Chronic-Disease Care in America," *New England Journal of Medicine* 385, no. 18 (October 28, 2021): 1633–36, https://doi.org/10.1056 /NEJMp2112063; and The Commonwealth Fund Commission on a National Public Health System, "Meeting America's Public Health Challenge: Recommendations for Building a National Public Health System That Addresses Ongoing and Future Health Crises, Advances Equity, and Earns Trust" (The Commonwealth Fund, June 2022), https://www.commonwealthfund.org/publications /fund-reports/2022/jun/meeting-americas-public-health-challenge.

2. For a recent much-discussed example, see Patrick Radden Keefe, *Empire of Pain: The Secret History of the Sackler Dynasty* (Doubleday Business, 2021).

3. See, for example, Jennifer Clawson, Josh Kellar, and Stefan Larsson, "Learning from COVID-19 to Transform Global Health Systems" (Boston Consulting Group, May 5, 2020), https://www.bcg.com/publications/2020/learning-from -covid-transforming-health-systems.; Lev Facher, "9 Ways Covid-19 May Forever Upend the U.S. Health Care Industry," *STAT*, May 19, 2020, https://www .statnews.com/2020/05/19/9-ways-covid-19-forever-upend-health-care/; and Zeynep Tufekci, "3 Ways the Pandemic Has Made the World Better," *The Atlantic*, March 18, 2021, https://www.theatlantic.com/health/archive/2021/03/three -ways-pandemic-has-bettered-world/618320/.

4. "COVID-19: Make It the Last Pandemic" (The Independent Panel for Pandemic Preparedness and Response, 2021), https://theindependentpanel.org/wp-content /uploads/2021/05/COVID-19-Make-it-the-Last-Pandemic_final.pdf.

5. See, for example, Rachel M. Werner and Sherry A. Glied, "Covid-Induced Changes in Health Care Delivery—Can They Last?," *New England Journal of Medicine* 385, no. 10 (September 2, 2021): 868–70, https://doi.org/10 .1056/NEJMp2110679; and Kojo Nimako and Margaret E Kruk, "Seizing the

Moment to Rethink Health Systems," *The Lancet Global Health*, September 2021, S2214109X21003569, https://doi.org/10.1016/S2214-109X(21)00356-9.

6. Michael E. Porter, and Elizabeth Olmstead Teisberg, *Redefining Health Care: Creating Value-Based Competition on Results* (Harvard Business Review Press, 2006).

7. See, for example, William H. Shrank, Teresa L. Rogstad, and Natasha Parekh, "Waste in the US Health Care System: Estimated Costs and Potential for Savings," *JAMA* 322, no. 15 (October 15, 2019): 1501–9, https://doi.org/10.1001/jama .2019.13978; and John N. Mafi et al., "Trends in Low-Value Health Service Use and Spending in the US Medicare Fee-for-Service Program, 2014–2018," *JAMA Network Open* 4, no. 2 (February 16, 2021): e2037328, https://doi.org/10.1001 /jamanetworkopen.2020.37328.

8. For an interesting account of what value-based health care has come to mean in practice in the United States, and a reasoned assessment of its strengths and limitations, see Sachin H. Jain, "Everybody's Talking About Value-Based Health Care. Here's What They're Not Saying," *Forbes*, April 12, 2022, https://www .forbes.com/sites/sachinjain/2022/04/12/what-is-value-based-healthcare-really/.

9. For a few illustrative examples from the extensive literature on models for the future of health care, see David L Sackett et al., "Evidence Based Medicine: What It Is and What It Isn't," *BMJ* 312, no. 71 (January 13, 1996): 2, https:// doi.org/10.1136/bmj.312.7023.71; Institute of Medicine (US) and Committee on Quality of Health Care in America, *Crossing the Quality Chasm: A New Health System for the 21st Century* (National Academies Press, 2001); National Research Council of the National Academies, *Toward Precision Medicine: Building a Knowledge Network for Biomedical Research and a New Taxonomy of Disease* (National Academies Press, 2011); Donald M. Berwick, Thomas W. Nolan, and John Whittington, "The Triple Aim: Care, Health, And Cost," *Health Affairs* 27, no. 3 (May 2008): 759–69, https://doi.org/10.1377/hlthaff.27.3.759; Michael Sagner et al., "The P4 Health Spectrum—A Predictive, Preventive, Personalized and Participatory Continuum for Promoting Healthspan," *Progress in Cardiovascular Diseases* 59, no. 5 (April 2017): 506–21, https:// doi.org/10.1016/j.pcad.2016.08.002; and Eric Topol, *Deep Medicine: How Artificial Intelligence Can Make Medicine Human Again* (Basic Books, 2019).

CHAPTER 1

1. Steven Johnson, *Extra Life: A Short History of Living Longer* (Riverhead Books, 2021).

2. For details of our analysis, see the sidebar "Why Growing Investment in R&D Isn't Solving the Evidence Crisis," later in this chapter.

3. See, for example, Stephen Bezruchka, "Increasing Mortality and Declining Health Status in the USA: Where Is Public Health?," *Harvard Health Policy Review*, October 11, 2018, http://www.hhpronline.org/articles/2018/10 /8/increasing-mortality-and-declining-health-status-in-the-usa-where-is-public -health; Atheendar S. Venkataramani, Rourke O'Brien, and Alexander C. Tsai, "Declining Life Expectancy in the United States: The Need for Social Policy as

Health Policy," *JAMA* 325, no. 7 (February 16, 2021): 621–22, https://doi.org/10 .1001/jama.2020.26339; and Anne Case and Angus Deaton, *Deaths of Despair and the Future of Capitalism* (Princeton University Press, 2021).

4. Lucinda Hiam et al., "Why Is Life Expectancy in England and Wales 'Stalling'?," *Journal of Epidemiology and Community Health* 72, no. 5 (May 2018): 404–8, https://doi.org/10.1136/jech-2017-210401; and Jessica Y. Ho and Arun S. Hendi, "Recent Trends in Life Expectancy across High Income Countries: Retrospective Observational Study," *BMJ* 362 (August 15, 2018): k2562, https://doi.org/10.1136 /bmj.k2562.

5. José Manuel Aburto et al., "Quantifying Impacts of the COVID-19 Pandemic Through Life-Expectancy Losses: A Population-Level Study of 29 Countries," *International Journal of Epidemiology*, 51, no. 1 (February 2022): 63–74, https:// doi.org/10.1093/ije/dyab207.

6. Joseph L. Dieleman et al., "Future and Potential Spending on Health 2015–40: Development Assistance for Health, and Government, Prepaid Private, and Out-of-Pocket Health Spending in 184 Countries," *The Lancet* 389, no. 10083 (May 2017): 2005–30, https://doi.org/10.1016/S0140-6736(17)30873-5.

7. KFF (Kaiser Family Foundation), "Employer Health Benefits—2020 Summary of Findings," October 8, 2020, https://www.kff.org/report-section/ehbs-2020 -summary-of-findings/.

8. "Medical Doctors (per 10,000 Population)," World Health Organization Global Health Observatory, accessed March 7, 2022, https://www.who.int/data/gho/data /indicators/indicator-details/GHO/medical-doctors-%28per-10-000-population %29.

9. Kingsley Inghobor, "Diagnosing Africa's Medical Brain Drain," *Africa Renewal*, November 25, 2016, https://www.un.org/africarenewal/magazine/december -2016-march-2017/diagnosing-africa%E2%80%99s-medical-brain-drain.

10. Shannon Brownlee et al., "Evidence for Overuse of Medical Services Around the World," *The Lancet* 390, no. 10090 (July 8, 2017): 156–68, https://doi.org/10 .1016/S0140-6736(16)32585-5; Paul Glasziou et al., "Evidence for Underuse of Effective Medical Services Around the World," *The Lancet* 390, no. 10090 (July 8, 2017): 169–77, https://doi.org/10.1016/S0140-6736(16)30946-1; and Adam G. Elshaug et al., "Levers for Addressing Medical Underuse and Overuse: Achieving High-Value Health Care," *The Lancet* 390, no. 10090 (July 8, 2017): 191–202, https://doi.org/10.1016/S0140-6736(16)32586-7.

11. Mark Smith et al., *Best Care at Lower Cost: The Path to Continuously Learning Health Care in America* (National Academies Press, 2013).

12. William H. Shrank, Teresa L. Rogstad, and Natasha Parekh, "Waste in the US Health Care System: Estimated Costs and Potential for Savings," *JAMA* 322, no. 15 (October 15, 2019): 1501–9, https://doi.org/10.1001/jama.2019.13978.

13. Marty Makary, "A Path to Lowering Health Care Costs," *RealClearHealth*, June 8, 2017, https://www.realclearhealth.com/articles/2017/06/08/a_path_to _lowering_health_care_costs__110623.html.

14. World Health Organization, "The World Health Report" (World Health Organization, 2010), https://www.who.int/publications/i/item/9789241564021.

15. Brownlee et al., "Evidence for Overuse of Medical Services Around the World."
16. Brownlee et al.; Hyeong Sik Ahn, Hyun Jung Kim, and H. Gilbert Welch, "Korea's Thyroid-Cancer 'Epidemic'—Screening and Overdiagnosis," *New England Journal of Medicine* 371, no. 19 (November 6, 2014): 1765–67, https:// doi.org/10.1056/NEJMp1409841; and Salvatore Vaccarella et al., "World-wide Thyroid-Cancer Epidemic? The Increasing Impact of Overdiagnosis," *New England Journal of Medicine* 375, no. 7 (August 18, 2016): 614–17, https:// doi.org/10.1056/NEJMp1604412.
17. Brownlee et al., "Evidence for Overuse of Medical Services Around the World."
18. For example, a December 2020 study by the nonprofit Kaiser Family Foundation estimated that between June and November of 2021, unvaccinated American adults accounted for $13.8 billion in preventable Covid hospitalization costs nationwide. See Krutika Amin and Cynthia Cox, "Unvaccinated COVID-19 Hospitalizations Cost Billions of Dollars," *Peterson-KFF Health System Tracker* (blog), accessed May 23, 2022, https://www.healthsystemtracker.org/brief /unvaccinated-covid-patients-cost-the-u-s-health-system-billions-of-dollars/.
19. A 2017 review of the sources of underuse identified four key drivers: obstacles to access to health care, inadequate supply of medical resources, lack of adoption on the part of physicians of innovations and best practices, and lack of com-pliance on the part of patients with prescribed treatments. See Glasziou et al., "Evidence for Underuse of Effective Medical Services Around the World."
20. Matthew J. Eckelman et al., "Health Care Pollution and Public Health Damage in the United States: An Update," *Health Affairs* 39, no. 12 (December 2020): 2071–79, https://doi.org/10.1377/hlthaff.2020.01247. The US health system is responsible for about a quarter of all global health-care greenhouse gas emis-sions, more than any other national health system. See Jeanette W. Chung and David O. Meltzer, "Estimate of the Carbon Footprint of the US Health Care Sec-tor," *JAMA* 302, no. 18 (November 11, 2009): 1970–72, https://doi.org/10.1001 /jama.2009.1610; and Manfred Lenzen et al., "The Environmental Footprint of Health Care: A Global Assessment," *The Lancet Planetary Health* 4, no. 7 (July 1, 2020): e271–79, https://doi.org/10.1016/S2542-5196(20)30121-2. In addition to its social and economic costs, health-care pollution also contributes to poorer health outcomes. According to Eckelman et al., health damages from US health care pollution are on the same order of magnitude as deaths from preventable medical errors, representing a total disease burden of approximately 388,000 lost disability-adjusted life years (DALYs) in 2018.
21. Peter-Paul Pichler et al., "International Comparison of Health Care Carbon Footprints," *Environmental Research Letters* 14, no. 6 (May 2019): 064004, https://doi.org/10.1088/1748-9326/ab19e1.
22. For more on the Costa Rican health care system, see Atul Gawande, "Costa Ricans Live Longer Than We Do. What's the Secret?," *New Yorker*, August 23, 2021, https://www.newyorker.com/magazine/2021/08/30/costa-ricans-live -longer-than-we-do-whats-the-secret.
23. All data on diabetes prevalence and cost is from International Diabetes Founda-tion, *IDF Diabetes Atlas*, 9th edition, 2019, https://diabetesatlas.org/atlas/ninth -edition/. The analysis includes adults with both type 1 and type 2 diabetes.

24. Fabrizio Carinci et al., "Lower Extremity Amputation Rates in People with Diabetes as an Indicator of Health Systems Performance. A Critical Appraisal of the Data Collection 2000–2011 by the Organization for Economic Cooperation and Development (OECD)," *Acta Diabetologica* 53, no. 5 (2016): 825–32, https://doi.org/10.1007/s00592-016-0879-4.

25. Shiwani Mahajan et al., "Trends in Differences in Health Status and Health Care Access and Affordability by Race and Ethnicity in the United States, 1999–2018," *JAMA* 326, no. 7 (August 17, 2021): 637–48, https://doi.org/10.1001/jama.2021.9907.

26. Lauren Paremoer et al., "Covid-19 Pandemic and the Social Determinants of Health," *BMJ* 372, no. 129 (January 28, 2021), https://doi.org/10.1136/bmj.n129; and World Health Organization, "Health Inequity and the Effects of COVID-19: Assessing, Responding to and Mitigating the Socioeconomic Impact on Health to Build a Better Future" (Copenhagen: WHO Regional Office for Europe, 2020), https://apps.who.int/iris/handle/10665/338199.

27. Barry L. Rosenberg et al., "Quantifying Geographic Variation in Health Care Outcomes in the United States Before and After Risk-Adjustment," *PLOS ONE* 11, no. 12 (December 14, 2016): e0166762, https://doi.org/10.1371/journal.pone.0166762.

28. John E. Wennberg, "Time to Tackle Unwarranted Variations in Practice," *BMJ* 342, no. 3 (March 17, 2011): d1513, https://doi.org/10.1136/bmj.d1513.

29. OECD, *Geographic Variations in Health Care: What Do We Know and What Can Be Done to Improve Health System Performance?*, OECD Health Policy Studies (OECD, 2014), https://doi.org/10.1787/9789264216594-en.

30. Wennberg, "Time to Tackle Unwarranted Variations in Practice."

31. For example, in some regions in the United States, less than 45% of Medicare patients receive pneumococcal vaccinations (which prevent some cases of pneumonia, meningitis, and sepsis), whereas in others, 95% do. And among primary care clusters in the United Kingdom, there is more than a fivefold variation in the percentage of diabetic patients who receive nine care processes recommended by that country's National Institute for Health and Care Excellence (NICE). See Wennberg, "Time to Tackle Unwarranted Variations in Practice."

32. Unwarranted variations in preference-sensitive care are mainly due to flaws in clinical decision-making and inadequate doctor-patient dialogue about care options. One study, for example, shows that in Ontario, Canada, only 15% of patients who met the clinical guidelines for hip or knee arthroplasty (based on symptom level and radiological changes) actually wanted surgery when asked which treatment they preferred. See G. A. Hawker et al., "Determining the Need for Hip and Knee Arthroplasty: The Role of Clinical Severity and Patients' Preferences," *Medical Care* 39, no. 3 (March 2001): 206–16, https://doi.org/10.1097/00005650-200103000-00002.

33. In the United States, for example, such supply-driven overuse accounts for most of the twofold regional variation in total per capita spending on patients over 65. And yet, according to Wennberg, the evidence suggests that patients living in regions with a high-intensity pattern of care have worse, or at least no better, survival than those living in low-intensity regions.

34. Wennberg, "Time to Tackle Unwarranted Variations in Practice."

35. For more on the history of evidence-based medicine as a concept and practice, see Gordon H. Guyatt, "Evidence Based Medicine," *American College of Physicians Journal Club* (April 1991): A–16, https://www.jameslindlibrary.org/guyatt -gh-1991/; David L. Sackett et al., "Evidence Based Medicine: What It Is and What It Isn't," *BMJ* 312, no. 71 (January 13, 1996): 2, https://doi.org/10.1136/bmj .312.7023.71; and Roger Sur and Philipp Dahm, "History of Evidence-Based Medicine," *Indian Journal of Urology* 27, no. 4 (2011): 487, https://doi.org/10.4103 /0970-1591.91438.

36. "Products | Dr.Evidence," accessed February 2, 2022, https://www.drevidence .com/products-old.

37. Daniel Kahneman, Olivier Sibony, and Cass R. Sunstein, *Noise: A Flaw in Human Judgment* (Little, Brown and Company, 2021), p. 275.

38. As described in Dawn Stacey et al., "Decision Aids for People Facing Health Treatment or Screening Decisions," *Cochrane Database of Systematic Reviews* 4 (April 12, 2017): CD001431, https://www.cochranelibrary.com/cdsr/doi/10.1002 /14651858.CD001431.pub5/full.

39. Sean R. Tunis, Daniel B. Stryer, and Carolyn M. Clancy, "Practical Clinical Trials: Increasing the Value of Clinical Research for Decision Making in Clinical and Health Policy," *JAMA* 290, no. 12 (September 24, 2003): 1624–32, https://doi .org/10.1001/jama.290.12.1624.

40. Pierluigi Tricoci et al., "Scientific Evidence Underlying the ACC/AHA Clinical Practice Guidelines," *JAMA* 301, no. 8 (February 25, 2009): 831–41, https://doi .org/10.1001/jama.2009.205.

41. Chi Heem Wong, Kien Wei Siah, and Andrew W Lo, "Estimation of Clinical Trial Success Rates and Related Parameters," *Biostatistics* 20, no. 2 (April 1, 2019): 273–86, https://doi.org/10.1093/biostatistics/kxx069.

42. John-Arne Røttingen et al., "Mapping of Available Health Research and Development Data: What's There, What's Missing, and What Role Is There for a Global Observatory?," *The Lancet* 382, no. 9900 (October 12, 2013): 1286–1307, https:// doi.org/10.1016/S0140-6736(13)61046-6.

43. Iain Chalmers et al., "How to Increase Value and Reduce Waste When Research Priorities Are Set," *The Lancet* 383, no. 9912 (January 11, 2014): 156–65, https:// doi.org/10.1016/S0140-6736(13)62229-1.

44. Maria Elena Flacco et al., "Head-to-Head Randomized Trials Are Mostly Industry Sponsored and Almost Always Favor the Industry Sponsor," *Journal of Clinical Epidemiology* 68, no. 7 (July 2015): 811–20, https://doi.org/10.1016 /j.jclinepi.2014.12.016.

45. D. N. Lathyris et al., "Industry Sponsorship and Selection of Comparators in Randomized Clinical Trials," *European Journal of Clinical Investigation* 40, no. 2 (February 2010): 172–82, https://doi.org/10.1111/j.1365-2362.2009.02240.x; and Flacco et al., "Head-to-Head Randomized Trials Are Mostly Industry Sponsored and Almost Always Favor the Industry Sponsor."

46. "Home—ClinicalTrials.Gov," accessed March 14, 2022, https://clinicaltrials.gov/.

47. Steven A. Schroeder, "We Can Do Better—Improving the Health of the American People," *New England Journal of Medicine* 357, no. 12 (September 20, 2007): 1221–28, https://doi.org/10.1056/NEJMsa073350.

48. Robert M. Kaplan, *More Than Medicine: The Broken Promise of American Health* (Harvard University Press, 2019), pp. 31–32.

49. Connor A. Emdin et al., "Association Between Randomised Trial Evidence and Global Burden of Disease: Cross Sectional Study (Epidemiological Study of Randomized Trials—ESORT)," *BMJ* 350 (January 28, 2015): h117, https://doi.org/10.1136/bmj.h117.

50. Amitabh Chandra, Dhruv Khullar, and Thomas H. Lee, "Addressing the Challenge of Gray-Zone Medicine," *New England Journal of Medicine* 372, no. 3 (January 15, 2015): 203–5, https://doi.org/10.1056/NEJMp1409696.

51. JoAnn E. Kirchner et al., "Getting a Clinical Innovation into Practice: An Introduction to Implementation Strategies," *Psychiatry Research* 283 (January 2020): 112467, https://doi.org/10.1016/j.psychres.2019.06.042.

52. Kaveh Shojania, "How Quickly Do Systematic Reviews Go Out of Date? A Survival Analysis," *Annals of Internal Medicine* 147, no. 4 (August 21, 2007): 224–33, https://doi.org/10.7326/0003-4819-147-4-200708210-00179.

53. Paul G. Shekelle, Eduardo Ortiz, and Shannon Rhodes, "Validity of the Agency for Healthcare Research and Quality Clinical Practice Guidelines: How Quickly Do Guidelines Become Outdated?," *JAMA* 286, no. 12 (September 26, 2001): 1461–67, https://doi.org/10.1001/jama.286.12.1461.

54. Michael Farias et al., "Standardized Clinical Assessment and Management Plans (SCAMPs) Provide a Better Alternative to Clinical Practice Guidelines," *Health Affairs* 32, no. 5 (May 1, 2013): 911–20, https://doi.org/10.1377/hlthaff.2012.0667.

55. One recent sign of that importance: the *New England Journal of Medicine* has recently launched a new online publication, *NEJM Evidence*, dedicated to the principle that "understanding the nuances of study design and execution is key to understanding how the results of a study can, or cannot, influence our clinical practice." See Chana A. Sacks et al., "NEJM Evidence—a New Journal in the NEJM Group Family," *New England Journal of Medicine* 386 (January 10, 2022): 182–83, https://doi.org/10.1056/NEJMe2118588.

56. For a recent review of the problem of clinician burnout, see Committee on Systems Approaches to Improve Patient Care by Supporting Clinician Well-Being, National Academy of Medicine, and National Academies of Sciences, Engineering, and Medicine, *Taking Action Against Clinician Burnout: A Systems Approach to Professional Well-Being* (National Academies Press, 2019).

57. Scott W. Yates, "Physician Stress and Burnout," *The American Journal of Medicine* 133, no. 2 (February 2020): 160–64, https://doi.org/10.1016/j.amjmed.2019.08.034.

58. Shasha Han et al., "Estimating the Attributable Cost of Physician Burnout in the United States," *Annals of Internal Medicine* 170, no. 11 (June 4, 2019): 784–90, https://doi.org/10.7326/M18-1422.

59. See The Lancet, "Physician Burnout: A Global Crisis," *The Lancet* 394, no. 10193 (July 13, 2019): 93, https://doi.org/10.1016/S0140-6736(19)31573-9; and Nicola McKinley et al., "Resilience, Burnout and Coping Mechanisms in UK Doctors: A Cross-Sectional Study," *BMJ Open* 10, no. 1 (January 2020): e031765, https://doi.org/10.1136/bmjopen-2019-031765.

60. Ed Yong, "Why Health-Care Workers Are Quitting in Droves," *The Atlantic*, November 16, 2021, https://www.theatlantic.com/health/archive/2021/11/the-mass-exodus-of-americas-health-care-workers/620713/.

61. Yates, "Physician Stress and Burnout."

62. For more on the growth in business complexity and how organizations need to respond to it, see Yves Morieux and Peter Tollman, *Six Simple Rules: How to Manage Complexity Without Getting Complicated* (Harvard Business Review Press, 2014).

63. For an early version of this argument, see Stefan Larsson and Peter Tollman, "Health Care's Value Problem—and How to Fix It," (BCG Henderson Institute, October 23, 2017), https://www.bcg.com/en-us/publications/2017/smart-simplicity-health-care-value-problem-how-fix-it.

64. On health care as a "complex adaptive system," see Paul Plsek, "Redesigning Health Care with Insights from the Science of Complex Adaptive Systems," in Institute of Medicine Committee on Quality of Health Care in America, *Crossing the Quality Chasm: A New Health System for the 21st Century* (National Academies Press, 2001); William B. Rouse and Nicoleta Serban, *Understanding and Managing the Complexity of Health Care* (MIT Press, 2014); and Joachim P. Sturmberg, *Health System Redesign: How to Make Health Care Person-Centered, Equitable, and Sustainable* (Springer, 2017).

65. For a recent call for more alignment in the goals of stakeholders across health systems, see Holger J. Schünemann et al., "The Ecosystem of Health Decision Making: From Fragmentation to Synergy," *The Lancet Public Health* 7, no. 4 (April 1, 2022): e378–90, https://doi.org/10.1016/S2468-2667(22)00057-3.

66. Donald M. Berwick, Thomas W. Nolan, and John Whittington, "The Triple Aim: Care, Health, And Cost," *Health Affairs* 27, no. 3 (May 2008): 759–69, https://doi.org/10.1377/hlthaff.27.3.759.

67. Rishi Sikka, Julianne M Morath, and Lucian Leape, "The Quadruple Aim: Care, Health, Cost and Meaning in Work," *BMJ Quality & Safety* 24, no. 10 (October 2015): 608–10, https://doi.org/10.1136/bmjqs-2015-004160.

68. See, for example, Institute of Medicine Committee on Quality of Health Care in America, *Crossing the Quality Chasm*; National Research Council of the National Academies, *Toward Precision Medicine: Building a Knowledge Network for Biomedical Research and a New Taxonomy of Disease* (National Academies Press, 2011); and Organisation for Economic Co-operation and Development, World Health Organization, and World Bank Group, *Delivering Quality Health Services: A Global Imperative for Universal Health Coverage* (OECD Publishing, 2018).

69. Michael Sagner et al., "The P4 Health Spectrum—A Predictive, Preventive, Personalized and Participatory Continuum for Promoting Healthspan," *Progress in Cardiovascular Diseases* 59, no. 5 (April 2017): 506–21, https://doi.org/10.1016/j.pcad.2016.08.002.

70. We have adapted this list from Paul Plsek, "Redesigning Health Care with Insights from the Science of Complex Adaptive Systems;" and William B. Rouse and Nicoleta Serban, *Understanding and Managing the Complexity of Health Care*.

71. For more on the Value in Healthcare project, see "Value in Healthcare: Laying the Foundation for Health System Transformation" (World Economic Forum, April 2017), https://www.weforum.org/reports/value-in-healthcare-laying-the-foundation-for-health-system-transformation/; "Value in Healthcare: Mobilizing Cooperation for Health System Transformation" (World Economic Forum, February 2018), https://www.weforum.org/reports/value-in-healthcare-mobilizing-cooperation-for-health-system-transformation/; and "Value in Healthcare: Accelerating the Pace of Health System Transformation" (World Economic Forum, December 2018), https://www3.weforum.org/docs/WEF_Value_in_Healthcare_report_2018.pdf.

CHAPTER 2

1. For a recent example, see Lisa Rosenbaum, "Metric Myopia—Trading Away Our Clinical Judgment," *New England Journal of Medicine* 386 (May 5, 2022): 1759–63, https://doi.org/10.1056/NEJMms2200977.

2. The idea that the health outcomes delivered are the most direct way to measure health care quality is not new. As early as the mid-1960s, Dr. Avedis Donabedian, the founder of the study of quality in health care and medical-outcomes research, acknowledged that "many advantages are gained by using outcome as the criterion of quality in medical care." See Avedis Donabedian, "Evaluating the Quality of Medical Care," *Milbank Memorial Fund Quarterly* 44, no. 3, pt. 2, 1966 (pp. 166–203), https://doi.org/10.1111/j.1468-0009.2005.00397.x. In his article, Donabedian also pointed out some of the limitations of outcomes as a measure of health-care quality, including the, sometimes, long time lag between treatment and outcomes and the poor quality of the medical records of the time for accurately tracking outcomes. We will address these and other limitations throughout our book.

3. Michael E. Porter, Stefan Larsson, and Thomas H. Lee, "Standardizing Patient Outcomes Measurement," *New England Journal of Medicine* 374, no. 6 (February 11, 2016): 504–6, https://doi.org/10.1056/NEJMp1511701.

4. And even systems for tracking adverse effects are far from comprehensive. Some 20 years after the Institute of Medicine highlighted the problem of medical errors in the US health system and called for a 50% reduction over a 5-year period, there is still no mandatory, nationwide system for reporting adverse events from medical errors. See Daniela J. Lamas, "The Cruel Lesson of a Single Medical Mistake," *New York Times*, April 15, 2022, sec. Opinion, https://www.nytimes.com/2022/04/15/opinion/radonda-vaught-medical-errors.html.

5. On the general problem of the incomparability of international health data, see Irene Papanicolas and Ashish Jha, "Challenges in International Comparison of Health Care Systems," *JAMA* 318, no. 6 (2017): 515–16, https://doi.org/10.1001/jama.2017.9392; and Erik Meijer, Arie Kapteyn, and Tatiana Andreyeva, "Internationally Comparable Health Indices," *Health Economics* 20, no. 5 (May 2011): 600–619, https://doi.org/10.1002/hec.1620.

6. See, for example, Robert S. Kaplan and Michael E. Porter, "The Big Idea: How to Solve the Cost Crisis in Health Care," *Harvard Business Review*, September 1, 2011, https://hbr.org/2011/09/how-to-solve-the-cost-crisis-in-health-care; Robert

S. Kaplan et al., "Using Time-Driven Activity-Based Costing to Identify Value Improvement Opportunities in Healthcare," *Journal of Healthcare Management* 59, no. 6 (December 2014): 399–412; and George Keel et al., "Time-Driven Activity-Based Costing in Health Care: A Systematic Review of the Literature," *Health Policy* 121, no. 7 (July 1, 2017): 755–63, https://doi.org/10.1016/j.healthpol.2017.04.013.

7. The research project was funded by the Swedish industrialist and philanthropist Carl Bennet and Anders Ekblom, then head of R&D at AstraZeneca, with a pro bono in-kind contribution from BCG.

8. Sheng-Chia Chung et al., "Acute Myocardial Infarction: A Comparison of Short-Term Survival in National Outcome Registries in Sweden and the UK," *The Lancet* 383, no. 9925 (April 12, 2014): 1305–12, https://doi.org/10.1016/S0140-6736(13)62070-X.

9. We first wrote about Swedeheart and the registry phenomenon in general in Stefan Larsson et al., "Use of 13 Disease Registries in 5 Countries Demonstrates the Potential to Use Outcome Data to Improve Health Care's Value," *Health Affairs* 31, no. 1 (January 1, 2012): 220–27, https://doi.org/10.1377/hlthaff.2011.0762.

10. Tomas Jernberg et al., "The Swedish Web-System for Enhancement and Development of Evidence-Based Care in Heart Disease Evaluated According to Recommended Therapies (SWEDEHEART)," *Heart* 96, no. 20 (October 15, 2010): 1617–21, https://doi.org/10.1136/hrt.2010.198804.

11. Rickard Carlhed et al., "Improved Clinical Outcome After Acute Myocardial Infarction in Hospitals Participating in a Swedish Quality Improvement Initiative," *Circulation: Cardiovascular Quality and Outcomes* 2, no. 5 (September 1, 2009): 458–64, https://doi.org/10.1161/CIRCOUTCOMES.108.842146.

12. Stefan Larsson and Peter Lawyer, "Improving Health Care Value: The Case for Disease Registries" (Boston Consulting Group, January 8, 2011), https://www.bcg.com/publications/2011/health-care-payers-providers-public-sector-value-based-health-care-interactive.

13. Swedeheart, "Hur Används Swedeheart? Resultat från enkätstudien 2016 (Utförd av Jönköpings Academi) [How is Swedeheart used? Results from the 2016 survey (conducted by Jönköpings Academi)]," n.d.

14. S. Lori Brown et al., "Tumor Necrosis Factor Antagonist Therapy and Lymphoma Development: Twenty-Six Cases Reported to the Food and Drug Administration," *Arthritis & Rheumatism* 46, no. 12 (2002): 3151–58.

15. Johan Askling et al., "Haematopoietic Malignancies in Rheumatoid Arthritis: Lymphoma Risk and Characteristics After Exposure to Tumour Necrosis Factor Antagonists," *Annals of the Rheumatic Diseases* 64, no. 10 (October 2005): 1414–20, https://doi.org/10.1136/ard.2004.033241.

16. Sean R. Tunis, Daniel B. Stryer, and Carolyn M. Clancy, "Practical Clinical Trials: Increasing the Value of Clinical Research for Decision Making in Clinical and Health Policy," *JAMA* 290, no. 12 (September 24, 2003), https://doi.org/10.1001/jama.290.12.1624.

17. Ole Fröbert et al., "Thrombus Aspiration During ST-Segment Elevation Myocardial Infarction," *New England Journal of Medicine* 369, no. 17 (October 24, 2013): 1587–97, https://doi.org/10.1056/NEJMoa1308789; and Bo Lagerqvist et al.,

"Outcomes 1 Year After Thrombus Aspiration for Myocardial Infarction," *New England Journal of Medicine* 371, no. 12 (September 18, 2014): 1111–20, https://doi.org/10.1056/NEJMoa1405707.

18. Sergio Buccheri et al., "Assessing the Nationwide Impact of a Registry-Based Randomized Clinical Trial on Cardiovascular Practice: The TASTE Trial in Perspective," *Circulation: Cardiovascular Interventions* 12, no. 3 (March 7, 2019): e007381, https://www.ahajournals.org/doi/10.1161/CIRCINTERVENTIONS.118.007381.

19. Michael S. Lauer and Ralph B. D'Agostino, Sr., "The Randomized Registry Trial—The Next Disruptive Technology in Clinical Research?," *New England Journal of Medicine* 369, no. 17 (2013): 1579, https://doi.org/10.1056/NEJMp1310102.

20. Siavash Foroughi et al., "Re-inventing the Randomized Controlled Trial in Medical Oncology: The Registry-Based Trial," *Asia-Pacific Journal of Clinical Oncology* 14, no. 6 (2018): 365–73, https://doi.org/10.1111/ajco.12992.

21. Philip Crosby, *Quality Is Free: The Art of Making Quality Certain* (McGraw Hill, 1979).

22. See also the discussion of diabetes care in Sweden in Chapter 3 and the discussion of Santeon Group in the Netherlands in Chapter 4.

23. John F. Crowe, Thomas P. Sculco, and Barbara Kahn, "Revision Total Hip Arthroplasty: Hospital Cost and Reimbursement Analysis," *Clinical Orthopaedics and Related Research®* 413 (August 2003): 175–82, https://doi.org/10.1097/01.blo.0000072469.32680.b6. When the cost of post-acute care is taken into account, the costs are, of course, higher. For example, a 2016 analysis found that the combined costs for revision surgery and 90-day post-acute care in the United States was between approximately $37,000 and $74,000, on average, depending on a variety of factors, such as the number of patient comorbidities, the existence of surgical complications, whether the patient was discharged to home or to a skilled nursing facility, and the need for hospital readmission after discharge. See Christine I. Nichols and Joshua G. Vose, "Clinical Outcomes and Costs Within 90 Days of Primary or Revision Total Joint Arthroplasty," *Journal of Arthroplasty* 31, no. 7 (July 2016): 1400–1406.e3, https://doi.org/10.1016/j.arth.2016.01.022.

24. Brian J. McGrory, Caryn D. Etkin, and David G. Lewallen, "Comparing Contemporary Revision Burden Among Hip and Knee Joint Replacement Registries," *Arthroplasty Today* 2, no. 2 (May 27, 2016): 83–86, https://doi.org/10.1016/j.artd.2016.04.003. According to data from the Swedish hip-arthroplasty registry, since this 2016 study, Sweden has reduced its revision burden even more: to 8.8% in 2019.

25. Larsson et al., "Use of 13 Disease Registries in 5 Countries Demonstrates the Potential to Use Outcome Data to Improve Health Care's Value."

26. Steven M. Kurtz et al., "Future Clinical and Economic Impact of Revision Total Hip and Knee Arthroplasty," *Journal of Bone & Joint Surgery* 89, no. suppl_3 (October 2007): 144–51, https://doi.org/10.2106/JBJS.G.00587.

27. Steven Kurtz et al., "Prevalence of Primary and Revision Total Hip and Knee Arthroplasty in the United States from 1990 Through 2002," *Journal of Bone &*

Joint Surgery 87, no. 7 (July 2005): 1487–97, https://doi.org/doi:10.2106/JBJS .D.02441.

28. American Joint Replacement Registry, "Annual Report 2021" (American Academy of Orthopaedic Surgeons, 2021).

29. Nathanael Heckmann et al., "Early Results from the American Joint Replacement Registry: A Comparison with Other National Registries," *Journal of Arthroplasty* 34, no. 7, Supplement (July 2019): S125-S134.e1, https://doi.org/10 .1016/j.arth.2018.12.027.

30. Another methodological complexity that makes comparison difficult: the recent rapid growth in US procedures reported to the registry may contribute to oversampling of the denominator (initial hip-replacement operations) and undersampling of the numerator (eventual revisions) in the most recent AJRR data.

31. Atul Gawande, "The Bell Curve," *New Yorker*, December 6, 2004, https://www .newyorker.com/magazine/2004/12/06/the-bell-curve.

32. Mats Lundström et al., "European Registry for Quality Improvement in Cataract Surgery," *International Journal of Health Care Quality Assurance* 27, no. 2 (2014): 140–51, https://doi.org/10.1108/IJHCQA-10-2012-0101.

33. "International Prosthesis Benchmarking Working Group Guidance Document: Hip and Knee Arthroplasty Devices" (International Society of Arthroplasty Registries, May 2018), https://drive.google.com/file/d/0BwKvdROo5Eg-MjZYc2 VHQUZGYzNJMlRaenZEVUN3cTdMYlBj/.

34. "Mission," ICHOM, accessed March 2, 2022, https://www.ichom.org/mission/.

35. ICHOM's initial funding also came from in-kind and cash contributions from the Harvard Business School and Swedish industrialist and philanthropist Carl Bennet. In the 10 years since its founding, ICHOM has also received financial support from patient advocacy groups such as Movember and the American Heart Association, and a variety of public and private organizations, including the United Kingdom's National Health Service, Humana, Medtronic, and Philips.

36. Freddie Bray et al., "Global Cancer Statistics 2018: GLOBOCAN Estimates of Incidence and Mortality Worldwide for 36 Cancers in 185 Countries," *CA: A Cancer Journal for Clinicians* 68, no. 6 (2018): 394–424, https://doi.org/10.3322 /caac.21492.

37. Prashanth Rawla, "Epidemiology of Prostate Cancer," *World Journal of Oncology* 10, no. 2 (April 2019): 63–89, https://doi.org/10.14740/wjon1191.

38. The term *localized prostate cancer* refers to cancer that is only inside the prostate gland and has not spread to other parts of the body. ICHOM also has an outcome-measurement set for advanced prostate cancer.

39. Neil E. Martin et al., "Defining a Standard Set of Patient-Centered Outcomes for Men with Localized Prostate Cancer," *European Urology* 67, no. 3 (March 2015): 460–67, https://doi.org/10.1016/j.eururo.2014.08.075.

40. Jason Arora et al., "Implementing ICHOM's Standard Sets of Outcomes: Cleft Lip and Palate at Erasmus University Medical Centre in the Netherlands" (International Consortium for Health Outcomes Measurement, December 2016), https://www.ichom.org.

41. Jason Arora et al., "Implementing ICHOM's Standard Sets of Outcomes: Parkinson's Disease at Aneurin Bevan University Health Board in South Wales, UK"

(International Consortium for Health Outcomes Measurement, March 2017), https://www.ichom.org.

42. Dermot McGrath, "French Centres Adopt ICHOM Standards," *EuroTimes*, September 1, 2019, https://www.eurotimes.org/french-centres-adopt-ichom-standards/.

43. Jason Arora, Rosanna Tavella, and Matthew Salt, "Implementing ICHOM's Standard Sets of Outcomes: Coronary Artery Disease in the Coronary Angiogram Database of South Australia (CADOSA)" (International Consortium for Health Outcomes Measurement, January 2017), https://www.ichom.org.

44. "Prostate Cancer in Australian and New Zealand Men: Patterns of Care, Patient-Reported Outcomes and Selected Treatment Analyses, 2015–2018" (PCOR-ANZ Annual Report, 2020), https://prostatecancerregistry-org.s3.amazonaws.com/pcor_cms/media/filer_public/ce/9c/ce9cd8eb-2cb0-4be9-8473-4087b277fb1e/pcor-anz_2020_annual_report_final.pdf.

45. Sue M. Evans et al., "Cohort Profile: The TrueNTH Global Registry—an International Registry to Monitor and Improve Localised Prostate Cancer Health Outcomes," *BMJ Open* 7, no. 11 (September 2017): e017006, https://doi.org/10.1136/bmjopen-2017-017006.

46. Daniel J. George et al., "IRONMAN: The International Registry for Men with Advanced Prostate Cancer," *Journal of Clinical Oncology* 40, no. 6S (February 20, 2022): TPS190, https://doi.org/10.1200/JCO.2022.40.6_suppl.TPS190.

47. Mathias C. Blom et al., "Harmonization of the ICHOM Quality Measures to Enable Health Outcomes Measurement in Multimorbid Patients," *Frontiers in Digital Health* 2 (December 15, 2020): 606246, https://doi.org/10.3389/fdgth.2020.606246.

48. David Lansky, "Reimagining a Quality Information System for US Health Care," *Health Affairs Forefront* (blog), January 25, 2022, https://www.healthaffairs.org/do/10.1377/forefront.20220120.301087/full/.

49. Lisa Rosenbaum, "Reassessing Quality Assessment—The Flawed System for Fixing a Flawed System," *New England Journal of Medicine* 386 (April 28, 2022): 1663–67, https://doi.org/10.1056/NEJMms2200976. See also Lisa Rosenbaum, "Metric Myopia—Trading Away Our Clinical Judgment;" and Lisa Rosenbaum, "Peers, Professionalism, and Improvement—Reframing the Quality Question," *New England Journal of Medicine*, 386 (May 12, 2022): 1850–54, https://doi.org/10.1056/NEJMms2200978.

CHAPTER 3

1. "EUROSPINE Patient Line—The Dialogue Support," accessed March 8, 2022, https://www.eurospinepatientline.org/en/the-dialogue-support.htm.

2. Ivbar Institute, "Dialogue Support for Spine Surgery—Based on Swespine, the Swedish Spine Register," Molnify, accessed April 12, 2022, https://app.molnify.com/custom.jsp.

3. For a similarly expansive view of the critical components of a value-based health system, see Rifat Atun and Gordon Moore, *Building a High-Value Health System* (Oxford University Press, 2021).

4. Assessing the relative contribution of different determinants of health outcomes and of the costs associated with them poses complex methodological issues. Studies suggest that, in general, individual behavior accounts for roughly half the relative contribution to health outcomes, with a small number of behavioral determinants—for example, smoking or physical exercise—having an outsized impact. When considering the impact of individual behavior on health outcomes, however, it is important to recognize that health behaviors occur within a larger social context. Behaviors are often heavily influenced by social and environmental factors that are outside the individual's control. Unhealthy eating habits, for example, may be a function of lack of access to affordable healthy foods. See Laura McGovern, "The Relative Contribution of Multiple Determinants to Health," *Health Affairs Health Policy Brief*, August 21, 2014, https://doi.org/10.1377/hpb20140821.404487.

5. Eurídice Martínez Steele et al., "Ultra-Processed Foods and Added Sugars in the US Diet: Evidence from a Nationally Representative Cross-Sectional Study," *BMJ Open* 6, no. 3 (January 1, 2016): e009892, https://doi.org/10.1136/bmjopen-2015-009892.

6. For a comparison of United States and Swedish spending on health care and social welfare, see Elizabeth H. Bradley and Lauren A. Taylor, *The American Health Care Paradox* (Public Affairs, 2013).

7. See Centers for Disease Control, "National Diabetes Statistics Report," January 20, 2022, https://www.cdc.gov/diabetes/data/statistics-report/index.html; and Suzanne V. Arnold et al., "Heart Failure Documentation in Outpatients with Diabetes and Volume Overload: An Observational Cohort Study from the Diabetes Collaborative Registry," *Cardiovascular Diabetology* 19, no. 1 (December 2020): 212, https://doi.org/10.1186/s12933-020-01190-6.

8. For more on the idea of integrator roles, see Yves Morieux and Peter Tollman, *Six Simple Rules: How to Manage Complexity Without Getting Complicated* (Harvard Business Review Press, 2014).

9. Harris Meyer, "Medicare Diabetes Prevention: Enrollment Short of Projections," *Health Affairs* 40, no. 11 (November 2021): 1682–87, https://doi.org/10.1377/hlthaff.2021.01292.

10. Puneet Kaur Chehal et al., "Diabetes and the Fragmented State of US Health Care and Policy," *Health Affairs* 41, no. 7 (July 2022): 939–46, https://doi.org/10.1377/hlthaff.2022.00299.

11. This description of Martini Klinik is based, in part, on Michael E. Porter et al., "Martini Klinik: Prostate Cancer Care," Harvard Business School Case 714–471, March 2014, https://www.hbs.edu/faculty/Pages/item.aspx?num=46332. For German-language readers interested to learn more about Martini, see Hartwig Huland, Markus Graefen, and Jens Deerberg-Wittram, (eds.), *Das Martini-Prinzip: Spitzenmedizin Durch Spezialisierung, Ergebnistransparenz Und Patientenorientierung* [*The Martini Principle: Cutting-Edge Medicine Through Specialization, Transparency of Results and Patient Orientation*] (MWV Medizinisch Wissenschaftliche Verlagsgesellschaft, 2018).

12. Sophie D. Fosså et al., "Improved Patient-Reported Functional Outcomes After Nerve-Sparing Radical Prostatectomy by Using NeuroSAFE Technique,"

Scandinavian Journal of Urology 53, no. 6 (November 2, 2019): 385–91, https://doi.org/10.1080/21681805.2019.1693625.

13. Thorsten Schlomm, Hartwig Huland, and Markus Graefen, "Improving Outcome of Surgical Procedures Is Not Possible Without Adequate Quality Measurement," *European Urology* 65, no. 6 (June 1, 2014): 1017–19, https://doi.org/10.1016/j.eururo.2013.11.042.

14. Colin B. Begg et al., "Variations in Morbidity After Radical Prostatectomy," *New England Journal of Medicine* 346 (April 11, 2002): 1138–44, https://doi.org/10.1056/NEJMsa011788.

15. Jens Deerberg-Wittram and Laura Lüdtke, "Value-Based Healthcare Delivery in Diabetes" (Medtronic, September 2016), https://diabeter.nl/media/cms_page_media/130/Value%20Based%20Healthcare%20Diabeter%20White%20Paper.pdf.

16. Vijay Govindarajan and S. Manikutti, "What Poor Countries Can Teach Rich Ones About Health Care," Harvard Business Review, April 27, 2010, https://hbr.org/2010/04/how-poor-countries-can-help-so.html.

17. Peter Dohmen et al., "Implementing a Comprehensive Value-Based Healthcare System to Improve Pregnancy and Childbirth Outcomes in Urban and Rural Kenya," *Research Square*, Preprint, November 23, 2021, https://doi.org/10.21203/rs.3.rs-1071399/v1.

18. Kevin Grumbach et al., "Revitalizing the U.S. Primary Care Infrastructure," *New England Journal of Medicine* 385, no. 13 (September 23, 2021): 1156–58, https://doi.org/10.1056/NEJMp2109700.

19. Eric Larsen, "Patrick Conway Led the Industry in Health Care Transformation at CMS. At Blue Cross NC, He's Not Stopping.," *Lessons from the C-Suite* (blog), September 12, 2019, https://www.advisory.com/Blog/2019/09/patrick-conway.

20. Michael E. Porter, Thomas H. Lee, and Meredith A. Alger, "Oak Street Health: A New Model of Primary Care," Harvard Business School Case 717-437, February 2017, https://www.hbs.edu/faculty/Pages/item.aspx?num=52357.

21. Andis Robeznieks, "Medicare-Only Oak Street Health Isn't Shy About Taking Big Risks," American Medical Association, July 23, 2019, https://www.ama-assn.org/practice-management/payment-delivery-models/medicare-only-oak-street-health-isn-t-shy-about-taking.

22. Griffin Myers and Thomas H. Lee, "Rebuilding Health Care as It Should Be: Personal, Equitable, and Accountable," *NEJM Catalyst*, August 3, 2018, https://catalyst.nejm.org/doi/full/10.1056/CAT.18.0120.

23. Myers and Lee, "Rebuilding Health Care as It Should Be: Personal, Equitable, and Accountable".

24. Myers Griffin, Geoffrey Price, and Mike Pykosz, "A Report from the Covid Front Lines of Value-Based Primary Care," *NEJM Catalyst*, May 1, 2020, https://catalyst.nejm.org/doi/full/10.1056/CAT.20.0148.

25. Surabhi Bhatt et al., "Interpretable Machine Learning Models for Clinical Decision-Making in a High-Need, Value-Based Primary Care Setting," *NEJM Catalyst* 2, no. 4 (April 2021): CAT.21.0008, https://doi.org/10.1056/CAT.21.0008.

26. Tom Debley, "How It All Started," accessed March 9, 2022, https://about.kaiserpermanente.org/our-story/our-history/how-it-all-started.

27. "Search for Medicare Plans—NCQA," accessed December 4, 2021, https://healthinsuranceratings.ncqa.org/2019/search/Medicare.

28. Michaela Schiøtz et al., "Something Is Amiss in Denmark: A Comparison of Preventable Hospitalisations and Readmissions for Chronic Medical Conditions in the Danish Healthcare System and Kaiser Permanente," *BMC Health Services Research* 11, no. 1 (December 2011): 347, https://doi.org/10.1186/1472-6963-11-347.

29. Monti Khatod, "Kaiser Permanente: Joint Arthroplasty in an Integrated Capitated Care Delivery Model," *Journal of Arthroplasty* 33, no. 6 (June 2018): 1649–51, https://doi.org/10.1016/j.arth.2018.01.029.

30. Michael H. Kanter et al., "Complete Care at Kaiser Permanente: Transforming Chronic and Preventive Care," *Joint Commission Journal on Quality and Patient Safety* 39, no. 11 (November 2013): 484–94, https://doi.org/10.1016/S1553-7250(13)39064-3.

31. Yi Yvonne Zhou, Warren Wong, and Hui Li, "Improving Care for Older Adults: A Model to Segment the Senior Population," *The Permanente Journal* 18, no. 3 (2014): 18–21, https://doi.org/10.7812/TPP/14-005.

32. Richard Brumley et al., "Increased Satisfaction with Care and Lower Costs: Results of a Randomized Trial of In-Home Palliative Care," *Journal of the American Geriatrics Society* 55, no. 7 (July 2007): 993–1000, https://doi.org/10.1111/j.1532-5415.2007.01234.x.

33. Loel Solomon, "Health Care Steps Up to Social Determinants of Health: Current Context," *The Permanente Journal*, 22, no. 4S (October 2018), https://doi.org/10.7812/TPP/18-139.

34. Nicole L Friedman and Matthew P Banegas, "Toward Addressing Social Determinants of Health: A Health Care System Strategy," *The Permanente Journal* 22, no. 4S (October 22, 2018), https://doi.org/10.7812/TPP/18-095.

35. Michael H. Kanter and Courneya, Patrick T., "Promising Methods for Improving Quality Through the Faster Spread of Best Practices," *The Permanente Journal* 23 (April 19, 2019): 19–39, https://doi.org/10.7812/TPP/19-039.

36. Benjamin Chesluk et al., "Physicians' Voices: What Skills and Supports Are Needed for Effective Practice in an Integrated Delivery System? A Case Study of Kaiser Permanente," *INQUIRY: The Journal of Health Care Organization, Provision, and Financing* 54 (January 2017): 004695801771176, https://doi.org/10.1177/0046958017711760.

37. Chesluk et al., "Physicians' Voices: What Skills and Supports Are Needed for Effective Practice in an Integrated Delivery System? A Case Study of Kaiser Permanente."

38. Chesluk et al., "Physicians' Voices: What Skills and Supports Are Needed for Effective Practice in an Integrated Delivery System? A Case Study of Kaiser Permanente."

CHAPTER 4

1. For more on Cleveland Clinic, see Toby Cosgrove, *The Cleveland Clinic Way: Lessons in Excellence from One of the World's Leading Health Care Organizations*, 1st edition (McGraw Hill, 2014); and Chibueze Okey Agba et al., "Global Horizons

for Value-Based Care: Lessons Learned from the Cleveland Clinic," *NEJM Catalyst*, June 18, 2022, https://catalyst.nejm.org/doi/full/10.1056/CAT.22.0123.

2. For more on the Santeon experience, see "How Dutch Hospitals Make Value-Based Health Care Work" (Boston Consulting Group; Santeon Group, June 2018), https://www.bcg.com/publications/2018/how-dutch-hospitals-make-value-based -health-care-work.

3. "How Dutch Hospitals Make Value-Based Health Care Work."

4. Unless, otherwise indicated, the quotations from Santeon-affiliated physicians are from "How Dutch Hospitals Make Value-Based Health Care Work."

5. Santeon Group, "Birth Care" (Santeon Group, March 2021), https://santeon.nl /app/uploads/2021/04/Santeon-Birth-Care_march-2021.pdf.

6. The description of the Erasmus breast cancer pilot is based, in part, on Arvind Oemrawsingh, Jan Hazelzet, and Linetta Koppert, "The State of Patient-Centered Breast Cancer Care: An Academic Center's Experience and Perspective," in Nico van Weert and Jan Hazelzet (eds.), *Personalized Specialty Care: Value-Based Healthcare Frontrunners from the Netherlands* (Springer, 2021).

7. L. S. E. van Egdom et al., "Implementation of Value Based Breast Cancer Care," *European Journal of Surgical Oncology* 45, no. 7 (July 1, 2019): 1163–70, https:// doi.org/10.1016/j.ejso.2019.01.007.

8. van Egdom et al., "Implementation of Value Based Breast Cancer Care."

9. Wee Loon Ong et al., "A Standard Set of Value-Based Patient-Centered Outcomes for Breast Cancer: The International Consortium for Health Outcomes Measurement (ICHOM) Initiative," *JAMA Oncology* 3, no. 5 (May 1, 2017): 677–85, https://doi.org/10.1001/jamaoncol.2016.4851; and van Egdom et al., "Implementation of Value Based Breast Cancer Care."

10. Yolima Cossio-Gil et al., "The Roadmap for Implementing Value Based Healthcare in European University Hospitals—Consensus Report and Recommendations," preprint, *Health Economics* (May 22, 2021), https://doi.org/10.1101 /2021.05.18.21257238.

11. Before 2019, Region Stockholm was known as the Stockholm County Council.

12. Jacqui Wise, "Melvin Samsom: Rebuilding Hospitals for Patients," *BMJ* 357, no. 8104 (May 2, 2017): j2088, https://doi.org/10.1136/bmj.j2088.

13. "Bästa sjukhuset 2013: Här är den längre listan på rankade sjukhus [Best Hospital 2013: Here is the longer list of the ranked hospitals]," *Dagens Medicin*, January 22, 2014, https://www.dagensmedicin.se/alla-nyheter/basta-sjukhuset /har-ar-den-langre-listan-pa-rankade-sjukhus/.

14. As reported in "Överlevnaden steg när färre opererade mer [Survival increased as fewer surgeons operated on more patients]" *Dagens Medicin*, March 23, 2021, https://www.dagensmedicin.se/specialistomraden/hjarta-karl/overlevnaden -steg-nar-farre-opererade-mer/.

15. "Överlevnaden steg när färre opererade mer [Survival increased as fewer surgeons operated on more patients]."

16. Twenty-three percent of the Swedish population lives in the Stockholm region. But at the height of the pandemic, 36% of all Swedish Covid inpatients were treated in Stockholm. Of that group, 38% were treated at Karolinska, including 54% of those needing ICU beds.

17. "World's Best Hospitals 2022," *Newsweek*, March 2, 2022, https://www.newsweek.com/worlds-best-hospitals-2022.

18. As this book went to press, Intermountain announced that Marc Harrison is stepping down as CEO in the fall of 2022 to run a new health-care platform business for the venture capital firm General Catalyst. In May 2022, General Catalyst and Intermountain entered a partnership to develop technology that advances value-based care.

19. "Intermountain Announces New Company to Elevate Value-Based Care Capabilities," intermountainhealthcare.org, accessed May 23, 2022, https://intermountainhealthcare.org/about/who-we-are/trustee-resource-center/newsletter/newsletter-archive/intermountain-announces-new-company-to-elevate-value-based-care-capabilities/.

20. Marc Harrison, "What One Health System Learned About Providing Digital Services in the Pandemic," *Harvard Business Review*, December 11, 2020, https://hbr.org/2020/12/what-one-health-system-learned-about-providing-digital-services-in-the-pandemic.

21. Marc Harrison, "What One Health System Learned About Providing Digital Services in the Pandemic."

CHAPTER 5

1. Sunil Eappen et al., "Relationship Between Occurrence of Surgical Complications and Hospital Finances," *JAMA* 309, no. 15 (April 17, 2013): 1599–1606, https://doi.org/10.1001/jama.2013.2773.

2. Brad Smith, "CMS Innovation Center at 10 Years—Progress and Lessons Learned," *New England Journal of Medicine* 384, no. 8 (February 25, 2021): 759–64, https://doi.org/10.1056/NEJMsb2031138.

3. Medicare is the US government program that covers some 52 million Americans who are 65 and older or who suffer from chronic disabilities or end-stage renal disease. Medicaid is an assistance program for low-income patients' medical expenses and covers approximately 75 million low-income Americans, nearly 40% of whom are children. In 2020, the combined expenditures for the two programs were approximately $1.5 trillion, representing about 36% of total US health care spending. See "NHE Fact Sheet," Centers for Medicare and Medicaid Services, accessed August 23, 2022, https://www.cms.gov/Research-Statistics-Data-and-Systems/Statistics-Trends-and-Reports/NationalHealthExpendData/NHE-Fact-Sheet.

4. Smith, "CMS Innovation Center at 10 Years—Progress and Lessons Learned."

5. Rajender Agarwal et al., "Comparing Medicare Advantage and Traditional Medicare: A Systematic Review," *Health Affairs* 40, no. 6 (June 1, 2021): 937–44, https://doi.org/10.1377/hlthaff.2020.02149.

6. Thomas W. Feeley and Namita Seth Mohta, "New Marketplace Survey: Transitioning Payment Models: Fee-for-Service to Value-Based Care," *NEJM Catalyst*, November 8, 2018, https://catalyst.nejm.org/doi/full/10.1056/CAT.18.0056. For a systematic review of value-based payment in non-Medicare commercial insurance, see Marina A. Milad et al., "Value-Based Payment Models in the Commercial Insurance Sector: A Systematic Review," *Health Affairs* 41, no. 4 (April 2022): 540–48, https://doi.org/10.1377/hlthaff.2021.01020.

7. Ben Horner et al., "Paying for Value in Health Care" (Boston Consulting Group, September 2019), https://web-assets.bcg.com/img-src/BCG-Paying-for-Value-in -Health-Care-September-2019_tcm9-227552.pdf.

8. For example, in February 2021, Brad Smith, the Biden administration's new head of CMMI, published a 10-year assessment of the agency's $20 billion Alternative Payment Models program in the *New England Journal of Medicine*. His conclusion: while some of the models tested resulted in substantial financial savings and produced significant improvements in quality, "the vast majority of the Center's models have not saved money, with several on pace to lose billions of dollars. Similarly, the majority of the models do not show significant improvements in quality, although no models show a significant decrease in quality." See Smith, "CMS Innovation Center at 10 Years—Progress and Lessons Learned." Other observers, however, have argued that this assessment, based on extremely strict evaluation criteria, undersells the considerable achievements of the APM program. For more on what has been, perhaps, the most successful APM model, the Maryland All-Payer model, see Ezekiel J. Emanuel et al., "Meaningful Value-Based Payment Reform, Part 1: Maryland Leads the Way," *Health Affairs Forefront* (blog), February 9, 2022, https://www.healthaffairs.org/do/10.1377 /forefront.20220205.211264/full/.

9. Amol S. Navathe et al., "Effect of Financial Bonus Size, Loss Aversion, and Increased Social Pressure on Physician Pay-for-Performance: A Randomized Clinical Trial and Cohort Study," *JAMA Network Open* 2, no. 2 (February 8, 2019): e187950, https://doi.org/10.1001/jamanetworkopen.2018.7950.

10. See, for example, Michael E. Porter and Robert S. Kaplan, "How to Pay for Health Care," *Harvard Business Review*, July 1, 2016, https://hbr.org/2016/07/how-to -pay-for-health-care; and Brent C. James and Gregory P. Poulsen, "The Case for Capitation," *Harvard Business Review*, July 1, 2016, https://hbr.org/2016/07/the -case-for-capitation.

11. For an interesting example, see Ezekiel J. Emanuel, *Which Country Has the World's Best Health Care?* (Public Affairs, 2020).

12. Robert A. Berenson and John D. Goodson, "Finding Value in Unexpected Places—Fixing the Medicare Physician Fee Schedule," *New England Journal of Medicine* 374, no. 14 (April 7, 2016): 1306–9, https://doi.org/10.1056 /NEJMp1600999.

13. As a point of comparison, in the Netherlands, which also has a regulated private-insurance market, the ratios for administrative costs and profit are much lower: 3% and 2%, respectively, for a total of 5%. For an explanation of the US federal government's rules for calculating medical loss ratios, see "Medical Loss Ratio (MLR)—HealthCare.Gov Glossary," HealthCare.gov, accessed April 16, 2022, https://www.healthcare.gov/glossary/medical-loss-ratio-mlr/.

14. HMOs, or health maintenance organizations, are one (but not the only) type of Medicare Advantage health plan. See Bruce E. Landon et al., "Analysis of Medicare Advantage HMOs Compared with Traditional Medicare Shows Lower Use of Many Services During 2003–09," *Health Affairs* 31, no. 12 (December 1, 2012): 2609–17, https://doi.org/10.1377/hlthaff.2012.0179.

15. Roseanna Sommers et al., "Focus Groups Highlight That Many Patients Object to Clinicians' Focusing on Costs," *Health Affairs* 32, no. 2 (February 1, 2013): 338–46, https://doi.org/10.1377/hlthaff.2012.0686.

16. Jon Kaplan et al., "Alternative Payer Models Show Improved Health-Care Value" (Boston Consulting Group, May 2013), https://www.bcg.com/en-au/publications /2013/health-care-payers-providers-alternative-payer-models.

17. Take the example of diabetes. Two key HEDIS standards for patients suffering from diabetes are frequent (at a minimum, once a year) testing for glycated hemoglobin (HbA1c), high levels of which have been correlated with cardiovascular disease and other conditions, and regular nephropathy screenings to monitor kidney function. The average number of HbA1c tests per patient increased from 0.75 in the fee-for-service matched sample to 1.36 in the capitated matched sample. And the average number of nephropathy screenings per patient more than doubled, from 0.17 to 0.40. What's more, whereas the fee-for-service matched diabetic sample had an average of 11.5 amputations per 1,000 patients, the capitated matched diabetic sample had only 0.3. And whereas the fee-for-service sample had an average of 212.3 foot-ulcer procedures per 1,000 patients, the capitated sample had only 25.4. See Jon Kaplan et al., "Alternative Payer Models Show Improved Health-Care Value."

18. Agarwal et al., "Comparing Medicare Advantage and Traditional Medicare."

19. As this book went to press, Will Shrank announced that he was leaving Humana in August 2022.

20. "Value-Based Care Report: Physician Progress and Patient Outcomes" (Humana, 2020), https://digital.humana.com/VBCReport/VBC_Report_2020_digital.pdf.

21. On post-acute care, see Adriane W. Casebeer et al., "Post-SNF Outcomes and Cost Comparison: Medicare Advantage vs. Traditional Medicare," *American Journal of Managed Care* 27, no. 4 (April 2021): 140–46, https://doi.org/10.37765/ajmc .2021.88616. On better utilization of home health care services, sees Adriane W. Casebeer et al., "A Comparison of Home Health Utilization, Outcomes, and Cost Between Medicare Advantage and Traditional Medicare," *Medical Care* 60, no. 1 (January 1, 2022): 66–74, https://doi.org/10.1097/MLR.0000000000001661. On addressing social determinants of health, see Tristan Cordier et al., "A Bold Goal: More Healthy Days Through Improved Community Health," *Population Health Management* 21, no. 3 (June 2018): 202–8, https://doi.org/10.1089/pop.2017.0142.

22. For a comprehensive critique of Medicare Advantage and Medicare's related direct-contracting program, see Richard Gilfillan and Donald M. Berwick, "Medicare Advantage, Direct Contracting, and the Medicare 'Money Machine,' Part 1: The Risk-Score Game," *Health Affairs Forefront* (blog), September 29, 2021, https://www.healthaffairs.org/do/10.1377/forefront.20210927.6239/; and Richard Gilfillan, and Donald M. Berwick, "Medicare Advantage, Direct Contracting, and the Medicare 'Money Machine,' Part 2: Building on the ACO Model," *Health Affairs Forefront* (blog), September 30, 2021, https://www.healthaffairs.org/do/10 .1377/forefront.20210928.795755/full/.

23. Joan Stephenson, "Federal Investigators Find Medicare Advantage Plans Too Often Deny, Delay Needed Care," *JAMA Health Forum* 3, no. 5 (May 10, 2022): e221781, https://doi.org/10.1001/jamahealthforum.2022.1781.

24. See Agarwal et al., "Comparing Medicare Advantage and Traditional Medicare;" and Medicare Payment Advisory Commission, "June 2021 Report to the Congress: Medicare and the Health Care Delivery System," June 15, 2021, http:// www.medpac.gov/-documents-/reports.

25. For a review of the counterarguments to the critiques of Medicare Advantage, see George C. Halvorson, "Medicare Advantage Delivers Better Care and Saves Money: A Response to Gilfillan and Berwick," *Health Affairs Forefront* (blog), January 7, 2020, https://www.healthaffairs.org/do/10.1377/forefront.20220106 .907235/full/; and Donald Crane, "The Important Roles of Medicare Advantage and Direct Contracting: A Response to Gilfillan and Berwick," *Health Affairs Forefront* (blog), February 7, 2022, https://www.healthaffairs.org/do/10.1377 /forefront.20220203.915914/.

26. Chris Gervenak and David Mike, "Value to the Federal Government of Medicare Advantage," Millman Client Report (Center for Innovation in Medicare Advantage, Better Medicare Alliance, October 2021), https://www.milliman .com/-/media/milliman/pdfs/2021-articles/10-20-21-value-federal-government -of-medicare-advantage.ashx.

27. Jeroen N. Struijs et al., "Bundled-Payment Models Around the World: How They Work and What Their Impact Has Been," Issue Brief (The Commonwealth Fund, April 6, 2020), https://www.commonwealthfund.org/publications/2020/apr /bundled-payment-models-around-world-how-they-work-their-impact.

28. Aaron Glickman, Claire Dinh, and Amol S. Navathe, "The Current State of Evidence on Bundled Payments," Issue Brief (Leonard Davis Institute of Health Economics, University of Pennsylvania, October 2018), https://ldi.upenn.edu /wp-content/uploads/archive/pdf/LDI%20Issue%20Brief%202018%20No.%203 _41.pdf.

29. "Comprehensive Care for Joint Replacement Model," CMS.gov, accessed March 22, 2022, https://innovation.cms.gov/innovation-models/cjr.

30. Although the CJR bundled-payment program was initially scheduled to end after five years in 2020, in 2021 CMS issued a rule finalizing changes to the payment model which will continue through 2024, but only in the 34 metropolitan statistical areas where participation is mandatory.

31. Struijs et al., "Bundled-Payment Models Around the World: How They Work and What Their Impact Has Been."

32. Rajender Agarwal et al., "The Impact of Bundled Payment on Health Care Spending, Utilization, and Quality: A Systematic Review," *Health Affairs* 39, no. 1 (January 2020): 50–57, https://doi.org/10.1377/hlthaff.2019.00784.

33. Dr. Holger Stalberg, senior physician, Region Stockholm, personal communication, April 2022. According to Dr. Stalberg, these clinical and cost improvements have been sustained in the subsequent years of the bundled-payment program. However, recent research suggests that the bundled-payment program and associated changes have had little to no positive impact on patient-reported health outcomes after surgery. See Fanny Goude et al., "The Effects of Competition and Bundled Payment on Patient Reported Outcome Measures After Hip Replacement Surgery," *BMC Health Services Research* 21, no. 1 (April 26, 2021): 387, https://doi.org/10.1186/s12913-021-06397-1.

34. Dr. Holger Stalberg, senior physician, Region Stockholm, personal communication. Like the hip replacement bundle, the spine surgery bundle appears to have had little or no positive income on patient-reported health outcomes after surgery. See Thérèse Eriksson et al., "A Pain Relieving Reimbursement Program? Effects of a Value-Based Reimbursement Program on Patient Reported Outcome Measures," *BMC Health Services Research* 20, no. 1 (August 27, 2020): 805, https://doi.org/10.1186/s12913-020-05578-8.

35. On the critical importance of value-based health care in low-income countries, see Margaret E. Kruk et al., "High-Quality Health Systems in the Sustainable Development Goals Era: Time for a Revolution," *The Lancet Global Health* 6, no. 11 (November 2018): e1196–1252, https://doi.org/10.1016/S2214-109X(18)30386-3; and Kojo Nimako and Margaret E Kruk, "Seizing the Moment to Rethink Health Systems," *The Lancet Global Health*, 9, no. 12 (December 2021): e1758–62, https://doi.org/10.1016/S2214-109X(21)00356-9.

36. This example is based on Benedict Stanberry, Gerhard Bothma, and Katie Harrison, "Using the MEAT VBP Framework to Analyse and Understand the Value of Surgical Gloves: An Explanatory Case Study," *Health Economics Review* 11, no. 1 (December 2021): 23, https://doi.org/10.1186/s13561-021-00325-z.

37. J. M. Badia, et al., "Impact of Surgical Site Infection on Healthcare Costs and Patient Outcomes: A Systematic Review in Six European Countries" *Journal of Hospital Infection* 96, No. 1 (May 1, 2017): 1–15, https://doi.org/10.1016/j.jhin.2017.03.004.

38. Alice Mannocci et al., "How Much Do Needlestick Injuries Cost? A Systematic Review of the Economic Evaluations of Needlestick and Sharps Injuries Among Healthcare Personnel," *Infection Control & Hospital Epidemiology* 37, no. 6 (June 2016): 635–46, https://doi.org/10.1017/ice.2016.48.

39. Munir Pirmohamed et al., "Adverse Drug Reactions as Cause of Admission to Hospital: Prospective Analysis of 18,820 Patients," *BMJ* 329, no. 7456 (July 3, 2004): 15–19, https://doi.org/10.1136/bmj.329.7456.15.

40. "Health Resources—Pharmaceutical Spending—OECD Data," accessed March 24, 2022, http://data.oecd.org/healthres/pharmaceutical-spending.htm.

41. Corinna Sorenson et al., "National Institute for Health and Clinical Excellence (NICE): How Does It Work and What Are the Implications for the U.S.?" (National Pharmaceutical Council, May 2008), https://www.npcnow.org/resources/national-institute-health-and-clinical-excellence-nice-how-does-it-work-and-what-are.

42. "Our History & Impact | Who We Are," ICER, accessed October 30, 2021, https://icer.org/who-we-are/history-impact/.

43. Peter Glassman et al., "VA And ICER At Three Years: Critics' Concerns Answered," *Health Affairs Forefront* (blog), June 15, 2020, https://www.healthaffairs.org/do/10.1377/forefront.20200611.662048/full/.

44. "Patient Outcomes Management | Philips," accessed April 12, 2022, https://www.usa.philips.com/healthcare/services/population-health-management/patient-engagement/patient-reported-outcomes/patient-outcomes-measurement-platform.

45. Benjamin Chesluk et al., "Physicians' Voices: What Skills and Supports Are Needed for Effective Practice in an Integrated Delivery System? A Case Study of Kaiser Permanente," *INQUIRY: The Journal of Health Care Organization, Provision, and Financing* 54 (January 2017): 004695801771176, https://doi.org/10.1177/0046958017711760.

46. Kyle H. Sheetz and Michael J. Englesbe, "Expanding the Quality Collaborative Model as a Blueprint for Higher-Value Care," *JAMA Health Forum* 1, no. 5 (May 27, 2020): e200413, https://doi.org/10.1001/jamahealthforum.2020.0413; and Ryan Howard et al., "Improving the Quality of Health Care through 25 Years of Statewide Collaboration in Michigan," *NEJM Catalyst* 3, No. 9 (September 2022): CAT.22.0153; https://catalyst.nejm.org/doi/10.1056/CAT.22.0153.

47. Ryan Howard et al., "Optimizing Postoperative Opioid Prescribing Through Quality-Based Reimbursement," *JAMA Network Open* 2, no. 9 (September 18, 2019): e1911619, https://doi.org/10.1001/jamanetworkopen.2019.11619.

48. Smith, "CMS Innovation Center at 10 Years—Progress and Lessons Learned." For a description of CMMI's future strategic priorities, see John E. McDonough and Eli Y. Adashi, "The Center for Medicare and Medicaid Innovation—Toward Value-Based Care," *JAMA* 327, no. 20 (May 24, 2022): 1957–58, https://doi.org/10.1001/jama.2022.6927.

49. "Health Care Payment Learning and Action Network," HCPLAN, accessed November 12, 2021, https://hcp-lan.org/.

50. Lola Butcher, "Geisinger Scraps Physician Pay-for-Performance," Healthcare Financial Management Association, June 9, 2017, https://www.hfma.org/topics/article/54513.html.

CHAPTER 6

1. RBC Capital Markets, "The Convergence of Healthcare and Technology," accessed February 8, 2022, https://www.rbccm.com/en/gib/healthcare/episode/the_healthcare_data_explosion#content-pane.

2. EMC Digital Universe, "The Digital Universe: Driving Data Growth in Healthcare," EMC Vertical Brief, 2014, https://www.cycloneinteractive.com/cyclone/assets/File/digital-universe-healthcare-vertical-report-ar.pdf.

3. David Reinsel, John Gantz, and John Rydning, "The Digitization of the World from Edge to Core," IDC White Paper, 2018, https://www.seagate.com/files/www-content/our-story/trends/files/idc-seagate-dataage-whitepaper.pdf.

4. Transparency Market Research, "Digital Health Market: Global Industry, Size, Share, Growth, Trends, and Forecast, 2017–2025," 2017.

5. IQVIA Institute for Human Data Science, "Digital Health Trends 2021" (IQVIA Institute for Human Data Science, July 2021), https://www.iqvia.com/insights/the-iqvia-institute/reports/digital-health-trends-2021.

6. "Digital Health Market Size and Forecast Report, 2030," P&S Intelligence, accessed March 9, 2022, https://www.psmarketresearch.com/market-analysis/digital-health-market.

7. "Product Library," Digital Therapeutics Alliance, accessed October 27, 2021, https://dtxalliance.org/understanding-dtx/product-library/.

8. Robert L. Grossman et al., "Toward a Shared Vision for Cancer Genomic Data," *New England Journal of Medicine* 375, no. 12 (September 22, 2016): 1109–12, https://doi.org/10.1056/NEJMp1607591; and Michael S. Lawrence et al., "Discovery and Saturation Analysis of Cancer Genes across 21 Tumour Types," *Nature* 505, no. 7484 (January 23, 2014): 495–501, https://doi.org/10.1038/nature12912.

9. "Digital Health Market Size and Forecast Report, 2030."

10. "VC Investment in the U.S. by Industry 2021," Statista, accessed October 27, 2021, https://www.statista.com/statistics/277506/venture-caputal-investment-in-the-united-states-by-sector/.

11. See Adriana Krasniansky, Bill Evans, and Megan Zweig, "2021 Year-End Digital Health Funding: Seismic Shifts Beneath the Surface," Rock Health Voice of the Market, January 10, 2022, https://rockhealth.com/insights/2021-year-end-digital-health-funding-seismic-shifts-beneath-the-surface/; and Ashwini Nagappan and Adriana Krasniansky, "H1 2022 Digital Health Funding: Two Sides to Every Correction," Rock Health Voice of the Market, July 10, 2022, https://rockhealth.com/insights/h1-2022-digital-health-funding-two-sides-to-every-correction/.

12. "The Complete List of Global HealthTech Unicorns," HolonIQ, October 25, 2021, https://www.holoniq.com/healthtech-unicorns/.

13. Artificial intelligence (AI) is the theory and development of computer systems able to perform tasks normally requiring human intelligence, such as visual perception, speech recognition, language translation, and decision-making. Machine learning (ML) is a subcategory of AI referring to the use and development of computer systems that are able to learn and adapt without following explicit instructions, by using algorithms and statistical models to analyze and draw inferences from patterns in data. The function of a ML system can be *descriptive*, using data to explain what happened; *predictive*, using data to predict what will happen; or *prescriptive*, using data to make suggestions about what action to take. See Brown, Sara, "Machine Learning, Explained," MIT Sloan, April 21, 2021, https://mitsloan.mit.edu/ideas-made-to-matter/machine-learning-explained.

14. Eric Topol, *Deep Medicine: How Artificial Intelligence Can Make Healthcare Human Again* (Basic Books, 2019), p. 9.

15. Eric Stegman et al., "IT Key Metrics Data 2022: Industry Measures" (Gartner, December 16, 2021), https://www.gartner.com/en/documents/4009145.

16. Michael Hammer, "Reengineering Work: Don't Automate, Obliterate," *Harvard Business Review*, August 1990, https://hbr.org/1990/07/reengineering-work-dont-automate-obliterate.

17. For example, some observers have suggested the biggest impact of artificial intelligence in health care will be in making administrative processes more efficient, thus radically reducing administrative costs which represent roughly one-third of health care spending. See Thomas H. Davenport and Randy Bean, "Clinical AI Gets the Headlines, but Administrative AI May Be a Better Bet," *MIT Sloan Management Review*, April 11, 2022, https://sloanreview.mit.edu/article/clinical-ai-gets-the-headlines-but-administrative-ai-may-be-a-better-bet/.

18. This example was originally described in Karalee Close et al., "Making Big Data Work: Health Care Payers and Providers" (Boston Consulting Group, September

8, 2014), https://www.bcg.com/publications/2014/making-big-data-work-health -care-payers.

19. This example was also originally described in Close et al.

20. Ohad Arazi, "AI Won't Replace Radiologists, But It Will Change Their Work. Here's How," *World Economic Forum* (blog), October 5, 2020, https://www .weforum.org/agenda/2020/10/how-ai-will-change-how-radiologists-work/.

21. Marc Raynaud et al., "Dynamic Prediction of Renal Survival Among Deeply Phenotyped Kidney Transplant Recipients Using Artificial Intelligence: An Observational, International, Multicohort Study," *The Lancet Digital Health* 3, no. 12 (December 1, 2021): e795–e805, https://doi.org/10.1016/S2589-7500(21)00209-0.

22. Ittai Dayan et al., "Federated Learning for Predicting Clinical Outcomes in Patients with COVID-19," *Nature Medicine* 27, no. 10 (October 2021): 1735–43, https://doi.org/10.1038/s41591-021-01506-3.

23. Sushravya Raghunath et al., "Deep Neural Networks Can Predict New-Onset Atrial Fibrillation from the 12-Lead ECG and Help Identify Those at Risk of Atrial Fibrillation–Related Stroke," *Circulation* 143, no. 13 (March 30, 2021): 1287–98, https://doi.org/10.1161/CIRCULATIONAHA.120.047829.

24. Nicholas J. Schork, "Personalized Medicine: Time for One-Person Trials," *Nature* 520, no. 7549 (April 2015): 609–11, https://doi.org/10.1038/520609a.

25. Katherine Baicker and Ziad Obermeyer, "Overuse and Underuse of Health Care: New Insights from Economics and Machine Learning," *JAMA Health Forum* 3, no. 2 (February 17, 2022): e220428, https://doi.org/10.1001/jamahealthforum .2022.0428. For a recent example of the use of machine learning to define population subsegments more precisely, see Faraz Faghri et al., "Identifying and Predicting Amyotrophic Lateral Sclerosis Clinical Subgroups: A Population-Based Machine-Learning Study," *The Lancet Digital Health* 4, no. 5 (May 1, 2022): e359–69, https://doi.org/10.1016/S2589-7500(21)00274-0.

26. Baicker and Obermeyer, "Overuse and Underuse of Health Care."

27. Ariel D. Stern et al., "Advancing Digital Health Applications: Priorities for Innovation in Real-World Evidence Generation," *The Lancet Digital Health* 4, no. 3 (March 2022): e200–e206, https://doi.org/10.1016/S2589-7500(21)00292-2.

28. Joann G. Elmore and Christoph I. Lee, "Artificial Intelligence in Medical Imaging—Learning from Past Mistakes in Mammography," *JAMA Health Forum* 3, no. 2 (February 25, 2022): e215207, https://doi.org/10.1001/jamahealthforum .2021.5207.

29. Timo M. Deist et al., "Distributed Learning on 20,000+ Lung Cancer Patients— The Personal Health Train," *Radiotherapy and Oncology* 144 (March 1, 2020): 189–200, https://doi.org/10.1016/j.radonc.2019.11.019.

30. Paul Nadrag, "Industry Voices—Forget Credit Card Numbers. Medical Records Are the Hottest Items on the Dark Web," Fierce Healthcare, January 26, 2021, https://www.fiercehealthcare.com/hospitals/industry-voices-forget-credit-card -numbers-medical-records-are-hottest-items-dark-web.

31. Nanibaa' A. Garrison et al., "A Systematic Literature Review of Individuals' Perspectives on Broad Consent and Data Sharing in the United States," *Genetics in Medicine* 18, no. 7 (July 2016): 663–71, https://doi.org/10.1038/gim.2015.138.

32. Michelle M. Mello, Van Lieou, and Steven N. Goodman, "Clinical Trial Participants' Views of the Risks and Benefits of Data Sharing," *New England Journal of Medicine* 378, no. 23 (June 7, 2018): 2202–11, https://doi.org/10.1056/NEJMsa1713258.

33. Salem T. Argaw et al., "Cybersecurity of Hospitals: Discussing the Challenges and Working towards Mitigating the Risks," *BMC Medical Informatics and Decision Making* 20, no. 1 (December 2020): 146, https://doi.org/10.1186/s12911-020-01161-7.

34. Davey Winder, "The University of California Pays $1 Million Ransom Following Cyber Attack," *Forbes*, June 29, 2020, https://www.forbes.com/sites/daveywinder/2020/06/29/the-university-of-california-pays-1-million-ransom-following-cyber-attack/.

35. The HHS data is available at "Breach Portal: Notice to the Secretary of HHS Breach of Unsecured Protected Health Information," U.S. Department of Health & Human Services—Office for Civil Rights, accessed November 1, 2021, https://ocrportal.hhs.gov/ocr/breach/breach_report.jsf.

36. Argaw et al., "Cybersecurity of Hospitals."

37. Ron Schmelzer, "The Achilles' Heel of AI," *Forbes*, March 7, 2019, https://www.forbes.com/sites/cognitiveworld/2019/03/07/the-achilles-heel-of-ai/.

38. This discussion of the main categories for common digital health standards builds on work that BCG did in 2017 for the World Economic Forum. See "Value in Healthcare: Mobilizing Cooperation for Health System Transformation" (World Economic Forum, February 12, 2018), https://www.weforum.org/reports/value-in-healthcare-mobilizing-cooperation-for-health-system-transformation/.

39. Tim Benson and Graham Grieve, *Principles of Health Interoperability—FHIR, HL7 and SNOMED CT*, 4th ed. (Springer, 2021).

40. Micky Tripathi, "Delivering on the Promise of Health Information Technology in 2022," *Health Affairs Forefront* (blog), February 22, 2022, https://www.healthaffairs.org/do/10.1377/forefront.20220217.71427.

41. See Benson and Grieve, *Principles of Health Interoperability—FHIR, HL7 and SNOMED CT*.

42. See Jianxing He et al., "The Practical Implementation of Artificial Intelligence Technologies in Medicine," *Nature Medicine* 25, no. 1 (January 2019): 30–36, https://doi.org/10.1038/s41591-018-0307-0.

43. Other commonly used semantic standards include the Anatomical Therapeutic Chemical (ATC) classification standard, used to characterize medicines; the Logical Observation Identifiers Names and Codes (LOINC), originally a standard for clinical laboratory orders and reports; and the Digital Imaging and Communications in Medicine (DICOM) standard, which specifies a nonproprietary data interchange protocol, digital image format, and file structure for biomedical images and image-related information. Indeed, the existence of the widely used DICOM standard is an important reason why many of the most advanced uses of AI in health care to date are in the domain of image analysis and interpretation. See Benson and Grieve.

44. See, for example, Dayan et al., "Federated Learning for Predicting Clinical Outcomes in Patients with COVID-19"; and Stefanie Warnat-Herresthal et al.,

"Swarm Learning for Decentralized and Confidential Clinical Machine Learning," *Nature* 594, no. 7862 (June 10, 2021): 265–70, https://doi.org/10.1038/s41586 -021-03583-3.

45. The Personal Health Train concept is based on the GO FAIR data initiative developed by Dr. Barend Mons, a molecular biologist and professor of biosemantics in the Department of Human Genetics at Leiden University Medical Centre in the Netherlands. According to the FAIR concept, all health data should be "findable" (easy to locate, and not only by humans but by automated computer systems), "accessible" (permanently stored with well-defined rules for licensing and criteria for access), "interoperable" (sharing the same semantic and data model, so that it is ready to be combined with other data sets), and "reusable" (able to be used in future research and further processed to address new research questions). For more, see Oya Beyan et al., "Distributed Analytics on Sensitive Medical Data: The Personal Health Train," *Data Intelligence* 2, no. 1–2 (January 2020): 96–107, https://doi.org/10.1162/dint_a_00032; and Virginia Graciano Martinez et al., "A Framework for Staging Personal Health Trains in the Cloud," *Proceedings of the 17th International Conference on Web Information Systems and Technologies*, 2021, 133–44.

46. Casey Ross, "Mayo Clinic Patient Data Fuels AI Companies, and Consent Concerns," *STAT*, June 3, 2020, https://www.statnews.com/2020/06/03/mayo-clinic -patient-data-fuels-artificial-intelligence-consent-concerns/.

47. Kelly N. Michelson, James G. Adams, and Joshua M. M. Faber, "Navigating Clinical and Business Ethics While Sharing Patient Data," *JAMA* 327, no. 11 (February 25, 2022): 1025–26, https://doi.org/10.1001/jama.2022.1942.

48. Ross, "Mayo Clinic Patient Data Fuels AI Companies, and Consent Concerns."

49. Kayte Spector-Bagdady et al., "Sharing Health Data and Biospecimens with Industry—A Principle-Driven, Practical Approach," *New England Journal of Medicine* 382, no. 22 (May 28, 2020): 2072–75, https://doi.org/10.1056 /NEJMp1915298.

50. "Value in Healthcare: Accelerating the Pace of Health System Transformation" (World Economic Forum, December 2018), https://www3.weforum.org/docs /WEF_Value_in_Healthcare_report_2018.pdf.

51. For more information on Estonia's e-health initiative, see "E-Health Record," e-Estonia, accessed March 29, 2022, https://e-estonia.com/solutions/healthcare /e-health-records/.

52. Eric D. Peterson and Robert A. Harrington, "Evaluating Health Technology Through Pragmatic Trials: Novel Approaches to Generate High-Quality Evidence," *JAMA* 320, no. 2 (July 10, 2018): 137, https://doi.org/10.1001/jama.2018 .8512.

53. For FDA policy on digital-health applications, see "Artificial Intelligence and Machine Learning (AI/ML)-Enabled Medical Devices," US Food and Drug Administration (FDA, September 22, 2021), https://www.fda.gov/medical -devices/software-medical-device-samd/artificial-intelligence-and-machine -learning-aiml-enabled-medical-devices. In Europe, Germany has also passed a Digital Healthcare Act, which, among other things, includes a "fast track"

pathway to regulatory approval and reimbursement for digital health applications. See Stern et al., "Advancing Digital Health Applications."

54. Kat Jercich, "Addressing AI Bias with an Algorithmic 'Nutrition Label,'" *Healthcare IT News*, August 9, 2021, https://www.healthcareitnews.com/news /addressing-ai-bias-algorithmic-nutrition-label.

55. See also Xiaoxian Liu et al., "The Medical Algorithmic Audit," *The Lancet Digital Health* 4, no. 5 (April 5, 2022): e3394-e97, https://doi.org/10.1016/S2589-7500 (22)00003-6; and The Lancet Digital Health, "Holding Artificial Intelligence to Account," *The Lancet Digital Health* 4, no. 5 (May 1, 2022): e290, https://doi.org /10.1016/S2589-7500(22)00068-1.

56. Office of the National Coordinator for Health Information Technology, "National Trends in Hospital and Physician Adoption of Electronic Health Records," Health IT Quick-Stat #61, March 2022, https://www.healthit.gov/data /quickstats/national-trends-hospital-and-physician-adoption-electronic-health -records.

57. Micky Tripathi, "Delivering on the Promise of Health Information Technology in 2022."

58. Office of the National Coordinator for Health Information Technology, "FY 2022 President's Budget: Justification of Estimates to the Appropriations Committees" (Department of Health and Human Services, n.d.), https://www.healthit .gov/sites/default/files/page/2021-07/FY%202022%20ONC%20CJ.pdf.

CHAPTER 7

1. Even in the United States, where private insurance continues to play the dominant role, the government remains, by far, the single largest payer. Of the $3.8 trillion in 2019 US health expenditures, roughly $1.4 trillion, or 37%, was paid by Medicare and Medicaid. Other government programs, such as the Children's Health Insurance Program (CHIP), the Indian Health Service, and the Department of Veterans Affairs fund targeted health coverage for children, Native Americans, and veterans, respectively. See "National Health Expenditures 2020 Highlights" (Centers for Medicare & Medicaid Services, 2020), https://www.cms .gov/files/document/highlights.pdf.

2. Mariana Mazzucato, *Mission Economy: A Moonshot Guide to Changing Capitalism* (Harper Business, 2021), p. xxiv.

3. "Cancer Moonshot^SM—National Cancer Institute," accessed July 10, 2022, https://www.cancer.gov/research/key-initiatives/moonshot-cancer-initiative.

4. Albert Bourla, *Moonshot: Inside Pfizer's Nine-Month Race to Make the Impossible Possible* (Harper Business, 2022).

5. Mazzucato, *Mission Economy*, pp. 4–5.

6. Michael E. Porter and Elizabeth Olmstead Teisberg, *Redefining Health Care: Creating Value-Based Competition on Results* (Harvard Business Review Press, 2006).

7. "Goal 3: Good Health and Well-Being," The Global Goals, accessed December 23, 2021, https://www.globalgoals.org/3-good-health-and-well-being.

8. Directorate-General for Research and Innovation (European Commission) et al., "Conquering Cancer: Mission Possible" (Publications Office of the European Union, September 22, 2020), https://data.europa.eu/doi/10.2777/045403.

9. "Cancer Moonshot^SM—National Cancer Institute."

10. UK Department for Business, Energy & Industrial Strategy, "Industrial Strategy: Building a Britain Fit for the Future," November 27, 2017, https://assets .publishing.service.gov.uk/government/uploads/system/uploads/attachment _data/file/664563/industrial-strategy-white-paper-web-ready-version.pdf.

11. WHO South-East Asia, "Monitoring the Health-Related Sustainable Development Goals (SDGs)" (World Health Organization, Regional Office for South-East Asia, 2017), https://www.who.int/docs/default-source/searo/hsd/hwf/01-monitoring-the -health-related-sdgs-background-paper.pdf?sfvrsn=3417607a_4.

12. David B. Agus, Elizabeth M. Jaffee, and Chi Van Dang, "Cancer Moonshot 2.0," *The Lancet Oncology* 22, no. 2 (February 1, 2021): 164–65, https://doi.org/10.1016 /S1470-2045(21)00003-6.

13. For details on the Dutch government's five-year plan, see "Outcome-Based Healthcare 2018–2022," Government of the Netherlands (Ministerie van Algemene Zaken [Ministry of General Affairs], July 28, 2016), https://www .government.nl/topics/quality-of-healthcare/information-on-the-quality-of -care.

14. For more on the Danish experience, see Danske Regioner [Danish Regions], "Værdibaseret Sundhed [Value-Based Health]," accessed April 4, 2022, https:// www.regioner.dk/sundhed/kvalitet-og-styring/tema-vaerdibaseret-sundhed; and Danske Regioner [Danish Regions], "Det Tværregionale Projekt Om Værdibaseret Sundhed [The Interregional Project on Value-Based Health]," accessed April 4, 2022, https://www.regioner.dk/services/publikationer/sundhed /det-tvaerregionale-projekt-om-vaerdibaseret-sundhed.

15. Value in Health, "Putting Value at the Center of Health and Care in Wales: A Three-Year Action Plan, 2019–2022" (Welsh Government, NHS Wales, 2019), https://vbhc.nhs.wales/files/vbhc-national-action-plan/.

16. For more on the Leading Better Value Care program, see Elizabeth Koff and Nigel Lyons, "Implementing Value-Based Health Care at Scale: The NSW Experience," *Medical Journal of Australia* 212, no. 3 (February 17, 2020): 104–06.e1, https://doi.org/10.5694/mja2.50470.

17. "Leading Better Value Care," accessed April 4, 2022, https://www.health.nsw.gov .au/Value/lbvc/Pages/default.aspx.

18. "IT Platform (HOPE)," Agency for Clinical Innovation, Government of New South Wales, accessed March 31, 2022, https://aci.health.nsw.gov.au/statewide -programs/prms/hope-platform.

19. Porter and Teisberg, *Redefining Health Care: Creating Value-Based Competition on Results.*

20. Amol S. Navathe, Risa Lavizzo-Mourey, and Joshua M. Liao, "The US Should Change Payment to Make Health Care More Equitable," *Health Affairs Forefront* (blog), October 26, 2021, https://www.healthaffairs.org/do/10.1377/forefront .20211025.5858/full/.

21. "CCO 2.0: The Future of Coordinated Care," Oregon Health Authority, Oregon Health Policy Board, accessed April 11, 2022, https://www.oregon.gov/oha/OHPB/Pages/cco-2-0.aspx.

22. Oregon Health Authority, "Oregon Health Plan Health Plan Services Contract" (State of Oregon, October 1, 2019), https://www.oregon.gov/oha/OHPB/CCODocuments/Final-CCO-contract-terms-for-5-year-contract-awardees.pdf.

23. For more on TioHundra's innovative delivery model, see Sofia Widén, "TioHundra Case Study Part One: Company Overview" (Access Health International, February 2015), https://accessh.org/interviews/tiohundra-case-study-part-one-company-overview/; and Sofia Widén and William A. Haseltine, "TioHundra Case Study Part Two: Care Homes and Integrated Elder Care" (Access Health International, February 2016), https://accessh.org/interviews/tiohundra-case-study-part-two-care-homes-and-integrated-elder-care/.

24. See Figure 1.3 in Chapter 1.

25. "RIE 2025: Human Health and Potential" (National Research Foundation, Government of Singapore, December 2020), https://www.nrf.gov.sg/rie2025-plan/human-health-and-potential.

26. Jeremy Lim, "Singapore Is Radically Changing Its Healthcare System with Healthier SG. Here's How to Make It Work," *TODAY*, March 21, 2022, https://www.todayonline.com/commentary/singapore-radically-changing-its-healthcare-system-healthier-sg-heres-how-make-it-work-1849661.

27. Mazzucato, *Mission Economy*, p. 25.

28. Elizabeth H. Bradley and Lauren A. Taylor, *The American Health Care Paradox* (Public Affairs, 2013).

29. The proposed mission of ARPA-H is "to make pivotal investments in breakthrough technologies and broadly applicable platforms, capabilities, resources, and solutions that have the potential to transform important areas of medicine and health for the benefit of all patients and that cannot readily be accomplished through traditional research or commercial activity." See "ARPA-H," National Institutes of Health (NIH), accessed May 19, 2022, https://www.nih.gov/arpa-h.

30. Jennifer Clawson, Josh Kellar, and Stefan Larsson, "Learning from COVID-19 to Transform Global Health Systems" (Boston Consulting Group, May 5, 2020), https://www.bcg.com/publications/2020/learning-from-covid-transforming-health-systems.

31. "COVID-19: Make It the Last Pandemic" (The Independent Panel for Pandemic Preparedness and Response, 2021), https://theindependentpanel.org/wp-content/uploads/2021/05/COVID-19-Make-it-the-Last-Pandemic_final.pdf.

32. "John F. Kennedy Moon Speech, Rice Stadium, September 12, 1962," National Aeronautic and Space Administration (NASA), accessed March 17, 2022, https://er.jsc.nasa.gov/seh/ricetalk.htm.

CHAPTER 8

1. Rich Hutchinson et al., "The Bionic Company" (BCG Henderson Institute, November 17, 2019), https://www.bcg.com/publications/2019/bionic-company.

2. For more on the concept of health ecosystems, see Ulrich Pidun et al., "The Untapped Potential of Ecosystems in Health Care" (BCG Henderson Institute, April 1, 2021), https://www.bcg.com/publications/2021/five-principles-of-highly -successful-health-care-ecosystems.

3. Adam M. Brandenberger and Barry J. Nalebuff, *Co-Opetition* (Doubleday Business, 1996).

4. For more on the role of health care integrators, see Donald M. Berwick, Thomas W. Nolan, and John Whittington, "The Triple Aim: Care, Health, and Cost," *Health Affairs* 27, no. 3 (May 2008): 759–69, https://doi.org/10.1377/hlthaff.27 .3.759.

5. For a recent call to rethink the current model of academic medicine so as to link scientific advances to "the goal of improving the health outcomes of the population," see Victor J. Dzau, Celynne A. Balatbat, and William F. Ellaissi, "Revisiting Academic Health Sciences Systems a Decade Later: Discovery to Health to Population to Society," *The Lancet* 398, no. 10318 (December 18, 2021): 2300–2304, https://doi.org/10.1016/S0140-6736(21)01752-9.

6. For an example, see Uwe E. Reinhardt, "Porter and Teisberg's Utopian Vision," *Health Affairs Blog* (blog), October 10, 2006, https://www.healthaffairs.org/do/10 .1377/hblog20061010.000063/full/.

7. Christophe Schweizer, "Why Business Must Leverage Climate Innovation," *Fortune*, December 8, 2021, https://fortune.com/2021/12/08/climate-change-green -technology-business-innovation-bcg/.

8. "Innovative Health Initiative," IMI Innovative Medicines Initiative, accessed July 13, 2022, http://www.imi.europa.eu/about-imi/innovative-health-initiative.

9. Tanja Stamm et al., "Building a Value-Based Care Infrastructure in Europe: The Health Outcomes Observatory," *NEJM Catalyst*, June 9, 2021, https://catalyst .nejm.org/doi/full/10.1056/CAT.21.0146.

10. For a recent, and typical, example, see Peter S. Goodman, *Davos Man: How the Billionaires Devoured the World* (Custom House, 2022).

11. For example, the Forum has been instrumental in launching the Gavi Vaccine Alliance (formerly the Global Alliance for Vaccines and Immunisation), a global health partnership of public and private sector organizations dedicated to increasing access to immunization in poor countries, and the Coalition for Epidemic Preparedness Innovations (CEPI), a partnership to accelerate the development of vaccines against emerging infectious diseases. See "Gavi, the Vaccine Alliance," accessed April 11, 2022, https://www.gavi.org/; and "CEPI | New Vaccines for a Safer World," CEPI, accessed April 11, 2022, https://cepi.net/.

12. Global Coalition for Value in Healthcare, World Economic Forum, accessed January 5, 2022, https://www.weforum.org/global-coalition-for-value-in-healthcare /home/.

INDEX

Page numbers followed by *f* refer to figures.

Academic medical centers, 115, 199
Accountable care organizations, 131
Activity-based payment models, 143–144
Adams, Greg, 254
Adelaide, 95
Advanced analytics, 170
Advanced Research Projects Agency for
   Health (ARPA-H), 233
Adverse effects, 273n4
Aetna, 163
Affordable Care Act, 11, 138, 146
Africa, 88
Agency for Care Effectiveness
   (Singapore), 229
AHRQ (Agency for Healthcare Research
   and Quality), 20, 34
AI (artificial intelligence):
   and administrative processes, 288n17
   applications, 183–185, 187–189, 192–
      193, 199
   China's investment in, 234
   clinical decision support systems, 198
   Dr. Evidence, 16
   lack of rigorous assessment, 201–202
   and predictive analytics, 115, 133, 178
   as term, 288n13
AJRR (American Joint Replacement
   Registry), 48

Åkerman, Christina Rångemark, 61
Alternative Payment Models program,
   138–139, 153, 169, 171, 231–232,
   283n8
Amazon, 177, 199
Ambulatory-care-sensitive conditions,
   183
American Academy of Orthopedic
   Surgeons, 48
American College of Cardiology, 16, 78
American College of Cardiology/
   American Heart Association
   guidelines, 16
American College of Physicians, 78
American Diabetes Association, 78
The American Health Care Paradox
   (Bradley and Taylor), 231
American Heart Association, 16, 256*f*,
   276n35
American Joint Replacement Registry
   (AJRR), 48
American Medical Association, 206
Amgen, 163
AMI (acute myocardial infarction),
   12–13, 153–154
Anatomical Therapeutic Chemical
   (ATC) classification standard,
   290n43

Aneurin University Health Board, 62, 219
Anthem, 95
Anticoagulants, 161–162
Apollo program, 210, 230
Apple, 177, 206
Aravind Eye Care System, 88
ARPA-H (Advanced Research Projects
    Agency for Health), 233
ARPANET, 229
Arthroplasty, 98, 154, 155, 157, 269n32,
    275n23
  hip, 47–48, 52–53, 56, 113, 228
  knee, 14
Ascension Health, 199
AstraZeneca, 256f
ATC (Anatomical Therapeutic
    Chemical) classification standard,
    290n43
Atrial fibrillation, 184–185
Australia, 5, 47, 52, 62, 182–183, 188, 219
Austria, 253
Autonomy, 21–25, 74–75, 101–102, 172

Balanced scorecard, 124–125
Bariatric surgery, 157
Barmer (German sick fund), 82
BCG (Boston Consulting Group):
  and Karolinska Hospital, 122, 125–126
  and Santeon hospitals, 110
  support of ICHOM, 55
  and Sweden's quality registries, 37, 53
  and Value in Healthcare Project, 254,
    256f
  and the World Economic Forum, 254
BCG Henderson Institute, 241
Behavioral interventions, 74
Belgium, 14
Benchmarking, 27f, 28
Berners-Lee, Tim, 203
Best practices, 28, 38, 43, 216
Biden, Joe, and administration, 204, 206,
    233
Biomedical literature, 2, 2f
Biomedical research and development
    funding, 17–19
Black Americans, 11
Blackstone (investment firm), 240
Blood thinners, 161–162
Blue Cross Blue Shield of Michigan, 168
BMJ Clinical Evidence (journal), 16
Bourla, Albert, 210
Bradley, Elizabeth, 231

Brandenburger, Adam, 241
Brazil, 5
Breast cancer, 8, 111–113, 116, 118, 119,
    157
British Medical Association, 21
Broussard, Bruce, 249
Brown, Nancy, 256f
Bruins, Bruno, 254
Buchanan, David, 92
Bundled payments, 140, 153–157, 285n29
Bürkner, Hans-Paul, 256f
Burnout, 21, 25, 271n56

CABG (coronary artery bypass grafting),
    14
Caesarean sections, 6, 14
CAHPS (Consumer Assessment of
    Healthcare Providers and Systems),
    97
Cambridge NHS Trust, 188
Canada, 188, 254, 269n32
Cancer Moonshot, 210, 213–214
Cancer patients, 184
Cancer treatment, 47
Capitation, 79–80, 140
Capsule Technologies (device-
    information platform), 239
Cardiac devices, implantable, 164
Cardiac surgery, 14, 154
Cardiac-related health outcomes, 8,
    39–44, 39f (See also Heart failure;
    Myocardial infarction)
Care:
  bundles, 86
  full cycle of, 168–170
Care pathways, 73–74, 83, 99, 103, 119,
    241
Care Solutions, 89
Career paths, 124–125
CareMore, 95
Carlyle (investment firm), 240
Castell (digital technology company),
    134
Cataract surgery, 52, 56, 155, 167, 256
Catharina Hospital, 114
CCOs (coordinated-care organizations),
    223
CDC (Centers for Disease Control and
    Prevention), 151
CDM (common data model), 194
Center for Medicare and Medicaid
    Innovation (CMMI), 138, 153, 282n8

Center for Medicare and Medicaid Services (CMS), 91–92, 95, 129, 138–139, 151, 232, 285n29
Centers for Disease Control and Prevention (CDC), 151
Centers of excellence, 116, 119
CenterWell, 148, 150
CEPI (Coalition for Epidemic Preparedness Innovations), 295n11
Cerebrovascular accident (*see* Stroke)
CERN (European Council of Nuclear Research), 204
Cerner (EMR), 177, 206
Chan, Margaret, 256*f*
Change, approaches to, 103–136
Change, disruptive, 127–128
Change initiatives:
  Erasmus University Medical Center, 115–120
  and health system transformation, 134–136
  Intermountain Healthcare, 128–134
  New Karolinska University Hospital, 120–128
  Santeon Group, 109–115
Chicago, Ill., 89–90
Child Investment Fund Foundation, 88
Children's Health Insurance Program (CHIP), 292n1
China, 6, 188, 234
Cholesterol, 163
Christie NHS Trust, 188
Chronic care coordinator, 148–149
Chronic diseases, 183
Chronic health conditions, 91
Chronic obstructive pulmonary disease (COPD), 225
Cigna, 163
CityBlock, 95
Civica Rx, 133–134
CJR (Comprehensive Care for Joint Replacement), 154, 285n29
Cleveland Clinic, 106–109, 123, 129
Clinical collaboration, 43
Clinical decision-making, 269n32 (*See also* Decision-support tools)
Clinical innovation, 143, 152, 188, 198
Clinical practice guidelines, 16–17, 19–20, 38, 40, 44
CMMI (Center for Medicare and Medicaid Innovation), 138, 153, 282n8

CMS (Center for Medicare and Medicaid Services), 91–92, 95, 129, 138–139, 151, 232, 285n29
CMS five-star ranking system, 151
Coalition for Epidemic Preparedness Innovations (CEPI), 295n11
Cochrane Collaboration, 16
Collaboration, interdisciplinary, 116
Collaborative Quality Initiatives (CQIs), 167–168, 252
Colombo, Francesca, 21, 256*f*
Common data model (CDM), 194
Commonwealth Fund, 153–154
Community benefits, 100
Community in Oncology for Rapid Learning (CORAL), 188–189, 189*f*, 196
Community-Based Care, 130
Comparative effectiveness research, 17–18, 186
Compassion, 33
Competition, in health care, 238–239
Complete Care, 99
Complex adaptive systems, 26–27, 272n64
Complexity, 233
  of health information, 192
  organizational, 22–26, 144, 168–169, 187, 272n62 .
Comprehensive Care for Joint Replacement (CJR), 154, 285n29
Consumer Assessment of Healthcare Providers and Systems (CAHPS), 97
Continuous quality improvement:
  culture of, 171–173
  as driver of value, 143
  at Erasmus University Medical Center, 115–116
  at Intermountain Health, 129
  at Kaiser Permanente, 100–101, 107, 167
  and market-shaping, 220–222
  at Martini Klinik, 83–84, 167
  in Michigan, 167
  at Santeon Group, 110–115
  in Singapore, 228
Contracts, risk-based, 134
Conviva, 148, 150
Conway, Patrick, 89
Cooperation, payer-provider, 23–25, 144
Coopetition, 241
Coordinated-care organizations (CCOs), 223

COPD (chronic obstructive pulmonary disease), 225
CORAL (Community in Oncology for Rapid Learning), 188–189, 189*f*, 196
Core data, 193
Coronary artery bypass grafting (CABG), 14
Coronary artery thrombosis aspiration, 45–46, 46*f*
Coronavirus pandemic (*see* Covid-19 pandemic)
Cosgrove, Toby, 107, 129
Cost:
  awareness, 165
  control, 24
  health care costs, 2–6, 4*f*, 47–49
  metrics, 32, 35–37
  transparency, 133
Costa Rica, 7, 268n22
Covid-19 pandemic:
  AI applications for, 184
  costs of, 3, 268n18
  deaths from, 2, 9
  destabilizing effect, 21
  in ICHOM outcomes metrics, 55
  impact on health care systems, 94, 127, 132, 216, 234, 281n16
  and telemedicine, 180
  vaccines for, 210, 230
CQIs (*see* Collaborative quality initiatives)
CVA (cerebrovascular accident) (*see* Stroke)
CVS Health, 256*f*
Cybersecurity, 179, 190–192, 196, 207, 222, 228, 232–233
Cystic fibrosis, 49–51
Cystic Fibrosis Foundation, 49
Cystic fibrosis registry, 249

Dagens Medicin, 127
DARPA (Defense Advanced Research Projects Agency), 203, 207, 229–230
Dartmouth Atlas of Health Care, 13, 14
Dashboards, 94, 114, 117, 165
Data:
  capture standards, 193
  de-identified, 199
  harnessing of, 175–177
  incomparability of, 273n5
  machine readable, 194
  sharing and analytics, 179, 196, 228

  storage, 196
  transparency, 38*f*, 40–43
  validation, 40
Data IQ, 95
Data security (*see* Cybersecurity)
De Bey, Pieter, 110, 114, 115
Decision-support tools, 27*f*, 28, 187, 198, 232
Deerberg-Wittram, Jens, 54
Defense Advanced Research Projects Agency (DARPA), 203, 207, 229–230
Dekker, Andre, 189
Denmark, 88, 153, 218–219, 256
Department of Defense, 203
Department of Health and Human Services, 191, 194, 204
Department of Veterans Affairs, 63, 292n1
DePuy ASR XL hip implant, 52–53
Diabeter (clinical research center), 88, 256
Diabetes:
  care in Canada, 254
  care in Sweden, 75–81, 157
  care in the United States, 75–81
  complications of, 9–10
  in Denmark and Germany, 88, 256
  and HEDIS standards, 283–284n17
  medication for, 134, 163
  nurses, 77, 80
  prevalence and cost of, 9–11, 10*f*, 268n23
  specialists, 76–78
  variation in care, 269n31
Diabetes Collaborative Registry, 78–79
Diabetes Prevention Program, 80
Digital health, 175–208
  action steps for, 207
  from automation to transformation, 179–185
  data security and patient privacy in, 190–192
  interoperability, 192–197
  patient bill of rights, 200–201, 207
  public-private partnership for, 202–206
  services, 132
  and sustainable innovation systems, 197–202
  and digital learning platforms, 185–189
Digital learning platforms, 186*f*, 220–222
Digitally Connected (app), 118
Digitization, of information, 228
Disease prevention, 130, 143, 145–147, 223

Dispatch (emergency care hotline), 150
Dr. Evidence, 16
Donabedian, Avedis, 273n2
Donley, Brian, 105–107
Donne, John, 257
Dual-eligible patients, 91
Duke University Clinical Research Unit, 16
Dutch Interoperability Maturity Model, 217
Dutch Ministry of Health, Welfare, and Sport, 215

Early intervention, 130, 145–146
ECGs (electrocardiograms), 184–185
Economies of scale, 132
EHealth exchange, 205–206
Electrocardiograms (ECGs), 184–185
Electronic health wallet, 158–159
Electronic medical records (EMRs), 97, 175, 180, 184, 192, 198, 204
Eli Lilly, 163
Emergency department visits, 147
Emerging economies, 4
EMRs (*see* Electronic medical records)
Entresto (heart failure drug), 163
Epic (EMR), 177, 206
EPIC-26 (Expanded Prostate Cancer Index Composite), 60–61
Erasmus University Medical Center, 61–62, 109, 115–120, 161, 188, 217, 248
Erectile dysfunction, 81–82
Estonia, 139
EUREQUO (European Registry of Quality Outcomes for Cataract and Refractive Surgery), 52, 253
European Council of Nuclear Research (CERN), 204
European General Data Protection Regulation (GDPR), 190
European Registry of Quality Outcomes for Cataract and Refractive Surgery (EUREQUO), 52, 253
European Society for Radiotherapy and Oncology, 188
European University Hospital Alliance, 118
Evidence-based medicine, 15–21, 270n35
Evidence crisis in health care, 3, 15–21
Expanded Prostate Cancer Index Composite (EPIC-26), 60–61
Expenses, out-of-pocket, 152

Fast Healthcare Interoperability Resources (FHIR), 195, 206
FDA (Food and Drug Administration), 44, 176, 202
Federated learning, 196
Fee-for-service payment, 79, 138, 143–144, 147, 165
Feick, Günter, 58–60
FHIR (Fast Healthcare Interoperability Resources), 195, 206
Financial metrics, 32, 35–37
Florida, 148, 188
Forcare (interoperability company), 239
4P Health Spectrum, 26
Fragmentation, 168–169, 191–192, 231, 234
France, 6
French Ministry of Health, 62
Fudan University, 188
Future Primary Care initiative, 227

Gavi Vaccine Alliance, 295n11
Gawande, Atul, 11, 127
Geisinger Health System, 172, 184
General Atlantic (investment firm), 240
General Data Protection Regulation (GDPR), 190
Generic drugs, 133–134, 181
Genetics, 72, 176, 186, 190
German Cancer Society, 58, 87
Germany, 6, 14, 88, 253, 256
Global Coalition for Value in Healthcare, 253, 255, 257
Global Digital Health Project, 206
Global System for Mobile Communications (GSM), 54
GO FAIR data initiative, 290n45
Goals, of health care system, 26–29
Google, 177, 199
Graefen, Markus, 81, 83, 85, 87, 248
Greenhouse gas emissions, 6, 268n20
GSM (Global System for Mobile Communications), 54
GUSTO study (Growing Up in Singapore Towards Healthy Outcomes), 226

Halamka, John, 202
Harrison, Marc, 109, 128–130, 134, 248, 251, 254, 256f, 282n18
Harvard Business Review, 179
Harvard Business School, 256f
Harvard Medical School, 137

Harvard Pilgrim Health Care, 163
Harvard T. H. Chan School of Public
    Health, 11
Hazelzet, Jan, 120
HCA Healthcare, 133
Heal (primary care startup), 150
Health Affairs (journal), 64, 65
Health care costs, 2–6, 4*f*, 47–49
Health care metrics, proliferation of,
    32–33
Health care spending, wasteful, 5–6
Health Cluster Portugal, 256
Health Effectiveness Data and
    Information Set (HEDIS), 34, 95, 97,
    99, 283–284n17
Health equity, 26, 151, 173, 177,
    223–224
Health Information and Management
    Systems Society (HIMSS), 202
Health Information Technology for
    Economic and Clinical Health
    (HITECH), 204
Health insurance:
    churn, 169
    premiums, 4
Health Insurance Portability &
    Accountability Act (HIPAA), 190,
    204
Health Level Seven International (HL7),
    195
Health maintenance organizations
    (HMOs), 147, 283n14
Health Outcomes and Patient
    Experience (HOPE), 219
Health outcomes measurement (*see*
    Outcomes measurement)
Health Outcomes Observatory (H2O),
    118, 253
Health Precinct, 227
Health technology, 177
Health technology assessment (HTA),
    159, 162–163
Health-adjusted life expectancy, 7*f*
Healthier Dining Program, 227
Healthy Ageing program, 214
Heart attack, 12–13, 45–46, 153–154
Heart failure, 163, 225, 228, 254
Heart surgery, 14, 154
HEDIS (*see* Health Effectiveness Data
    and Information Set)
HIMSS (Health Information and
    Management Systems Society), 202

Hip:
    arthroplasty, 47–48, 52–53, 56, 113, 228
    osteoarthritis, 112
Hip replacement (*see* Arthroplasty, hip)
HIPAA (Health Insurance Portability &
    Accountability Act), 190, 204
HITECH (Health Information
    Technology for Economic and
    Clinical Health), 204
HL7 (Health Level Seven International),
    195
HMOs (health maintenance
    organizations), 147, 283n14
Home health care, 284n20
HOPE (Health Outcomes and Patient
    Experience), 219
Horizon Program (European Union), 213
Hospital(s):
    beds, 161
    organizational structures, 70
    outcome variation among, 12
Hospitalizations, 147, 183
HTA (health technology assessment),
    159, 162–163
H2O (Health Outcomes Observatory),
    118, 253
Huff, Stanley, 198, 201
Huland, Hartwig, 60, 81, 82, 87, 248
Humana, 148–157, 206, 223, 249, 276n35

IBM, 199
ICD (International Classification of
    Diseases), 194
ICER (Institute for Clinical and
    Economic Review), 163
ICGC (International Cancer Genome
    Consortium), 85
ICHOM (International Consortium for
    Health Outcomes Measurement):
    2017 conference, 215
    breast cancer measures, 118
    funding, 276n35
    and Medicare Advantage plans, 151
    and NHS Wales, 219
    prostate cancer measures, 87
    role of, 32, 54–64, 55*f*, 57*f*
IDF (International Diabetes
    Foundation), 9–10
IDF Diabetes Atlas, 10
IHI (Innovative Health Initiative), 253
IHS Markit, 164
ImagineMD, 95

India, 88, 188
Indian Health Service, 292n1
Indonesia, 256f
Infant mortality, 8
Infections, hospital-acquired, 160–161
Informatics, 27f, 28
Information overload, 15
Ingvar, Martin, 54
Innovative Health Initiative (IHI), 253
Inovio, 230
Institute for Clinical and Economic
   Review (ICER), 163
Institute of Medicine, 5
Insurance companies, 115
Integrated General Hospital, 227
Integrated payment (*see* Bundled
   payment)
Integrated practice unit (IPU), 81, 126
Integrator roles, 80
Intermountain Healthcare, 109, 128–134,
   150, 223, 251, 254, 256f
International Cancer Genome
   Consortium (ICGC), 85
International Classification of Diseases
   (ICD), 194
International Consortium for Health
   Outcomes Measurement (*see*
   ICHOM)
International Diabetes Foundation
   (IDF), 9–10
International Registry for Men
   with Advanced Prostate Cancer
   (IRONMAN), 62
International Society of Arthroplasty
   Registries (ISAR), 52
Interoperability, 63, 179, 197, 207–208,
   222, 232 (*See also* FHIR)
Iora Health, 95, 251
IPU (integrated practice unit), 81, 126
IRONMAN (International Registry
   for Men with Advanced Prostate
   Cancer), 62
ISAR (International Society of
   Arthroplasty Registries), 52, 253
Ishrak, Omar, 254
Israel, 5, 7
Ivbar (digital-health company), 156–157

J. Craig Venter Institute, 185
JAMA (journal), 11, 137
James, Stefan, 42, 45
Jimenez, Joe, 254

Johns Hopkins School of Medicine, 5, 11
Johnson & Johnson, 52–53
Joint replacement (*see* Arthroplasty)
Joslin Diabetes Center, 78, 80

Kahneman, Daniel, 16
Kaiser Family Foundation, 4, 268n18
Kaiser Permanente, 71–72, 98f, 164–167,
   170, 206, 223, 254
   Kaiser Permanente Colorado, 99
   Kaiser Permanente Hawaii, 99
   Kaiser Permanente Joint Replacement
      Registry, 98
   Kaiser Permanente Northwest, 100
   KP Health Connect, 97–100
Kaplan, Jon, 147
Kaplan, Robert, 19
Karlstad Hospital, 42
Karolinska University Hospital, 109, 248,
   281n16 (*See also* New Karolinska
   University Hospital)
Kennedy, John F., and administration,
   210, 233, 235
Kenya, 88, 157
Key performance indicators (KPIs), 122
Kinnevik (investment firm), 240
KKR (investment firm), 240
Knee replacement, 14
Koelemji, Ron, 114
Koppert, Linetta, 116, 118, 119
KPIs (key performance indicators), 122
Kuenen, Jan Willem, 147
Kuipers, Ernst, 120, 218, 248

The Lancet (journal), 3, 17, 39
Landmark Health, 251
Lane, Bennett, 137
Larsson, Stefan, 54, 147
Leadership, 237–257
   strategic, 239–246
   system, 252–257
   transformational, 247–251
Leading Better Value Care program, 219
Learning systems, 37–44
Life expectancy, 1–2, 6–8, 49
Linnean Group, 215
LOGEX (Dutch health care analytics
   firm), 64
LOINC (Logical Observation Identifiers
   Names and Codes), 290n43
Los Angeles, Calif., 12
Low-income patients, 99–100

Lung cancer, 111
Lynch, Karen, 256*f*

MAASTRO Clinic, 189
Machine learning, 178, 183–184, 187, 288n13
  algorithms, training of, 192
  as term, 288n13
Martha, Geoff, 256*f*
Martini Klinik (Hamburg, Germany), 60, 71–72, 81–89, 84*f*, 113, 167, 239, 248
Maryland All-Payer model, 283n8
Maternal and newborn care, 88, 157–159
Maternal mortality, 8, 157
Matheson, Dave, 127
Mayo Clinic, 133, 202
Mazzucato, Mariana, 210–211, 220, 229–230, 235, 253
Medical devices, 159–164, 176, 191, 207, 232–233
Medical loss-ratio requirements, 146
Medical services:
  overuse, 269n33
  underuse, 14, 268n19
Medically inappropriate care, 5
Medicare, 282n3 (*See also* CMS)
Medicare Advantage, 131, 139, 145–163, 169, 232, 284n21
Medi-Save, 226–227
MedTech Europe, 252–253
Medtronic, 88, 164, 254, 256*f*, 276n35
Medumo (patient-engagement company), 239
Memorial Sloan Kettering Cancer Center, 199
Meta (company), 177
Metadata, 176, 193
Michigan, 167–168, 252
Michigan Medicine, 199–200
Michigan Opioid Prescribing and Engagement Network, 168
Microsoft, 199
Ministry of Health (Singapore), 227–229
Mission Economy: A Moonshot Guide to Changing Capitalism (Mazzucato), 210
MIT, 210
Moderna, 230
Moffitt Cancer Center, 188
MomCare, 88, 157–159
Mons, Barend, 290n45
More Than Medicine (Kaplan), 19

Morieux, Yves, 22–23, 144
Mortality rates, 39, 40, 133, 183 (*See also* Infant mortality; Life expectancy; Maternal mortality)
Movember, 60, 62, 276n35
Multipartner health systems, 241
My Health+ (app), 132
Myers, Griffin, 91, 92
Myocardial infarction, 12–13, 45–46, 153–154

Nalebuff, Barry, 241
Narasimhan, Vasant, 254, 256*f*
National Academies of Science, Engineering, and Medicine, 89 (*See also* Institute of Medicine)
National Center for Quality Assurance (NCQA), 97
National Committee for Quality Assurance, 34
National Institutes of Health (NIH), 19, 49
National Quality Forum (NQF), 65, 232
National Quality Measures Clearinghouse, 34
National Quality Registry for Diabetes (NDR), 78
National Quality Registry for Spine Surgery, 156
National Research Foundation (Singapore), 226
National University Hospital (Singapore), 228
NCQA (National Center for Quality Assurance), 97
NDR (National Quality Registry for Diabetes), 78
Needlestick injuries, 160
NEJM Catalyst, 92
NEJM Evidence, 271n55
Netherlands, 88, 109, 153, 188–189, 214–218, 230–231, 253–254 (*See also* Erasmus University Medical Center; Santeon Group)
Netherlands national breast cancer registry, 120
Netwalker (cybercrime group), 191
New England Journal of Medicine, 46, 65, 89, 271n55
New Karolinska University Hospital, 120–128
New Zealand, 153
Newsweek, 127

NHS (National Health Service), 161, 163, 190–191, 214, 254, 276n35
NHS Wales, 161, 219, 256
NICE (National Institute for Health and Clinical Excellence), 162, 269n31
Nigeria, 4, 89, 157
NIH (National Institutes of Health), 19, 49
Noise: A Flaw in Human Judgment (Kahneman, Sibony, and Sunstein), 16
Norway, 191
Novartis, 163, 254, 256f
NQF (National Quality Forum), 65, 232
Nursing shortages, 121

Oak Street Health, 71–72, 89–96, 90f, 240, 248
Observable Medical Outcomes Partnership (OMOP), 195
OECD (Organisation for Economic Co-operation and Development), 3, 8, 14, 21, 256f
Office of Healthcare Transformation (Singapore), 227
OMOP (Observable Medical Outcomes Partnership), 195
ONC (Office of the National Coordinator for Health Information Technology), 204–206, 222, 232
One Home Care, 150
One Medical, 95
Open source systems, 207
Oregon Health Authority, 223
Organisation for Economic Co-operation and Development (*see* OECD)
Organization of care delivery, 27f, 29, 69–103
    for diabetes, 75–81
    Kaiser Permanente model, 96–102
    for primary care, 89–96
    for prostate cancer, 81–89
    value-based model of, 71–75
Organizational metrics, 32
Osteoarthritis, hip, 112
Outcomes measurement:
    linking payment to, 166–168
    mandatory, 220–221, 236
    obstacles to, 63–65
    role of, 31–37, 35f
    (*See also* ICHOM; Quality registries)

Out-of-pocket expenses, 152
Overuse, of medical services, 269n33
Oxeon Partners, 251

Palliative care, 99
Parkinson's disease, 219
Partnerships, public-private, 252
Pathology, 184
Patient(s):
    adherence, 51
    consent, 196
    falls, 161
    length-of-stay, 147, 161, 225
    population segments, 70–75, 97–98, 103, 123–124, 226
    satisfaction and experience, 32, 57, 132, 134
    volume, 86, 155
Patient navigators, 100
Patient-centered outcomes, 56
Patient-provider engagement, 142
Patient-reported outcome measures (*See* PROMs)
Payer-providers, 97
Payers, health care, 145, 173, 175, 208, 243–244
Pay-for-participation, 167
Pay-for-performance bonuses, 139, 140
Payments:
    activity-based, 143-144
    bundled, 140, 153–157, 285n29
    outcomes-based, 166–168, 217–218
    value-based (*see* Value-based payment)
PCOR-ANZ (prostate cancer registry), 62
Percutaneous transluminal coronary angioplasty (PTCA), 14
Personal Health Train, 196–197, 290n45
Personalized care, 73
Pfizer, 210
PharmAccess, 88
Pharmaceutical industry, 18, 115, 163–164, 169, 239, 244–246
Pharmacy and pharmacists, 114
Philips (medical technology company), 164, 239, 249, 254, 256f, 276n35
Physician prescribing behavior, 181–182, 182f
Physician-led change, 111
Plan for Outcome-Based Healthcare, 215
Policymakers, action steps for, 174, 207, 236, 246
Politicians, 236, 246

Pollution, health care, 6, 268n20
Population health, 70–75, 97–98, 103, 123–124, 226
Porter, Michael, 53, 81, 212, 220, 247, 254, 256*f*
Portugal, 153, 256
Post-acute care, 284n20
Practice variation, 13–15, 15*f*, 38
Predictive analytics, 178, 184
Preference-sensitive care, 14
Pregnancy and childbirth, 8, 88, 157–159
Pressure ulcers, 161
Price, Geoff, 91–92
Price, Trevor, 250–251
Primary care, 69, 76–77, 79, 89–96, 148–150, 227
Princess Margaret Cancer Centre, 188
Private equity, 239–240
Privatization, 211–213
Process-related metrics, 34
PROMs (patient-reported outcome measures), 50, 56, 58, 60, 65, 116–118
Prostate cancer, 58–62, 72, 81–89, 111, 239, 276n38
Prostate Cancer Self-Help Association of Germany, 58
Prostatectomies, 81–82, 86
Providers, health care, 145, 208, 242–243
Pseudomonas infections, 50
PTCA (percutaneous transluminal coronary angioplasty), 14
PubMed, 2
Purpose crisis in health care, 21–26
Pykosz, Mike, 91, 93, 96, 248

Quadruple Aim, 26
Qualcomm Life, 254
Quality registries, 31–67
 and health care costs, 47–49
 implementation of standards for, 61–67
 international, 51–53, 253
 as learning systems, 37–44
 metrics for, 32–37
 national (*see names of specific countries*)
 procedure-based, 56
 and registry-based randomized controlled trials, 44–47
 and standardized outcomes measurement sets, 53–61
 in the United States, 49–51
 (*See also names of specific registries*)

Quality review, 83
Quality-of-life outcomes, 60

Racial and socioeconomic groups, 11
Radboud University Hospital, 121
Radiology, 184
Ransomware, 190–191
RCTs (randomized controlled trials), 202
Redefining Health Care: Creating Value-Based Competition on Results (Porter and Teisberg), 53
"Reengineer: Don't Automate, Obliterate" (Hammer), 179
Region Stockholm, 121
registry-based randomized clinical trials (R-RCTs), 44–47, 187, 232
Reimagining Primary Care, 131
Remote-monitoring equipment, 176
Reorganization of care delivery, 216
Repatha (cholesterol drug), 163
Resource allocation, 220, 222, 236
Rheumatoid arthritis, 44–45
Risk assessment and stratification, 93, 95, 97, 157, 169, 187
Risk management, 236
Robotic surgery, 85–86
Rosenberg, Barry, 11, 127
R-RCTs (registry-based randomized clinical trials), 44–47, 187, 232
Rubicon MD, 96
Rumsfeld, John, 63
Rutte, Mark, 120
Ryu, Jaewon, 172

Sadikin, Budi Gunadi, 256*f*
Sadoff, David, 127
Safran, Dana Gelb, 65
St. Antonius Hospital, 114
Samsom, Melvin, 121, 126, 127–128, 248
Santeon Group, 109–115, 111*f*, 217
Saudi Arabia, 88
Schippers, Edith, 254
Schork, Nicholas, 185
SCL Health, 134
Scripps Research, 178
SDGs (Sustainable Development Goals), 213
Security breaches (*see* Cybersecurity)
SelectHealth, 129–130
Semantic interoperability, 194–195
Sepsis, 198
Sequoia Project, 206

Shanghai Medical College, 188
Shared decision-making, 216, 217
Shrank, Will, 148–149, 151, 284n19
Sibony, Olivier, 16
Singapore, 225–229, 231, 256*f*
Slavitt, Andy, 251
Smokers, 72
SNOMED-CT (Systematized
　Nomenclature of Medicine-Clinical
　Terms), 195, 197
Social and behavioral determinants of
　health:
　addressing, in health care, 223–224
　and Humana patients, 150
　impact on health, 278n4
　incorporation into interventions, 103
　and Intermountain Health patients,
　　131–132, 134
　and Kaiser Permanente patients,
　　99–100
　and Oak Street patients, 91–92
Social interventions, 74
SONNET (Social Needs Network for
　Evaluation and Translation), 100
Soriot, Pascal, 256*f*
South Korea, 230
South-Eastern Norway Regional Health
　Authority, 191
Spain, 5, 88, 164, 253
Specialty-Based Care, 130
Spine surgery, 155–157, 169, 228, 285n33
STEMI (ST-segment elevation
　myocardial infarction), 45–46
Steno Diabetes Center, 256
Stevens, Simon, 254
Strategic leadership, 239–246
Stroke, 112, 157, 184–185
Sunstein, Cass, 16
Suppliers, in health care, 173–174, 208
Supply-sensitive care, overuse of, 14
Surgical complications, 137, 155
Surgical gloves, 160
Surgical volume, 126–127
Sustainable Development Goals (SDGs),
　213
Svenarud, Peter, 126
Svensson, Lars, 109
SVEUS (Swedish performance
　monitoring and payment program),
　156–157
Swarm learning, 196
Swedeheart, 39–47, 187, 249, 274n9

Sweden, 10–11, 37, 75–81, 109, 153, 155,
　157, 224, 230, 281n16
Swedish Medical Products Agency, 61
Swedish rheumatoid arthritis registry, 45
Swedish Society of Spinal Surgeons, 156
Swedish spine surgery bundle, 169
SweSpine (Swedish spine quality
　registry), 73
Switzerland, 7, 14, 139, 238–239
System leadership, 252–257
Systematic reviews, 20

Taiwan, 153
Takeda Pharmaceuticals, 256*f*
Tan, Chorh-Chuan, 229, 256*f*
Tanzania, 6, 88, 157
TASTE trial, 45–46, 46*f*
Tata Memorial Hospital, 188
Taylor, Lauren, 231
TCP/IP protocol, 203
Team-based approach to care, 76–77
Teisberg, Elizabeth, 53, 81, 212, 220, 247,
　256*f*
Telehealth, 132, 176
Tempus (health data company), 184
Terminal illness, 99
Tesla Motors, 230
Texas, 148
"Three Beyonds," 225–228
Thyroid cancer, 5
Tiohundra, 224–225
TNF (tumor necrosis factor) antagonists,
　44–45
Tollman, Peter, 22–23, 144
Topol, Eric, 178
Town Hall Ventures, 251
Transformational change, 120, 123–128
Transformational leadership, 247–251
Transparency:
　algorithmic, 201–202
　of data, 38*f*, 40–43
　of outcomes, 41*f*, 172, 240
　payment linked to, 166–168
　phased, 110–111
　of value-based payment models, 171
Treatment protocol metrics, 32
Tripathi, Micky, 204–206
Triple Aim, 26
TrueNTH Global Registry, 62
Trulicity (diabetes drug), 163
Trust, 101–102, 113, 123, 170–171
Tsinghua University, 256*f*

Tumor boards, 84
21st Century Cures Act, 194, 204–205
Tyson, Bernard, 254

UCSF (University of California San Francisco), 191
UKE (University Hospital Hamburg-Eppendorf), 71, 81
Underuse, of medical services, 14, 268n19
United Kingdom, 139, 153, 188
United Nations, 213, 235
United States:
  bundled payments in, 153
  diabetes care in, 75–81
  greenhouse gas emissions of, 6
  outcome variation across regions, 13f
  quality registries in, 49–51
  wasteful health care spending in, 5
University Hospital Hamburg-Eppendorf (UKE), 71
University of California San Francisco (UCSF), 191
University of Michigan, 199
University of Michigan Medical School, 11
University of Rochester Department of Public Health, 11
University of Texas, 247, 256f
University of Utah, 198
Uppsala Clinical Research Center, 43
Upstream Healthcare, 95
Urinary incontinence, 81
USCDI (United States Core Data Interoperability) standards, 194, 206
Utah, 128–129, 131
Utilization rates, 147

VA (Department of Veterans Affairs), 163, 292n1
Vaccinations, pneumococcal, 269n31
Valencia, Rick, 254
Value crisis in health care, 3–15
Value in Healthcare Project, 27, 200, 254
Value Institute for Health and Care, 247
Value-based contracting, 163–164
Value-based health care improvement cycle, 38f
Value-Based Health Care Project (Denmark), 219

Value-based health system, model of, 27–29, 27f, 71–75, 255f
Value-based payment, 64, 137–174
  behaviors driving value, 142–145
  bundled payment, 153–157
  context for success in, 166–172
  for drugs, devices, and medical supplies, 159–164
  in low-income countries, 157–159
  in Medicare Advantage programs, 145–153, 169
  models of, 27f, 28
  resource stewardship in, 164–166
  varieties of, 139–141
Value-based transformation, 209–236
  game-changing for, 229–233
  governments as leaders, 233–235
  market-shaping actions for, 220–229
  mission of, 213–214
  national strategies for, 214–219
Van Houten, Frans, 249, 254, 256f
Van Riet, Yvonne, 114
Venter Institute, 185
Venture capital, 177, 239–240, 250–251
VGZ (Dutch health insurer), 181–182, 182f
VillageMD, 251
Virtual care, 134
Virtual consults, 133
Virtual hospitals, 132–133
VitalHealth, 239
Vocabulary, common, 194

Wales, 219
Wallentin, Lars, 249
Walt Disney Company, 131
WannaCry (digital virus), 190–191
Warburg (investment firm), 240
Warwick, Warren, 49, 249
Wearable technologies, 176
Weber, Christophe, 254, 256f
Wellcentive (digital health platform), 239
Wennberg, John, 13–15, 269n33
WHO (World Health Organization), 5, 6, 89, 194, 235
World Economic Forum, 27, 200, 253, 295n11
World Health Summit, 254

Xerox Palo Alto Research Center, 203

Zoëga, Björn, 126

ABOUT THE AUTHORS

Stefan Larsson, MD, PhD, is a pioneer in the field of value-based health care. Dr. Larsson is an independent advisor to health care organizations and a board member of life science companies. He spent 25 years at Boston Consulting Group (BCG), where as a senior partner he was the founder and first global leader of the firm's health care payers and providers sector and of its health systems sector, which advises the leaders of national health systems around the world; he continues to serve as a BCG senior advisor. Dr. Larsson is also a cofounder and board member of the International Consortium for Health Outcomes Measurement (ICHOM), a nonprofit that works to create global standards for measuring health outcomes, and a distinguished fellow on the Health and Healthcare team of the World Economic Forum. He did his medical training and PhD research at the Karolinska Institute in Stockholm, Sweden, where he has an affiliation as an associate professor, and did postdoctoral research at the MRC Human Genomics Unit in Edinburgh, Scotland.

Jennifer Clawson is a partner and director in BCG's Madrid office and global head of the firm's Center for Value in Health Care. She has worked with both private- and public-sector organizations to create new value-based business models and evaluate strategic opportunities to improve health outcomes.

Josh Kellar, PhD, is a partner and managing director in BCG's Chicago office, leader of the firm's Global Scientist Network of more than 500 MDs and PhDs, and coleader of its medical response to Covid-19. He works with clients throughout the US health care industry, specializing in advanced analytics, value-based care delivery, and the application of digital technologies.

Robert Howard is a former senior editor at *Harvard Business Review* and *MIT Technology Review,* and the author of a number of books about work, technology, and organization. He has been collaborating for more than a decade with BCG on the topics of value-based health care and health-system transformation.